Capital Ideas and Market Realities

Capital Ideas and Market Realities

OPTION REPLICATION, INVESTOR BEHAVIOR, AND STOCK MARKET CRASHES

Bruce I. Jacobs

With a foreword by Harry M. Markowitz, Nobel Laureate

Dear David,

I'm delighted to share this work with you. Hope you enjoy it!

Bruce

BLACKWELL
Publishers

First published 1999

2 4 6 8 10 9 7 5 3 1

Blackwell Publishers Inc.
350 Main Street
Malden, Massachusetts 02148
USA

Blackwell Publishers Ltd
108 Cowley Road
Oxford OX4 1JF
UK

Library of Congress Cataloging-in-Publication Data

Jacobs, Bruce I.
    Capital ideas and market realities : option replication, investor
  behavior, and stock market crashes / Bruce I. Jacobs; with a
  foreword by Harry M. Markowitz.
      p.   cm.
    Includes bibliographical references and index.
    ISBN 0–631–21554–9 (hbk.). — ISBN 0–631–21555–7 (pbk.)
    1. Hedging (Finance)   2. Financial crises.   3. Stock options.
  I. Title.
  HG6024.A3J33   1999   99–12641
                                                         CIP

British Library Cataloguing in Publication Data

A CIP catalogue record for this book is available from the British Library.

Typeset in 10 on 12 pt Sabon
by Graphicraft Limited, Hong Kong
Printed in Great Britain by MPG Books, Bodmin, Cornwall

This book is printed on acid-free paper

Contents

Illustrations

Foreword

by Harry M. Markowitz, Nobel Laureate

In a documentary about Hannibal, retired General Norman Schwarzkopf said that Hannibal's crushing defeat of the Romans at Cannae in 216 BC inspired his own highly successful plan against Saddam Hussein's forces. The details, of course, are different between Hannibal's campaign and that of Schwarzkopf: one army numbering tanks, the other Carthaginian cavalry among its resources; one battle being fought in a day, the other (waged over greater distances) lasting one hundred hours. But the basic principle, of encircling an enemy whose forces are focused at the front, is remarkably similar between Cannae and Operation Desert Storm. Thus there are two reasons for studying the Battle of Cannae. One, as a momentous event that changed the course of history; the other, as a possible guide to action in military campaigns and, perhaps, to other kinds of decisive encounters between rivals.

Similarly, the causes of the great crash of October 19, 1987, "Black Monday," can be profitably studied, not only to understand a tumultuous event in stock market history, but also for their implications for stock market mechanisms and their possible consequences, today and tomorrow. In the present book, Bruce Jacobs analyzes the causes of the 1987 crash and the presence of similar market forces today.

Many observers, including Dr Jacobs and me, believe that the severity of the 1987 crash was due, in large part, to the use before and during the crash of an option replication strategy known as "portfolio insurance." In this book, Dr Jacobs describes the procedures and rationale of portfolio insurance, its effect on the market, and whether it would have been desirable for the investor even if it had worked. He also discusses "sons of portfolio insurance," and procedures with similar objectives and possibly similar effects on markets, in existence today.

In addition, Dr Jacobs considers alternate methods of investing, to achieve objectives similar to portfolio insurance without what he (and I) sees as its problems. In particular, in the penultimate chapter Dr Jacobs makes the (to me, crucial) distinction between portfolio *insurance* and portfolio *theory*. Broadly stated, the objective of portfolio *insurance* is to reduce risk, in some sense, perhaps at the expense of return on the average. This sounds very much like the objectives of portfolio *theory's* mean-variance analysis. The objective of the latter is to present the investor with "efficient" combinations of risk and return from which the investor picks an efficient combination according to her or his risk aversion, perhaps sacrificing return on the average in order to reduce risk.

I cannot add to Dr Jacobs's comprehensive account of portfolio insurance, its effects on markets, or the possible consequences of "sons of portfolio insurance." I can, however, amplify a bit on Dr Jacobs's remarks on the difference between portfolio theory and portfolio insurance. This may, in a small way, supplement the materials presented elsewhere in this book.

Portfolio *insurance* seeks to control risk by radically altering equity exposure. To facilitate comparison between portfolio *insurance* versus portfolio *theory*, in the present discussion it is sufficient to consider portfolios of two securities – cash and the market. Since portfolio insurance's movements back and forth between cash and equities are not motivated by shifting beliefs about the market, it is sufficient in the present discussion to assume that market performance per period is a sequence of random draws. (Technically speaking, we assume that returns are independent and identically distributed, or i.i.d.) We will also assume that the portfolio can be switched back and forth between cash and the market without cost. This will tend to favor portfolio insurance.

Even though I assume zero transaction costs, switching back and forth between cash and stocks is nevertheless "expensive" in terms of mean-variance efficiency. To illustrate, consider an extreme case. Suppose that at the beginning of every day (or month) the investor applies some rule that indicates that she or he should either be completely in cash or completely in the market. This rule can be any function of past observations. To be specific, rather than general, let us assume that after some period of time (like a year's worth of days, or five years' worth of months) the rule has directed the investor to be completely in cash half the days (months) and completely in the market the other half. Let us compute the realized mean and variance of this strategy, and compare them with those of a portfolio that was rebalanced each day (or month) to a half stock, half cash portfolio.

The strategy of switching back and forth, being all in cash half the time and all in stocks half the time, has the same mean return as but more than twice the variance of the strategy of rebalancing a 50/50 portfolio.[1] In particular, the rebalanced strategy will be on the market line, whereas the strategy of switching back and forth will be on the inefficient side of the market line. More generally, given our assumption of i.i.d. returns, the rebalanced portfolio will lie on the market line, whatever the proportions of stock and cash chosen, whereas the portfolio that switches back and forth will lie on the inefficient side of the market line.

Markowitz (1959: ch. 9) proposes semivariance or, equivalently, semideviation as an alternative measure of risk. Semivariance is like variance, except that it considers only returns below some target level. Specifically, semivariance is the expected square of deviations below the target. For the present discussion, it is most convenient if we use the risk-free rate as the target level.

There is a mean semideviation market line, just as there is a mean standard deviation market line. In general, the rebalanced portfolio will be on the market line, whereas the strategy that switches back and forth will be on the inefficient side of the line. In particular, a portfolio that is half the time in stocks and half the time in cash will have a daily semivariance twice as large as that of a 50/50 portfolio.[2]

The examples above, of course, present the easily calculated, extreme case in which the "portfolio insurer" is either in stocks or in cash, but not both simultaneously. The direction of the result is the same, however, if we take the more realistic, less extreme, case where the proportion of stocks held by the portfolio insurer varies over time as a function of past observations, but is not necessarily always 0 percent or 100 percent. In this general case, the portfolio will not lie on the market line (given our assumption of an unvarying probability distribution of the market).

The portfolio *insurance* supporter would surely counter that this inefficiency in terms of daily mean and variance (or mean and semivariance) is the price paid to reshape the probability distribution of returns over a longer interval of time, call it the "insured period." Often this insured period is a year, but to facilitate the present discussion in terms of ex post returns, assume that the insured period is a month; that we examine performance after many months; and that ex post frequencies, both for monthly and daily returns, are "close" to ex ante probabilities. Then the portfolio insurance supporter will point out that the greatest loss in any month is less for the portfolio insurance strategy than for the rebalanced strategy and, indeed (given our assumptions), no month has lost more than the preset floor for the portfolio.

The portfolio *theory* aficionado might counter by pointing out that, for the period of analysis as a whole, the rebalanced portfolio grew more than the switched-back-and-forth one. This is because the strategy with the greater average daily log (1 + return) will have grown the most during the period; average daily log (1 + return) is very closely approximated by a function of mean and variance (see Markowitz 1959: ch. 6) and Young and Trent 1969); and this (approximate) average log decreases with increasing variance. A particular point on the mean-variance frontier gives approximately maximum growth. More than that, every point on the frontier gives approximately maximum growth in the long run for given short-run fluctuations (in our case, day-to-day variance).

The portfolio *insurance* advocate might counter that, after one or two bad years, the "customer," the company in the case of a company-backed pension plan, might not wait for the long run, but might summarily fire the pension fund executive and/or pension portfolio manager. The portfolio *theory* aficionado might seek moral high ground by contrasting the needs of the client with those of its agent, the pension executive. The portfolio insurance supporter might remind the portfolio theory aficionado that, in practice, applications of portfolio theory sometimes put manager motives ahead of true client needs, as perhaps when mean-variance (or mean-semivariance) analysis is used to minimize tracking error, rather than total variability, for a given average return.

At this point, we interrupt this friendly discussion about whether portfolio insurance would have been the right thing to do had it worked. We recall that Dr Jacobs will show us that portfolio insurance did not in fact work, partly because it destabilized the market and then had liquidity problems as a consequence. We further note that the reason that portfolio insurance destabilized the market was because it bought when the market went up and sold when the market went down. The rebalancing strategies that portfolio theory implies – when we use it, for example, to maximize return for the long run – sell when the market rises and buy when the market falls, tending to stabilize the market. Thus such an application of portfolio *theory* is, if nothing else, more environmentally friendly than portfolio *insurance*.

Notes

1   Average daily returns (E) and variances (V) of daily returns of the two strategies are calculated from the following formulas and presented in the accompanying table. R_M is the market's return and r_0 is the risk-free rate. E_M is the average return on the market and V_M represents the variance of the market. The calculations assume that, ex post, the distribution of the stock market returns is independent of whether the strategy of switching back and forth is all in stocks or all in cash; this is also true of the ex ante probabilities, since the choice is a function only of prior observations.

In particular:

$$V_M = E(R_M^2) - E_M{}^2, \tag{1}$$

where

$$E_M = E(R_M).$$

Also, for any random variable v whose expected value $E(v \mid s)$ is conditional on a vector of state variables s, we have:

$$Ev = E[E(v \mid s)]. \tag{2}$$

Thus, for the switch-back-and-forth strategy (where R is the strategy return):

$$V = E(R^2) - E^2,$$
$$= \tfrac{1}{2}(V_M + E_M^2) + \tfrac{1}{2}r_0{}^2 - [(r_0 + E_M)/2]^2,$$
$$= \tfrac{1}{2}V_M + \tfrac{1}{4}(E_M - r_0)^2, \tag{3}$$

The formula for the rebalanced portfolio follows immediately from portfolio theory, since the portfolio is (1/2, 1/2) every time.

	E	V	S
Rebalanced portfolio	$(E_M + r_0)/2$	$V_M/4$	$S_M/4$
Switch-back-and-forth	$(E_M + r_0)/2$	$V_M/2 + (E_M - r_0)^2/4$	$S_M/2$

2   As shown in Markowitz (1959: ch. 9), the semivariance of any portfolio satisfies a formula like that of variance, except using only the portfolio's underperformance "years" (here, days) to compute the entries of the "semi-covariance" matrix. With underperformance defined in terms of the risk-free rate, r_0, all convex (non-negative) combinations of cash and the market have the same underperformance years (days). Consequently, the formula given in the table for the rebalanced portfolio applies. The formula for the switch-back-and-forth strategy is derived by applying Equation (2) of footnote 1 to $(\min[R-r_0, 0])^2$ – that is, the square of the smaller of zero or the shortfall between the strategy return and the risk-free rate. The table gives the semivariances, S, below the risk-free rate for the two strategies; S_M is the semivariance of the market.

References

Markowitz, H. 1959: *Portfolio Selection: Efficient diversification of investments.* New York: John Wiley & Sons; 1991: 2nd edn. Cambridge, MA: Blackwell.

Young, W. and Trent, R. 1969: Geometric mean approximation of individual security and portfolio performance. *Journal of Financial and Quantitative Analysis,* 4, 179–99.

Acknowledgments

Anyone who has written a book in their "spare" time, as an avocation and a labor of love, rather than mere duty, knows that it doesn't get done (even over a decade) without a lot of help and support from others. I have first to thank my partner at Jacobs Levy Equity Management (and former coworker at Prudential), Ken Levy. Without his encouragement, wisdom, and good advice (not to mention his willingness to put up with a part-time author as a full-time business partner), this book truly could never have come to be.

I am indebted to others at Jacobs Levy. Judy Kimball has provided editorial support through much of the book's genesis, helping to shape the work through its various incarnations and to ensure both sense and sensibility. David Starer has applied his sound engineering skills to many readings of the work; it has benefited from his fine-tuning and valuable insights. Thanks to Janie Kass, Mitch Krask, and Pete Rudolph for reading and advising on the manuscript, and to Marji Carano, my administrative assistant, who cheerfully provided the support services without which no work gets done.

One of the great pleasures in writing this book was the opportunity it gave me to talk with and benefit from the insights of Harry Markowitz. Harry was kind enough to write the foreword to the book, but his encouragement and creative suggestions have improved the entire work.

I am grateful to Jane Buchan for providing suggestions for further research and to Charles Kindleberger for his moral support. Barry Burr, Mike Clowes, and Roger Lowenstein were valuable sounding-boards.

Any book with as long a history as this one has deep roots. In at the beginning of my involvement with option replication, and encouraging me to publish my early findings, was my colleague at Prudential, Jim Gately.

Finally, my thanks to Al Bruckner, Executive Editor at Blackwell Publishers.

Readers may send comments, questions, or corrections via e-mail to cimr@jlem.com.

To Ilene, Lauren, Julie, Sam, and Erica
for their love, patience, and support.

Introduction

This book sifts through the recent history of financial markets to unravel the complex ways in which investment ideas, and the products born of those ideas, are linked to each other and to the behavior of capital markets. In particular, it examines how some investment strategies, especially those based on theories that ignore the human element, can self-destruct, taking markets down with them. Ironically, the greatest danger has often come from strategies that purport to reduce the risk of investing.

The summer and fall of 1998, for example, witnessed some of the most turbulent markets the world has ever seen. The troubles began with investor panic in the wake of the collapse of the Russian currency and bond market. As investors flew to safety, the contagion of fear spread, first to other emerging markets, then to the equity markets of more developed nations. Contributing to the general disorder, however, were trading activities related to the supposedly low-risk investment strategies of many large investors.

The near-collapse of the hedge fund giant Long-Term Capital Management (LTC) exemplified one of the problems. LTC had engaged in strategies that attempt to profit from pricing discrepancies between related markets; for example, it held long positions in low-quality, high-yielding bonds and short positions in high-quality, low-yielding securities such as US Treasury bonds. Such arbitrage trades are theoretically low risk because the offsetting price moves of the securities held long and sold short cushion the overall portfolio from the full impact of changes in underlying fundamentals such as interest rates. In fact, LTC's investments were perceived as so low risk that tremendous amounts of leverage were piled on to amplify the fund's profit margins.

As the global flight to safety sank the values of the fund's long positions and elevated the values of its short positions, the fund's leverage amplified its risk, and the risk to markets generally. LTC, and other hedge funds and investment banks and brokers with hundreds of billions of dollars in similar strategies, were forced to unwind their positions. Their trading exacerbated asset price moves, increased market volatility, and further widened the wedge between risky and safer assets.

At the same time, another institutional trading force was also contributing to instability. With the increase in equity market volatility in the summer and fall of 1998, investors had flocked to purchase put options on their equity portfolios. Such options give the purchaser the right to sell stock at a specified price, hence provide a minimum floor value for the stock. The seller of the put option, however, takes on the risk that the stock's value will fall below this floor. To mitigate this exposure, the option seller is likely to engage in dynamic hedging in underlying markets – buying stock as its price rises and selling as it falls. In 1998, dynamic hedging by option sellers exacerbated market volatility, which in turn magnified the losses on dynamic hedges.

The same basic investor behavior and investment trading strategies behind the upheavals of 1998 underlie other notable episodes of market turmoil. The unwinding of highly leveraged positions upset the market in 1929, for example, just as it did in 1998. Investors' purchase of stock had accelerated through the 1920s as increases in the value of their stock positions allowed more borrowing to purchase more stock. As the market began to become undone in the fall of 1929, however, the value of the shares collateralizing this massive borrowing declined. Margin calls forced investors to liquidate their positions, accelerating the market downturn into the crash.

In 1987, the same dynamic hedging that roiled the market in 1998 led to a one-day US market decline of over 22 percent, which in turn ignited crashes in stock markets throughout the world. In the 1980s, the dynamic hedging was being done by institutional investors engaged in a strategy known as "portfolio insurance," rather than by option sellers, but the effects were the same.

In 1987, as in 1998, strategies supported by the best that finance theory had to offer were overwhelmed by the oldest of human instincts – survival. In 1929, in 1987, and in 1998, strategies that required mechanistic, forced selling of securities, regardless of market conditions, added to market turmoil and helped to turn market downturns into crashes. Ironically, in 1987 and 1998, those strategies had held out the promise of reducing the risk of investing. Instead, they ended up increasing risk for all investors.

This book reveals the links between stock market crashes and trend-following trading strategies such as portfolio insurance and the option replication underlying hundreds of billions of dollars in new equity derivatives products in today's global markets. It uncovers the dangers posed by these strategies when they collide with market realities. And it sounds a warning for investors who would shield themselves from the resulting implosions of investment value.

The Story of Option Replication

Markets have always been driven by fear and greed, by investors' aversion to loss and desire for gain. But advances in financial theory, statistical analysis, and computing power, particularly over the last thirty years, have often seemed to be on the verge of taming the human element. Perhaps the apotheosis of this thinking was the development in the 1970s of the theories of market efficiency and rational pricing. With investors acting rationally and exploiting fully and instantaneously all available information, market prices were believed to be securely tied to underlying fundamentals.

On the heels of rational pricing of basic financial assets came the development of models for pricing instruments contingent on those assets. In 1973, Fischer Black, Myron S. Scholes, and Robert C. Merton published their solutions to the option pricing problem (a feat for which Scholes and Merton received the Nobel Prize in Economic Sciences in 1997). It was a problem that had long stumped economic researchers, from Louis Bachelier at the turn of the century through Paul Samuelson in the 1960s. Black, Scholes, and Merton cracked it by viewing an option as essentially equivalent to a portfolio with positions in the simple asset underlying the option and a simple riskless asset such as Treasury bills, where the proportions invested in each position are changed as the value of the underlying asset changes.

Option pricing theory opened the door to an explosion in new derivatives instruments and markets. Organized exchanges for trading options and futures emerged in the 1970s and 1980s; burgeoning markets in over-the-counter trading of options, forwards, and swaps on currency, interest rates, and equities developed in the 1980s and 1990s. Trading strategies, too, were soon developed to exploit these new tools, and to exploit the natural fear and greed of investors.

Futures and options on commodities had long provided agricultural and manufacturing concerns with a means of reducing their risks by locking in product prices. Now equity derivatives, and strategies based on them, held out the promise of being able to reduce the risk of common stock investing. Even if investors could not predict a market downturn, they could protect themselves against one.

Portfolio insurance was one of the first of these strategies to emerge, popularized by Los Angeles-based Leland O'Brien Rubinstein Associates (LOR) in the 1980s. LOR was founded by Mark Rubinstein and Hayne Leland, professors of finance at the University of California, Berkeley, and John O'Brien, who had been an investment consultant at his own firm, O'Brien Associates, and at A.G. Becker. The portfolio insurance strategy was born from the tenets of market efficiency, drew milk from the ideas of traditional insurance, and was given substance by Black–Scholes option pricing theory. That is, it promised to protect investment portfolios from unpredictable market moves, just as insurance protects homeowners from the risks of fire or flood; protection would be accomplished with a trading strategy based on the Black–Scholes pricing formula.

The option pricing formula had opened the door to the creation of synthetic options. A synthetic option was merely a real-life version of the hypothetical portfolio Black–Scholes assumed equivalent to the real option. By taking and dynamically trading positions in stocks and in cash equivalents, an investor could, in theory, construct a trading strategy that replicated the behavior of any desired equity option.

In the case of portfolio insurance, that option was an equity put, which allows an investor to sell a stock or a portfolio of stocks for a prespecified price at some future date (whatever its actual value at that date). Just as an actual put on an underlying stock portfolio protects the portfolio from stock price declines below a certain level while leaving the portfolio open to stock price advances, portfolio insurance aimed to maximize an investment portfolio's stock exposure while eliminating portfolio losses below a specified level. Computerized rules and program trading would move portfolio assets between stock and cash (often accomplished by selling short stock index futures) to replicate the behavior of a stock portfolio protected by a put option.

Option replication requires trend-following behavior – selling as the market falls and buying as it rises. Thus, when substantial numbers of investors are replicating options, their trading alone can exaggerate market trends. Furthermore, the trading activity of option replicators can have insidious effects on other investors. These investors will generally not know that the option-replicating sell orders are merely mechanistic reactions to market declines, or the buy orders mechanistic reactions to market rises. These investors may thus be inclined to interpret any price changes that result from the trading as reflective of new information, hence be encouraged to trade in the same direction as replicators.

By the time of the 1987 crash, for example, portfolio insurance had fueled a fad that threatened market stability. It had attracted up to $100 billion in assets (about 3 percent of the market's capitalization at the time). Almost every major asset management firm offered some form of insurance – LOR and its licensees Aetna, Wells Fargo, First Chicago, Kidder Peabody, and BEA, as well as J.P. Morgan, Bankers Trust, Chase Manhattan, Travelers, Mass Mutual, and Mellon Capital.

From 1982 well into 1987, the market had risen virtually uninterruptedly, buoyed by a sturdy underlying economy and hearty infusions of foreign capital. Many investors, concerned with elevated stock price levels and anxious to preserve the investment gains already under their belts, had turned to portfolio insurance as a safety net. Rather than retrenching and reducing their stock allocations, these investors had retained or even increased their equity exposures, placing even more upward pressure on stock prices. And, of course, as equity prices rose more, "insured" portfolios bought more stock, causing prices to rise even higher.

In the week before October 19, 1987, however, an increase in the prime rate, a large trade deficit, and fears of a weakening dollar depressed prices in both the stock and futures markets. These initial declines called for substantial selling by insured investors. The great majority of other investors, however, did not know these sell orders were purely mechanistic. Many of these investors inferred impending bad news and sold also. An avalanche of sell orders overwhelmed both the stock and futures markets at their openings on October 19.

Ironically, the dynamic trading required by option replication had created the very conditions portfolio insurance had been designed to protect against – volatility and instability in underlying equity markets. And, tragically, portfolio insurance failed under these conditions (because, as we will see, it was not true insurance). The volatility created by the strategy's dynamic hedging spelled its end. As investors pulled out of their insurance programs, or failed to renew them, the amount of assets synthetically insured dropped by two-thirds in the aftermath of the crash.

The crash of 1987 placed not just portfolio insurance, but stock market behavior generally under the microscope. Proponents of efficient markets and fundamental pricing fought it out with advocates of more intuitive views encompassing Keynesian spirits and Shillerian fads, and with newer-wave behavioral psychologists and chaotic theoreticians. In effect, the crash provided an ultimate test for some long-held ideas about how the market works, what Peter Bernstein (1992) has termed "capital ideas." Not all of them survived intact. But the crash gave rise to new theories about the way the investment world works, and new products and strategies to exploit them.

While the 1987 crash killed off portfolio insurance, it awakened investors to the potential for catastrophe in financial markets and reinforced their desire for protection. The spirit of portfolio insurance may have been forgotten, but it has not gone. Today, institutional investors can turn to an expanded menu of listed options or to over-the-counter (OTC) option dealers to supply directly the protection that synthetic puts promised to provide in the 1980s. And individual investors are relying in increasing numbers on "guaranteed equity" funds promising, through the use of options, upside participation with downside protection.

Options exchange market makers and sellers of OTC options now find themselves doing what portfolio insurers were doing in the 1980s. In satisfying the public's demand for long options (either puts or calls), market makers and dealers sell options. A short option position, however, is essentially a speculative posture, as it exposes the seller to potentially unlimited losses if the underlying assets move in the wrong direction. Exchange market makers and OTC dealers are generally not in the business of speculating. They will want to neutralize short option positions by taking on long option positions that offset them.

The ability of option sellers to offset their short positions is ultimately dependent on the presence of speculators and the price those speculators demand for assuming the risk of these short positions. For both market makers and dealers, purchase of offsetting long option positions may prove uneconomical. OTC dealers, of course, face the additional problem of having to hedge customized short option positions with specifications that are not available in exchange markets.

Option sellers unable to hedge short option positions by buying options must turn to the stock and stock futures markets to replicate long option positions with dynamic hedging. The same trend-following, dynamic hedging that portfolio insurers used to such ill effect in the 1980s destabilized the markets again in October 1989, November 1991, October 1997, and, as we have noted, August 1998.

Our Story

The core of our story constitutes a detailed examination of synthetic portfolio insurance and how it played out in the crash of 1987. As such, it tells the story of the people who sold it and those who studied its nature and impact, those in the universities, in the financial community, and in various government agencies. But, more broadly, it tells the story of the age-old desire to reduce risk in the pursuit of return.

The story of portfolio insurance is one of sophisticated marketing winning out over common sense. It is a story of the potential dangers of a complex financial theory taken up with little appreciation of its suitability for real-world conditions and applied mechanistically with little regard for its potential effects. It is a story about how a relatively small group of operators, in today's complicated and interconnected marketplaces, can wreak havoc out of all proportion to their numbers.

This story is in turn part of a much larger picture. For synthetic portfolio insurance itself remains only a small part of a history of financial ideas and innovations ranging from the efficient market theory of the 1970s to today's exotic derivatives. In particular, it is one small but representative part of the whole option revolution that began in 1973 with the publication of the Black–Scholes option pricing formula and the opening of the first US exchange for trading listed equity options.

It is a story of unintended consequences. For synthetic portfolio insurance, although born from the tenets of market efficiency, affected markets in very inefficient, destabilizing ways. And option replication, although envisioned as a means for investors to transfer and thereby reduce unwanted risk, came to be a source of risk for all market participants.

It is a story that intersects with other theories and strategies, including rational bubbles, informational cascades, index arbitrage, and program trading, and one that ranges across time and geography. A thread runs from margin buying and margin calls in the 1920s, through synthetic portfolio insurance in the 1980s, to today's option replication and arbitrage strategies, tying together trading strategies that rely on automatic selling dictates and their damaging effects on markets. As the 1987 crash showed, those effects may not be limited to markets that use such strategies; although synthetic portfolio insurance then was pretty much limited to the US, it brought down the rest of the world's markets via international price transmission.

Our story sounds a warning. As retail and institutional investors increasingly turn to options and option-like products to provide equity participation without loss or to protect portfolio values from market declines, option sellers depend more and more on the same destabilizing trading rules that have brought the markets down time and time again.

My Story

This is a warning that I have sounded in the wake of the Nobel Prize awards in 1997 and on the occasion of the tenth anniversary of the

1987 crash. My views have been published in the *New York Times* (October 19, 1997), the *Wall Street Journal* (November 6, 1997), *Pensions & Investments* (Burr 1997a; Jacobs 1997a; 1997b; and 1998a) and the *Journal of Investing* (Jacobs 1998d and 1999). I have argued the case that option-replicating strategies destabilize markets against representatives of the options industry (Jacobs 1998c) and option-industry advocates such as Nobel laureates Merton Miller and Myron Scholes (Burr 1997b). And, over fifteen years ago, I argued it against the purveyors of portfolio insurance.

In early 1982, I had left a teaching assignment at the Wharton School to join the asset management group of Prudential Insurance Company of America. Soon thereafter, I was delegated to attend LOR's introductory presentation at the Pierre Hotel in New York City to find out more about this new invention. My internal memorandum on "portfolio insulation," distributed to Prudential's client service and sales forces, is included in appendix A of this book. In it, I point out, "if a large number of investors utilized the portfolio insulation technique, price movements would tend to snowball. Price rises (falls) would be followed by purchases (sales) which would lead to further price appreciation (depreciation)."

That memorandum formed the basis for my first article on the issue, "The Portfolio Insurance Puzzle" (Jacobs 1983c), which examined how insurance would reduce portfolio returns in the long run. I also shared my insights on portfolio insurance as a long-term investment with Simon Benninga, a colleague at Wharton, who, along with Marshall Blume, fleshed out some of these ideas and eventually published the results (Benninga and Blume 1985).

Around this time, John O'Brien was attempting to persuade me that Prudential should license their portfolio insurance product, but I told him that, based on my research, we had no interest. LOR ended up forming a relationship with Aetna Life and Casualty. Announced in the fall of 1983, this was an exclusive license of LOR's product to an insurance company; by the time of the crash, the value of the assets under management in this arrangement alone had grown to at least $17 billion.

Mark Rubinstein once called me the "nemesis of portfolio insurance." I have indeed played the role of devil's advocate in the industry, debating LOR in print (see, for example, Jacobs 1983a; O'Brien 1983; and Jacobs 1987) and in person. I debated Hayne Leland and John O'Brien at a University of California, Berkeley, seminar in 1984 (see Leland 1984) and aired my views at a 1986 conference in New York on "dynamic hedging," which featured many of the key players in the portfolio insurance

FIGURE 0.1
The Options Debate

Source: *Wall Street Journal*, November 6, 1997, p. C1.
  Pensions & Investments, December 8, 1997, p. 30.
  Pensions & Investments, November 24, 1997, p. 14.
    Pensions & Investments, June 15, 1998, p. 12.

FIGURE 0.2

Tenth Anniversary of the 1987 Crash

Source: *New York Times*, October 19, 1997, S. 3, p. 1.
Pensions & Investments, September 29, 1997, p. 34.

story (see the conference brochure reproduced in appendix A; also Jacobs 1986 and Ring 1986c).

This is a debate in which I have no direct financial interest. For me, this book is an attempt to clarify the role of synthetic portfolio insurance in the crash of 1987 so as to reveal the potentially harmful effects of option replication and other short-sighted, trend-following strategies today. In that regard, I am proud to have been recognized (as I was, notably, by John O'Brien at that 1986 conference) as the Darth Vader of portfolio insurance!

FIGURE 0.3
The Portfolio Insurance Debate

Source: Reprinted from the June 14, 1982 issue of *Fortune* by special
permission; copyright 1982, Time Inc. Photo by Bonnie Schiffman.
Pensions & Investment Age, August 22, 1983.
Pensions & Investment Age, March 15, 1982.
Pensions & Investment Age, July 7, 1986.

A Look Ahead

This book begins with a look, in chapter 1, at how financial ideas are translated into products – in our case, from Black–Scholes option theory into synthetic option strategies. Chapter 2 highlights the excessive marketing hype used to promote portfolio insurance and details its extraordinary growth. Chapters 3 and 4 examine some weaknesses in portfolio insurance that should have been evident to insurance vendors, including its hidden costs, pitfalls in implementation, and lack of suitability for most investors.

In part II, the focus turns to the global market crash of 1987 and the various theories that emerged to explain it. Chapter 5 considers the case for informationally efficient markets and economic fundamentals. Chapter 6 discusses some of the ideas that emerged in the wake of the failure of fundamentals to explain the crash, including investor overreaction, fads, and feedback trading. Chapter 7 looks at theories of bubbles, cascades, and chaos, which may be consistent with both investor rationality and market crashes. Chapter 8 examines the effects of investment products and strategies, including futures contracts, index arbitrage, and program trading, on market liquidity and volatility.

Part III focuses directly on the effects of dynamic hedging on markets – its effects on the bull market of the 1980s, its contributions to market volatility and liquidity problems, and its role in the 1987 crash. Chapter 9 looks at several ways in which synthetic portfolio insurance, in combination with faddish investor behavior, problems in correctly aggregating disparate information, and stock index arbitrage, may have exacerbated the market's rise and its fall. Chapter 10 places synthetic puts at the nexus of events leading up to the crash and at the vortex of the turbulence of October 19 and 20. Chapters 11 and 12 consider and dismiss the various defenses raised by those seeking to exonerate synthetic portfolio insurance as a culprit in the crash. Chapter 13 discusses portfolio insurance's failure to live up to its name, and contrasts the more overreaching marketing statements made by its purveyors before the crash with their exculpatory statements following the crash.

Part IV warns of present dangers. Chapter 14 examines the role OTC portfolio puts played in the mini-breaks of 1989, 1991, and 1997. Chapters 15 and 16 describe new trading technologies and new investment instruments that purport to overcome the pitfalls of option replication. As we will see, these new products pose some familiar threats to markets and market participants.

Chapter 17 examines the relationship between equity risk and return and investment horizon. What is the tradeoff between short-term risk reduction and long-term investment return? What errors in thinking can bias investors toward accepting lower returns in exchange for less short-term risk? How can investors willing to take a long-term view benefit from the myopia of other investors?

Chapter 18 examines the volatile summer and fall of 1998, with a particular focus on option trading and on the near-collapse of the hedge fund giant Long-Term Capital Management. The volatility-amplifying effects of option replication were, in this recent financial crisis, compounded by the impact of a highly leveraged firm liquidating positions in global bond, equity, and currency markets. As we will see, the story of LTC in 1998 bears some eerie resemblances to the story of portfolio insurance in 1987; not least of these is the presence of LTC partners and option formulators Myron Scholes and Robert Merton.

An epilogue considers some lessons investors have, or haven't, learned since 1987. In particular, it is important to realize that, when investors flock to strategies that appear to eliminate the risk of investing, they may ironically end up creating risk, and courting disaster.

___ Part I ___

From Ideas into Products

In 1973, Fischer Black, Myron S. Scholes, and Robert C. Merton published the results of their work on how to value an option. It was a problem that, despite promising breakthroughs dating back to the turn of the century, had continued to stymie investors and researchers.

Black, Scholes, and Merton solved the problem by examining the essentially risk-free nature of a hedged option position. An option plus some continuously adjusted offsetting position in the risky asset underlying the option will yield a riskless rate of return. This allowed for a solution that was independent of investors' risk preferences and of the underlying asset's expected value.

The publication of the option pricing formula coincided with the establishment of the first US exchange for trading listed options on stocks. Together, these developments fostered a booming option industry. The pricing formula itself became the means for valuing and creating, not only listed options, but all sorts of option-like instruments. These included over-the-counter (OTC) options tailored to individual investor needs, exotic options with specialized payoff features, and more general corporate instruments and contracts and insurance company contracts.

Option pricing theory fostered the development of another product that would take the markets by storm in the 1980s. Synthetic portfolio insurance packaged one of the seminal ideas of option pricing theory – the theoretical equivalence between options and dynamic positions in the underlying risky asset and a risk-free asset. That is, by taking and trading positions in the underlying asset and a risk-free asset, investors could construct an actual portfolio that synthesized the behavior of any desired option.

Leland O'Brien Rubinstein Associates (LOR) launched the first synthetic portfolio insurance products in 1982. It was soon joined by licensees such as Wells Fargo Investment Advisors, a subsidiary of Wells Fargo Bank, and Aetna Life and Casualty. Estimates of the amount of equity assets insured just prior to the market crash of October 19, 1987 range from $60 to $100 billion.

The expanding popularity of synthetic portfolio insurance was not surprising, given the claims made for its performance. Purveyors of the strategies asserted that they could insure equity portfolios against market declines while allowing participation in any market advances over the insurance horizon. The strategies thus appealed to the two most basic human instincts of investors – both greed and fear.

Vendors claimed that synthetic portfolio insurance was equivalent to the insurance an individual would purchase for a home or car, or a corporate entity would purchase for its factory and equipment. Just as these assets' values could be insured against loss, the (often far greater) value of financial asset portfolios could now be protected. But could synthetic portfolio insurance provide true insurance?

Synthetic portfolio insurance differs from traditional insurance, where numerous insured parties each pay an explicit, predetermined premium to an insurance company, which accepts the independent risks of such unforeseeable events as theft or fire. The traditional insurer pools the risks of many participants and is obligated, and in general able, to draw on these premiums and accumulated reserves, as necessary, to reimburse losses. Synthetic portfolio insurance also differs critically from real options, where the option seller, for a premium, takes on the risk of market moves.

Synthetic portfolio insurance is essentially a form of self-insurance; it is the investors who "buy" the insurance who take on the risk. They give up some degree of portfolio return in exchange for the theoretical assurance of receiving no less than a chosen minimum return. They are not able to draw upon the premiums of many thousands or millions of other investors in the event of catastrophe. Instead, they are reliant upon the ability to get into or out of the market as needed, hence upon the willingness of other investors to take the offsetting sides of required trades.

Furthermore, synthetic portfolio insurance, in attempting to replicate the behavior of a long put option, must buy as markets rise and sell as they fall. This trend-following dynamic trading is inherently destabilizing to markets. It has the potential to create volatility and (as we will see) even crashes. In that case, it is not merely synthetic insurers who must bear the risk of their insurance, but all market participants.

Chapter 1 outlines the basics of options, option replication, and synthetic portfolio insurance. Chapter 2 reviews the marketing hype of the insurance purveyors. For many investors, vendors' talk of insured returns at no or negative costs amounted to an offer they couldn't refuse. As chapter 3 shows, however, many of the promises of insurance vendors were hollow: insurance strategies are by no means costless; nor are they as "riskless" as the option strategies they are designed to replicate.

Chapter 4 examines the appeal of portfolio insurance generally for different types of investors and the suitability of specific insurance strategies. For most long-term investors, alternative investment strategies will prove more rewarding than insurance.

1

Options and Option Replication

> If options on a particular stock or on a portfolio do not exist, we can create them by using the appropriate strategy for the underlying asset and cash. . . . Such an investment strategy would be tantamount to insuring the equity portfolio against losses by paying a fixed premium to an insurance company.
>
> *Mark Rubinstein and Hayne Leland, 1981*

No investor wants to lose money. Unfortunately, the risk of loss is intrinsic to the pursuit of gain. In fact, the two are positively related: the higher the return an investor aims for, the more risk he or she must incur.

This doesn't mean that attempts haven't been made to separate out the risk from the return component of investing. In the 1950s and 1960s, for example, the Edinburgh Insurance Company in the United Kingdom and Harleysville Mutual Insurance Company and Prudential Insurance Company of America in the United States offered insured mutual funds. These funds came with a guarantee of a minimum value for the funds' assets, which was backed by insurance company reserves.

These particular products found little acceptance in the marketplace (Gatto et al. 1980). Perhaps it was a matter of timing; the 1950s and 1960s, sandwiched between the deflationary era of the prewar period and the inflationary 1970s, offered relatively steady real returns and rising nominal returns, and investors may have felt little need for insurance. Perhaps it was lack of an effective marketing effort. In any case, it wasn't until the 1980s that the insurance of portfolios of financial assets really took off, and then it took its cue, not from the principles of the insurance industry, but from option pricing theory.

Options

Options provide a useful, if sometimes misused, instrument by which investors can enhance their investment returns or limit their investment risks. Options have been around for quite some time.

The Romans and the Phoenicians optioned the cargoes transported on their ships. Suppose you, as a Roman citizen, wanted to invest in a cargo of wine bound for Egypt or Syria. The wine can be purchased in Rome for a lot less than it is expected to sell for at its destination, so there is a sizable potential profit. But the ship may sink; the wine may spoil on its voyage; or the market may already be glutted by wine brought in by other exporters with the same idea. You could lose much or all of your investment.

For a mere percentage of what it would cost you to buy a direct investment in the cargo, you could purchase an option that effectively gives you the right to purchase a certain percentage interest in the cargo at a predetermined price (say, the cost of the wine in Rome) at some time in the future – presumably after the ship is expected to land. This is what is known as a call option. If the wine arrives safely, and is sold at a price that exceeds the price specified in the option contract, you exercise the call option, paying the specified price and pocketing a profit.

Of course, this profit will be somewhat reduced by the amount you paid for the option; you will thus not be as well off as an investor who purchased a share of the cargo outright. However, if the wine ends up at the bottom of the sea, or as vinegar, or has to be sold at a loss, you will be much better off. In that case, you will not exercise your call option, as shares in the ship's cargo will be worth less than the price specified in the option contract. You will be out the amount you paid for the option, but will have saved yourself the full expense of an investment in the cargo's shares.

There is an alternative option strategy that can give an equivalent result. You could purchase a share of the cargo but, at the same time, purchase a put option, which allows you to sell your share at a specified price at some future date. Say this price equals the cost of the wine in Rome. Now, if the ship arrives safely and the cargo is sold for a profit, you will not exercise the put; you will receive the profit from the sale of the wine, which will of course be reduced by what you paid for the option. If the profit does not materialize, however, you will exercise the put, receiving the specified price. So, as with the call option, rather than losing your entire investment, you are out only what you paid for the put option.

In both cases you, as the option holder, have the opportunity to participate in any profits from the sale of wine. Relative to the direct investor, you have reduced your potential profit by the amount you paid for the option, whether put or call. In exchange for this reduction in potential profit, however, you have limited the maximum amount of your potential loss to the cost of the option – the option premium.

Of course, someone must bear the risk you have gotten rid of. This is the seller of the option, or the option writer. The put writer stands ready to pay you the specified price for a worthless asset if the venture fails, and the call writer stands ready to turn over to you the profits of a successful voyage. Option sellers are thus at substantial risk. The price they charge the option holders for accepting this risk is the option premium.

The option premium can thus be likened to the premium paid for an insurance policy.[1] As with an insurance policy premium, an option premium may be expected to depend upon factors such as the time over which the option can be exercised (the term of the insurance); the difference between the initial value of the underlying asset and the price, specified in the contract, at which the option can be exercised, or struck (the deductible in an insurance policy); and the probability of the option being exercised (the actuarial rates in insurance). Until very recently, however, no one could describe with any precision how an option's value depended upon such factors.

How Options Took Off

Options reemerged in Europe, like much else of Classical civilization, after the Middle Ages. With the collapse of Dutch tulip prices in the 1630s, however, owners of put options on bulbs were left with near-worthless investments when put sellers reneged on their obligations (Gastineau 1988: 16). Their image deeply tarnished, options were driven to the underground economy, from whence they reemerged into public light only sporadically.

Options began trading in the US in the late eighteenth century. Up through the 1920s, however, when option-linked manipulation helped to fuel the stock market's pre-crash rise, their reputation left much to be desired. The securities laws passed in the wake of the 1929 crash eliminated many of the abuses options gave rise to.

Options on equity didn't really take off until 1973. That watershed year saw the establishment of the first centralized exchange for the trading of options – the Chicago Board Options Exchange (to be followed within a few years by the American, Pacific, and Philadelphia exchanges). Compared with over-the-counter option trading, which had prevailed until then, centralized option exchanges offered standardized strike prices, interchangeableness, and low transaction costs. They enabled investors to trade options more readily than ever before.[2]

Despite the convenience of centralized trading, option exchanges themselves may not have led to a booming option business had it not been for another development. In 1973, Fischer Black and Myron S.

Scholes published "The Pricing of Options and Corporate Liabilities," and Robert C. Merton published "Theory of Rational Option Pricing."[3] Together, their work constituted the first valid analytical formula for valuing options. They took ad hoc valuation techniques and replaced them with a closed-form formula that investors could use to value options more accurately than ever before.

Black and Scholes modeled a call and the stock underlying it in a way that allowed them to build a formula for deriving a "fair" option value from the current price of the stock, its price volatility, the risk-free interest rate, the strike price of the option, and its time to expiration.[4] Merton generalized the Black–Scholes formula for stocks paying a continuous dividend. Appendix B goes into what is known as the Black–Scholes option pricing formula in some detail.

A great deal of the beauty, and popularity, of Black–Scholes stems from the fact that the necessary ingredients are either observable or readily estimated, and from the fact that the results are fairly robust to relaxation of the simplifying assumptions used to derive the formula (see Ingersoll 1989).[5] Of equal importance, however, is the value of the insights gained from the way in which Black, Scholes, and Merton structured the valuation problem.

They solved the problem of option pricing by examining the essentially risk-free nature of a hedged option position. That is, an option plus some continuously adjusted offsetting position in the risky asset underlying the option will yield a riskless rate of return; the price movements of the risky asset offset, or hedge, the price movements of the option. This in turn implies the equivalence, at least in theory, between options and dynamic positions in the underlying risky asset and a risk-free asset. The value of an option must thus equal the value of the replicating portfolio of common financial assets. This follows from the no-arbitrage condition: if the values of the option and its replicating portfolio diverged, arbitragers could earn a riskless profit by selling the relatively expensive alternative and buying the relatively cheap one.

This essential insight was generalizable to a great many other derivative assets and financial contracts with option-like characteristics. Common shares and corporate debt, for example, can be seen to depend upon the value of the issuing firm in much the same way an option depends on the underlying stock. Many new derivatives products, including the booming over-the-counter option industry, owe their viability to Black, Scholes, and Merton.

The Royal Swedish Academy of Sciences recognized this contribution to finance in 1997 by awarding Merton and Scholes the Bank of Sweden Prize in Economic Sciences in Memory of Alfred Nobel. (Unfortunately, Fischer Black had died, at fifty-seven, in 1995.) The Academy noted:

Black, Merton and Scholes ... laid the foundation for the rapid growth of markets for derivatives in the last ten years. Their method had more general applicability, however, and has created new areas of research – inside as well as outside of financial economics. A similar method may be used to value insurance contracts and guarantees, or the flexibility of physical investment projects.

FIGURE 1.1
Fischer Black

Source: Debra Minter/Goldman, Sachs & Co.

FIGURE 1.2
Myron S. Scholes receiving his Nobel Prize

Source: Anders Wiklund/Pica Pressfoto AB.

FIGURE 1.3
Robert C. Merton receiving his Nobel Prize

Source: Jonas Ekströmer/Pressens Bild AB.

Replicating Options

The replicating portfolios implicit in the pricing formula opened the door to the creation of *synthetic* options. That is, not only could investors use the theoretical replicating portfolio to price its corresponding option, but, by taking and trading positions in the underlying asset and a risk-free asset, investors could construct an actual portfolio that synthesized the behavior of a desired option.

This idea was taken up in the late 1970s by Michael Brennan and Eduardo Schwartz (1976 and 1979), who demonstrated that insurance companies offering an asset value guarantee could hedge their liability through synthetic option replication. Brennan and Schwartz were the first scholars to simulate synthetic option strategies. They were not the first to put this notion into practice, however.

Hayne Leland and Mark Rubinstein, two scholars from the University of California at Berkeley, were the first to popularize these synthetic strategies as "portfolio insurance" (see Rubinstein and Leland 1981 and O'Brien 1982). Leland and Rubinstein joined forces with John O'Brien, formerly a practitioner at the investment consulting firms O'Brien Associates and A.G. Becker, to form Leland O'Brien Rubinstein Associates (LOR). LOR launched the first portfolio insurance products in 1982.

In 1982, despite the emergence of listed option markets and the publication of the option pricing formula, large institutional investors faced substantial hurdles when it came to using options. These consisted of tight position limits that were unsuitable for large-scale investors and the unavailability of options with longer-term horizons. Synthetic portfolio insurance offered a way around these obstacles.

Synthetic portfolio insurance was essentially an attempt to replicate a protective put – a put option on an underlying portfolio.[6] A real protective put strategy combines a put option on a stock or stock index and a long position in the underlying stock. The stock position affords the investor the opportunity to benefit from increases in the stock's price. The put allows the investor to sell the stock to the put writer at the specified price, so the investor is protected from declines in the stock price below this strike price. The investor thus achieves, at the cost of the put premium, participation in upside gains and protection from downside losses.

Option pricing theory indicates that put (or call) replication requires buying stock as the market rises and selling as it falls. The concept of buying as prices rise and selling as they fall may seem counterintuitive, but it makes sense within the context of portfolio insurance.

Intuitively, a decline in the price of the stock component of the insurance portfolio lowers the portfolio's return, jeopardizing achievement of better than the minimum insured return. Reducing the portfolio's commitment to stock (the risky asset) and increasing its commitment to cash (the riskless asset) firms up the portfolio's return. Conversely, increases in the price of the stock component of the portfolio lower the probability that the portfolio will fall below the guaranteed minimum. The portfolio's commitment to equity can be increased, increasing its participation in any market advances. (Appendix C provides a more formal description of option replication.)

Early synthetic insurance programs, including the strategy marketed as "Dynamic Asset Allocation" by LOR, were actually implemented by buying and selling stocks in order to alter the portfolio's allocations between risky and riskless assets.[7] Stock index futures were introduced in 1982, however, and within a few years had attracted more trading activity than their underlying stocks.

An investor can purchase a futures contract at today's price, secured with a small margin payment, and receive the underlying asset, upon payment of the remaining amount due, at a given future date. Alternatively, an investor can sell a futures contract short, in effect locking in a given price now in exchange for delivering the asset in the future. Like options, futures are derivatives contracts in that their value is contingent on the value of the underlying asset – in the case of stock index futures, the value of a stock index such as the S&P 500. Unlike options, futures require the transfer of the asset (or its cash equivalent) at contract expiration.

By the time of the 1987 crash, the volume of underlying shares represented by the average daily volume of trading in all index futures contracts equaled 150 to 200 percent of the trading volume on the New York Stock Exchange. Futures markets had come to be perceived as extremely liquid and as having low transaction costs compared with the underlying stock market. As a result, futures had become insurers' preferred means of hedging.[8] LOR had introduced its alluringly named "Fiduciary Hedge" strategy, implemented with futures, in early 1984.[9]

Stock index futures can be used to create cash synthetically or to provide exposure to the risky underlying stock. A long futures position offers exposure to the underlying risky asset. A short futures position held against underlying stock is equivalent to a synthetic cash position.

An insured portfolio can thus sell futures short to reduce risk or cover short futures positions to increase upside return potential. As the portfolio's value falls towards its assured minimum floor, the manager sells futures short, creating synthetic cash. If the market rallies, the manager covers short positions, substituting equity exposure for synthetic cash and restoring the portfolio's upside potential.

Real versus Synthetic Options

Although portfolio insurance via option replication was purportedly equivalent to an option or an insurance policy, in reality it differed from both real options and real insurance in several critical respects. A real put option, for example, provides a minimum floor value for a portfolio of risky assets; this minimum value is pegged by the option's strike price. The investor pays an explicit price for this protection – the option premium.

A put synthesized via option replication also promises a minimum floor value (although, as we will see later, this promise is not necessarily fulfilled). For this synthetic insurance, however, the investor does not have to pay an explicit premium to an option writer. This does not mean that synthetic portfolio insurance does not have costs; in fact, as we will see, its costs may be incurred, not only by the investor insuring the portfolio, but by the market as a whole.

The protection supposedly offered by a synthetic portfolio insurance program is for a specific investment horizon, analogous in option valuation to the time to expiration (or to the term of a regular insurance policy). The overall performance of the synthetically insured portfolio must be measured over this investment horizon.

If the market declines during this period, portfolio insurance should provide a minimum floor value via the reallocation of portfolio assets away from stock as its price falls and into cash. If the market rises, the insured portfolio should participate in the gain via the reallocation of portfolio assets away from cash and into stock.

Reductions in risk, however, usually cannot be accomplished without cost; in the investment world, cost often comes in the form of reduced return. For synthetic portfolio insurance, cost is incurred through a reduction in achievable return in periods when stock returns exceed cash returns. In such periods, the insured portfolio's return will fall short of the return to a portfolio fully invested in stock, because of the insured portfolio's commitment to cash. The difference between the insured portfolio's return over the horizon and the fully invested portfolio's return is called the shortfall.

The shortfall cost is likely to be larger, the riskier stocks are. Higher risk will, other things being equal, necessitate a larger commitment to cash in order to ensure a given minimum return. The higher the portfolio's commitment to cash, the lower, in general, its expected return will be.

The shortfall is likely to be smaller, the larger the potential loss the investor is willing to live with. An investor willing to accept a loss of 10 percent when the cash return is 5 percent will obviously be able to allocate a relatively larger percentage of the portfolio to stock than an investor who will tolerate a maximum loss of only 5 percent. The first investor will thus be positioned to capture more of any upside market moves.

The difference between an insured portfolio's initial value and the investor's maximum tolerable loss (or, equivalently, assured minimum floor) is comparable to the deductible in a regular insurance policy, or to the difference between the initial value of the underlying stock and the option strike price. The smaller the deductible, the higher the expected cost of the program, in terms of sacrifice of upside capture.

The cost of synthetic portfolio insurance, then, depends importantly on the percentage of the portfolio allocated to cash rather than stock. This constitutes a major difference between synthetic insurance and insurance with a real option or traditional insurance, where the cost of insurance is explicit in the premium paid up front. With portfolio insurance, the cost is implicit and is incurred, not at the start of the insurance program, but over its life.

The actual cost of a synthetic insurance program will be determined by the actual volatility of stock returns over the course of the program's horizon. If, over the insurance horizon, experienced volatility is in line with expectations at the outset of the insurance program, the actual cost of the insurance program will turn out to be roughly equal to the anticipated cost. If volatility turns out to be higher than expected, however, the cost of the insurance program will be higher than anticipated at the outset.

Higher than anticipated volatility will necessitate more frequent or larger adjustments of the cash and stock positions; as a consequence, transaction costs will be higher than expected. Higher volatility will also increase the likelihood of "whipsaw" price movements, whereby sudden stock price increases are followed by declines, which are in turn followed by increases. As portfolio insurance calls for buying when prices rise and selling when prices fall, it can put the investor on the unprofitable side of trades when the market is characterized by whipsaws. More frequent selling before price rises and buying before declines will erode portfolio return.

A Risk Posed

The costs of synthetic portfolio insurance may not be confined to its buyers. The trading requirements of the strategy may impose upon the overall market costs in the form of increased volatility and instability. These reflect the tendency of trend-following dynamic hedging to exacerbate and amplify departures of market prices from their fundamental values and its potential to add to the noise in market prices.

As we have noted, synthetic portfolio insurance is equivalent to replication of a long put position combined with an underlying stock portfolio. Replicating long option positions requires selling as the market falls and buying as it rises. This trend-following trading constitutes positive feedback, which is inherently destabilizing.

For example, when long put replication calls for buying, it can cause prices to rise more than they otherwise would. The higher prices rise, the more fragile the market becomes. At some point, even slightly bad news can trigger a price decline. At this point, the same dynamic hedging rules that required buying on the way up will require selling on the way down.

These dynamic hedging trades alone have the potential to exacerbate price moves. Moreover, their effects may be magnified by the actions of other investors who observe the results of the trades but not the reasons behind them. Investors unaware that the trades are mechanistic and informationless may misread them as reflecting new information. These investors may be encouraged to trade in the same direction as, or discouraged from taking the other side of, hedgers' trades. Thus insurers' trend-following trades can have a snowball effect.

The trading demands of long put replication may overwhelm other investors' ability, or willingness, to supply them. In the face of concentrated selling by put-replicating portfolio insurers, market prices can gap down; rather than moving smoothly through every increment on the way from one price to a lower one, prices may skip over intermediate intervals. In the presence of such price discontinuity, dynamic hedgers may not be able to execute their trades at the required prices. Synthetic insurance may fail to offer the protection it was designed to provide.

Worse, volatility and price discontinuities caused by dynamic hedging trades can lead to a market crash. As we will see in part III, this is what happened in 1987. In 1987, portfolio insurance amounted to a massive replicated put on the entire stock market. This put insured up to $100 billion in equity assets, or 3 percent of the market's capitalization back then.

Synthetic portfolio insurance exploited investors' human frailties by promising increased returns at reduced risk. In reality, the insurance proved a bad bargain. Its automated purchases helped fuel the market's rise in the mid 1980s, and its selling demands on October 19, 1987 turned a market correction into a major crash. The crash in turn trampled on the guarantees of most portfolio insurance programs – and on the toes of most investors as well.

While investors deserted synthetic portfolio insurance in droves in the wake of the crash, portfolio insurance has not disappeared; it has merely changed form. In particular, investors who had turned to option replication for synthetic insurance in the 1980s did so because they could not use real options in meeting their insurance needs. Today, these investors can turn to an expanded menu of listed options, with relaxed position limits, or to over-the-counter (OTC) options for portfolio protection. Listed and OTC options, unlike synthetic portfolio insurance, are not inherently destabilizing to markets. Once an investor purchases them, they provide the protection promised, and the investor does not have to engage in any further trading.

What is true for the option buyer, however, is not necessarily true for the option seller. As we have noted, option sellers expose themselves to substantial market risk. If they do not wish to assume the risk of their short option positions, they may be able to neutralize it by buying equivalent long option positions from speculators who are willing to take on the risk in exchange for the option premium. They may not be able to do so, however. Equivalent options may not be available. Or demand for long option positions may make buying options uneconomical. In either case, option sellers who want to reduce their own risks must turn to dynamic hedging in the futures or underlying stock markets. Their dynamic hedging, in turn, can raise market volatility for all investors.

As we will see, the risk of holding equity can be transferred from one market participant to another. It cannot be eliminated.

Summary

In an ideal world, an investor could insure the value of a portfolio by purchasing, at a quoted premium, a put option that would allow the portfolio to be sold at a predetermined price at the end of the investment horizon. If the portfolio's value declined below this price, the investor would exercise the option; if the portfolio's value rose, the investor would not exercise the option and the investor's return would be reduced only by the amount of the prepaid option premium. The investor would thus be able to establish a floor value for the portfolio, at the cost of a known option premium, while retaining upside potential.

In the real world, options may not be available to suit every need. Option pricing theory, however, suggests that any desired option can be replicated by a dynamic trading strategy. Synthetic portfolio insurance replicates a long put on an underling stock portfolio. By hedging with cash or short futures positions as portfolio value declines, synthetic portfolio insurance aims to ensure a floor or minimum return over the investment horizon. By increasing equity or covering short futures positions as portfolio value rises, portfolio insurance aims to maximize portfolio participation on the upside.

Synthetic portfolio insurance (and other forms of option replication), however, differs from real options in several critical ways. With real options, the cost of protection is limited to the option premium and known in advance. The cost of synthetic portfolio insurance is incurred over the insurance horizon, in accordance with the price behavior of the underlying asset. If price volatility turns out to be higher than anticipated, the synthetic option will end up costing more than was expected at the beginning of the insurance horizon. And, to the extent the trend-following dynamic trading required by option-replicating insurance strategies increases price volatility and market instability, it paves the way for disappointment.

Nevertheless, some of the early purveyors of synthetic portfolio insurance argued that these strategies would turn out to be not only riskless, but also costless. Some of the evidence even suggested that the strategies would "pay" insured investors in the form of enhanced returns over and above those on a fully invested equity portfolio. These claims are documented in the following chapter.

Notes

1 Although the examples we have just given are undoubtedly more soph-isticated than the actual derivatives contracts used 2,000 years ago, an Egyptian papyrus dating from the middle of the second century details an agreement, written as a loan, whereby the lender, in exchange for a 33 per-cent premium, paid out the agreed amount in the event a ship and its cargo were lost (Liversidge 1976: 181).
2 Although, at the outset, investors could not trade puts on these exchanges, only calls; puts were introduced in 1977. Stock index options began trading in 1983.
3 Interestingly, Black and Scholes' work was rejected by several leading fin-ance journals before finding a home at the University of Chicago's *Journal of Political Economy*, where it was fostered by Merton Miller and Eugene Fama. Black (1989b) later wrote that he suspected the rejections had more to do with the lack of an academic return address on the envelope than with the work's merits. Although Scholes was at MIT (where Black, too, subsequently taught after leaving the University of Chicago and before joining Wall Street's Goldman, Sachs), Black at that time was "merely" doing research and consulting in Cambridge.
4 The value of a put can be derived from a pricing relationship known as put-call parity. This simply indicates that, because puts can be used in conjunc-tion with stock to create call-like payoffs, put and call prices must be related in a given way; otherwise arbitrage would be possible. The Black–Scholes formula strictly applies only to European-style options, which cannot be exercised until expiration. There is no closed-form solution for American-style options, which can be exercised early, before expiration; within certain limitations, however, Black–Scholes can be used to approximate the values of American options.
5 The formula assumes away dividends, taxes, transaction costs, and restric-tions on short sales; it assumes a constant risk-free rate, continuous trading, no early exercise, and a stock price that evolves via geometric Brownian motion.

6   See Rubinstein and Leland (1981). They frame the argument in terms of a fiduciary call (cash plus call), which equals a protective put (stock plus put). Because insurance strategies are concerned only with value at termination, a European-style, rather than American-style, option was the appropriate replication target.

7   The term "dynamic asset allocation" has more recently been applied to other strategies that involve moving funds among various asset classes, particularly tactical asset allocation. Tactical asset allocation differs fundamentally from portfolio insurance, however. In the former, funds are allocated and reallocated among various asset classes, based on return forecasts, with the aim of timing asset class performance. As we have seen, portfolio insurance assumes that returns cannot be anticipated and mechanistically reallocates assets in response to stock price changes, with the aim of achieving the maximum return possible while at the same time not falling below a specified minimum return. As we will see in later chapters, tactical asset allocators may actually serve as a natural counterparty to portfolio insurance traders.

8   By the time of the crash, over 80 percent of portfolio insurance was implemented with futures (Leland 1988b: 81).

9   Because LOR's "Dynamic Asset Allocation" strategy called for the portfolio to sell or buy stocks in response to market moves, it interfered with the management of the underlying equity portfolio. LOR's "Fiduciary Hedge" strategy offered protection via a "transparent" futures position that did not disrupt the underlying portfolio. Note that predicting the volatility of an active manager's portfolio would be even more difficult than predicting the volatility of a passive stock index.

2

Synthetic Portfolio Insurance: The Sell

> Corporations insure many facets of business risk. Yet pension fund risks far outweigh most others. It takes a lot of smoke and fire to match a 20 percent decline in a $1 billion portfolio.
>
> *Hayne Leland, 1986*

Synthetic portfolio insurance became "the fastest growing investment strategy in the history of investment strategies" (Luskin 1988: xv) in part because it was intensely promoted as a product with universal appeal. LOR Executive Vice President Robert Ferguson (1983: 38) asserted that LOR's "Dynamic Asset Allocation" portfolio insurance program "is a new investment technology that can please virtually any investor. In fact, because dynamic asset allocation is a more efficient way of solving investment problems, it would be surprising if an informed investor chose not to use it." According to its promoters, portfolio insurance had numerous useful applications. We review these claims in this chapter.

Asset Protection

Portfolio insurance vendors appealed to investors' instinctive desire for protection. They likened the concept of insuring security portfolios to that of insuring automobiles, homes, and factories. As Ferguson and his LOR colleague Larry Edwards put it (1985: 1):

> Most corporations and individuals find it desirable to insure some or all of their property against loss. Automobile and home insurance are good examples of policies chosen by individuals. Corporations often insure factories and equipment.
>
> Portfolios of risky assets, such as stocks and bonds, are often just as important or more important to individuals and corporations as automobiles,

homes, and factories. If individuals and corporations want to insure these physical assets, logic suggests that they also will want to insure their securities portfolios.

LOR cofounder Hayne Leland (1986: 34) emphasized that pension investment risks can far exceed the property and casualty risks that corporations insure as a matter of course: "Corporations insure many facets of business risk. Yet pension fund risks far outweigh most others. It takes a lot of smoke and fire to match a 20 percent decline in a $1 billion portfolio."

Traditional insurance requires payment of a premium for coverage. The premium for synthetic insurance of risky assets, by contrast, was often promoted as negative. That is, portfolio insurance was frequently sold, not only as a means of protecting assets, but as a means of actually enhancing returns. Simulated backtests, demonstrating that returns on an insured portfolio far exceeded those on a fully invested (uninsured) equity portfolio, were used as a marketing tool.

Enhanced Returns

In a series of advertisements appearing in 1982, LOR reported the results of its "Dynamic Asset Allocation" strategy, which called for investment in a changing mix of the S&P 500 and US Treasury bills. One dollar invested in the dynamic strategy at the beginning of 1972 would have returned $2.61, or 10 percent per annum, by the end of 1981. Over this same period, the S&P 500 returned $1.89, or 6.5 percent, and Treasury bills $2.18, or 8.1 percent.[1]

Another LOR advertisement, made jointly with Aetna, began with the come-on: "Read what happened when the pioneer of dynamic asset allocation met the manager of $25 billion in pension funds." Appearing in the November 14, 1983 issue of *Pensions & Investment Age*, the ad continued, "They came up with GEM, Aetna Life and Casualty's Guaranteed Equity Management Strategy." As the name implies, GEM guaranteed a minimum return on Aetna's largest separate equity account. But the advertisement also touted the results of a simulation applying the strategy to the account over the ten years ending 1982 – a 170 percent cumulative return, versus 91 percent for the S&P 500.[2] (Aetna discontinued GEM after the crash.)

Steven Wunsch (1985c), then a vice president and futures trader at Kidder Peabody, an important futures broker for insurance vendors, used the analogy of a racing car to compare dynamic portfolio insurance strategies with static strategies:

FIGURE 2.1
LOR Ad: "Investing's Third Wave"

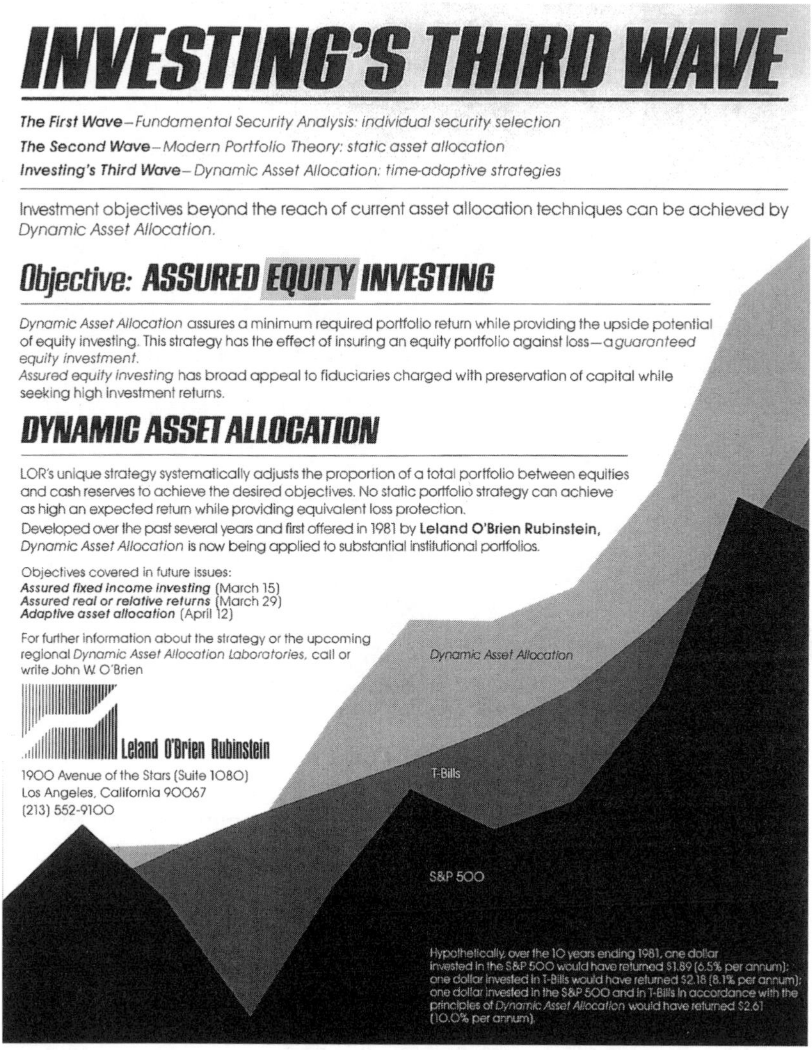

INVESTING'S THIRD WAVE

The First Wave — *Fundamental Security Analysis: individual security selection*
The Second Wave — *Modern Portfolio Theory: static asset allocation*
Investing's Third Wave — *Dynamic Asset Allocation: time-adaptive strategies*

Investment objectives beyond the reach of current asset allocation techniques can be achieved by *Dynamic Asset Allocation.*

Objective: ASSURED EQUITY INVESTING

Dynamic Asset Allocation assures a minimum required portfolio return while providing the upside potential of equity investing. This strategy has the effect of insuring an equity portfolio against loss — a *guaranteed equity investment.*
Assured equity investing has broad appeal to fiduciaries charged with preservation of capital while seeking high investment returns.

DYNAMIC ASSET ALLOCATION

LOR's unique strategy systematically adjusts the proportion of a total portfolio between equities and cash reserves to achieve the desired objectives. No static portfolio strategy can achieve as high an expected return while providing equivalent loss protection.
Developed over the past several years and first offered in 1981 by **Leland O'Brien Rubinstein,** *Dynamic Asset Allocation* is now being applied to substantial institutional portfolios.

Objectives covered in future issues:
Assured fixed income investing (March 15)
Assured real or relative returns (March 29)
Adaptive asset allocation (April 12)

For further information about the strategy or the upcoming regional *Dynamic Asset Allocation Laboratories,* call or write John W. O'Brien

Leland O'Brien Rubinstein

1900 Avenue of the Stars (Suite 1080)
Los Angeles, California 90067
(213) 552-9100

Dynamic Asset Allocation

T-Bills

S&P 500

Hypothetically, over the 10 years ending 1981, one dollar invested in the S&P 500 would have returned $1.89 (6.5% per annum); one dollar invested in T-Bills would have returned $2.18 (8.1% per annum); one dollar invested in the S&P 500 and in T-Bills in accordance with the principles of *Dynamic Asset Allocation* would have returned $2.61 (10.0% per annum).

Source: *Pensions & Investment Age*, March 1, 1982.

FIGURE 2.2
Aetna Ad: GEM

John O'Brien, President
Leland O'Brien Rubinstein Associates, Inc.

T. Jerald Moore, Vice President, Employee
Benefits Division, Ætna Life & Casualty

Read what happened when the pioneer of dynamic asset allocation met the manager of $25 billion in pension funds.

They came up with GEM, Ætna Life & Casualty's Guaranteed Equity Management strategy.

What makes GEM unique is the combination it offers: Dynamic asset allocation, coupled with a guaranteed minimum rate of return which you select.

What's more, GEM offers the highest equity participation of any dynamic strategy available.

What else makes our GEM strategy so remarkable? The investment technology credentials of Leland O'Brien Rubinstein Associates (LOR) are impeccable. They provide dynamic asset allocation services and nothing but. Currently, they are serving twenty other portfolios totaling over $600 million.

Ætna's equity management credentials are equally impressive. Cumulatively, over a ten-year period, our largest pooled account performance has ranked in the top 9% of the P.I.P.E.R. universe.

And we provide pension and financial services to one out of four of America's largest corporations.

If you would like to learn more about GEM, get in touch with your Ætna Employee Benefits Representative, or call T. Jerald Moore, Vice President, at (203) 273-4734.

You'll be glad you met Ætna.

Employee Benefits Division
Ætna Life Insurance Company
151 Farmington Avenue, Hartford, CT 06156

Source: *Pensions & Investment Age*, November 14, 1983, p. 22.

Imagine trying to win the Indy 500 by fixing your car's speed [static allocation]. If that speed were even close to fast enough to be competitive, the result would be a certain crash. On the other hand, if the fixed speed were slow enough to be safe for the turns, losing the race would be certain. A fixed speed strategy would be adequately competitive only if none of the other contestants had brakes or accelerators either. . . . Some corporations are using . . . [dynamic strategies] extensively to slow down for the curves so that when favorable market conditions do develop, they will be in the optimal position to power into the straightaways for maximum competitive advantage.

Unleashing the Aggressive Investor

Its vendors argued that portfolio insurance, by virtue of its guarantee of some minimum return, could unleash more aggressive approaches to equity investment. Leland (1980) asserted, for example, that investors with more optimistic return expectations than average would want to insure. The downside protection offered by an insurance program would allow such investors to raise equity allocations, thus increasing expected returns.

Leland and Mark Rubinstein, University of California, Berkeley and LOR colleagues, contended:

FIGURE 2.3

LOR Ad: Unleashing the Aggressive Investor

The Fiduciary Hedge Program

Using the Fiduciary Hedge Program (FHP) a plan sponsor can control the minimum return of his entire fund (except for illiquid and non-U.S. assets), without disturbing existing programs or managers. The FHP can apply annually or over multi-year periods.

When the FHP is used to apply Dynamic Asset Allocation, implementation is through stock index and bond futures contracts. The principle behind the use of futures contracts here is that holding stock and selling a stock index futures contract accomplishes the same end as selling stock and buying T-bills. The same is true for bonds and bond futures contracts.

The benefit of using futures contracts is that transaction and administrative expenses are greatly reduced, and no change in existing asset structures

or manager discretion is required.

There is a cost, or premium, for the minimum return assurance that the Fiduciary Hedge Program provides. However, with the FHP in effect more of the fund's assets can be placed in higher expected return albeit riskier asset classes. **The net effect can be to increase the total fund's expected return by 1 to 2 percent per annum.**

Establishing an FHP requires only that one additional account—the fiduciary hedge account—be opened with the master trustee. Authority is given to the manager of that account to use futures contracts to accomplish the hedge management directed by the DAA process.

Major pension funds are currently using the Fiduciary Hedge Program on assets totalling over one billion dollars. Programs in place currently cover investment horizons out to three years.

Leland O'Brien Rubinstein Associates

Source: LOR Sponsored Section, *Institutional Investor*, 1984, p. 7.

> Long-run returns can actually be raised, with downside risks controlled, when insurance programs are applied to more aggressive active assets. Pension, endowment, and educational funds can actually enhance their expected returns by increasing their commitment to equities and other high-return sectors, while fulfilling their fiduciary responsibilities by insuring this more aggressive portfolio. Compared with current static allocation techniques, annual expected returns can be raised by as much as 200 basis points [each basis point being one hundredth of 1 percent] per year. (Leland and Rubinstein 1988b: 9)

In fact, LOR claimed (in an undated LOR document entitled "Fiduciary Hedge Program") that its insurance program using futures could increase returns by up to 400 basis points a year! This return increment more than made up for the annual management fees of 20 basis points or less that LOR charged for providing such insurance of institutional portfolios.[3]

Continuing the racing car analogy, LOR Vice President Scott Grannis (1988: 49) compared dynamic insurance strategies to good brakes: "the driver with good brakes will likely be the winner since he can average a faster speed than the driver with poor brakes."

And if equity alone wasn't aggressive enough, one could always use leverage. LOR's Ferguson (1986b) claimed that an aggressive investor could "beat the S&P 500 without losing sleep." He and Leland simulated a strategy of insuring an S&P 500 index portfolio that had been leveraged to a point where its volatility was 50 percent higher than the market's (beta of 1.5). The reported returns, net of transaction costs, exceeded those of the unleveraged index (Leland 1984 and Ferguson 1986b). Leland (1984: 2) stated:

> Is it possible to use portfolio insurance to *increase* expected return over that of the uninsured S&P 500, while still protecting against downside risk? . . . consider running a protected portfolio with beta 1.5 . . . such a portfolio could be constructed, for example, by levering an index fund, or by using index futures. . . . Results of the simulations . . . show conclusively that portfolio protection programs can be used to increase returns, while limiting downside risks.

Locking in Gains

As the bulls charged through 1986 and into 1987, many investors began to worry about the possibility of being gored by a market about-face, and about preserving the exceptional gains they had made over the past four to five years. An LOR advertisement in the January 1987 issue

Source: Institutional Investor, January 1987, p. 88.

of *Institutional Investor* (p. 169) asked: "With the market at new highs, isn't it time to consider locking in your gains?"

Survey results reported in the November issue of *Institutional Investor* (p. 139) had indicated that "76.5 percent of investors that selected insurance did so primarily to protect the gains . . . made since the onset of the bull market in 1982." This suggests that insurers and vendors of insurance – contrary to the basic tenets and mechanics of portfolio insurance, which assume that price changes are unpredictable – elected portfolio insurance as a market timing device.

Pension Fund Benefits

Insured equity was promoted as offering downside protection while allowing capture of the generally higher long-term returns that equities provide. Leland and his LOR cofounder John O'Brien (1985: 2) enumerated the benefits for pension plans: "A substantial lowering of expected pension costs through the use of high-return (for example, equity) investments. Rigorous control of the maximum possible cost of pension funding. Raising of actuarial rates to levels close to that of the dedicated bond portfolio."

Actuarial rates generally increase with the perceived safety of the invested assets. Some actuaries stood ready to increase the actuarial assumption for pension plans that adopted portfolio insurance (Dreher 1986). A higher actuarial assumption increases expected returns, hence reduces plan contributions.

The advent in 1986 of Financial Accounting Standards Board Statement No. 87 (FASB #87) gave insurance vendors a new lure to attract pension plan sponsors (see Ring 1986a). FASB #87 requires that increases or decreases in a pension plan's surplus (pension fund assets minus plan liabilities) amounting to 10 percent or more of either assets or liabilities be reported as changes to corporate earnings. Short-term volatility in the pension fund's assets could thus have a substantial impact on a firm's bottom line.

Protection of plan surplus became a common marketing theme for insurance providers. An LOR advertisement in the March 1987 issue of *Institutional Investor* read: "You can turn FASB #87 into an asset, not a liability." Employment of a portfolio insurance program would presumably "lock in" surplus balances and prevent undesirable charges to corporate earnings.

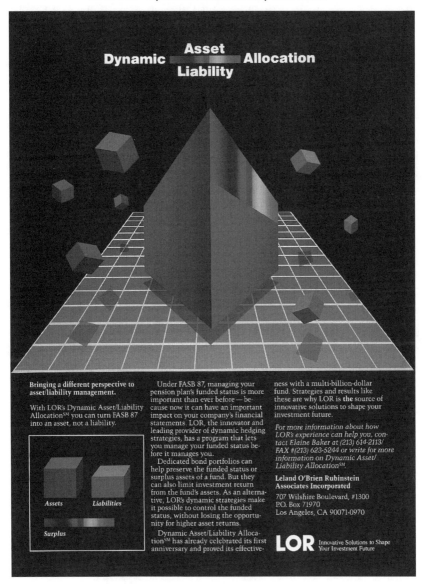
Source: *Institutional Investor*, March 1987, p. 128.

Beyond Equity

If insurance worked for stocks and T-bills, why not stocks and bonds? Currency? Foreign markets? James Tilley and Gary Latainer (1985) of Morgan Stanley, another insurance vendor, had run historical simulations demonstrating that a dynamic strategy allocating assets between stocks and bonds would have turned in a performance placing in the first decile of balanced fund managers.

Portfolio insurance vendors rapidly extended insurance applications beyond the stock market and beyond the US. Insurance strategies were offered for fixed income instruments, commodities, foreign stocks, and foreign currencies.[4] A strategy designed to achieve the highest return available in multiple markets was applied to international stocks and currencies (see Fong and Vasicek 1989).[5] By the time of the 1987 market crash, at least six mutual funds offered insurance on US and Japanese stocks and bonds.[6]

FIGURE 2.6
LOR/Aetna Ad: Job Security

Guaranteed Equity Management

Aetna Life Insurance Company, which already offers clients a variety of specialty investment approaches, has aggressively developed practical applications for Dynamic Asset Allocation. "We pride ourselves on being at the leading edge of investment technology," says Ralph S. Tate, Vice President and Director of Portfolio Management for Aetna's Common Stock Department, "and Dynamic Asset Allocation will play an important role in keeping us there."

Aetna now offers a full range of Dynamic Asset Allocation products, including the Fiduciary Hedge Program. Aetna has taken the additional step, moreover, of applying insurance guarantees to the process. Under Aetna's program, called Guaranteed Equity Management (GEM)℠, plan sponsors select both a minimum guaranteed return and the time period for which it applies. Assets in GEM accounts are invested in common stock and Treasury securities, with the initial asset mix and subsequent rebalancing based on the Dynamic Asset Allocation program. Clients may withdraw the market value of the account at any time. At the expiration of the guarantee period, clients are entitled to the market value in the account or the guarantee, whichever is greater.

T. Jerald Moore, Aetna's Vice President of Pension and Financial Services Marketing, describes Dynamic Asset Allocation as a "natural" for a company like Aetna. "It is a tool that allows us to combine our considerable investment expertise with our ability to offer traditional insurance company guarantees."

GEM gives plan sponsors an alternative approach to the problem of controlling portfolio risk by allowing them to participate in equity returns while placing absolute limits on downside exposure. "The key word is 'absolute,' " says Tate. ***"If a sponsor chooses a 0 percent return, he's never going to have to go to his pension committee and explain losses.*** *Even the most conservative balanced or bond manager can't offer that."*

Tate says many larger plans have expressed an interest in GEM with higher returns, guaranteed over periods of five years or more. "Longer guarantees usually mean the client has a better chance to participate in equity returns," Tate explains. Given current interest rates, a five-year program with an 8 percent minimum guarantee would initially be about 70 percent invested in stocks. If the period were extended to ten years, the initial equity investment would increase to 85 percent. Because Aetna's program allows the plan sponsor to withdraw assets at market value before the guarantee period expires, longer-term GEM programs combine many of the advantages of GICs with the liquidity and upside potential of equities or other assets with high expected returns.

"Right now," Tates says, "a lot of people see Dynamic Asset Allocation as some kind of magic black box technology. It isn't. It's a state of the art technology that works. We aren't just telling people it works, we're guaranteeing it."

ÆTNA LIFE INSURANCE COMPANY

Guaranteed Equity Management (GEM) *is a service mark of Aetna Life Insurance Company.*

Source: LOR Sponsored Section, *Institutional Investor*, 1984, p. 4.

Job Security

Beyond its risk reduction and return enhancement possibilities, portfolio insurance also appealed to the self-preservation instincts of investment managers and fund officers. Wunsch (1984) argued that "those who nearly lost their jobs maintaining static positions in the 1973–4 period would intuitively prefer the known and acceptable minimum result of the dynamic strategy to the unpredictable danger of the static allocation, just as drivers who crash trying to maintain some average speed on the sharpest curves would be wise to adopt a more flexible driving policy." Because synthetic portfolio insurance makes no use of market foresight, however, an insurance strategy is more akin to racing a car with a blindfold on. What Wunsch and Grannis (1988) failed to appreciate was that, even with good brakes and a powerful engine, this car is doomed to crash.

The job security tack was taken, not only with pension officers, but also with their attorneys: "O'Brien says he ultimately was able to face down corporate attorneys who objected to futures by warning them they were preventing their own plans from being protected and might incur liabilities themselves" (Gamlin 1986: 46).

"No Unhappy Surprises"

The integrity of synthetic implementations was, according to its promoters, beyond reproach. LOR's Ferguson and Edwards (1985: 2) asserted that "It doesn't matter that formal insurance policies are not available. The mathematics of finance provide the answer. . . . The bottom line is that financial catastrophes can be avoided at a relatively insignificant cost."

Wunsch (1984) claimed that a guaranteed minimum return was assured even under "the worst of all worst case scenarios." Similarly, a marketing display entitled "What LOR's Sophistication Means" (discussed in the *Wall Street Journal*, January 4, 1988: B4) assured that "all the implications and expectations of the selected strategy are known in advance. No unhappy surprises."

LOR used a catchy marketing gimmick to validate their strategy:

After saturating potential clients with the theories behind "dynamic asset allocation" . . . when first marketing the idea, they concluded their seminars with a challenge. Managers were invited to step up to the computer and adjust the market in such a way that LOR's asset management theories would fail. The reward if it was done: 1,000 dollars. Many left the seminars convinced that, if someone was really worried about risk, the idea was foolproof. (Falloon 1984: 36)

Summary

Its vendors claimed that synthetic portfolio insurance provided a hard floor for portfolio values while at the same time enhancing portfolio returns. They showed that a synthetically insured portfolio could outperform a comparable uninsured portfolio. Furthermore, by providing the assurance of a minimum specified return, portfolio insurance could afford investors the security to reach for still higher returns by increasing or even leveraging equity positions.

According to its proponents' claims, synthetic portfolio insurance could serve as a virtual cure-all for pension funds. By reducing short-term fluctuations in pension portfolio values, insurance could stare down the lion of FASB #87, which threatened increased volatility for corporate earnings. By allowing increased equity return along with reduced risk of loss, insurance could pave the way for increased actuarial rates and a resultant diminution in required corporate contributions. And for portfolio managers and fund officers alike, insurance offered a Kevlar vest for protection against the career-threatening bullets of poor performance.

Its purported ability to "lock in" portfolio gains attracted even more adherents to synthetic insurance as the equity market rose throughout the mid-1980s. Yet a close examination of the mechanics underlying synthetic insurance would have laid bare the inherent weaknesses that were to prove the undoing of portfolio insurance come October 1987.

Notes

1   These advertisements, which appeared in the March 1, 15, and 19 and April 12, 1982 issues of *Pensions & Investment Age*, introduced the institutional investment community to LOR's assured equity, fixed income, inflation-adjusted real return, and total investment program applications.

2   But the 1973–82 period, like the 1972–81 period touted in LOR's "Dynamic Asset Allocation" ads, was a very uncharacteristic one for asset returns, in that T-bills outperformed stock. Chapter 3 discusses this apparent free lunch in more detail and gives results for more typical asset returns.

3   Based on LOR's rates, annual vendor fees for management of a futures-overlay insurance strategy ranged from $50,000 for insuring portfolios of $25 million to $287,500 for portfolios worth $500 million.

4   From a survey reported in the September 1987 issue of *Intermarket*, p. 26.

5   For the theory behind the insurance of two risky assets, see Margrabe (1978) and Stulz (1982).

6   From the September 1987 issue of *Intermarket*.

3

A Free Lunch?

It doesn't matter that formal insurance policies are not available. The mathematics of finance provide the answer. . . . The bottom line is that financial catastrophes can be avoided at a relatively insignificant cost.

Robert Ferguson and Larry Edwards, 1985

The early simulations of synthetic insurance strategies suggested that insurance would not only provide downside protection, it would also generate more wealth than a comparable uninsured strategy. Portfolio insurance, in other words, could be both riskless and costless. But the principles of synthetic insurance, as described in chapter 1, suggest that dynamic strategies cannot provide insurance of a minimum return without some give-up in the potential maximum return.

Consider, for example, an omniscient investor who has perfect market foresight. This investor will be fully invested in cash when stocks decline and fully invested in stocks when they rise. This perfect market timer is perfectly insured against market declines and incurs no opportunity costs when the market rises.

Synthetic portfolio insurance is not omniscient. Rather, redeployments of assets between stock and cash are made solely in response to (not in anticipation of) market movements. Synthetic insurance strategies are essentially reactive, rather than proactive. They do not use return predictions, hence do not possess market foresight.

For a synthetic insurer with no market foresight trading against a perfect market timer, the cost of creating an insured return pattern equals the windfall earned by the perfect timer. In effect, the portfolio insurer pays a premium identical to the perfect timer's windfall (see Merton 1981).

Of course, the perfect market timer does not exist. In fact, according to efficient market theory, which had become the reigning paradigm of market behavior by the 1980s, all attempts to forecast stock prices are futile, because their movements are essentially random. In such an environment, synthetic insurance strategies, with no market foresight, are at no innate disadvantage to strategies that presume market foresight.

Sacrificing Wealth

It is possible to arrive at an estimate of the portfolio insurance premium by comparing returns to simulated insured portfolios with returns to an alternative investment that is equally blind to future market performance – buying and holding the market. Obviously, a synthetically insured portfolio is not truly comparable with an all-equity holding, in that an investor who chose the former would be unlikely to find the latter equally desirable. Nevertheless, such a comparison is valuable for several reasons.

As noted, neither investment requires any market foresight. Furthermore, the all-equity return serves as a reasonable gauge of the *maximum* return give-up that can be expected from a synthetically insured portfolio. Most importantly, perhaps, the vendors of synthetic portfolio insurance frequently touted its performance in relation to an all-equity market alternative.

I simulated the performance of a synthetically insured portfolio over the ten years ending 1982, a period often highlighted by insurance vendors when marketing their product (Jacobs 1983a; 1983c; 1984). The portfolio dynamically hedged the S&P 500 to insure protection of 95 percent of its value; that is, it was designed to allow for no more than a 5 percent loss by the end of each year of the period (a 5 percent annual deductible policy). Given one-way transaction costs of 0.5 percent (a reasonable assumption for hedging using stocks and cash), one dollar invested in the insured strategy would have grown to $2.29. Given zero transaction costs (the best futures-based implementation), one dollar would have grown to $2.43. An investment in the S&P 500 (with dividends reinvested) would have grown to only $1.90. No wonder insurance vendors liked this comparison!

Synthetic insurance did provide a negative cost – a profit – compared with the alternative of a straight, uninsured investment in equity. But Treasury bill returns during this period also exceeded S&P 500 returns. (One dollar would have grown to $2.27 if invested in T-bills, versus $1.90 if invested in the S&P 500.) This is a phenomenon not representative of long-run expectations. Over most historical periods, returns to equity have exceeded returns to cash; this is the well known equity risk premium (discussed in detail in chapter 17), which provides compensation for the added risk of stock investing.

The fact is that it pays to be insured (that is, less than fully invested) in very weak markets, because holding cash is then more profitable than owning stock. But such periods have not been the norm. My simulations of the insurance strategy's performance over a much longer period, the fifty-five years from 1928 to 1982, revealed the more likely costs of insurance.

One dollar invested in 1928 in an insured S&P 500 strategy with a 5 percent annual deductible would have grown to $36.97 by the end of 1982, after one-way transaction costs of 0.5 percent. Given zero transaction costs, one dollar would have grown to $52.36. But that same dollar, had it been fully invested in the S&P 500 over the period, would have grown to $104.25! Thus the cost of insurance would have constituted an enormous wealth sacrifice over this time span.[1]

In general, relative to an uninsured strategy, insurance results in a downward shift in returns above the insured floor, reflecting payment of the (explicit or implicit) insurance premium. Insurers accept this downward shift in returns in exchange for the upward shift in returns that insurance can provide when underlying asset returns fall below the insured floor. The combination of these shifts in outcomes, however, results in a high probability of returns at or near the insurance loss limitation (see Jacobs 1984 and Rendleman and McEnally 1987a). Overall, the opportunity costs represented by the downward shift in returns on the upside can wash out any savings represented by the upward shift in returns on the downside. C.B. Garcia and F.J. Gould (1987: 44) find that, "with a zero floor, the opportunity cost of insurance can be as much as or more than the opportunity cost of not insuring."

Implementation Pitfalls

The performance of a synthetic portfolio insurance strategy can be compared with that of the protective put strategy it is designed to replicate. As we have noted, the premium for a publicly traded put is paid up front. The price of a put will depend upon investors' expectation of the volatility of the underlying asset over the term of the option; the higher the expected volatility, the higher the premium. The cost of a protective put strategy will also depend upon the level of protection desired by the put purchaser; protecting 100 percent of the value of the underlying portfolio (having no deductible) will require more insurance than protecting 95 percent of its value (a 5 percent deductible).

Once the premium is paid for a publicly traded put option, the buyer incurs no further costs. The buyer receives in exchange for the premium payment the assurance of a minimum portfolio value. If the asset underlying the put subsequently falls below the put's strike price, the option holder can exercise the put and receive the predetermined minimum value. If the asset subsequently rises in value, the option holder does not exercise the put (it expires worthless) and earns the full value of the increase in asset value, less the put premium.

Can synthetic portfolio insurance provide the same levels of downside protection and upside capture as an option-insured strategy? The answer will depend on how well the initial insurance program anticipates the actual behavior – that is, the volatility – of the underlying assets over the insurance horizon. For, although synthetic insurance strategies may assume no ability to forecast market returns, they are critically dependent on forecasts of the volatility of returns!

When volatility over the course of the program turns out to be higher than anticipated at the outset, and especially when it takes the form of sudden jumps in price, either up or down, a synthetic insurance strategy will fall short of the performance of the option it is designed to replicate. That is, the return on the synthetically insured portfolio will fall short of the net return (after premium payment) on the assets underlying the put option. Worse yet, when volatility takes the form of downward price spikes (gap-downs), synthetic insurance can even fail to deliver the level of protection promised.

Of course, if the market's actual volatility turns out to be lower than expected, the synthetic strategy can cost less than a real protective put. But, as we will see later, the very actions of synthetically insured investors contribute to market volatility, increasing the likelihood that actual volatility will exceed the levels anticipated by their insurance programs.

Falling Through the Floor

When volatility turns out to be substantially higher than anticipated, the synthetically insured portfolio may find itself playing a catch-up game that is impossible to win. As it becomes apparent that the initial cash position is not enough to insure the minimum portfolio value in the face of increased volatility, a larger cash position may be established. But if volatility continues to increase, the insured portfolio may find its riskless position inadequate to insure the required return.

I found that misspecified volatility could cause portfolio insurance to fail (Jacobs 1983c), but Mark Rubinstein dismissed these concerns: "Bruce [Jacobs] is looking at the vanilla version of portfolio insurance, which is what we started with. But we have modified our program to cope with this. Even though there are two balls in the air [stock prices and interest rates] and we don't know when they will come down, the strategy will still work" (in Falloon 1984: 35).

However, Yu Zhu and Robert Kavee (1988), too, find violations of the insurance floor when stock market volatility turns out to be much higher than expected. For example, when volatility is expected to be 15 percent, but turns out to be 30 percent, the portfolio falls 11.3 percent below the promised floor.

An even more serious problem with synthetic portfolio insurance is its inability to hedge against jumps or gaps in prices. Intuitively, it is clear that any strategy demanding that a trade must take place at a specific price will fail if the price jumps from a level above that price to a level below it. Vasanttilak Naik and Moon Lee (1990: 506–7) demonstrate that random jumps in stock prices invalidate the portfolio insurance.

In a discussion of synthetic call strategies, Rubinstein and Hayne Leland (1981: 66) recognize that "the possibility of gap openings or jump movements in the stock price means that a call can provide something that a levered stock position [synthetic option] cannot. To take an extreme case, suppose a catastrophic event suddenly causes the stock price to collapse to zero. This may happen too fast for us to adjust our stock/cash position."[2] Nevertheless, Rubinstein and Leland argue, a synthetic insurance strategy is "tantamount to insuring the equity portfolio against losses by paying a fixed premium to an insurance company." They qualify this statement only in a footnote: "the analogy to insurance breaks down under a sudden catastrophic loss that does not leave sufficient time to adjust the replicating portfolio" (Rubinstein and Leland 1981: 72).

Synthetic portfolio insurance may thus be far from riskless. And the risk will be magnified if the insurer adopts one of the portfolio insurance applications advocated in the previous chapter, which calls for insuring a leveraged equity portfolio in order to increase returns.[3] In reality, holding such an aggressive asset could prove devastating in the event of a market break: in that case, the insurance may fail, and the leverage will magnify the loss.[4]

Missing the Upside

When excessive volatility or a gap-down in prices causes an insured portfolio to fall below its floor, the insurance strategy will call for a full commitment to cash. The investor will not only suffer a shortfall from the insurance floor, but will be "stopped out" of any subsequent rallies and may have to bear significant opportunity costs (see Jacobs 1983a; 1983c; 1984). The synthetic insurance strategy will fail to replicate the return on a protective put because it is shut out of upside moves in the underlying asset.

My historical simulations of an insured S&P 500 strategy with a 5 percent annual deductible show that major stop-outs would have occurred in 1933 and 1938 (Jacobs 1983a and 1983c). In 1933, the S&P 500 fell 17 percent by the end of February; at that point, the strategy would have stopped out and thereby missed the 85.5 percent market rise during the rest of the year. In 1938, the strategy stopped out by March, after an 18.6 percent decline; the S&P 500 subsequently rallied by 61.1 percent.

John O'Brien (1983) criticized these findings as evidence of "flawed implementation," but his LOR colleague Robert Ferguson (1986b: 45) later reported stop-outs in the same two years: "The market was abnormal enough to result in disappointing upside capture in only two years, 1933 and 1938." In fact, Ferguson reports virtually no upside capture in these years. He dismisses his own results, however, as the product of a too simple hedging method; a "well-designed portfolio insurance product," he claims, would not stop out (Ferguson 1986a: 79). (After the 1987 crash, Rubinstein [1988: 40] admitted that stop-outs were "virtually impossible to prevent.")

Unexpected Transaction Costs

There is yet another reason that insurance conducted via dynamic asset allocation may fail to replicate insurance with publicly traded puts – the costs of transacting. As we have noted, insuring an underlying portfolio with options requires a one-time premium payment, with no further transactions required of the option buyer. By contrast, synthetic insurance strategies necessitate high portfolio turnover.[5] My findings suggest that turnover for an annual 5 percent deductible policy averages 66 percent (Jacobs 1984). And this trading activity is in addition to that associated with the management of the underlying portfolio. Zhu and Kavee (1988) find turnover of over 300 percent for an annual 0 percent deductible policy.

With such levels of turnover, synthetic strategies can incur substantial transaction costs. This was certainly true in the early days, when synthetic strategies were implemented in the stock market, using stocks and Treasury bills. Stock index futures, however, soon became insurers' preferred hedging vehicle.

If the futures market is more liquid than the spot market, it should offer lower transaction costs. In the mid-1980s, Steven Wunsch (1985b), then a vice president at Kidder Peabody, found that a $20 million stock trade had a price impact of 0.27 percent, compared with 0.04 percent for a comparable futures trade.

These findings assume that futures contracts are fairly priced. Fair price is conventionally defined as a function of the underlying index price and the relevant interest rate (for futures) and dividend rate (for stock).[6] It is assumed that futures will normally trade at fair prices because movements away from fair price will attract arbitragers. If futures appear to be expensive relative to the underlying index, for example, index arbitrage will occur: arbitragers, seeing a profit opportunity, will sell index futures and buy the stock index itself. These actions will push futures prices down and stock prices up. On average, then, fair prices should be maintained.

Arbitragers will consider the transaction costs of a position in the stock market when deciding whether futures can be profitably bought or sold against the underlying index. Futures prices lying within the range determined by the underlying index price plus the transaction costs do not present arbitrage opportunities. Only when futures prices move outside this range do arbitragers step in.[7]

Futures prices thus generally lie within a "fair range" of spot prices, and the price at which a contract is actually traded may deviate substantially from the conventionally determined fair price. In fact, Joanne Hill and her colleagues at Kidder Peabody (1988) find that the level of futures mispricing averaged 0.32 percent from June 1983 to August 1986. There will obviously be times, then, when transacting in the spot market is cheaper than transacting in the futures market.[8]

This is most likely to be the case when markets are rising or falling sharply. Because the futures market reflects new information more quickly than the spot market does, index futures prices generally lead stock market indexes (see Chan 1992). Gould (1988) demonstrates that futures prices are thus likely to be at the high point of their range (farthest above fair price) in bullish markets and at the low point of their range (farthest below fair price) in bearish markets (see also Hill et al. 1988).[9] This finding is of particular relevance to synthetic portfolio insurance, because insurers trade "with the trend," buying in rising markets and selling in falling markets. Insurers are thus likely to be "bagged" by buying futures "rich" on up market days and selling them "cheap" on down market days.

Hill et al. (1988) conjecture that round-trip transaction costs (including commission and market impact of 0.23 percent) are 1 percent in periods of moderate futures mispricing and 1.75 percent in periods of extreme mispricing. Using the average market volatility over the 1926–85 period, they find that portfolio insurance with a one-year term and a 5 percent deductible would have cost 2.9 percent per year, assuming modest futures transaction costs of 0.5 percent round-trip. If transaction costs were 1.75 percent round-trip, however, the insurance cost would rise to 3.8 percent.

But these estimates are based on average market volatility. If volatility increases, the cost of trading an insured portfolio is also likely to increase, as more and/or larger adjustments in futures positions will be required to keep the portfolio within the insurance program's parameters. When the market experiences extreme volatility, the insurance program's cost could rise to a whopping 13.4 percent (Hill et al. 1988). This estimate was surpassed in October 1987, when transaction costs exploded (see SEC 1988 and Wang et al. 1990).

To adjust for the impact of transaction costs, Leland (1985: 1300) once proposed basing the initial insurance hedge ratio on an overestimate of market volatility: "Inclusive of transaction costs, the net price of purchasing stock is slightly higher than the price without transaction costs. Similarly the net price of selling is slightly lower. The accentuation of up or down movements of the stock price can be modeled as if volatility of actual stock price was higher." But Peter Abken (1988) finds this approach insufficient to avoid replication failures. John Merrick (1988) also attempts to adjust hedge ratios for the futures market's tendency to overshoot the underlying stock market, but hedging errors persist in the face of his adjustments.

In short, synthetic portfolio insurance is not riskless, in the sense of providing guaranteed downside protection; nor is it costless, in the sense of being able to capture upside returns that will offset or exceed the costs incurred to implement it. Furthermore, rather than being fixed and knowable in advance, synthetic insurance costs are highly sensitive to market volatility. Leland and Rubinstein's assertions that the synthetic premium is "fixed" and "tantamount" to that paid to a third-party insurance company are misleading. In fact, even prior to the crash it was reported that portfolio insurance "cost some pension funds 50 to 100 basis points more than expected in 1986, largely because of the stock market's volatility" (Ring 1987c: 50).

Leland (1986: 33) concedes that "greater than expected volatility raises the program's cost or premium." Nevertheless, he argues that "volatile markets are precisely when protection is most valuable." As we have seen, however, unexpected increases in market volatility increase the possibility that a synthetic insurance strategy will fall below its floor and be stopped out, missing out on any subsequent price gains. Unexpected volatility will also increase transaction costs. Further, as we will see later, the trading demands of synthetic portfolio insurers themselves increase the likelihood of discontinuous price jumps, which can prove catastrophic for insured portfolios.

Job Insecurity

An editorial in *Pensions & Investment Age* on February 23, 1987 (p. 10) suggested that portfolio insurance's popularity might relate more to the needs of pension executives than to the needs of the pension plan:

> Judging by its acceptance, the product [portfolio insurance] fulfills a need. However, the question needs to be asked: whose need? Some pension executives, presumably those skeptical about the use of portfolio insurance, have begun to refer to it as "job insurance." The implication is that portfolio insurance is being bought by some pension executives more to protect their own jobs than because it is the right thing for the pension fund and the sponsoring entity.

The popularity of portfolio insurance may have reflected the presence of agency costs. These are costs incurred by a principal when the incentives provided to an agent employed on his or her behalf do not motivate the agent to act in the principal's best interests. According to Brennan and Schwartz (1989: 456–7):

> Portfolio insurance strategies are employed not to maximize the welfare of the investor, but to protect the interests of an agent who is delegated the task of managing a portfolio; such an agent may have no interest in the return on the portfolio, per se, but only insofar as it affects his wage. If agents' incentive schemes are inappropriately defined, these dynamic investment strategies may enable them to game the reward scheme.

Garcia and Gould (1987: 50) conclude that, rather than enhancing job security for pension officers, portfolio insurance actually creates a dilemma: "You may be damned if you do and damned if you don't." That is, if you are insured, you are likely to be in the hotseat when the market rises and uninsured portfolios outperform yours; but if you do not insure, you are likely to be penalized when the market falls and you underperform insured portfolios.

And synthetic portfolio insurance will certainly jeopardize the pension officer's job if it fails to work. In this case, rather than providing a free lunch, insurance may simply be setting the table for a fast. Richard Rendleman and Thomas O'Brien (not affiliated with LOR) simulate portfolio insurance under the crash conditions of October 1987. With a 5 percent deductible policy, their typical portfolio falls 20 percent short of its floor, and the shortfall below achievable returns is as high as 40 percent (Rendleman and O'Brien 1990).

Summary

Despite the aggressive promotions in the early advertisements for portfolio insurance programs, synthetic insurance is neither riskless nor costless. When stocks offer a return premium over cash (as they do in most periods and over the course of time), synthetic insurance will under-perform an uninsured position in the stock because of the required commitment to cash.

Furthermore, although designed to replicate the performance of a port-folio with a protective option position, synthetic insurance may fail to deliver. As actual volatility exceeds anticipated volatility, the likelihood increases that an insured portfolio will fall through its floor, failing to provide the promised level of protection, and be stopped out, thereby being shut out of subsequent market rises. Despite the arguments of portfolio insura-nce vendors that increasing volatility heightens the need for portfolio insurance, it would appear that increasing volatility merely augments the likelihood that a synthetic insurance program will fall short of matching either the downside risk reduction or upside return poten-tial of the option it supposedly replicates.

Even if unanticipated market volatility does not lead to replication fail-ures or violations of the insured floor, it imposes higher trading costs, which diminish portfolio return. Higher-than-anticipated volatility will call for larger or more frequent trades, leading to higher transaction costs. High volatility may also increase futures mispricing, thereby magnify-ing the trading costs of trend-following insured portfolios, which tend to be selling as futures prices are furthest below fair values and buying as futures prices are furthest above fair values.

The purveyors of synthetic portfolio insurance once argued that it would help to insure the job security of portfolio managers and other investment professionals. But, in truth, synthetic strategies' imple-mentation pitfalls can undermine the safety of both portfolios and their fiduciaries.

Notes

1 Prior to March 1957, the S&P composite index consisted of 90, rather than 500, stocks. While simulations with different parameters may yield somewhat different results, my general conclusions still hold. Furthermore, Singleton and Grieves (1984: 63) observe that "several major security firms . . . promise that these [portfolio insurance] strategies provide risk insurance for a very small premium." They demonstrate that synthetic puts can be cre-ated only at a fair price, and not at a bargain price.

2   A synthetic call strategy is a margined long position in stock, with borrow-
    ing increased to buy stock as stock price rises and stock sold to retire
    margin debt as stock price declines.

3   The magnifying effects of leverage on risk were vividly demonstrated in
    1998, with the near-collapse of the Long-Term Capital Management hedge
    fund. Its extremely high leverage of theoretically low-risk positions proved
    devastating, both to the fund and to markets generally, when asset prices
    failed to conform to the fund's expectations. See chapter 18 for a description.

4   Investors with the ability to leverage an asset may wish to consider instead
    the "growth-optimal" strategy of Rendleman and McEnally (1987a). Such
    a strategy is specifically designed to maximize the expected growth rate of
    assets over time, and it provides a higher expected compound return than an
    insured leveraged strategy. See Rubinstein's critique of this strategy (1987)
    and Rendleman and McEnally's reply (1987b). See also the comment by Borger
    (1988) and Ferguson's reply (1988). The growth-optimal strategy has been
    touted for some time; see Latane (1959) and Markowitz (1959: ch. 6).

5   Portfolio turnover depends on such factors as market volatility, the deduct-
    ible set by the insured party, and the insurance horizon (see Etzioni 1986).
    It will also depend importantly on the rebalancing interval. In theory, the
    Black–Scholes model calls for continuous rebalancing; the longer the delay
    in rebalancing in response to underlying asset price moves, the larger the
    potential discrepancy between the perfect hedge and the actual hedge. In prac-
    tice, of course, continuous rebalancing would lead to untenable transaction
    costs. There is thus a tradeoff between hedge accuracy and transaction costs.
    Leland (1985) discusses this tradeoff in the context of rebalancing intervals
    of from one week to two months. Recent controversial research by Gilster
    (1997) argues that, at some of the longer rebalancing intervals suggested in
    the literature, the resulting hedge can introduce more risk than the equival-
    ent non-hedged position contains. Jarrow (1997), however, disputes Gilster's
    methodology. For a discussion of various models of transaction costs for strat-
    egies requiring discrete hedging, see Whalley and Wilmott (1997).

6   Historically, the futures market has traded at a premium to the spot mar-
    ket, because interest rates have been higher than dividend rates, but this need
    not be the case.

7   For more on arbitrage bounds, see MacKinlay and Ramaswamy (1988).

8   See also Finnerty and Park (1987); Kawaller et al. (1987); Stoll and Whaley
    (1990).

9   Hill et al. (1988) also find a reversal of the mispricing on the next day.
    On the basis of this evidence, they suggest that it may be beneficial for an
    insurer to delay adjusting a hedge until the day following the market move
    that necessitates an adjustment. But this would leave the portfolio unpro-
    tected and would have been disastrous on October 19, 1987.

4

Who Needs It?

When favorable market conditions do develop, they [insurers] will be in the optimal position to power into the straightaways for maximum competitive advantage.

Steven Wunsch, 1985c

The marketing claims of portfolio insurance vendors were designed to appeal to all sorts of investors. While the safety element of insurance appealed to risk-averse, conservative investors, for example, more aggressive investors were lured by promises of enhanced returns. Insurance vendors claimed that, by raising and simultaneously insuring equity exposures, portfolio insurance could increase overall returns without increasing risk. They described synthetic portfolio insurance as a strategy that accelerates for the straightaways and brakes for the turns. (Of course, as synthetic insurance strategies have no market foresight, it is hard to imagine how they know when to accelerate and when to brake, except after the fact; a more apt analogy might be to a race car being towed around the track by the leading "market" car.)

According to LOR's Scott Grannis (1988: 51–2), "a dynamic strategy can increase the expected return of a portfolio when it is used to replace a . . . fixed-allocation strategy." Grannis makes his point by comparing two strategies designed to eliminate or to minimize portfolio losses in excess of a specified amount. One uses a static 55/45 percent allocation of stocks and Treasury bills (a buy-and-hold strategy) to constrain the chance of a loss exceeding 5 percent to no more than one in twenty. The other calls for dynamic hedging, with an initial stock/bill mix of 72/28 percent and an average mix during the year of 78/22 percent; it promises to limit losses in any one year to no greater than 5 percent. The static allocation has an expected return of 14.4 percent and the dynamic strategy an expected return of 16.2 percent. Thus the dynamic strategy has a net advantage of 1.8 percentage points. LOR's Hayne Leland (1984) and Robert Ferguson (1983) make similar arguments.

A static-mix strategy cannot provide an absolute floor on losses; the larger its allocation to the riskless asset, however, the better the chance that returns will not fall below a given floor (see appendix D for an example). A dynamic strategy can provide a higher expected return than such a fixed allocation, because it allows for a higher average commitment to the risky asset over the investment horizon.[1] It also promises an absolute loss limitation. As we saw in chapter 3, however, whether this promise will be fulfilled in practice is questionable.[2] Only a real option can, in fact, provide an absolute loss limitation.

A dynamic strategy will dominate a static buy-and-hold strategy when an absolute limit on losses is required. But is an absolute loss limitation necessary, or even desirable, for most investors?

Investors who insure implicitly seek portfolios with asymmetric, or skewed, return distributions – in particular, portfolios whose returns are skewed to the right, providing ample probability of positive returns and no chance of returns below a given floor. These investors are concerned, not with risk or volatility as conventionally measured (as the asset's return dispersion about the average), but only with that portion of volatility that represents returns below some cut-off value. Such investors have zero tolerance for returns below this cut-off.[3]

Such investors undoubtedly exist. Consider, for example, an investor in a rising bull market who expects that the market will continue to rise but who also faces payment of a specific obligation. Such an investor may be loath to sell off stock, thereby missing out on expected gains, but will also want to be sure of having the funds available to meet the obligation. For such an investor, insurance may provide a good solution (although synthetic insurance will not, as we have noted, provide the same level of reliability as an actual put).

Portfolio insurance vendors targeted institutions such as pension and endowment funds as ideal customers for their product, touting it as a means by which such institutions could reap higher returns while ensuring the safety of their funds over the short term. But why would such long-term investors need an absolute limitation on short-term losses? As I pointed out in the early 1980s, it seems extremely dubious to assign a skewness preference to long-term investors such as pension and endowment funds (Jacobs 1984).

An Alternative: Buy Low and Sell High

Investors unconcerned with skewness (or any other higher-order moment of the return distribution) will not be willing to pay a premium in order to obtain a return distribution that is skewed to the right. Rather, according to the tenets of modern portfolio theory as developed by Nobel laureate Harry Markowitz, they will seek the portfolio that can provide the highest expected return at any given level of volatility (as measured statistically by variance). That is, they will seek a portfolio on the mean-variance efficient frontier (see Markowitz 1952 and 1959).[4]

A fixed-allocation portfolio on this frontier will provide a higher expected return than a dynamic insurance strategy having the same variance. For the mean-variance investor, an insured portfolio will always be suboptimal, because it lies below the efficient frontier.[5]

In fact, because a mean-variance investor places no value on skewness, this investor is willing to "sell" skewness; doing so will improve upon the portfolio's mean-variance efficiency.[6] By "selling" portfolio insurance, the investor can achieve, for a given level of variance, a higher expected return than either a dynamic insurance strategy or a static strategy on the efficient frontier can provide.[7]

Intuitively, it has often been said that portfolio insurers buy equities as prices rise and sell as prices fall; they thus tend to "buy high and sell low." By contrast, sellers of portfolio insurance tend to sell equities as prices rise and buy as prices fall; they thus "buy low and sell high." This characterization is particularly true in volatile markets with mean reversion. In such an environment, insurers will get bagged by buying before price declines and selling before price rises; and insurance sellers will bag the profits!

An investor who writes a put (sells a put to insurers) and holds the underlying stock maintains full exposure to upside market moves and receives, in exchange for assuming more risk from downside market moves, a premium from insurance buyers. Covered call writers (stock plus short call), too, can be considered insurance sellers, as synthetic strategies designed to replicate covered calls follow trading rules opposite to those of portfolio insurance (see Rubinstein and Leland 1981). Covered call writers sell off the desirable right tail (the upside) of the return distribution, while protective put buyers eliminate the undesirable left tail (the downside). The market provides compensation for selling the upside and extracts a cost (in the form of the premium to the put seller) for unloading the downside.[8]

In general, any investor willing to buy as prices decline and sell as they rise acts as a counterparty for portfolio insurers. Market timers, including tactical asset allocators, value investors, and contrarians may all provide a natural other side to portfolio insurance trades. (Part III will examine the consequences for market stability when the demand for synthetic portfolio insurance exceeds the supply of portfolio insurance sellers.)

For some short-term investors, in particular those with zero tolerance of losses beyond a specified level, insurance will be appealing. Longer-term investors should be aware, however, of some of the less sanguine implications of synthetic insurance as practiced. In particular, multiperiod renewals of short-term insurance strategies lead to some paradoxical consequences. We review these issues below.

Strategies in Practice

Early on, Leland (1980) posited that investors requiring absolute loss limitations, but whose willingness to take on risk (risk tolerance) increases with wealth more rapidly than the average investor's, should insure. The portfolio insurance strategies being offered at that time were option-replication strategies with fixed expiration dates and multiple renewals. I showed that this type of insurance (repeated application over consecutive periods) has some rather unusual implications for investor preferences (Jacobs 1984).

In particular, portfolio insurers buy stock when the market rises and sell stock when the market falls. Investors following this type of trading rule exhibit increasing relative risk tolerance. That is, they commit an increasing proportion of their wealth to stock as their wealth rises and a decreasing proportion as their wealth declines.

But now consider an investor who decides to renew the same insurance policy at each expiration. Within each insurance policy's horizon, this investor will follow a trading rule consistent with increasing relative risk tolerance. At the expiration of each insurance program, however, the investor will reestablish the same stock/cash allocation (assuming market conditions are unchanged and the same level of insurance protection is desired). The investor will thus rebalance to the same stock/cash mix at each expiration/renewal date. Across expiration dates, the investor will appear to be following a constant-mix strategy.

A constant-mix strategy is favored, not by investors with increasing relative risk tolerance, but by investors with constant proportional risk tolerance; these investors commit a fixed proportion of their wealth to stock, irrespective of their wealth level.[9] With repeated renewal of a policy, the insured investor is displaying increasing relative risk tolerance during the life of the policy and constant proportional risk tolerance across expiration/renewal dates! As I claimed, "these characteristics are at odds with one another" (Jacobs 1984: 17).

Furthermore, whether or not an investor chooses the same or a different insurance policy at each renewal date, a discontinuity occurs with the imposition of each policy's initial stock/cash allocation. If the portfolio's value is above the floor at expiration, it will be fully invested in stock; if at the floor, it will be fully committed to cash. With renewal of the insurance policy (or adoption of a new policy), the portfolio will have to reallocate a substantial portion of assets to either stock or cash. This abrupt change in the investment mix is mandated solely by the expiration/renewal date, which may have been set arbitrarily.

In fact, John Cox and Hayne Leland (1982) show that a multiperiod application of portfolio insurance is inefficient. They demonstrate that multiple renewals of insurance lead to path-dependence, meaning that ending wealth is dependent on the particular price path taken by the underlying asset.[10] Only path-independent strategies, however, have the desirable characteristic of maximizing investor utility; their outcomes depend only on the ending price, without regard to its history. This implies that the repeated application of portfolio insurance is suboptimal. By contrast, a constant-mix policy is path-independent, hence consistent with expected utility maximization.

Philip Dybvig (1988) has measured the loss in efficiency that results from repeated applications of portfolio insurance. He compares the cost of such a strategy with what it would cost to obtain the same terminal distribution of wealth in the most efficient manner. For an insurance strategy that is renewed annually for each of ten years, he concludes (p. 83): "While following this strategy for one year is efficient, following it repeatedly with a one-year horizon is poorly diversified over time and is very costly: in ten years, the strategy throws away over five percent of the initial investment!"[11]

"Perpetual" insurance strategies were designed to overcome the path-dependence associated with fixed expiration dates (see Bookstaber and Langsam 1988). Perpetual strategies are time-invariant; that is, the amount allocated to stock does not depend on a fixed time horizon or on the time remaining in the program.[12] Such strategies therefore avoid the problems associated with a fixed expiration date, including the need to reset the asset mix at expiration.[13]

New and Improved

Insurance vendors soon designed perpetual insurance strategies that addressed one major problem with standard synthetic insurance – its dependence on the stochastic process driving the underlying assets. All insurance strategies that seek to replicate option performance are process-dependent. The insurance program's hedge ratio, for example, will depend upon the insurer's assumptions about the volatility of the underlying stock. Divergence of actual behavior from assumed behavior will cause replication difficulties.

Constant proportion portfolio insurance (CPPI) is "process-free," independent of the stochastic process of the underlying stock.[14] Rather than replicating an option position, CPPI uses a simple linear trading rule: maintain a position in stock equal to a constant multiple of the portfolio's value in excess of the specified floor.[15] As well as being process-free, CPPI is time-invariant.

CPPI can be path-dependent, however. With the linear trading rule, the strategy will call for the portfolio's position in stock to increase proportionally as the portfolio's value in excess of the floor rises. Unless the insurer has access to borrowing with which to leverage an ever-increasing investment in stock, portfolio performance will be path-dependent.[16]

A CPPI strategy with some modifications may nevertheless be optimal for some investors. George Constantinides (1988 and 1990) has demonstrated that "habit formation" may lead some rational investors to ratchet up the insurance floor as their wealth rises. Rather than increasing their commitment to stock as their wealth increases, these investors, as they become accustomed to new, higher levels of wealth, may choose to protect this additional wealth by raising their levels of insurance. These investors exhibit state-dependent utility functions.

A CPPI strategy that permits ratcheting and that caps the portfolio's allocation to stocks may be suitable for state-dependent investors (even though it remains path-dependent because of the upper limit on the fraction of the portfolio that can be invested in stocks). As with basic CPPI, such a strategy would call for investing in stocks a constant multiple of the difference between the portfolio's value and the floor. But whenever the portfolio's value hit a new high, a new, higher level of insurance would be chosen. Furthermore, the fraction of the portfolio to be invested in stocks would be capped at a level the investor found comfortable.

As we noted above, an option-based insurance strategy that is renewed frequently and maintained over horizons of constant length will be equivalent to a constant-mix strategy (Jacobs 1984). Similarly, a "rolling" CPPI strategy with a floor that is adjusted to be a constant fraction of assets is equivalent to a constant-mix strategy (Perold and Sharpe 1988). Furthermore, like other synthetic insurance strategies, CPPI requires dynamic portfolio adjustment; it may thus suffer from the implementation pitfalls detailed in chapter 3.[17]

Summary

Portfolio insurance may be optimal for certain investors under certain limited conditions. In general, however, investors unconcerned with skewness will be better off with a portfolio on the mean-variance efficient frontier than they will with an insured portfolio, which lies below this frontier. They can expect to do better still if they act as sellers of portfolio insurance. Sellers of insurance tend to buy low and sell high. They can expect to benefit at the expense of insurers, who tend to buy high and sell low.

Short-term investors with an absolute limit on portfolio losses may find insurance appealing. But longer-term investors should be aware that renewing short-term insurance policies over multiple horizons can give rise to some strange behavior. It implies, for example, that investors exhibit contradictory risk impulses – specifically, increasing relative risk tolerance within the insurance horizon and constant relative risk tolerance across renewal dates. Furthermore, because multiple renewals are path-dependent, they are inefficient, hence incapable of maximizing investor utility. Properly designed perpetual strategies can overcome some of these difficulties, but they will retain the inherent weakness of all synthetic insurance strategies – the susceptibility to failure under market stress.

We have discussed portfolio insurance's pitfalls both from a practical and a theoretical point of view. We now turn to the stock market crash of October 1987 and to the creative turmoil it generated in the world of financial ideas.

Notes

1   Absent replication failures, a dynamic insurance strategy provides the highest expected return of any path-independent strategy requiring an absolute loss limitation. To understand this, consider an investment in stock protected against loss by the purchase of a put option. The premium paid for the put option provides an absolute loss limitation, while the remaining funds, invested in stock, provide maximum expected return.

2   Bird et al. (1988) find that stop-loss techniques (instructions to a broker to sell stock should its price fall to a specified level) can offer a harder floor than synthetic insurance, given the latter's failure to replicate an option position when volatility is underestimated. When replication failures occur, synthetic insurance strategies become path-dependent. A stop-loss approach is always path-dependent, however, as price declines of sufficient magnitude call for a complete liquidation, at which point there will be no benefit from any subsequent price rebound. Furthermore, stop-loss orders are as susceptible as synthetic insurance to gap-downs in prices (as many investors learned on October 19, 1987).

3   See, e.g., Benninga and Blume (1985), who refer to insurers as having "an unbounded coefficient of relative risk aversion" below the insured floor.

4   Mean-variance analysis will closely approximate the optimal solutions for a wide range of plausible investor utility functions (Markowitz 1990: 67).

5   See Jacobs (1984); Ferguson (1987: 57); and Ring (1987b). For an empir-
    ical analysis of the attractiveness of insured strategies using a stochastic
    dominance criterion, see Trennepohl et al. (1988). Bookstaber and Clarke
    (1985) point out, correctly, that mean-variance analysis is deficient for
    evaluating option-related portfolio strategies when investors are concerned
    with higher moments of the return distribution, such as skewness. Clarke
    (1991), however, finds that insurance is suboptimal under general utility
    functions that account for skewness. Using stochastic dominance tests
    applied to the complete probability distribution of returns, together with
    the general utility function characteristics of nonsatiety, risk-aversion, and
    skewness preference, he concludes that a portfolio insured by fairly priced
    puts does not dominate an uninsured portfolio. The results hold for all
    risk-averse investors, independent of the pattern of risk-aversion of the
    investor's utility function. In particular, the test results are more general than
    those that rely only on mean-variance optimality conditions, and account
    for such issues as skewness preference. Brennan and Solanki (1981) show
    that portfolio insurance is not in general an optimal policy for an expected
    utility maximizer. Brennan and Schwartz (1989) measure the opportunity
    cost of following the insurance strategy relative to the expected utility-
    maximizing strategy.
6   In fact, an investor who sells options is said to be selling volatility.
7   See Jacobs (1984); Ritchken (1985); Ferguson (1987); and Trippi and
    Harriff (1991).
8   Selling insurance is also consistent with a growth-optimal strategy
    (Rendleman and McEnally 1987a). Maximization of the growth rate of a
    portfolio's value over the investment horizon is consistent with a logarith-
    mic utility function. Over time, a portfolio managed in order to maximize
    logarithmic utility will, with certainty, accumulate more wealth than any
    other significantly different strategy involving the same assets. (Rubinstein
    [1991] agrees that this result is true, but points out that the time required
    to achieve this outcome may be very long.) Strategies that continuously rebal-
    ance to a constant mix over time (assuming risk and return expectations
    remain unchanged) can maximize logarithmic utility. Rebalancing to a con-
    stant mix implies the sale of insurance. Maintaining constant proportions
    invested in stock and cash, for example, requires selling off stocks as the
    value of stock holdings rises and buying stocks as the value of stock hold-
    ings falls. These trading rules are opposite to those of portfolio insurance.
9   On the basis of extensive empirical analysis, Friend and Blume (1975)
    conclude that most investors can be characterized as having constant pro-
    portion risk aversion. Hakansson (1970) and Merton (1971) showed that
    if the investment opportunity set is constant, an investor having constant
    proportion risk tolerance would maintain a constant proportion of wealth
    in stocks. Mossin (1968), Leland (1971), and Hakansson (1974) find that,
    for broad classes of utility functions defined over terminal wealth, the
    optimal investment strategy becomes constant as the horizon recedes.
10 Leland (1985) also points out that the transaction costs inherent in option-
    replication strategies lead to path-dependence. See also Rubinstein (1985).

11 This is consistent with Trippi and Harriff's (1991: 24) finding that, "if the investor is risk-averse, it is possible over a short investment horizon for a convex rule [like portfolio insurance] to produce a return distribution with greater expected utility than an optimal static portfolio, although as the number of iterations of the rule increases . . . it will tend to outperform a decreasing percentage of the time."

12 Because these strategies are perpetual, the floor is often set to increase automatically over time to reflect increases in the value of the portfolio. For a complete characterization of portfolio insurance strategies that are time-invariant, see Brennan and Schwartz (1988). They find time-invariant strategies to be the appropriate long-term portfolio insurance strategy for a broad class of insurance payoff functions.

13 It should be noted that the strategy LOR marketed as perpetual, the "Zero-Upside [Cost] Loss Perpetual," was path-dependent (see Bookstaber and Langsam 1988). Furthermore, although it promised zero cost, as premiums would be incurred only as needed, this was accomplished by starting out with a fully invested position. The strategy would thus be costless only if the market rose; if the market declined, the strategy would incur costs in the form of a loss of portfolio value relative to having started out with the appropriate allocation to cash.

14 This approach was introduced by Fischer Black, by this time a partner at Goldman, Sachs, and Andre Perold of Harvard in 1987 (for the final version of the original article, see Black and Perold 1992). See also Perold (1986); Black and Jones (1987); Black and Rouhani (1987); Black and Rouhani (1988); Perold and Sharpe (1988); and Grossman and Vila (1992). For an application of CPPI to fixed income instruments, see Hakanoglu et al. (1989).

15 There is some theoretical support for such a constant proportion strategy. See Mossin (1968); Hakansson (1970); Leland (1971); Merton (1971); and Hakansson (1974). Bookstaber and Langsam (1988) find, however, that process-free strategies are dominated by the properly specified process-specific strategy.

16 Black and Perold (1992) find that being at the maximum equity exposure limit just reduces volatility cost. They also demonstrate a parallel between CPPI and perpetual American calls where early exercise corresponds to reaching the exposure limit.

17 See, for example, Zhu and Kavee (1988).

— Part II —

The Crash of 1987: A Reality Check

By October 1987, the US economy had been expanding for fifty-nine straight months. Between August 12, 1982 and August 25, 1987, the Dow Jones industrial average (DJIA) climbed from 777 to 2722. In 1987 alone, from the beginning of the year to the August 25 peak, the DJIA rose by 826 points, or 43.6 percent. Then came October.

During the week of October 5, the DJIA declined by 159 points, its biggest weekly point drop ever. This included a record one-day drop of 91 points on Tuesday, October 6, on heavy New York Stock Exchange (NYSE) trading volume of 175 million shares. The slide intensified during the week of October 12. On Wednesday the 14th, the DJIA dropped a record 95 points, or 3.8 percent; on Thursday, 57 points, or 2.4 percent; and on Friday, a new record 108 points, 4.6 percent. These declines occurred on increasing NYSE trading volume of, respectively, 210, 266, and a record 344 million shares. By the close on Friday, October 16, the Dow had fallen to 2246, down almost 500 points, or 17.5 percent, from its August 1987 peak.

On Monday, October 19, the market suffered its worst percentage decline in history. On this single day, the DJIA plummeted 508 points to close at 1738, off 22.6 percent, and other stock market indexes experienced similar declines. Among individual issues, IBM stock fell over 31 points to $103, Digital Equipment over 42 points to $130, and Eastman Kodak over 27 points to $63. NYSE volume skyrocketed to an unprecedented 604 million shares, just under $21 billion.

In New York, state pension portfolios lost 32 percent of their value over the two weeks leading up to and including the crash (*New York*

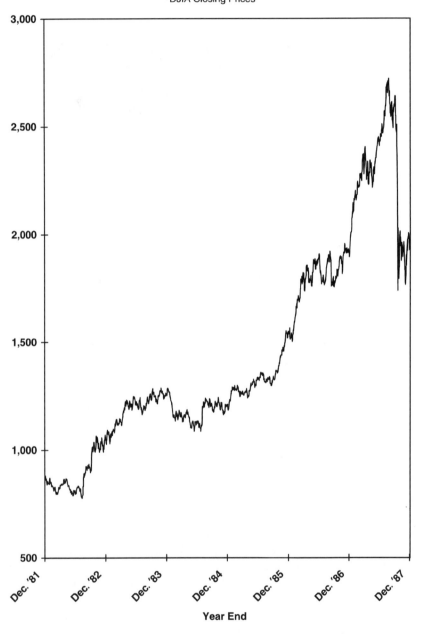

FIGURE PII.1
The Market Rises (and Falls)

DJIA Closing Prices

Times, October 20, 1987: D32). In Chicago, pawnbrokers harvested a bumper crop of Rolexes off investors and commodities traders. At the Pacific Stock Exchange, the falling ticker quickened the rumor that exchange officials had posted a suicide watch at the Golden Gate Bridge.

The *New York Times* reported the next day (p. 1) that "the losses were so great they sent shock waves to markets around the world." The London market fell 10 percent on the 19th and 11.5 percent on the 20th, while Tokyo, down on the 19th (before New York's open on that date), lost a record 14.9 percent on the 20th. The specter of recession raised its fearsome head. Democrats immediately began blaming Republicans, and Republicans Democrats. Nevertheless, the markets on the 19th weathered the storm. The next day provided a sterner test.

On Tuesday morning, before the markets opened, the Federal Reserve Board released a statement from Chairman Alan Greenspan that the Fed stood ready to provide liquidity to support the financial system (a statement backed up by the Fed's infusion of over $11 billion in new reserves to money center banks in the week of and the week following the crash). The Dow climbed almost 200 points in the morning. It then, however, proceeded to drop to an intraday low of 1709, with trading in many stocks and on most futures markets breaking down completely. The afternoon saw a turnaround, with massive corporate buy-back programs starting a rally that lifted the DJIA to a close of 1841. It ended up being a record point-day advance for the DJIA, and a record volume day for the market.

S&P 500 futures contract prices experienced even more extreme fluctuations. On October 19, S&P 500 futures fell 28.6 percent. Volume was 162,000 contracts, almost $20 billion. The futures contract traded at a substantial discount to the stock market throughout the day. At its intraday low on October 20, the contract was at a DJIA equivalent level of 1444, totally unhinged from the underlying stock market (SEC 1988: 2.1).

From its intraday high of 2747 on August 25 to the intraday low of 1709 on October 20, the market had declined by over 1000 points, or 37 percent. More than a trillion dollars in investment value had evaporated. Investors were understandably upset and worried about the future.

New York City real estate tycoon and casino magnate Donald Trump advised: "I'm not going back in the market, and I suggest the little guys just sit on the sidelines. Instead of playing the market, they should go to Atlantic City" (*New York Times*, October 25, 1987: F6). Many of the "little guys" did just that. Although many mutual fund holders weathered the brunt of the turmoil on Monday and Tuesday, mutual fund investors began pulling out more serious money in the wake of the crash, and fund redemptions outpaced investments in fifteen of the following seventeen months.

In a more forceful and tragic reaction, a disgruntled Florida investor, an employee of the Social Security Administration, shot his broker and shot and killed the brokerage firm's manager before committing suicide. Follow-up reports by Martha Brannigan and Sydney Freedberg in the *Wall Street Journal* revealed that the perpetrator, formerly a lawyer, had been living under an assumed name in the Federal Witness Protection Program, having pleaded guilty in the mid-1970s to charges stemming from an insurance fraud case. While serving a six-month prison term, he had also aided the prosecution in a federal case that sent a long-time associate of Miami mob figure Meyer Lansky to prison on stock-manipulation charges (October 30, 1987: 25). He had opened a margin account at Merrill Lynch in 1981 with $500,000, and had reportedly traded an average of $2 to $3 million a month, amassing a portfolio valued at some $11 million, $7 million of which was margin debt, before the crash (October 29, 1987: 6). At the time of the murder, all that was left of the portfolio were 30,000 margined Telex Corp. shares (October 30, 1987: 30).

The crash put a crimp in many business plans. Two brokerage houses that had planned to expand in Stamford, Connecticut, pulled out. A number of proposed mergers and acquisitions, including Carl Icahn's offer for TransWorld Airlines, fell through. Mary Tyler Moore had to postpone an IPO for her MTM Enterprises. But Hollywood read the crash as "bullish" for *Wall Street*, its forthcoming film of unbridled greed and unbounded egos.

Nevertheless, a *New York Times* telephone poll, conducted between October 18 and 22, found Americans still largely optimistic (October 28, 1997: D14). Many large investors were complacent, if not happy. Wal-Mart founder Sam Walton, whose family reportedly lost half a billion dollars in the crash, called it a "paper loss" (*New York Times*, October 21, 1987: D14). The future would prove these investors right.

On October 18, 1988, almost one year to the day after the crash, the DJIA was at a post-crash high. Within a decade of the crash, the DJIA had more than quadrupled in value. Equity mutual fund assets had grown from well under $200 billion to over $2 trillion. On the ten-year anniversary of the market's 1987 peak, hedge fund guru Michael Steinhardt noted in the *Wall Street Journal* (August 25, 1997: C1): "The stock market is supposed to be an indicator of things to come, a discounting mechanism that is telling you of what the world is to be. All that context was shattered. In 1987, the stock market crash was telling you nothing."

Ten years after the crash, Robert Glauber, executive director of the Brady Commission that investigated the event, looked back with some resignation: "It's ironic that we concluded the markets nearly fell apart in 1987, and just ten years later people treat it like ancient history" (*Boston Sunday Globe*, October 19, 1997: F1). Floyd Norris noted in the *New York Times*'s commemoration of the tenth anniversary date (October 19, 1997: C4): "In 1987, the crash traumatized investment bankers and small investors alike. A decade later it has produced something that no one could have forecast: complacency."

While the crash may have signified little economically, however, it had profound effects on investment thinking. In the decade or two preceding the crash, it had seemed that the market mavens, with theories of efficiency and ever more precise measurements of risk and return, had come close to understanding, if not taming, the unwieldy beast. The crash put many of their accepted truths to the test and gave rise to several competing, though not necessarily mutually exclusive, theories.

The following chapters explore these perceptions of the crash of 1987. Chapter 5 examines the case for the crash as a rational investor response to fundamental information. Chapter 6 discusses some evidence against stock market rationality. Research in this area (spurred by the crash itself) suggests that the markets may be moved as much by investor sentiment as by investment logic. When investors do not behave rationally, equity prices can roam far and wide from the prices that would be determined to be fair on the basis of fundamentals.

Chapter 7 looks at three broad theories of crashes that do not depend on individual investor irrationality but that do result in markets that are far from fundamentally efficient. The concepts of rational speculative bubbles, informational cascades, and chaotic markets are all consistent with the kind of behavior exhibited by the markets in October 1987. According to these views of market behavior, investors may behave rationally as individuals, seeking to maximize wealth on the basis of known information; yet markets may nevertheless become detached from fundamental values because of speculative "gambling," because of inherent limitations on the human ability to gather and interpret information, or simply because it is their nature.

Finally, chapter 8 discusses the role of trading in the then relatively new stock futures market and its impact on the volatility and liquidity of the underlying stock market. According to some market observers, the 1987 crash, if it did not exactly begin in the futures market, was substantially exacerbated by futures market instability, which was transmitted to the stock market via index arbitrage. As we will see in part III, synthetic portfolio insurance played a major role in these complex interactions.

5

The Fall of a Reigning Paradigm

The October [1987] price drop has the look of an adjustment to a change in fundamental values.

Eugene Fama, 1989

Option replication does not rely on evaluating market prices vis-à-vis underlying business and economic data, or on forecasting the future performance of individual companies, the economy, or the market. Rather, option replication merely *reacts* to market price changes; it is essentially insightless and foresightless.

This is no handicap in the theoretical world of market efficiency and rational expectations. According to these theories, investors base their investment decisions on expectations formed from the rational analysis of all available relevant information – fundamental information on underlying firms, industrial sectors, and the economy – and act so as to maximize the potential of achieving their investment goals. When market participants' analyses and actions are rational and timely, market prices reflect, almost instantaneously, all information pertinent to value as the information becomes available. Market prices are thus fair indicators of the real, or fundamental, value of the underlying firms.

Furthermore, only the arrival of new fundamental information has the potential to affect prices, and it will do so only to the extent that it contains surprises; any information anticipated by investors will already have been discounted in security prices. As surprises are by definition unexpected, price changes should be unpredictable and unrelated to past or subsequent price changes. This means that price changes will be uncorrelated over time, or random. Option-replicating portfolio insurance and other "passive" investment strategies such as indexing eschew prediction as impossible in theory and unprofitable in practice.[1]

Market efficiency was the dominant doctrine, at least in academic circles, throughout most of the 1970s and 1980s. It is thus hardly surprising that the 1987 crash was largely viewed at the time (and is still viewed by many) as a fundamental readjustment of investor expectations.

An Efficient Crash

The theory of market efficiency posits that security prices fully reflect all publicly available information. It is only unexpected changes in this information, in fundamental factors related to the economy, the markets, and specific companies, that cause investors to change their expectations and securities prices to move.

The University of Chicago's Eugene Fama (1970 and 1991), a leading proponent of this view, has documented substantial evidence that prices are informationally efficient. He has also discerned linkages between market returns and economic fundamentals (Fama 1981 and Fama and French 1989). Similar linkages at the individual security level have been reported by me and my colleague Ken Levy (Jacobs and Levy 1989a; see also Chen et al. 1986).

Fama views the 1987 crash within the context of an efficient market driven by fundamentals. In his view, the suddenness and severity of the market's decline, rather than challenging market efficiency, are evidence of its triumph: "The October price drop has the look of an adjustment to a change in fundamental values. In this view, the market moved with breathtaking quickness to its new equilibrium, and its performance during this period of hyperactive trading is to be applauded" (Fama 1989: 81).

On the basis of a simple valuation model, Fama (1989) reasons that price changes arise from changes in earnings expectations and/or changes in the rates of return required by investors. In the 1980s, an extended period of economic growth produced expectations of continued good times and high stock prices. Stock prices plummeted in October 1987 as the result of the confluence of a downward adjustment in expectations for growth and an upward shift in investors' required rates of return.

Fama advances no explanation for this shift in expectations, but cites the post-crash rise in the market's dividend yield as evidence that it did occur. The S&P 500's dividend yield, the ratio of its weighted average dividend to its weighted average price, had been 2.8 percent at the end of September 1987. By the end of the year, it had risen to 3.7 percent – more in line with the historical average yield of 3.8 percent during the 1957–86 period. He also finds that the default spread between high- and low-grade corporate bonds increased, and interprets this as further evidence of an increase in investors' required returns.[2]

Avner Arbel and his colleagues (1988) also view the crash as a rational, informationally motivated event. Stratifying securities by equity attributes (such as dividend yield, price-earnings ratio, company size, and risk measures), and tracking their returns from October 1 through October 19, Arbel et al. find that stocks with high dividend yields fell 21.2 percent, while stocks paying no dividends declined 32 percent. They conclude that the returns to securities followed an orderly process consistent with a risk-averse fundamental approach to stock valuation.

From an international perspective, Richard Roll (1988b: 27) sees the US crash and the various overseas crashes as the outcomes of some unidentified worldwide fundamental factor. (Roll is a UCLA professor and cofounder with Stephen Ross of a firm that offers strategies based on Ross's arbitrage pricing theory, which maintains that prices are driven by fundamentals.) He finds that the magnitude of the decline in each country's market can be explained by the usual relation between the market and a worldwide market index. That is, each market's decline was proportional to its historical sensitivity to world market movements.

These studies, however, focus primarily on the results of the crash, rather than its causes. Each begs the question of what change or changes in fundamentals caused investors to alter so abruptly their desire to hold equities. There are a number of plausible candidates.

The Fundamental Things

As the market began to falter in the weeks preceding the crash, newspapers were quick to point an inky finger at interest rates, trade wars, budget deficits, oil, and Robert Prechter. During the week of October 5, for example, the prime rate had risen to 9.25 percent and the market had dropped. Chemical Bank raised its prime another half a percentage point on the 15th. And the day before that, yields on long-term bonds hit a psychological barrier, rising to 10 percent.

These increases played out against a complex backdrop of international economic brinkmanship. In February of 1987, the US and its major trading partners (Japan, Germany, Britain, France, Italy, and Canada) had agreed to prop up the US dollar, which was under heavy selling pressure due to an ever-widening US trade deficit. In the months following the so-called Louvre Accord, however, Japan and Germany proceeded to raise their rates, in seeming contradiction to their February promises. To keep the dollar in line with Louvre standards, the US had had to increase its own rates.

Higher interest rates could draw money away from equity into fixed income investments. They could also increase the rate used to discount future income streams to present values, leading to a decline in current equity prices.

Higher rates would also raise borrowing costs. This could have put a damper on the hot LBO market. Leveraged buyouts, in which companies were taken over by private partnerships funded by heavy borrowing, had helped feed the merger and acquisition activity that had grown with the market in the mid-1980s. Higher rates would make debt-financed takeovers more expensive, perhaps even unviable.

But there was nothing exactly new about rising rates. Although rates had fallen through much of 1986, the Federal Reserve had switched to a tighter monetary regime in early 1987. Yet the market had continued to rise through most of August. And merger and acquisition activity had proceeded apace.

There was, however, a political factor that may have kicked in right around the time of the crash. A bill before Congress in October would have severely limited tax deductions for the interest paid on debt used to finance corporate takeovers. Mark Mitchell and Jeffry Netter (1989) present evidence that this bill was the specific trigger for the crash. And, indeed, acquisition candidates seem to have been especially heavily hit on several days leading up the crash, particularly on October 16.

Nevertheless, the market fell along a broad front during the week of October 12, and all stocks fell, and fell hard, on the 19th, not just takeover targets. In an empirical study, Nejat Seyhun (1990) argues that, if price declines in the crash had primarily reflected the proposed tax legislation, insiders in takeover-related firms would have been net sellers of their firms' shares just before and during the crash; he finds otherwise. Furthermore, as a *Wall Street Journal* editorial pointed out on the eve of the crash (October 16, 1987: 28), President Reagan was expected to veto the tax bill, if it passed Congress.

Perhaps it was the US economy in general. On October 14, US trade figures for August were released. At $15.8 billion, the trade deficit had shrunk from previous record levels, but it remained huge. The *New York Times* reported on October 16 (p. 1) that US Treasury Secretary James Baker 3rd was raising the possibility of allowing the dollar to weaken in the face of the general lack of support from foreign central banks. A weaker dollar could help the US trade deficit.

A weaker dollar would also customarily imply lower interest rates. That had been the case in 1985 and 1986, when the Fed was engineering a drop in the dollar's value. If high interest rates were bad for equity, wouldn't a hint of lower rates be good?

Not if it meant higher inflation. And there may have been some justification to fear such an outcome. A stubborn US budget deficit persisted despite the generally healthy economy and strong equity market, and many political observers doubted President Reagan's ability or resolve to make the necessary compromises with Congress to raise taxes and/ or cut spending. At the same time, Iranian threats to shipping in the Persian Gulf were generating fears of rising oil prices.

Preliminary reports on the budget deficit, published on the Tuesday preceding the crash, showed that it remained substantial. It was, however, down at least $60 billion from the previous year's record $220 billion (*New York Times*, October 13, 1987: D5). And although oil prices had increased considerably (but throughout the year, not merely since the market's peak in August), inflation seemed well under control. In fact, Federal Reserve Chairman Alan Greenspan, speaking at a Congressional conference on October 14, had emphasized that the Fed saw no evidence of any significant inflation.

George Soros, who reportedly lost $800 million, blamed the crash on Robert Prechter (*New York Times*, October 28, 1987: D1). Prechter was a technical analyst, a follower of the Elliot Wave theory of repetitive price patterns, who had been very bullish on the market during its rise. Rumors had begun circulating in early October that he had turned bearish. Of course, Prechter – or the propensity of numbers of investors to act in accordance with his prognostications (or rumors thereof) – is hardly a fundamental factor.

Although there are plenty of fundamentals that could serve as likely candidates for the cause of the 1987 crash, it is difficult to intuit how (or even in what direction) these fundamental things apply. Merton Miller (1991: 101), a Nobel laureate for his contributions to modern corporate finance, suggests that an aggregation of fundamentals, including the increase in interest rates, the proposed tax treatment of takeovers, and hostilities in the Persian Gulf, combined with market declines in the week preceding the crash, may have led many investors simultaneously to revise their relative desires for equity and fixed income securities:

> The long-sought missing ("fundamental") explanation for the Crash of 1987 may . . . come down to nothing more than this: on October 19, after some weeks of external events, minor in themselves, but that cumulatively may have signaled a possible change in what had been up to then a very favorable political and economic climate for equities . . . many investors simultaneously . . . came to believe that they were holding too large a share of their wealth in risky equities and too little in safer instruments.

But more rigorous attempts to model the crash with specific fundamentals have met with, at best, only mixed success. Robert Barro (1989) models stock returns using interest rates, net exports, and the federal budget deficit as explanatory variables. While his model can account for unusually low stock returns in the fourth quarter of 1987, driven primarily by rising interest rates earlier in the year, it cannot begin to account for the hit that stocks took. He concludes that economic developments in 1987 are unable to explain the crash.

Jeremy Siegel (1992a) meets with similar lack of success. Examining equity risk premiums and corporate profit forecasts during the crash period, Siegel finds that the dispersion of short-term profit forecasts narrowed in the period from April to October preceding the crash, while the dispersion of long-term profit forecasts widened. While the former development may have contributed to a lowering of the equity risk premium prior to the crash, the latter may have left the market vulnerable to negative shocks. He finds, however, that neither equity risk premiums nor profit forecasts can explain the crash.

Political pundit Michael Kinsley (*Wall Street Journal*, October 22, 1987: 39) views attempts to explain the crash rationally with some skepticism, but proffers the following with tongue firmly in cheek:

> The Cholesterol Market. Recent government approval of a new drug that reduces blood cholesterol will cut heart attacks and thus increase the impact of Social Security payments on the federal deficit beginning in the year 2000. In addition, consumption of ice cream is expected to increase, beginning after lunch and continuing through "Nightline," thus slowing our economy during the very hours when the Japanese are asleep and we have a brief window of opportunity to play catch-up ball.

The Psychic Crash

Soon after the crash, LOR's Mark Rubinstein (1988: 42) drew up a list of a dozen fundamental items, including increasing interest rates and budget and trade deficits, that could have triggered the event. But writing elsewhere with his colleague Hayne Leland (1988a: 45), he is forced to conclude that, given the strong economic conditions after the crash, news about fundamentals such as the US budget and trade deficits was probably not the cause of the crash.

In the absence of definitive evidence that prior economic conditions can explain the crash, some researchers have looked to the future to explain it. Using a predictive model for real gross national product based on the previous year's stock market return, Barro (1989 and 1990) finds that the crash augured relatively slow economic growth in 1988. Similarly, Joe Peek and Eric Rosengren (1988: 48) conclude that real economic growth in 1989 should have slowed to below 2 percent to be consistent with historical relationships between stock market declines and subsequent economic activity. Using a Minneapolis Federal Reserve Bank model of the economy, David Runkle (1988) also finds that the crash predicted a weakening in economic growth.

But economic growth after the crash remained robust through 1990, despite the close to one-trillion-dollar drop in the market value of common stock in October 1987. In fact, Runkle's forecast of economic growth had returned to its precrash path by early 1988, primarily because of the economy's resilience. As a possible explanation, Runkle notes (p. 7) that the 1987 rise in equity values may have been generally viewed as "temporary wealth," so that its disappearance had little or no real impact on the economy.

Summary

Some evidence, including the behavior of dividend yields and the international character of the crash, suggests that the sharp drop in stock prices on October 19 reflected changes in fundamental factors. It has proved difficult, however, to pin the crash on any one fundamental factor or combination of factors. Interest rates, budget deficits, and corporate profit forecasts cannot explain investors' behavior in October 1987. Nor can the state of the economy subsequent to the crash.

This does not mean that fundamentals played no role. It is probable that, as the Securities and Exchange Commission concluded (1988: 3.6, 3.9), economic news about the US trade and budget deficits, a possible decline in the value of the dollar, increases in interest rates, and the proposed anti-takeover bill triggered the market's downturn in the week preceding the crash. As we will see, however, it took substantial input from non-fundamental factors to bring the market to its knees on the 19th.

Notes

1   In fact, one of the most successful firms in attracting portfolio insurance business was Wells Fargo Investment Advisors, the country's largest manager of passive funds in the mid-1980s. According to Wells Fargo President Fred Grauer (*Pensions & Investment Age*, February 9, 1987: 31): "What makes for good indexation also makes for good portfolio insurance management," as both index funds and portfolio insurance must be managed within narrow boundaries to produce the desired results at the lowest possible cost.

2   See Fama and French (1989) for empirical evidence on the dividend yield and the default spread as business cycle variables.

6

Animal Spirits

Social movements, fashions, or fads are likely to be important or even the dominant cause of speculative asset price movements.

Robert Shiller, 1984

Even at the time of the 1987 crash, many questioned the informational efficiency of a market that could drop so precipitously. Corporate leaders reached by the *New York Times* (October 20, 1987: D32) on the day of the crash, for example, could see no economic fundamentals behind the market's move. They attributed it to such non-fundamental factors as investor overreaction and herd behavior.

Steven Wunsch (1988: 1) ridicules the notion that the crash represented a highly efficient market response to new information:

> We must really have efficient markets now, if they're so sensitive to new information that they can drop 23 percent on October 19 (an 18 sigma event), and no one can even agree on what the bad news was; and then jump 17 percent by 10 a.m. the next morning . . . then efficiently adjust to another wave of bad news by falling 25 percent in the next two hours (a 40 sigma event). . . . I guess you'd believe the next move was the most impressive display of efficiency we have seen in this country: a 32 percent rise in the MMI (Major Market Index) in thirty-two minutes (a 101 sigma event), once again caused by phenomenal, but unidentified, good news.

Of course, John Maynard Keynes had observed long ago that stock market fluctuations were often self-fulfilling prophecies arising from investors' "animal spirits." He likened the stock market to a beauty contest, in which each investor's goal is not to pick the prettiest contestant, but rather to choose the contestant the other judges deem the prettiest. Keynes (1936: 157) asserted that "investment based on genuine long-term expectations is so difficult . . . as to be scarcely practicable.

FIGURE 6.1
Perceived Reasons for Crash*

Factor

Fundamental	20%
Technical	40%
Psychological	40%

* Results from 172 responses to a survey of market participants and observers.
Source: *Report of the Presidential Task Force on Market Mechanisms*
(Brady Commission), 1988.

He who attempts it most surely . . . run[s] greater risks than he who tries to guess better than the crowd how the crowd will behave."[1]

The magnitude and apparent inexplicability of the crash fueled renewed interest in the role of non-fundamental factors in security pricing. Theories holding that stock prices responded only, and efficiently, to fundamentals came into question. New paradigms of market behavior were born.

Research in the wake of the crash has often focused on the shortcomings of efficient market theory. David Cutler et al. (1989), for example, find that a large fraction of the market's variability remains unexplained by macroeconomic, political, and world news events. They conclude that market moves often occur in the absence of any discernible news event. Jeremy Siegel's (1998a) analysis of days on which the DJIA changed by more than 5 percent could detect an identifiable news event on only twenty-eight of the 123 days.

Testing the dividend discount model, my colleague Ken Levy and I conclude that fundamental value is just a fraction of the security pricing story (Jacobs and Levy 1988c). Richard Roll (1988a), too, finds that pervasive macroeconomic factors, industry influences, and firm-specific news can account for only a small portion of the variability of security returns.

Furthermore, a great deal of research has detected persistent, perhaps exploitable, patterns in stock price movements, which are anomalous in the context of efficient market theory. In an efficient market, only the arrival of new, fundamental information has the potential to affect prices, and it will do so only to the extent that it contains surprises not already anticipated in prices. Price changes should thus be unpredictable, and prices should move randomly about a trend line reflecting the premium investors demand for bearing risk, the equity risk premium. (Chapter 17 discusses the equity risk premium in light of protective strategies such as portfolio insurance.)

Patterns

Market participants have long noted anecdotally patterns of abnormal returns to small-firm or low-P/E stocks, or to specific time periods, such as Mondays or Januaries. Jacobs and Levy (1988a and 1989b) test a number of these effects jointly, in order to control for the possibility of overlapping impacts on stock returns. They find several return patterns associated with calendar turning points, such as day-of-the-week and holiday effects, which cannot be adequately explained by fundamentals such as tax-loss selling, cash flow patterns, or the distribution of news.

Jacobs and Levy (1988b) also find overall patterns of short-term positive price momentum, or price trends, related to upgrades in analysts' earnings estimates and positive earnings surprises (see also Jacobs et al. 1997). For example, stocks whose earnings estimates have been upgraded by Wall Street security analysts tend to produce positive returns that persist, at a receding rate, up to a few months after the revision. Andrew Lo and Craig MacKinlay (1988) find significant positive serial correlation in weekly and monthly returns, particularly for small-firm stocks; they consider such correlation to be inconsistent with random walk behavior.[2]

Frank Fabozzi and his colleagues (1995) find systematic intraday price reversals, with large price changes generally followed by price reversals, then price stabilization, and reversals following large increases generally twice the magnitude of reversals following large declines. Jacobs and Levy (1988b) document the predictive power of reversals in one-month market-adjusted returns. Werner De Bondt and Richard Thaler (1985) find evidence of longer-run price reversals.

Efficient market theorists Eugene Fama and Kenneth French (1988b) also document large negative autocorrelations (reversals) for horizons beyond one year. Stocks that perform better than average in one period tend to have below-average returns in a subsequent period, and vice versa. This predictable price variation accounts for between 25 and 40 percent of the variability in three-to-five-year returns.[3]

Although patterns in stock prices seem to fly in the face of rational pricing and market efficiency, they could be consistent with rational pricing based on fundamental information. It may be, for example, that fundamental factors evolve in such a way that the premium investors require for bearing the risk associated with equity investments exhibits discernible systematic changes.

In support of this view, Fama and French (1988a) find that dividend yields can explain a large fraction of the variability in long-term returns. They also find (1989) that dividend yields and corporate bond default spreads (the yield spread between high-grade and low-grade bonds) capture similar variations in expected bond and stock returns, and that both are related to changes in economic conditions over business cycles. They see this as evidence (although not conclusive) of rational pricing and market efficiency.[4]

Fama (1991: 1585) notes, however, that "deciding whether return predictability is the result of rational variation in expected returns or irrational bubbles is never clearcut." Paul Kupiec (1993: 2), surveying the literature on patterns of price reversion and price overreaction in stock movements, concludes that "there is little evidence that establishes strong and convincing links between time variation in economic factors and time variation in expected stock returns – links that should be apparent if markets are efficient."

To the contrary, Narasimhan Jegadeesh and Sheridan Titman (1993) document short-term price trending that cannot be explained by risk. They hypothesize that investors tend to buy past winners and sell past losers, causing prices to overreact.

Similarly, Navin Chopra and his colleagues (1992) document long-term price reversion that cannot be explained by fundamentals. They form portfolios on the basis of the prior five years' returns and find that the extreme prior "losers" outperform the extreme prior "winners" by 5 to 10 percent a year over the next five years. Portfolios formed on the basis of one year of data, however, tend to exhibit positive price momentum, or trending. The authors find their results cannot be explained by risk-related factors, by firm size, or by a January effect.

James Poterba and Larry Summers (1988) find that the predictable variation in long-horizon returns is too large to be accounted for by changing risk. Cutler, Poterba, and Summers (1991), examining data on stock, bond, and other asset returns in thirteen countries, find that excess returns demonstrate positive serial correlation over short horizons and weak negative correlation over longer horizons. They believe that fundamentals such as changing risk premiums are an unlikely explanation for these patterns.

Noise

Fischer Black (1986) terms that portion of price that cannot be explained by fundamental information "noise." Noise in security pricing can be substantial. According to Black, markets are efficient if price is within a factor of two of true value; that is, prices can range from half to twice their fundamental values without violating efficiency.

Noise can be created in any number of ways. A portion of the noise present in security prices undoubtedly reflects simple errors by investors in interpreting information or extrapolating its implications. Of course, errors are to be expected; no one can have perfect foresight. Theoretically, however, individual errors will cancel out over the aggregate of investors. For each investor who is too optimistic about a stock, for example, there will presumably be an investor who is too pessimistic.

But investors may at times tend to err systematically in the same direction. This can happen if investors are driven, not merely by fundamentals, but by a common behavior. A growing body of literature investigating the role of investor psychology in stock pricing suggests that individual investors share common cognitive defects that may cause them to err in the same direction (see works by Kahneman and Tversky 1979 and Thaler 1993 on behavioral finance).

Nobel laureate economist Kenneth Arrow (1982), for example, finds that investors in general tend to overreact to current information – that is, to overemphasize the importance of it – if it appears to be "representative" of a possible future event. Thus investors may tend to believe the highest earnings estimate of analysts following a firm, overlooking other analysts' lower estimates, if the underlying firm has enjoyed high earnings over the recent past and if its management is considered to be good.

David Dreman and Michael Berry (1995b) examine the price responses of high-P/E and low-P/E stocks when actual company earnings come in higher or lower than Wall Street security analysts had anticipated. They find a pattern of price reversion over the long term. Positive earnings surprises are followed by significant above-market returns for low-P/E stocks but only modest gains for high-P/E stocks, while negative earnings surprises are followed by significant below-market returns for high-P/E stocks but have only a modest impact on low-P/E stocks. They hypothesize that analysts extrapolate too far into the future, anticipating continuing high returns for high-priced stock and continuing low returns for low-priced stock. Analysts are forced to reevaluate their assumptions only when unexpected trigger events, such as low earnings for high-P/E firms or high earnings for low-P/E firms, force them to.

Robert Shiller (1984), a proponent of a psychological element in price volatility, suggests that investing is as susceptible as any other social activity to fads and fashions. As an example, he cites the post-World War II boom in stock prices, which he attributes in part to a general increase in the availability of information about stocks and individuals' increased awareness of and participation in the market. Presenting evidence that stock prices are far too volatile to be explained by fundamentals alone, Shiller maintains (1984: 497) that "social movements, fashions, or fads are likely to be important or even the dominant cause of speculative asset price movements."[5] Although he does not dismiss rational expectations and fundamentals, he sees them as only part of the pricing mosaic:

> I think the truth may well be that financial prices can be successfully modeled as reflecting proper anticipations of those future movements in dividends that can be predicted plus a term reflecting the anticipation of fashions or fads among investors. (Shiller 1987: 318)

Larry Summers (1986) argues that the empirical tests used to evaluate market efficiency have no power against the alternative hypothesis that fads cause prices to deviate widely and frequently from fundamental values. He maintains (in Shiller 1984: 509) that "the existing evidence does not establish that financial markets are efficient in the sense of rationally reflecting fundamentals." Of the crash, he had this to say: "The efficient market hypothesis is the most remarkable error in the history of economic theory. This is just another nail in its coffin" (*Wall Street Journal*, October 23, 1987: 7).

Overoptimism

Systematic price trending and reversing may reflect overoptimism on the part of investors. De Bondt and Thaler (1990), examining the behavioral dimensions of investing, analyze changes in security analysts' earnings per share forecasts and actual earnings changes.[6] They find that analysts' forecasts tend to be too optimistic and too extreme, and that these characteristics become stronger as the forecast period is lengthened. As a result, stock prices tend to exhibit mean reversion, first rising above fundamental values, then falling as expectations meet reality.

Dreman and Berry (1995a) also uncover evidence of significant overoptimism in analysts' earnings estimates. Comparing actual earnings with the consensus of analysts' earnings forecasts, they find that analysts overestimated earnings by several percentage points. Furthermore, the overoptimism was present in down as well as up markets.

Earnings forecasts may tend toward overoptimism for a number of reasons. Companies, for example, are understandably loath to publicize bad news; they may thus delay its release, or attempt to disguise it via window-dressing (or, in rare cases, commit actual fraud). This, however, seems an unlikely explanation for the type of across-the-board optimism that has been documented.

Overoptimism may exist because brokers and analysts favor buy over sell candidates. Such bias may reflect practical business concerns. Publishing negative opinions about a company can jeopardize investment banking relationships and even threaten analyst job security (Regan 1993). Optimism may reflect basic economics. Buy recommendations elicit more commissions than sell recommendations, as all customers are potential purchasers, whereas commissions from sales are primarily limited to customers who already own the stock, as there are few short-sellers.[7]

The latter rationale is supported by Lex Huberts and Russell Fuller (1995), who find that the level of analysts' overoptimism about a company's earnings can be forecast on the basis of the predictability of its past earnings. On the basis of actual and estimated earnings, they find that the less predictable a company's earnings history is, the more optimistic analysts' earnings estimates are likely to be. They hypothesize that brokerage firms have an incentive to produce optimistically biased earnings estimates, and that those companies with the least stable earnings histories are the prime candidates for such upwardly biased estimates because the very instability of their earnings makes the overestimation difficult to detect.

To the extent that investors buy (and sell) on the basis of analysts' forecasts, overly optimistic forecasts can lead stock prices to overreact – to rise above levels justified by the fundamentals. When actual earnings come in below forecasts, the (now) disappointed investors sell, and prices drop.[8]

Nejat Seyhun (1990) hypothesizes that, if prices during and after the 1987 crash reflected investor overreaction, rather than fundamental factors, corporate insiders should have been purchasing their own firms' shares as prices fell below fundamental values. He finds that the number of insider purchases and the ratio of insiders' purchases to total transactions did, in fact, set records in the week of October 19. Furthermore, insiders bought more, the further their firms' share prices fell, and top executives purchased more than other corporate insiders. This suggests that the crash was characterized by overreaction.

Jeremy Siegel (1992a) wonders whether shifts in investors' inclinations toward optimism or pessimism can account for differences between actual market levels and consensus market valuations. He examines actual market levels, consensus market valuations, and the variability of analysts' forecasts about the consensus forecast over the period from April 1987 through March 1988. He finds that sharp shifts in investor sentiment from the optimistic to the pessimistic camp correspond closely to changes in stock price levels.

Feedback Trading

Large numbers of investors caught up in fashions or fads or responding to overly optimistic earnings or return forecasts can create noise. This noise can take the form of waves of price increases followed by price declines. Furthermore, such systematic patterns may persist even in the face of fundamentals that would be expected to nullify them.

The patterns persist in part because the noise they introduce into prices creates substantial uncertainty, or risk (Black 1986). This uncertainty limits the ability of fundamental values to assert themselves, because it limits the activity of informed traders who base their trading decisions on fundamentals alone. Even if informed traders are sure that securities are substantially over- or underpriced, they will be unwilling to take unlimited offsetting positions because they cannot be sure that continuing noise won't move prices further away from fundamental values.

Andrei Shleifer and Robert Vishny (1997), for example, model the behavior of arbitragers who would theoretically be expected to bet against noise traders, in the expectation that any mispricing introduced by noise will eventually disappear in the glare of fundamental truth. Under real world constraints, such as their dependence on outside investors willing to capitalize them, such arbitragers may decline to bet against mispricings, even if they know with certainty that the mispricing will eventually be corrected. This is true because they will be forced to expend capital as long as the mispricing persists. The longer it persists, the less willing investors may be to supply them with capital. Thus, to the extent that the duration of mispricing is related to its degree, arbitragers may in fact be least willing to bet against noise, the "louder" it is.

De Long et al. (1991) point out that those who base their trading decisions on noisy information may tend to underestimate risk. In that case, noise traders can end up (unwittingly) taking on more risk and earning higher returns (at least over finite periods) than informed traders. Noise can thus persist in the face of informed traders.

Investors who trade on noise in prices as if it represented information are called "feedback" traders (Black 1986). Prices and price changes, rather than fundamental factors, are the prime (or sole) determinants of trading decisions for such investors. Feedback traders can amplify noise, exacerbating price deviations from fundamental values.[9]

Investors following a fad or speculators participating in a bubble (see chapter 7) may use current prices as a guide to trading. But certain trading strategies depend upon price movements to the virtual exclusion of all other information. Market technicians, for example, base their decisions on changing price patterns. Their trading may not consistently amplify noise-related overreaction, however, because they do not consistently buy into rising markets (or sell out of falling markets); at times they will be exerting a stabilizing influence by selling or buying against the general market trend. Portfolio insurers, by contrast, are feedback traders who will consistently amplify market movements. As long as their programs are not stopped out, they will be buying as prices increase and selling as prices decline.

Cutler et al. (1990) propose a model of asset price dynamics that depends upon the presence of feedback traders as well as investors who base their trading decisions on fundamentals. Given a sufficient number of feedback traders who buy on price increases, "prices will overreact to fundamental news. In the long run, however, prices must change by only the amount of the fundamental shock. This implies that returns must be negatively serially correlated over some horizons," in line with the documented mean reversion in securities prices (Cutler et al. 1990: 66).[10]

Shiller (1989: 23) uncovers some anecdotal evidence for feedback trading during the October 1987 crash. Surveying investors shortly after the crash, he found that respondents could recall no major news story, over the weekend or on Monday the 19th, that could have accounted for the precipitous decline. He did find, however, a correspondence between the crash and the "internal dynamics of investor thinking." Two "feedback channels" were at work: investors reacted to price declines, and investors reacted to each other. Shiller cites in support of this observation the frequency with which investors checked prices and communicated with each other during the crash.

Summary

The crash spurred researchers to look beyond fundamentals to understand market behavior. Some have considered the human element in the pricing equation and see investors herding to fads or fashions, creating waves of overpricing followed by gradual corrections. Others find evidence for overoptimism in security analysts' forecasts, motivated perhaps by greed, leading to overly optimistic price levels that subside only as the rosy future fails to materialize.

Divergence of prices from fundamental underpinnings constitutes noise. Noise makes it difficult for informed traders to discern fundamental values and to trade profitably against prevailing trends. Overpricing (or underpricing) can thus persist in the face of fundamental evidence to the contrary. Deviations from fundamental values can also be amplified by feedback traders, who base their trading decisions primarily on prices and price changes, rather than fundamentals. Portfolio insurers are the archetypal feedback traders because they always buy on price advances and sell on price declines.

Notes

1 Aiyagari (1988) presents a theoretical model in support of this view.
2 Froot and Perold (1995) find that positive serial autocorrelation in stock prices disappeared in the course of the 1980s and attribute this to increased efficiency in the dissemination of information.
3 Several researchers dispute the findings of mean reversion in stock prices. Kim et al. (1991), for example, examine 1926–86 data adjusted for non-normal distribution of the relevant variables and find that mean reversion is entirely a prewar phenomenon. Variance ratios in the postwar period exhibit, if anything, persistence rather than mean reversion.
4 Fama and French surmise (1989) that the observed patterns in predictive variables such as dividend yield may reflect return expectations that are consistent with intertemporal pricing models that assume consumption smoothing. If investors seek to maintain a fairly constant level of consumption in relation to wealth, they will tend to save more when income is high relative to wealth and less when income is low. High demand for investments when business conditions are good may thus pull expected security returns down, whereas low demand for investments when business conditions are poor may push expected returns up. (See also Cecchetti et al. 1990.) Additionally, expected returns may vary in response to variations in capital investment opportunities or in response to changes in perceived risks as economic conditions change.
5 The evidence is presented in Shiller (1981) and is controversial. For a summary of the debate, see Kleidon (1988) and West (1988).
6 Chan (1988) claims that De Bondt and Thaler's long-run reversal effect is explained by changing risk. However, De Bondt and Thaler (1987) find contrary evidence.
7 For discussion of the relationship between short-selling and overly optimistic pricing, see E.M. Miller (1990); Jacobs and Levy (1996); and Jacobs and Levy (1997).
8 Investor overoptimism based on analysts' forecasts may be consistent with evidence presented in Chopra et al. (1992), who find the strongest indications of overreaction in stocks not owned heavily by institutions; that is, return reversals are strongest for stocks dominated by retail investors, who are more likely to rely on brokerage recommendations. A similar connection between individual investors and overoptimism has been made by Lee et al. (1991), who hypothesize that closed-end fund performance should be correlated with small-company stock performance, as retail investors dominate both types of investments; they indeed find that closed-end fund discounts narrow when small-company stocks perform well.

9 Feedback is studied extensively in control engineering, which deals with methods and apparatus to regulate the behavior of systems such as the flight dynamics of spacecraft or, more familiarly, the household thermostat. Control is often effected by comparing a sample of the system's output with the desired goal. For example, a thermostatic control system samples indoor air temperature and compares it with the setting on the thermostat; if the temperature is too high, an error signal is generated, which initiates cooling action until the error signal diminishes to zero. Note that a higher-than-desired temperature (a positive error signal) causes the system to lower the temperature (a negative response); a lower-than-desired temperature (negative error signal) would cause the system to raise the temperature (a positive response). A stable control system uses negative feedback to produce a stable output; positive feedback almost invariably produces unstable systems (or systems that exhibit unbounded output for a bounded input). Thus, in our example, positive feedback corresponds to an increase in temperature when the house is already too hot, or a decrease when the house is too cold. See Dorf and Bishop (1994) and Franklin et al. (1994).

10 See also De Long et al. (1990a); Shleifer and Summers (1990); and Campbell and Kyle (1993).

7

Bubbles, Cascades, and Chaos

Prices on competitive markets *need not* be continuous, and they are conspicuously *discontinuous*.

Benoit Mandelbrot, 1983

Trading strategies that rely on interpretations of other investors' actions as revealed in current prices can create and amplify noise. The result may be markets characterized by price overreaction and instability, with intermittent price run-ups followed by abrupt price reversals. That such patterns are observable in the history of stock prices is indisputable. What remains in doubt is the mechanism underlying these patterns. One of the more popular explanations, and the one perhaps most firmly entrenched in the public's mind as the cause of the 1987 crash, is that speculative investors drive prices up to unsustainable levels, from which they are bound to fall.

Bubbles

Prices propelled upward by fads tend to return to their former levels slowly, over time. In contrast, speculative bubbles are fragile and tend to burst suddenly, creating a crash.

A speculative bubble can represent collective market irrationality. The market is irrational in the sense that prices rise above the levels justified by fundamentals. The run-up in prices, however, is fueled by speculators who may be seen to be behaving quite rationally as individuals. That is, speculators may choose to invest in a rising market, despite their knowledge that it is overpriced, with the expectation of being able to get out, at a profit, before the bubble bursts.

Some have argued that, if bubbles are certain to burst (as they are if the number of traders, their wealth, or their horizons are finite), they should not exist in the first place. But if traders have differing beliefs about the limits of the market, then a bubble may start and some "greater fool" will be caught when the burst occurs.[1] Jack Treynor (1998: 70) asserts: "It is not obvious that, if the market level is temporarily perturbed, equilibrium forces will return it to its original level. If not, then the mere presence of heterogeneous expectations sets the stage for market bubbles, in which the equilibrium level is no longer uniquely defined and market level changes are no longer random."

Eugene Fama (1989) admits that there is no scientific way to discriminate between rational and irrational pricing, since true values are inherently unknowable. But addressing the possibility that the 1987 bull market was irrational, Fama asserts (p. 77): "If there are bubbles, economic efficiency is served by letting them burst rather than leak."

Avner Arbel and his colleagues (1988: 124) find that a Benjamin Graham (1974) valuation model shows the market to have been overvalued by 17 percent on September 30, but undervalued by just 4 percent on October 19. (This model, according to the authors, also accurately predicted the October 19 closing prices of some leading companies.) In light of this evidence, they tend to view the crash as the bursting of a bubble, with rational behavior restoring sobriety and rationality:

> The steep market descent that the world witnessed actually prevented a long, gradual descent. . . . Portfolio insurance and program trading did not worsen the crash, they kept it from lasting longer. In the language of statistics, they increased its amplitude and compressed its duration. With sudden swiftness, the crash imposed the rational rules of a remarkable exercise of analytic intelligence. (Arbel et al. 1988: 124)

Edward Renshaw (1988: 1, 5) finds evidence for a speculative bubble using a model based on a theory forwarded by Vernon Smith. Smith and his colleagues (1988) found that experimental markets (markets characterized by inexperienced participants) are prone to bubble creation followed by crashes; as investors become more experienced, the likelihood of bubbles is reduced but not eliminated. Renshaw's model suggests that the size of a bubble is proportional to the number of traders who have not lived through a crash. According to the model, prices were due to fall about 20 percent in October 1987, because it had been a relatively long time since the previous collapse, in 1973–4.

But was the precrash run-up in prices truly a speculative bubble? Olivier Blanchard and Mark Watson (1982) observe that a bubble produces a sequence of positive returns while it is growing and a single negative return when it bursts. The run of positive returns will be longer than is the case for a purely random sequence, and the crash will produce an outlier of a large negative return. They propose two statistical tests – a runs test and a test for large outliers – to identify a speculative bubble.

Gary Santoni (1987) uses a runs test to examine market returns prior to the crash and finds no evidence of a speculative bubble. (See also Santoni and Dwyer 1990.) Gikas Hardouvelis (1988, 1990b) confirms Santoni's findings but concludes that the runs test is not powerful enough to reject the hypothesis that the returns were random. He proposes a more powerful test that models the bubble premium directly. Using this approach, he finds evidence of a positive and rising bubble premium in US and Japanese markets over the one and a half years prior to October 1987. (The evidence of a bubble in the UK market is weak.)

While his evidence is consistent with a speculative bubble and subsequent crash, Hardouvelis notes that it does not provide a complete answer, because the Japanese market returned to its precrash level within six months of the crash, while the US and UK markets recovered only slightly. Nor does Hardouvelis examine German and other markets where stock returns, rather than rising, had been weak prior to the crash.[2]

Mustafa Chowdhury and Ji-Chai Lin (1993), examining stock returns between 1982 and 1990, find strong evidence for dependence on past returns and past shocks to small-capitalization stocks prior to the crash, but no return autocorrelations after the crash. Based on this, they conclude that the crash was a rational response to overpricing. But they admit that they could find little evidence of return autocorrelations in large-capitalization stocks.

Gerald Dwyer and R.W. Hafer (1990), using daily index values for Australia, Canada, France, Germany, Japan, the UK, and the US from the end of June 1986 through December 1987, find scarce support for a rational bubble. They hypothesize that proportional changes in stock price should be an increasing function of time when a bubble is evolving. Examining proportional changes in stock price over time, they find no significant trend that would indicate the presence of a bubble. Nor do they find (except for Canada) the positive serial correlation that would exist in the presence of a bubble. But the researchers also admit that their tests of economic fundamentals (including long-term interest rates, real exchange rates, and industrial production) are no more successful in explaining stock price variation.[3]

Richard Roll (1988b) finds an inverse relationship between the magnitudes of the crashes in twenty-three international markets and the prior market run-ups from January to September; that is, the bigger the run-up, the bigger the crash. While this is consistent with the bursting of a worldwide speculative bubble, Roll interprets it as evidence of an efficient worldwide response to some unidentified fundamental factor.

In another study, Roll (1989) tests for serial dependence in international market returns. Here Roll finds positive dependence prior to the crash and none thereafter, which is consistent with the bursting of a speculative bubble. But the observed serial dependence is not related to the magnitude of the price rises, as would be expected in the case of a bubble. Roll concludes that his findings are not definitive.[4]

David Bates (1991) argues that if the crash popped a rational speculative bubble, there would have been reliable signals that investors expected it. That is, speculators, aware that stocks were overpriced, would have acted to protect themselves. He examines Chicago Mercantile Exchange (CME) data on options on S&P 500 futures from 1985 through early 1987 to see if out-of-the-money puts ("crash insurance") became more expensive than out-of-the-money calls over the 1985–7 period.

Bates finds that crash insurance was indeed relatively expensive before and at the market's peak in August 1987, but that this was not the case in September and October. Examining hourly data from October 1987, he finds (p. 1022) that "the crash came as a surprise." He concludes that, if a bubble did pop, it popped in mid-August, rather than in October. Mark Mullins (undated), too, finds that monthly price data give no evidence of a bubble, while daily data suggest, if anything, an August bubble.

James Grant (1990) calculates the stock market risk levels implied by option pricing models at the time of the crash. That is, as expected volatility is one of the inputs used to price options, one can "back out" of the observed prices of given stock index options the expected market volatility implicit in those prices. But, while the implied volatilities rose in September and early October 1987, they remained below long-term averages. Grant concludes that October 19 came as a surprise, a finding one would not expect if speculators, aware of overpricing, had been the primary movers of prices leading up to the crash.

One might also note that the *Wall Street Journal* of Monday, October 19, 1987, in a page-one article covering the market's substantial decline on the previous Friday, made the soon-to-become ironic observation: "No one is forecasting a crash like that in 1929–30."

Informational Cascades

Unlike speculative bubbles, informational cascades do not reflect the behavior of rational speculators betting on the continuance of overpricing. But neither are the investors in a cascade necessarily behaving irrationally, as are those investing on the basis of a fad. Rather, they are attempting to make rational decisions based on all the information available to them, but their aggregation of that information results in mispricing relative to fundamentals.[5]

Sushil Bikhchandani et al. (1992) explain how imperfect information aggregation may occur when individuals follow the behavior of preceding individuals rather than acting on their own information. Ivo Welch (1992) applies this theory to underwriting and issuing practices, examining the behavior of individuals signing up early or late for new share offerings.

In Welch's model, later investors, unaware of the information that motivated earlier signers, will be tempted to base their decisions on the actions of those investors – that is, on whether demand was high or low – and ignore their own information. Prices can thus get detached from fundamental values, much as the message passed in the children's game of "telephone" begins to lose all resemblance to the original as the telephone line lengthens. The result can be self-feeding "information bubbles," price rises induced by investors' interpretation of the information imparted by other investors' actions.[6]

Following Welch, In Ho Lee (undated) constructs a model in which agents base their decisions on the past decisions of other agents, as well as their own private information. In such a market, traders with privately held bad news may discount its import when the prior actions of other traders indicate that they hold good news. As the number of traders sitting, and not acting, on bad news increases, however, the possibility increases of a distinguishable bad news trade starting an avalanche of bad news trades. (See also Bikhchandani et al. [1998].)

David Scharfstein and Jeremy Stein (1990) posit a model in which the investing public can choose between "smart" managers who receive informative signals and "dumb" managers who receive only noise. Given systematic unpredictability in stock price behavior, managers acting on informative signals may perform as poorly as the managers acting on noise; because they are all acting on signals radiating from the same truth, however, their actions will tend to be correlated. To the extent the investing public perceives such correlation as evidence of smartness, they will reward managers who act like each other and punish managers who act on their own. Managers may thus have an incentive to "herd," even if herding moves them away from known fundamentals.

Kenneth Froot, together with Scharfstein and Stein (1992), proposes a trading model in which speculators with short horizons may find it beneficial to focus on noise, rather than fundamentals. Over a short term, it may be rational for speculators to attempt to infer what other traders know, and trade on that information, much along the lines of Keynes's beauty contest. These speculators may be able to maximize their profits by herding around a given piece of information, even if that information is mere noise, and ignoring other information.

Kenneth French (1988) believes that, prior to the crash, investors put too much weight on market signals such as prices and volume and not enough on their own private information, which was more pessimistic than the information implied by prices. Because of this overreliance on market information, prices rose above their fundamental values.[7] When news announcements on October 14 through 16 corroborated investors' private information, however, that information suddenly became weightier, and prices declined sharply.

In the three trading days prior to the crash, the drop in prices actually exceeded any one-, two-, or three-day decline since May 13–14, 1940, when German forces broke through France's defenses, sealing Europe's short-term fate in World War II (Mitchell and Netter 1989: 63). These price declines convinced investors that others also had pessimistic private information. French (1988: 282) concludes: "The big news that drove prices down on October 19 may have been the market's large response to moderately bad news over the previous three trading days." The SEC (1988: 2.6, 3.9) agrees that the declines on these days led to a widespread shift in investor sentiment.

Chaos

Physicists Per Bak and Kan Chen (1991) develop a theory of "self-organized criticality" based on their observations of sand piles. When grains of sand are poured onto a flat surface, a critical point of equilibrium is reached where the amount of sand added is balanced by the amount of sand it dislodges, so that the pile stops growing. At this point, the addition of more sand can create an avalanche. In a market that exhibits self-organized criticality, prices can behave very similarly to those in an information cascade.

Bak and Chen (1991: 52–3) note their model's implications for the economy:

> Conventional models assume the existence of a strongly stable equilibrium position for the economy, whereby large aggregate fluctuations can result only from external shocks that simultaneously affect many different sectors in the same way. . . . If, on the other hand, the economy is a self-organized critical system, more or less periodic large-scale fluctuations are to be expected even in the absence of any common jolts across sectors.

A major difference between an informational cascade and a system characterized by self-organized criticality is that the dynamics of the latter are intrinsic (hence "self-organized"), and do not require extrinsic inputs such as changes in economic variables. In essence, the sand pile alternates between a self-defined state of equilibrium and the disequilibrium of an avalanche. Self-organized criticality is behavior that borders on the chaotic.

Chaotic behavior has been the pet subject of physical scientists over the last several decades. Research into weather prediction, thermal dynamics, and population growth patterns has shed light on how systems that should be governed by laws and subject to observable events (deterministic systems) can have outcomes that appear to be chaotic or random. Conversely, it explains how observations that appear to be chaotic or solely random can be manifestations of deterministic systems.

A random system is the product of innumerable, equally probable events. As a result, its behavior over time is uncorrelated and essentially unpredictable. A deterministic system, by contrast, can be modeled using a finite number of observable parameters. It is thus, theoretically at least, predictable.

In a deterministic system, however, the "state of the universe at one time determines its state at any other time" (Ruelle 1991: 15). Because the state of a deterministic system at any point depends upon earlier states, it is very sensitive to preceding conditions.

In his introduction to chaos theory and its history, James Gleick (1987: 16–17) relates the experiments of meteorologist Edward Lorenz. Working on a weather simulation one day in 1961, Lorenz entered some figures to set the initial conditions for a computer run, and then left the room. As the numbers he had entered were simply rougher forms of numbers he had used earlier (rounded from six to three decimal places), he expected to find a similar pattern on his return. But Lorenz returned to find a new pattern, one that diverged so rapidly and so drastically from the earlier one that it lost all resemblance to it within several simulated months. Lorenz took these results at face value and realized their significance: contrary to much conventional scientific belief, very small differences in initial conditions can lead to extremely large variations in outcome.

Thus, on the one hand, a system characterized by deterministic chaos may be predictable, if one can identify the parameters governing its dynamics. On the other hand, the same system is inherently susceptible to bouts of chaotic behavior, during which it may appear to be random and unpredictable. According to Jenny Ellis (1994: 188): "The appeal of chaos theory is that the type of complex dynamic behavior apparent in actual time series is intrinsic to the model and does not require the introduction of exogenous shocks."

William Brock and his colleagues (1992: 26) point out some of the implications for economics and finance of the difference between the traditional view, which holds that fluctuations in activity reflect exogenous shocks, and the view of deterministic chaos, in which such fluctuations primarily reflect "*internal* self-magnifying dynamics, where an increase in activity in one part of the economy magnifies upward activities in other parts of the economy." Brock et al. suggest that forecasts (at least over the very short term) may be improved by more complex models that capture the dynamics of chaos.

Vance Martin and Kim Sawyer (1994) note that deterministic patterns in stock prices would contradict the theory of market efficiency. This in turn has severe implications for security trading strategies. In particular, inefficiency in pricing may favor strategies such as technical analysis, market timing, and tactical asset allocation over such efficiency-based strategies as portfolio insurance.

Is the stock market a chaotic system? Edgar Peters (1991: 5–6) thinks so. He believes the market is not primarily in an equilibrium state and is characterized by the long-term correlations and recycling trends typical of deterministic chaos, as investors' memories of past events affect their present decisions.

Jose Scheinkman and Blake LeBaron (1989) examine daily returns on stock portfolios and find that the series displays more dependence than would be predicted by a nonlinear model that assumes stock behavior is random. Using weekly stock returns, they conclude that variations from week to week are nonlinear but not random.

In general, however, evidence for deterministic chaos in stock prices is weak.[8] The lack of evidence in part reflects the difficulty of detecting chaotic behavior. A major problem is that behavior consistent with chaos, including serial dependence and discontinuity, can also be consistent with nonlinear stochastic (random) systems.[9] Thus David Hsieh (1991), although his tests of weekly stock returns strongly reject the hypothesis that returns are random, cannot distinguish between chaos and stochastic nonlinearity.[10]

Tonis Vaga (1990) makes a case for a nonlinear statistical model that can forecast transitions from random walk markets to periods of coherent price trends and periods of chaotic fluctuations. Vaga uses the Theory of Social Imitation, a nonlinear statistical model, as an alternative to chaos theory.

The Theory of Social Imitation extends a model from the physical sciences, the Ising model, which describes the magnetism of the molecules in a bar of iron, to the behavior of social groups. As applied to the stock market, the Ising model has three key inputs: investor sentiment, which measures the level of "group think"; biases, created by external fundamentals, toward bullish or bearish markets; and the number of industry groups, a relatively constant factor (Vaga 1990: 36–40). As the first two factors change, the market may move from a random walk state to a coherent bull market, a coherent bear market, or a chaotic state. Vaga concludes that the market is not extremely efficient and that various forms of both fundamental and technical analyses may prove useful.

Either chaos or stochastic nonlinearity has grave implications for investment trading strategies. Benoit Mandelbrot, the "father of fractals" (and one of the first researchers to apply chaos theory to financial data), avers that "prices on competitive markets *need not* be continuous and they are conspicuously *discontinuous*" (Mandelbrot 1983: 334). In other words, any strategy that requires that a stock trade at, say, $40 at some point on its way down from $60 to $20 is doomed to failure. The implications for portfolio insurance are obvious.

Summary

Investors behaving rationally as individuals may in concert lead to prices that are inefficient in the sense of rising above (or falling below) price levels justified by fundamentals alone. Several theories of investor behavior are consistent with the boom-and-bust pattern typical of the 1987 and other market crashes.

In rational speculative bubbles, investors buy into an overpriced market, creating more overpricing, with the expectation of being able to get out unscathed, at a profit, before the bubble bursts. Some evidence suggests that the 1982–7 run-up in prices was speculative in nature. Other research finds that, if a speculative bubble did exist, it burst in August. October came as a surprise to investors, which would not have been the case if the precrash increase in prices had been fueled primarily by speculators aware of an eventual market collapse.

It may be that, as prices rose in the months leading up to the crash, many investors found in the price advance itself evidence that led them to emphasize their most optimistic interpretations of underlying fundamentals and to ignore more pessimistic thinking. Based on investors' imperfect aggregation of information, prices continued to rise, until some investors discerned that even the most optimistic scenarios could not support the price levels attained. Sales by these investors in the week preceding the crash led a large number of other investors to recalibrate their assumptions. The market opened on Monday the 19th to an informational cascade.

Or it may be that the crash was an inherent, and unavoidable, manifestation of a deterministic system subject to chaos. While research may

never be able to determine whether the market is chaotic, the events of
October 1987 did prove that it is subject to the discontinuous price movements characteristic of chaos.

Notes

1 See the following for surveys of the rational bubble literature: West (1988);
   Camerer (1989); and Allen and Gorton (1993). For the history of bubbles,
   and notably the tulip mania of Holland in the 1630s, see MacKay (1932)
   and, for a countervailing view, Garber (1990).
2 Roll (1989: 214) has raised some questions about Hardouvelis's techniques.
3 Von Furstenberg and Nam Jeon (1990) criticize Dwyer and Hafer for requiring that bubbles follow a particular dynamic and argue that Dwyer and
   Hafer do not find evidence of an international contagion effect because their
   tests are time-dependent and sensitive to the timing of information releases.
4 Roll (1989) notes that the degree of serial dependence can be highly non-
   stationary during a speculative bubble. Traditional methods for measuring
   serial dependence, such as autocorrelation, generally assume stationarity.
   Roll uses a volatility comparison, or variance ratio test, to detect nonsta-
   tionary serial dependence.
5 Kurz (1997), for example, posits a "rational beliefs" model of security pricing in which investors process information efficiently but make mistakes in
   evaluating it because they do not know the true conditional expectations
   of a process. The result can be gross over- or undervaluation and "local
   bubbles" characterized by no bounce back.
6 See also Diamond and Verrecchia (1981); Camerer (1989); and Friedman
   and Aoki (1992).
7 This view is consistent with French and Roll (1986). They find that the
   disclosure of private information through the trading activity of informed
   investors accounts for part of the market's volatility. They also find that
   to some extent trading is self-generating, as investors overreact to each
   others' trades. Such overreaction is consistent with imperfect information
   aggregation. Barclay et al. (1990) find, in an analysis of the Japanese stock
   market, that volatility is caused by private information revealed by trading, and that trading is not self-generating.
8 For a review of some of the evidence, see Brock et al. (1992) and Creedy
   and Martin (1994).
9 As Brock et al. (1992) point out, the problem is compounded by technical
   difficulties such as lack of computer power, limited data, and nonstationarity of the data.
10 Furthermore, the behavior of a chaotically deterministic system becomes
   empirically indistinguishable from randomness as the number of the parameters governing its behavior increases beyond a certain level. In effect, one
   can know that a market's behavior is deterministic but can never hope to
   identify and measure all the relevant variables, let alone model them.

8

Futures and Index Arbitrage

There is no such thing as liquidity of investment for the community
as a whole.

John Maynard Keynes, 1936

It was not only theory but also practice, in the form of specific investment instruments and strategies, that came under fire in the aftermath
of the 1987 crash. In particular, early responses to the crash, especially
in the popular press, focused attention on the then relatively new markets for futures and options and on related trading practices.

For example, according to investment adviser and author David
Dreman (*New York Times*, October 23, 1987: D8), "the fall . . . was
accentuated by the new instruments we have such as index options and
program trading." The *Wall Street Journal* (October 20, 1987: 38) termed
the event a "computerized panic." In the immediate aftermath of the
crash, in fact, the NYSE began restricting so-called "program trades" –
the trading of large numbers of stocks via computer – and the futures
exchanges began imposing daily price-movement limits on stock index
futures contracts.

Futures contracts on the S&P 500, introduced in 1982, provide
market participants with a quick and easy means of taking or reducing positions in a broad portfolio of underlying stocks. As we noted in
chapter 3, the cost of transacting in the futures market is also perceived
as cheap compared with transacting in the underlying securities market.

Futures quickly became primary trading vehicles, not only for synthetic
portfolio insurance strategies, but also for stock indexing, asset allocation, and speculation. With the rapid growth of trading volume in futures
and other derivatives markets, some market observers began to fear for
the stability of the underlying stock market. Of particular concern were
the so-called "triple witching days," the third Friday of every quarter

FIGURE 8.1

LOR/Kidder Peabody Ad: Brokers Laud Liquidity of New Futures Market

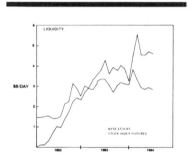
Source: LOR Sponsored Section, *Institutional Investor*, 1984, p. 6.

when stock index futures contracts, stock index options, and options on stock index futures expired. The exercise or expiration of index contracts often elicited large volumes of trading in the underlying stocks, which created much higher than normal stock volatilities on these days (Stoll and Whaley 1987).[1]

Others, including the SEC (1988: 3.6–3.8, 3.25), had discerned a more general increase in stock market volatility, not confined to expiration days. According to these observers, volatility in the futures market was transmitted to the underlying equity market via the mechanism of index arbitrage.

The Futures – Stock Interface

Because of its lower margin requirements, its absence of short-selling restrictions, and perceived lower transaction costs and higher liquidity, the futures market may be preferred to the underlying stock market as an arena for trading stocks. Merton Miller (1991: 26) points out, for instance, that futures market participants essentially operate as traders, with market makers providing immediacy of execution; in contrast, participants in the stock market operate as investors, with specialists (except in the case of relatively illiquid stocks) operating more as auctioneers.

Futures trading may be motivated by the arrival of new information, by speculative activity, or by the liquidity requirements of portfolio rebalancing, portfolio insurance, or indexing strategies. Whatever the motivation, trading in the futures market is likely to result in price changes. These may be transmitted to the underlying stock market – called the "spot" market – via the mechanism of index arbitrage.

Index arbitragers take advantage of price discrepancies between the futures and spot markets. They buy (sell) futures contracts and sell (buy) the underlying stocks when futures are underpriced (overpriced) relative to spot prices.[2] Their purchases and sales in the stock market are likely to be executed through program trading, using computers to trade many securities at the same time. Portfolio insurers, indexers, and portfolio rebalancers may also use program trades to realign their equity portfolios. On the NYSE, program trades are executed through the automated order-delivery mechanism of the Designated Order Turnaround (DOT) system.

The transmittal from the futures to the spot market of volatility representing receipt of new information should not be destabilizing per se. If futures price changes reflect new information, for example, then index arbitrage merely transmits that information from the futures market to the stock market. Furthermore, any price changes resulting from the arbitrage are limited to the movement necessary to restore futures and spot prices to a fair range of values, given the new information. Arbitragers should thus actually increase the fairness of prices and, by deepening trading participation, add to stock market liquidity (see Merrick 1990: 200).

Futures trading and associated index arbitrage may prove destabilizing to the underlying stock market, however, if trading in futures is noisy (or noisier than trading in equities). This may be the case if the perceived ease and cheapness of trading in the futures market encourages more noisy trading than would occur in the absence of such a market. Speculators and market technicians, for example, may take advantage of the lower margin requirements and transaction costs in the futures market to take larger or more frequent positions. And, as we have already noted, the perceived advantages of trading in futures early on attracted most synthetic portfolio insurance programs away from trading in the spot market.

As discussed in chapter 6, portfolio insurance traders are theoretically capable of significantly increasing noise in security pricing, because their trading decisions are based, not on underlying fundamentals, but on price changes themselves. Ronald Anderson and Mehmet Tutuncu (1988) develop a model that shows that portfolio insurers can exaggerate price movements, whether their insurance programs are implemented via futures or directly in the stock market. The same model shows that index arbitrage in the absence of portfolio insurance enhances market stability.

Futures trading may also have destabilizing effects on the underlying stock market if it encourages a volume of trading that cannot be easily accommodated by existing sources of liquidity. Gregory Duffee and his colleagues (1992: 39) find that index arbitrage may prove destabilizing when heavy arbitrage volume exhausts liquidity in the underlying spot market. This is conceivable because of the substantial volume of futures contracts traded relative to the value of the underlying shares outstanding.

Merton Miller (1991: 188) notes that, given the perceived ease and relative cheapness of trading in futures markets, the advent of these markets may have encouraged an increase in the frequency and volume of trading, hence an increase in velocity – the frequency of price moves. The transmission of this velocity to the spot market, through index arbitrage, may prove detrimental to market liquidity if it increases losses to market makers, discouraging them from committing to limit orders or encouraging them to widen bid-ask spreads. Miller (1991: 189) suggests that "the real case against index arbitrage might . . . be not that it increases volatility in the standard academic sense . . . but that by increasing the risks and hence costs of market-making, it effectively imposes an excise tax on market liquidity."

The Mixed Evidence

Because of the perceived ease and economy of trading in futures, the advent of stock index futures markets may have attracted an increased level of trading that has led, via index arbitrage, to higher volatility in the underlying stock market. Higher market volatility may prove destabilizing if it reflects a significant increase in the amount of noise trading and/or a significant reduction in liquidity.

Edwin Maberly and his colleagues (1989), examining various time periods both before and after the 1982 introduction of stock index futures, find evidence of increased stock market volatility in some, but not all, periods. They postulate that the introduction of futures may have increased information-based trading, hence the frequency and magnitude of price changes in response to economic fundamentals.

Lawrence Harris (1989a) compares the volatilities of the individual stocks in the S&P 500 (which underlie the most widely traded stock index futures contract) with the volatilities of a matched set of non-S&P 500 stocks over the 1975–87 period. He finds that the volatility of the S&P 500 rose significantly beginning in 1985; the increase was especially apparent over short (daily) intervals, but held to a lesser extent over longer intervals as well. He concludes that his evidence is consistent with a number of theories. The relatively higher volatility for S&P 500 stocks could signal an increased flow of information. Alternatively, the volatility increase over shorter intervals might reflect temporary liquidity problems induced by portfolio insurance and index arbitrage trading, while the less marked increase over longer intervals might be associated with residual but longer-lasting noise effects created by speculative trading.

Kenneth Froot and Andre Perold (1995) hypothesize that faster dissemination of information leads to a decline in autocorrelation (a symptom of overreaction and inefficiency) and an increase in volatility. They find that, over the 1983 to 1989 period, S&P 500 index returns measured over fifteen-minute intervals went from being very highly autocorrelated to practically uncorrelated. They attribute this to faster incorporation of information and consequent compression of market moves, resulting in an improvement in efficiency attributable to the facilitating role played by stock index futures. Wade Brorsen (1991), too, finds decreased autocorrelation in spot market returns over the 1980s, associated with an increase in the daily volatility of stock price changes (but unchanged volatility over longer intervals).

Hendrik Bessembinder and Paul Seguin (1992), examining daily data on S&P 500 and NYSE composite indexes and futures over the 1978–89 period, find that futures trading enhances stock market depth – the capacity of the market to absorb trades without a large price impact – and, as a result, reduces volatility. They hypothesize that the ease of trading in the futures market increases the level of informed trading.

A study by Aswath Damodaran (1990), however, concludes that derivatives contributed to both noise and volume of trading in S&P 500 index stocks versus non-index stocks. He examines daily returns for S&P 500 and non-S&P 500 NYSE stocks over the five-year period surrounding the April 21, 1982 introduction of S&P 500 futures trading. In the post-introduction period, the S&P 500 stocks exhibited significantly higher systematic risk (versus no change for the non-index stocks), and a marginal increase in volatility (versus a decline for non-index stocks). The increase in risk cannot be explained by accounting statement fundamentals.

Duffee et al. (1992: 29) find that the frequency of extreme daily price movements ("jump volatility") increased in the 1980s, following the advent of the futures market, although movements in one direction tended to reverse within a short period of time. But Ali Darrat and Shafiqur Rahman (1995), on the basis of sophisticated tests of monthly futures trading volume and open interest over the May 1982 to June 1991 period (using OTC volatility to control for the impact of information), find that futures trading has not led to an increase in jump volatility. And Sean Becketti and Dan Roberts (1990), looking at the frequency of S&P 500 intraday price jumps (defined as price rises or falls in excess of 1.75 percent), find that, while jump frequency almost doubled between the 1962–82 and 1982–90 periods, it was uncorrelated with the frequency of futures trading, even in October 1987.[3]

Many studies of the effects of futures trading, however, find little evidence of increased volatility in general, but a significant increase in the period surrounding the 1987 crash. Franklin Edwards (1988a), for example, finds no evidence for a long-term increase in volatility but does note a sharp short-term rise in the latter part of 1986 and in 1987 (which he attributes to economic fundamentals). Robert Wood (1989) detects a dramatic increase in the intraday volatility of the S&P 500 in 1987, followed by a sharp drop in 1988. He also finds high intraday volatility in September 1986 and January 1987, both significant dates as precursors of the crash (see chapter 9). And according to William Schwert (1990a, 1990b), while monthly, daily, and fifteen-minute data indicate that NYSE volatility has been generally stable since the nineteenth century, volatility was exceptional in October 1987.

Andreas Pericli and Gregory Koutmos (1997) examine volatility in S&P 500 prices from 1953 to 1994 and find that the shift from fixed to floating exchange rates was associated with a significant change in stock price behavior. The introduction of stock index futures (and options) caused no further volatility shifts, however, with the exception of October 1987.

Other studies have examined the impact of program trading in particular. Neither Duffee et al. (1992) nor Robert Neal (1993) finds any convincing evidence of a relationship between program trading and increased stock market volatility. Sanford Grossman (1988c) discovers no systematic relationship between interday market volatility and program trading intensity, but he does find that program trading intensity was substantially above average during the three trading days prior to the 1987 crash and on October 19 itself.

Arbitrage and the Crash

Many studies of the 1987 crash have noted the potential for market instability created by the prices of futures relative to stocks in the weeks preceding the crash. In particular, futures began selling at substantial discounts to the underlying stocks a few weeks before the crash. In the normal course of events, one would expect this kind of differential to induce index arbitragers to sell the "expensive" stocks and purchase the "cheap" futures.

According to Stephen Newmark (in Lerner et al. 1987: 450), interest rates had begun to rise faster than the implied spread between Major Market Index (MMI) futures and the underlying spot index starting in September 1987. This led many arbitragers to expect a down expiration and to engage in anticipatory selling. It also led longer-term investors to anticipate a substantial market decline.

Dean Furbush (1989) contends that discounts between the futures and spot markets on October 14 through 16 triggered index arbitrage, which narrowed this mispricing. On October 19 and 20, however, the arbitrage relationship broke down. Futures prices fell to unprecedented discounts to spot, 20 points on the 19th and 40 points on the 20th.

According to the task force appointed by President Reagan to study the crash (the Brady Commission, chaired by Wall Street investment banker Nicholas Brady), the unprecedented futures discounts helped to depress the stock market:

> The enormous futures discounts signaled to prospective stock buyers that future declines were imminent. . . . This "billboard effect" inhibited some stock purchases. Moreover, the futures discount made stocks appear expensive, inhibiting buying support for the market. The pathology of disconnected markets fed on itself. Faced with a surfeit of sellers and a scarcity of buyers, both markets (futures and stock) were at times on October 19 and 20 nearly in freefall. (Brady Commission 1988: 56–7)

Some have argued that the large futures discounts during the crash itself were more apparent than real. A stock index can lag behind the true value of its underlying stocks because of nonsynchronous trading. That is, prices of stocks that have not recently traded will not be accurately reflected in the index price. The Commodity Futures Trading Commission (CFTC 1988: v–vi) claims that, "during the periods when the reported futures discount was extreme . . . a significant portion of those discounts was illusory since a substantial number of stocks included in the S&P 500 index were not actively trading." The CFTC concludes that "these findings cast substantial doubt upon . . . the supposition that

FIGURE 8.2

S&P Index and Futures Contract Spread, October 19

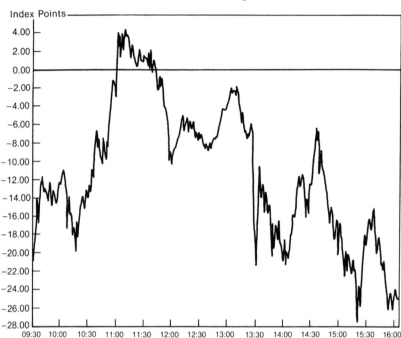

Source: *Report of the Presidential Task Force on Market Mechanisms*
(Brady Commission), 1988.

futures prices were leading the stock market . . . during the morning of October 19."

Gilbert Bassett and his colleagues (1991) use a technique to interpolate stock prices during non-trading intervals. Examining minute-by-minute price changes for the twenty MMI securities and the MMI futures contract, they find this technique does reduce the absolute value of the observed cash-futures spread on October 19 and 20, although sometimes by less than 50 percent. They conclude that studies that rely on the prices of stocks that have traded cannot capture the true values of stocks or indexes when order imbalances cause substantial numbers of stocks to cease trading.

A study by Harris (1989b), looking at the S&P 500 futures-stock spread, shows that only part of the discount can be explained by nonsynchronous trading. Eugene Moriarty and his colleagues (1990) reach a similar conclusion, as do Allan Kleidon and Robert Whaley (1992).[4] Studying the pricing relationship between London's FT-SE 100 index

FIGURE 8.3

S&P Index and Futures Contract Spread, October 20

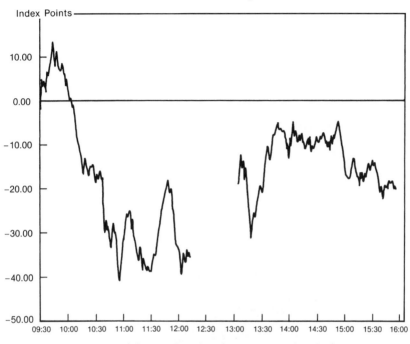

Source: *Report of the Presidential Task Force on Market Mechanisms*
(Brady Commission), 1988.

and the index futures contract in the UK during the crash, Antonios
Antoniou and Ian Garrett (1993) also find that nonsynchronous trading cannot fully explain the futures discounts.

According to these observers, the anomalous futures discounts that
prevailed during the crash primarily reflected, not nonsynchronous trading, but breakdowns in the market mechanisms that tie the futures and
stock markets together. As noted, index arbitrage serves to link market
makers in the futures and underlying stock markets. In effect, as Sanford
Grossman and Merton Miller (1988: 633) note, if there are order imbalances in one market, arbitrage acts to transmit them to the other market.
Market makers' resources are thus employed more effectively, much as if
the number of market makers were increased. Inhibiting index arbitrage
can thus result in reduced, rather than enhanced, market-making capacity.

A look at the events that unfolded on October 19 and 20 shows that
both program trading and index arbitrage were effectively knocked out
long before formal trading restrictions delivered the coup de grace.

FIGURE 8.4
Specialists "Blown Away"

BLOWN AWAY
BY BLACK MONDAY

Pete Haas, center, presides at Post 12 on the Big Board. An abrupt sale to Merrill Lynch put an end to 60 years of independence for his firm, A.B. Tompane.

Source: *New York Times Magazine*, December 20, 1987. Copyright 1987
by *The New York Times*. Reprinted by permission.
Photo by Frank Fournier/Contact Press Images.

A Massive Liquidity Event

Grossman and Miller (1988: 631) find that a "massive liquidity event"
occurred at the opening of the markets on October 19, as both futures
and stocks "were hit simultaneously with a flood of sell orders of unprecedented size." The demand to sell futures in the Chicago Mercantile

Exchange (CME) was so great that the contracts gapped down by 7 percent at the opening on the 19th. With futures trading at a discount, arbitragers were dumping stock (McClain 1988: 81–2).

But as Keynes (1936: 155) once observed, "there is no such thing as liquidity of investment for the community as a whole." Selling pressure in stocks severely strained specialists' ability to provide orderly, continuous markets. There were 195 opening delays and trading halts on the NYSE on October 19 (GAO 1988: 55–8); a third of the well-known stocks that comprise the DJIA had not begun trading one hour after the opening bell. Before trading in all stocks had even commenced, opening prices had gapped down an unprecedented 10 percent from Friday's close.

The futures and stock markets were hit with another wave of sell orders in the afternoon. By this time, both markets had become highly illiquid and virtually incapable of supplying immediacy at almost any price. NYSE computer systems were strained well beyond their capacities. Operating problems in nine of the twelve major automated systems resulted in sporadic delays and system outages. Deliveries of orders to the floor were delayed by as much as seventy-five minutes (GAO 1988: 73). The breakdown in DOT created enormous problems for arbitragers. Unsure of settlement prices and hampered by regulations such as the exchange's uptick rules (limiting short sales), they were finally sidelined completely, as they watched the futures-stock gap widen even further (McClain 1988: 83, 86).

The over-the-counter market was also strained. On Monday, 1,192 OTC stocks (and on Tuesday, 1,575 stocks) locked or crossed quotations; that is, the best bid and ask prices were identical, or the bid-ask spreads were inverted. This made the National Association of Securities Dealers' (NASDAQ's) electronic system, the Small Order Execution System, virtually inoperative. Market makers' telephone lines were overloaded, and there were widespread reports of calls going unanswered. Price quotations were questionable, market depth evaporated, and trading delays were commonplace (GAO 1988: 59–61).

Despite this situation, the influx of sell orders to all markets continued throughout Monday. On the morning of Tuesday, October 20, investors faced a temporary reversal of fortune. Buy-side, rather than sell-side, demand kept some stocks from opening at first (McClain 1988: 93).

By 10:00 a.m. on Tuesday, however, selling pressure in the S&P 500 index futures contract had reappeared, coming largely from portfolio insurance programs (McClain 1988: 94). By 10:30, futures were selling at discounts of 20 to 25 percent. These were larger than the discounts seen on the 19th, even allowing for the effects of nonsynchronous trading.[5] Rumors circulated that the exchange would close, fostering even more

FIGURE 8.5

DJIA Price Levels and Index Arbitrage on October 19

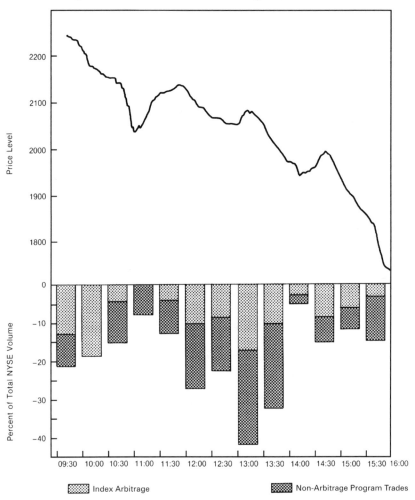

Source: *Report of the Presidential Task Force on Market Mechanisms*
(Brady Commission), 1988.

panic (GAO 1988: 48). By Tuesday afternoon, trading in many NYSE stocks had been suspended as market-making capacity had become exhausted.

At this point, the NYSE formally barred program trading from its DOT system, effectively severing the arbitrage link between futures and stock markets (although most index arbitrage had already ceased). Both

FIGURE 8.6
DJIA Price Levels and Index Arbitrage on October 20

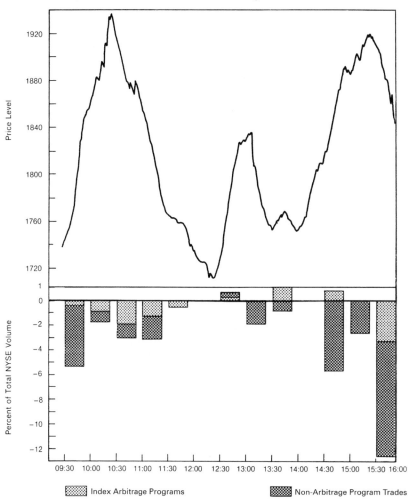

Index Arbitrage Programs   Non-Arbitrage Program Trades

Source: *Report of the Presidential Task Force on Market Mechanisms*
(Brady Commission), 1988.

the Chicago Board Options Exchange (CBOE) and the CME had called temporary trading suspensions on stock index options and futures. And with market participants frequently unable to determine prices in the underlying stock market, "simultaneous buying and selling under panic conditions was virtually impossible" (GAO 1988: 46).

Harris (1990: 173) blames the severity of the crash on this break-down in market mechanisms, particularly the drying up of index arbitrage because of exchange regulations and congestion in order flows. Antoniou and Garrett (1993: 1460) find likewise for futures and stock market mechanisms in the UK: "Because of liquidity problems in the stock market . . . the arbitrage link broke down, the outcome being a vicious downward spiral in prices in both markets."

Bruce Greenwald and Jeremy Stein (1991) develop a model of the market's absorption of large volume shocks that accords well with the events of October 19 and 20. They examine what happens if value investors are required to submit their orders without knowing execution prices. In this scenario, value buyers become reluctant to submit orders, particularly in times of falling prices when there is a greater risk that the transactions will not be made at the most favorable prices. Market makers in turn become wary of taking on large volume, and liquidity dries up. In their view, the volume of trading in the crash caused a breakdown in the mechanism linking sellers and potential buyers.

Summary

Advances and declines in stock index futures prices will be trans-mitted to the underlying stock market via arbitrage. To the extent that the perceived ease and economy of trading in futures contracts attracts more noise trading, or merely encourages informed traders to take more frequent and/or larger positions, it may increase volatility in the under-lying spot market. The evidence on stock market volatility since the advent of futures trading is sometimes contradictory, but the bulk of it suggests that futures trading is not generally destabilizing for the underlying stocks. A notable exception, however, is found in the period immediately sur-rounding the 1987 crash.

Whether or not index arbitrage prompted by sell-offs in the futures market in the week prior to the crash contributed to the dramatic collapse on October 19, the evidence during the crash itself suggests that the lack of arbitrage, rather than its presence, may have exacerbated the decline once it began.

The crash itself was a massive liquidity (or, more precisely, illiquidity) event. In the wake of an unprecedented volume of sell orders, market mechanisms, including computerized trading systems, proved inadequate. Their failures effectively halted index arbitrage, which further restricted the overall market's capacity to supply liquidity.

We noted in passing in this chapter some of the troubling problems synthetic portfolio insurance may pose for market liquidity and volatility.

In the next part, which examines the body of evidence on synthetic portfolio insurance and the crash, we will see how insurance trading, when
mixed with futures and index arbitrage, can create a potentially poison-
ous brew.

Notes

1 In the spring of 1987, expiration procedures were changed to ameliorate
   destabilizing effects on the stock market.
2 Note that the ability to initiate a "short" arbitrage (sell stock short and
   buy futures) is limited by the short-sale rule, which requires that stock sold
   short be executed on a "plus" tick or "zero-plus" tick for each stock in the
   program trade. This tick-test provision of the short-sale rule can, however,
   be circumvented by those institutional investors managing index funds. Such
   investors hold a long position in the index and can initiate a short arbitrage
   by shorting, or selling, the stock held long (see SEC 1988: 3–7).
3 See chapter 11 for a possible explanation for this lack of correlation.
4 See also Kleidon (1992). Kleidon distinguishes between two different aspects
   of nonsynchronous trading: nontrading and stale prices. Nontrading occurs
   when a stock has not traded for some time, so that the price recorded in the
   stock index does not represent the current executable price. Stale prices occur
   when there is a delay between the time a limit order is submitted and when
   it is executed. By considering these two aspects of nonsynchronous trading,
   Kleidon is better able to explain the price discrepancies between futures and
   stock prices than is Harris (1989b), who controlled solely for nontrading.
5 In addition, futures prices were gapping even more than on the 19th. According to a study by Bodurtha (noted in SEC 1988: 3.14), the average price
   change between reported trades in the December S&P 500 futures contract,
   which had been 0.02 percent of the index value in September 1987, reached
   0.66 percent on the 19th and 0.89 percent on the 20th.

Part III

How Dynamic Hedging Moved Markets

The crash opened the door to new lines of inquiry into what makes the market tick. Fundamental information no longer seemed to be the sole key that wound stock prices up (and down). Research on cognitive errors in investor thinking, overoptimism in analysts' forecasts, and fads and fashions in investment instruments and techniques suggested that market prices can diverge in systematic ways from levels justified by fundamentals alone.

Fundamentals remain important, of course, providing the underlying structure for the pricing of financial assets. In that capacity, fundamentals may be said to exert a gravitational pull on market prices. An overvalued market will tend to recede and an undervalued one rise. But it may take some time for the tides to turn.

In 1987, however, prices changed sharply – a decline of over 20 percent in a single day. Chapter 7 discussed a number of models that might explain market crashes, including speculative bubbles and informational cascades. Both theories rely on noise traders, who base their trading decisions on prices or changes in prices. When speculators bet on the continuance of price increases, or when investors interpret price increases as a signal of coming good news, prices can rise substantially above levels justified by fundamentals. Such speculative or informational bubbles are prone to burst suddenly.

Investors using synthetic portfolio insurance are noise traders. They buy simply because prices increase and sell simply because prices fall. Portfolio insurance can thus amplify price movements away from fundamental values.

The noise trading of portfolio insurers may exacerbate price-inflating fads and speculative bubbles by adding heat to the underlying buying pressure. Portfolio insurance can also contribute to informational cascades. Synthetic portfolio insurance is essentially self-insurance; there are no insurance premiums to give investors an idea of the cost of (and enable them to infer the demand for) protection. Nor can investors easily distinguish between trades motivated by information and those motivated by the mandates of insurance programs. When they mistake insurance trades as information-motivated, they may be encouraged to ignore fundamental information in favor of trading along with insurers.

Some examinations of the crash, particularly the formal inquiries of the Brady Commission and the US Securities and Exchange Commission, pointed a finger at synthetic portfolio insurance. Most of these examinations noted the destabilizing effects of trend-following trading. The Brady Commission also drew attention to the potentially inflammatory outcome of combining synthetic portfolio insurance with index arbitrage.

In fact, synthetic insurance interacts with a number of the theories presented in part II. The following chapters examine how these interactions turned what might have been an average market correction into a market crash, and how the crash in turn revealed the fatal flaws in portfolio insurance.

Chapter 9 looks at synthetic portfolio insurance in the context of investment fads, informational cascades, stock index arbitrage, and futures market liquidity. It shows how insurance trading contributed to the run-up in prices preceding the crash and to the crash itself. Chapter 10 examines the evidence against synthetic portfolio insurance, including the extent of insurance trading just prior to the crash and during the day of the crash and the day after. It shows how insurance sales in the week preceding the crash led to index-arbitrage-related sell-offs in the stock market at the open on Monday, and how delays in the sales required by insurance programs acted as a drag on the market on October 19 and the morning of October 20 as well.

Chapters 11 and 12 address some of the "alibis" that advocates of portfolio insurance have offered in its defense. Chapter 11 takes up, among others, the question of how portfolio insurers, constituting only a small portion of all investors, could have exerted such a powerful force during the crash. Chapter 12 addresses the defenders' claims that the absence of synthetic insurance in the 1929 crash and its absence in market crashes outside the US in 1987 prove that it cannot have played a crucial role in the US crash of 1987. As we will see, however, synthetic portfolio insurance had antecedents in the form of margined buying and margin calls in 1929, just as it has successors that pose a threat to markets today. Furthermore, to the extent the US crash in 1987 triggered the crashes in non-US markets, insurance may be said to have contributed to those crashes, as well as to the US crash.

Finally, chapter 13 examines how the conditions during the crash caused synthetic portfolio insurance to falter and, in many cases, fail to provide the level of protection promised. To the extent that insurance strategies themselves contributed to the conditions of the crash, they may be said to have contributed to their own demise.

9

Synthetic Puts and the 1987 Crash: Theory

The bearishness [of portfolio insurance] may be lurking in the weeds, only to spring out on a less than perfectly forewarned public.

Merton Miller, 1992

Market observers, even before the crash, had worried about the effects of futures trading and index arbitrage on the stability of the underlying stock market; some had also pointed to the potentially destabilizing effects of synthetic portfolio insurance trading. But prior to the crash, insurers had maintained that the amount of insured assets would not pose a problem for market stability. For example, Ralph Tate, president of Aetna's Portfolio Hedging Group, saw no reason to be anxious at current levels of insured assets: "If the business exploded, going from $50 billion to $500 billion, then we'd have to worry" (*New York Times*, February 1, 1987: 12). Even after the crash, Eugene Fama (1989: 79) wrote that "any price pressure created by portfolio insurance is more a marketing problem for insurance vendors than a market problem."

But portfolio insurance as carried out via dynamic hedging is potentially destabilizing because it trades in the same direction as the market. Insurers sell stocks as the market falls and buy stocks as the market rises. As I have pointed out (see memorandum in appendix A and Jacobs 1986), this tends to amplify market movements, thereby raising market volatility. The higher the level of insured assets, the greater the potential amplification.

Gew-Rae Kim and Harry Markowitz (1989) simulate a market with varying numbers of portfolio insurers, and they find that market volatility increases dramatically with the number of insurers present. Glen Donaldson and Harald Uhlig (1993: 1952–3) find that portfolio insurance generally increases volatility and can lead to price crashes.

In an efficient market, if synthetic insurance trading were to cause prices to rise above or fall below fundamental values, one would expect an influx of informed investors happy to take the offsetting side of insurance trades. Their actions would serve to correct any mispricings caused by insurance. However, the trading demands of insurers will not always attract sufficient interest from potential counterparties, for several reasons.

For instance, value-based investors, who tend to buy as the market falls and sell as it rises, are the natural trading partners for insurers, in effect the natural sellers of portfolio insurance. As Joanne Hill and Frank Jones (1988) point out, whether there will be sufficient value trading to offset the destabilizing effects of synthetic insurance trading depends on several factors, including: first, the amount of insured assets; second, the percentage of the insured portfolio traded versus that of the value-based portfolio; and third, the speed at which the trading occurs.

In regard to the first point, estimates of the amount of assets synthetically insured just prior to the crash range from about $60 to $100 billion. Whether or not this would have been enough to have had a destabilizing trading impact remains a controversial question even today, but the theories outlined below and the evidence presented in the next chapter suggest strongly that it was.

The second and third points of Hill and Jones's argument are perhaps more readily addressed. According to the Brady Commission (1988: 29), insurers trade about 2 percent of their portfolio in response to a 1 percent market move. According to Jack Treynor (1988), value-based investors often require a discount of 15 to 20 percent before they are motivated to trade. Furthermore, insurers often react to market moves in a matter of minutes, while value investors generally react over a matter of days (Treynor 1988). The trading of synthetic insurers is thus likely to be far more intensive than that of their potential counterparty traders. The evidence presented in chapters 10 and 11 indicates that indeed it was, at least during the crash period.

More generally, price changes brought on by synthetic insurance trading represent noise, as the trades do not directly reflect any fundamental information. We have already noted in chapter 6 that informed investors will be reluctant to take fully offsetting positions against noise traders because of the substantial uncertainty introduced by noise trading. In the case of synthetic portfolio insurance, uncertainty introduced by noise is augmented by uncertainty about intent. Potential counterparties to insurance trades may be unable to distinguish the extent to which a price change reflects noisy insurance trades simply because synthetic insurance trades are not revealed as such. Investors may thus interpret insurance-induced price changes as reflective of real information, and decline to trade against them for fear of getting bagged.

To the extent that synthetic insurance trading introduces price movements that are not offset by informed traders, market prices can be expected to move away from fundamental values. Synthetic insurance trading can thus contribute to a fad element in market movements.

A Fad

Portfolio insurance is by no means an orphan among investment products and strategies. There has always been a demand for strategies that can limit stock market losses. A "run with your winners, cut your losses" rule of thumb is one such approach. Others include stop-loss orders, put options on securities, and puts on stock indexes. But the aggressive marketing of synthetic insurance strategies may have increased the perceived need (hence the demand) for all types of insurance. As I wrote shortly after the crash (Jacobs 1987: 79): "The explosive growth of the portfolio insurance industry has exhibited the characteristics of a fad, whose bubble has now burst."

Insurance "buyers" included the corporate pension and profit-sharing plans of A.G. Becker (the financial consulting firm and former employer of LOR principal John O'Brien), Aluminum Co. of America, Bayer USA, Bechtel Power Corp., Boeing, Burlington Industries, Caterpillar Tractor, Chrysler, Detroit Edison, Gates (Rubber) Corp., Honeywell, Hughes Aircraft, J.P. Stevens & Co., Manville Corp., Mead Corp., San Diego Gas & Electric, Sunkist Growers, Times Mirror, and Trans World Airlines. Other corporations leased the software to run insurance programs internally. General Motors, for example, used the software to insure $10 billion of its pension plan.

The Episcopal Church Pension Fund adopted portfolio insurance. So did public pension plans, including the Minneapolis Teachers' Retirement Fund, the Southern California Rapid Transit District, and the State University Retirement Systems of Illinois. The endowment funds of Alfred University, the College of Wooster, and Duke University were "insured." In the twelve months ending June 1987, at least 198 institutional clients had signed up for portfolio insurance, almost doubling the amount of insured assets.[1]

From a survey taken after the crash, Robert Shiller (1989) finds that 10.2 percent of institutional investors had some form of stop-loss policy in place prior to the crash; this figure includes 5.5 percent using synthetic insurance strategies. In addition, 10.1 percent of wealthy individuals were using some form of stop-loss rule. Shiller (1988: 291) suggests that "stop-loss behavior increased as a result of the publicity that portfolio insurance had received, and of the publicity campaign launched

FIGURE 9.1

Kidder Peabody Ad: "Don't let your pension plan destroy your bottom line."

Don't let your pension plan destroy your bottom line.

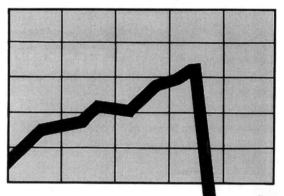

New financial accounting standards, called FASB '87, now link a company's pension plan performance directly to its bottom line. To the extent that its pension plan is actually under-performing or underfunded, the company's profits will be reduced.

For many companies, this will be a serious blow; for those in delicate financial health, FASB '87 could be fatal. Recognizing this, Kidder, Peabody offers CEOs, CFOs and treasurers a unique combination of strategic programs that could help keep their pension plans' performance from diminishing their bottom lines.

The key to the success of these programs is your Kidder, Peabody Corporate Services Specialist, who has been extensively trained to understand your business needs and pressures, as well as the many options open to you (such as PRIME—Portfolio Review and Investment Management Evaluation and AREM—Assured Return Equity Management). Your corporate representative will assist you in finding the appropriate structure and manager for your investments.

PRIME, for example, is an asset management consulting service that offers several

advantages: it helps you establish realistic investment objectives, it assists you in meeting your fiduciary liability and it helps you stream-line your administrative responsibilities. The result is a more cost effective program which should suit your financial objectives.

Another alternative that your corporate representative may suggest is AREM (Assured Return Equity Management). AREM is a form of what is popularly called "portfolio insurance" designed for fund managers seeking to substantially eliminate downside risk and still participate in the upside potential of the equity market. At its heart is a sophisticated computer-driven hedging mechanism that indicates optimal shifts in portfolio allocation from equities to cash in response to stock market behavior.

AREM is directed by Webster Management Corporation, the Kidder, Peabody investment subsidiary which currently manages over $5 billion in assets.

For more information on PRIME and AREM, as well as other services and products that Kidder, Peabody can offer the pension fund manager, please send in the coupon, or call (800) 345-8600 Ext. 28.

Kidder, Peabody & Co. Incorporated
20 Exchange Place—12th Fl.
New York, New York 10005
Attn: Corporate Services

Tel: (800) 345-8600 Ext. 28

Please send me more information on AREM and PRIME.

Name_____
Company_____
Address_____
City_____State_____Zip_____
Bus. Phone_____

⬛ KIDDER, PEABODY

© Kidder, Peabody & Co. Incorporated • Founded 1865 • Members New York and American Stock Exchanges • Member SIPC • Over 60 offices worldwide

Source: *Pensions & Investment Age*, March 9, 1987, p. 22.

Source: *Pensions & Investment Age*, January 26, 1987, p. 19.

Source: *Institutional Investor*, July 1987, p. 139.

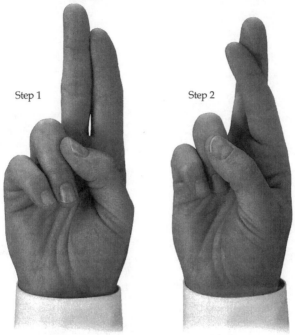

Source: *Pensions & Investment Age*, October 5, 1987, p. 37.

FIGURE 9.5
First Chicago Ad: "Protected Equity Program"

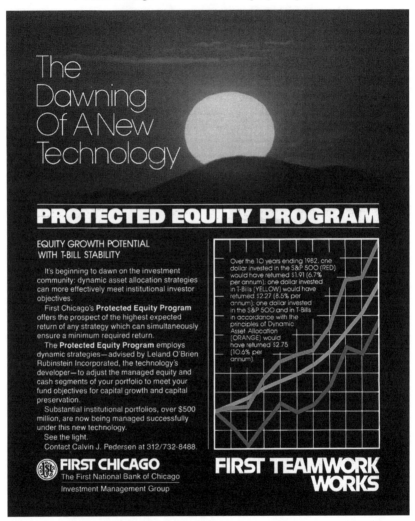

Source: *Pensions & Investment Age*, October 3, 1983, p. 37.

FIGURE 9.6

Aetna Ad: "Aetna got the most new business in dynamic hedging in 1986"

Ætna got the most new business in dynamic hedging in 1986

Most portfolio insurance new business in 1986

Company	$ mils.
Ætna	**14,476**
Wells Fargo Investment, San Francisco	7,505
J.P. Morgan Investment Mgmt., New York	3,460
Bankers Trust–Invest. Mgmt., New York	2,083
Skye Investment Advisors, Cupertino, Calif.	840
RepublicBank, Dallas, Texas	800
Oppenheimer Capital, New York	425
BEA Associates, New York	309
Advanced Investment Mgmt. Inc., Pittsburgh	205
Northern Trust Co., Chicago	120
Boston Co., Mass.	100
Citicorp Investment Mgmt., New York	100

Ætna uses technology developed by Leland O'Brien Rubinstein Associates

WORK WITH THE BEST IN THE BUSINESS

Ætna Capital Management, Inc.
Ætna Life Insurance Company, Hartford, CT 06156

Source: *Pensions & Investment Age*, April 20, 1987, p. 9.

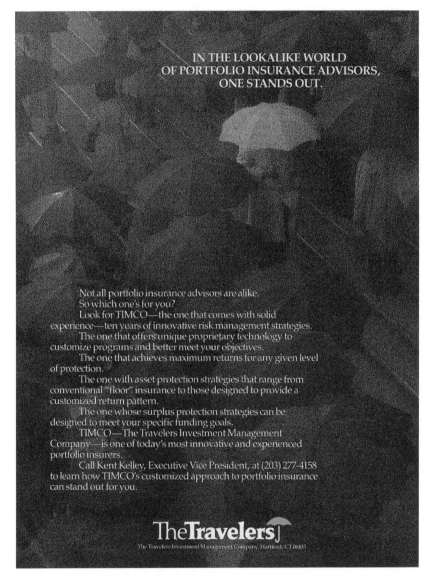

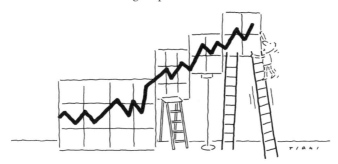
Source: Pensions & Investment Age, October 19, 1987, p. 47.

FIGURE 9.9

BEA Ad: "The Hedge with the Dynamic Edge"

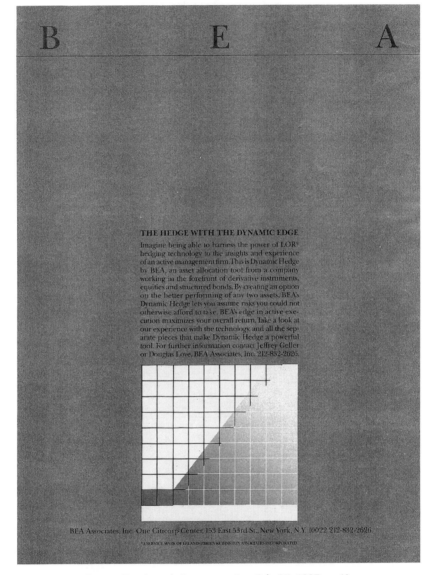

Source: *Pensions & Investment Age*, July 27, 1987, p. 43.

by entrepreneurs who found a new way, by selling portfolio insurance, to profit from such stop-loss behavior." He concludes that "portfolio insurance is best thought of as an investor fad that, like other fads, had caused an important change in investor behavior."[2]

Steven Wunsch (1985a) of Kidder Peabody had predicted that the availability of insurance would lead to higher stock prices: "Futures-based portfolio insurance is an advance in investment technology capable of increasing the portion of savings available for equity investment by hundreds of billions of dollars. . . . Major benefits that would follow include . . . higher stock prices." The Brady Commission (1988: 9) finds that: "The rapid rise in the popularity of portfolio insurance strategies . . . contributed to the market's rise. Pension fund managers adopting these strategies typically increased the fund's risk exposure by investing more heavily in common stock during this rising market. The rationale was that portfolio insurance would cushion the impact of a market break by allowing them to shift quickly out of stocks."

Indeed, Massachusetts Mutual Life Insurance Company, together with Skye Investment Advisors, had advertised their Enhanced Stock Protection (ESP) plan as "a profitable alternative to pulling capital out of the equities market and committing it to lower-risk vehicles."[3] Mass Mutual Vice President Edmond F. Ryan (quoted in Ring 1986b: 29) further noted the role portfolio insurance could play in converting employees with defined contribution plans to the benefits of equity investment: "If you can somehow protect the downside, you'll get more employee money in equities."

According to Girish Reddy (1987: 50), then of Leland O'Brien Rubinstein (LOR), clients often substituted insured stocks and bonds for cash: "A lot of our clients who used to hold large amounts of cash because they were nervous about the market and didn't know when the market would crash, have now committed that money into equities or long bonds because they are able to protect themselves with our dynamic hedging strategy."

Aetna's Tate noted the ambiguity in the minds of pension fund executives, who had "concerns about losses in a market that has been very good to them" (in Ring 1987a: 76). Portfolio insurance, he suggested, helped to resolve this ambiguity by lessening fears of loss while allowing funds to keep reasonably high levels of equity exposure. Aetna's own $1.9 billion pension fund, primarily invested in equity, was about one-third hedged.

Inasmuch as synthetic portfolio insurance served to increase the demand for equities, the market's rise prior to the crash may have been accelerated by the growing popularity of portfolio insurance. Hayne Leland and Mark Rubinstein (1988a: 46), however, deny that portfolio insurance was a factor in the market's rise: "Even if one believes that portfolio insurance was a major factor in the precipitous decline of the stock market, we believe it is stretching the imagination too far to extend this theory to explain the market rise in the year preceding the crash." They claim that, of the $60 to $80 billion they estimated to be invested in insurance strategies, at most $10 billion represented additional commitments to stock; this would account for less than a third of 1 percent of total stock market capitalization at the time.

A similar conclusion is reached by a report undertaken on behalf of the Chicago Mercantile Exchange (Miller et al. 1988: 9–11) by Merton Miller, random-walk enthusiast Burton Malkiel, option pricing theorist Myron Scholes, and attorney John Hawke. Miller (1991: 98) also finds the orders of magnitude out of line. He questions how $10 to $20 billion in added demand for equity, distributed over the many months preceding the crash, can be said to account for the half a trillion dollar increase in US equity value that occurred between January and August 1987.

But as well as encouraging additional, marginal commitments to equity, synthetic insurance strategies also encouraged investors to maintain levels of equity exposure that would, absent insurance, have been reduced. The purchase of insurance increased investors' willingness to bear risk. Insured investors were thus willing to hold more risky assets than they would have held had they been uninsured. Furthermore, their greater tolerance for risk led them to buy still more risky assets as the prices of those assets, hence the insured investors' wealth, appreciated.[4]

According to a Securities and Exchange Commission survey (SEC 1988: 3.15), investors maintained relatively high equity exposures in part because of the risk-reduction capability of portfolio insurance. The SEC found that institutional investors using portfolio insurance had an average equity commitment of 56 percent, compared with 46 percent for those not insured. The Katzenbach study (1987: 28), undertaken for the New York Stock Exchange (NYSE), concludes that portfolio insurance served to "encourage institutional investors to remain with a higher percentage of equity longer than might, in view of market fundamentals, seem prudent." A study by the US General Accounting Office (GAO 1988: 38) finds that portfolio insurance "gave institutional investors a false sense of security, thereby encouraging overinvestment in the stock market."

Synthetic portfolio insurance may be seen to encourage somewhat paradoxical investment behavior. In the normal course of events, as prices climb and investors become wary of a market set-back, one would expect them to reduce their equity exposures. With synthetic insurance, however, the opposite may occur. As market uncertainty increases, the demand for insurance increases. But as long as prices continue to climb, synthetic insurance will call for increased equity exposure. The contradiction between the anxiety of insured investors and their actions may pose problems for market stability that could undermine the integrity of their own market positions.

An Informational Cascade

John Cox and Rubinstein (1985: 428, 444, 456) underscore the importance of prices for economic decision-making and identify the links between option prices and anticipated volatility:

> It is a basic principle of economics that prices produced in competitive markets provide participants in the economy with useful information for making a variety of economic decisions. . . . The prices of options, like those of other securities, contain implicit predictions about future events. An option's price will depend on and contain information about anticipated future volatility. . . . Index option prices provide important, otherwise unobtainable, information to the economy.

With publicly traded options, investors can look to published prices, as well as volume and open interest figures, to glean some idea of the demand for put protection and the expectations for market volatility. For synthetic insurance strategies, these vital pieces of information are lacking. The price of the insurance is unknown even to its sellers, let alone its potential buyers.

The very extent of insurance programs was largely unknown prior to the crash (and remains a matter of some conjecture even today). *Intermarket*'s "1987 Portfolio Insurance Directory & Survey" reported insured assets at $45 billion as of June 30, 1986, and at $61 billion as of July 1, 1987. The latter figure, however, excludes LOR insured assets, as LOR did not respond to the 1987 survey.

According to Ring (1987b: 50), as of September 30, 1987, the largest providers of insurance – LOR ($22 billion) and two of its licensees, Aetna ($17 billion) and Wells Fargo ($9.2 billion) – accounted for about $48.2 billion of an estimated total of $68.1 billion of insured assets. LOR licensees BEA Associates, Centerre Trust, and Webster Capital Management accounted for another $1.9 billion. Not included in any of these figures, however, are other LOR licensees such as First Chicago, General Motors, Rosenberg Capital Management, Stein Roe & Farnham, and Western Asset Management, and licensees in Canada, Australia, Japan, and the UK. On a conservative basis, LOR and its licensees accounted for over 75 percent of all insured assets.

FIGURE 9.10

Estimate of Amount of Externally Managed Assets Insured as of
September 30, 1987 (millions of dollars)

Firm

Advanced Investment Mgmt.	580
Aegis Capital Mgmt.	55
Aetna Life & Casualty	17,000
American Nat'l Bank of Chicago	100
BEA Associates	1,200
Bankers Trust-Investment Mgmt.	4,000
The Boston Co.	300
Centerre Trust	620
Drexel Burnham Lambert	2,000
Leland O'Brien Rubinstein	22,000*
Lotsoff Capital Mgmt.	280
Mellon Bond Associates	NA
Mellon Capital Mgmt.	1,000
J.P. Morgan Investment Mgmt.	7,000
Morgan Stanley	NA
Northern Trust	150
Oppenheimer Capital	1,500
Skye Investment Advisors	813
The Travelers	150
Webster Capital Mgmt.	80
Wells Fargo Investment Advisors	9,200
Westridge Capital Mgmt.	40
TOTAL	68,068

* *Pensions & Investment Age* estimate

Source: *Pensions & Investment Age*, November 2, 1987, p. 50.

Even after the crash, estimates of the amount of assets insured in October 1987 vary widely. The Brady Commission (1988: 27) estimates insured assets at $60 to $90 billion. The SEC's (1988: 3–4) report on the crash identifies a minimum of $55 billion in insurance programs. Leland and Rubinstein (1988b: 46) estimate $60 to $80 billion and Gennotte and Leland (1990: 999) $70 to $100 billion.

Grossman (1988b) argues that lack of information about the demand for insurance will effectively reduce the number of trading partners willing to take the other side of insurance trades. This may cause prices to rise above the levels that would obtain if investors knew the extent of portfolio insurance and, consequently, could anticipate the level of market volatility.[5]

In fact, the paradoxical behavior of insurers may lead investors other than insurers to contribute actively to departures from fundamental values. Chapter 7 discussed how prices can become detached from underlying fundamentals when investors err in aggregating information. This can occur when investors place too much emphasis on the public information incorporated in prices and too little on their own private interpretations of information. Because the magnitude of synthetic insurance trading is obscured, its impact on market prices can easily be misinterpreted by other investors.

As the market rose from 1982 to 1987, the demand for synthetic insurance also increased. There were thus more and more insurance clients increasing their equity exposures as prices continued to climb. Marginal price rises resulting from these trades essentially reflected growing uncertainty. To investors unaware of the extent of insured strategies, however, it would have been all too easy to interpret the price rises as positive signals for the market. These investors may have been encouraged to maintain or even increase their own equity exposures, setting the stage for an informational cascade. When sales by insurers on October 16 revealed the extent of prior uninformed purchases, investors in general reassessed their information.[6]

Fischer Black's (1988) view of the crash also fits this paradigm. In Black's scenario, investors underestimated the market's tendency toward mean reversion because they underestimated the flexibility of investor tastes. Investors have flexible tastes if their appetite for risk-taking increases with rising wealth and decreases with declining wealth. The tastes of portfolio insurance buyers exhibit more flexibility than those of the average investor because insurers buy as equities rise and sell as they fall (as did some mutual fund shareholders during the crash).

A rise in the flexibility of tastes implies greater mean reversion. But investors discounted the probability of price reversals in the years preceding the crash, thereby facilitating the market's rise. The market rose more, and subsequently fell more, than it would have otherwise. Black describes the crash as follows:

> By the morning of October 19, investors had become aware of how the typical investor's tastes had changed. Some people had added up the assets used in portfolio insurance strategies and realized that lots of sell orders were due that day. The market's behavior during the day gave further clues to the typical investor's tastes. As investors became aware that the typical investor had more flexible tastes than they thought, they increased their estimates of the market's mean reversion and reduced their estimates of the market's expected return. This made them less willing to hold stocks. The market fell sharply. (Black 1988: 273)

David Eagle (1994) argues that the possibility of cascade-like behavior, with discontinuous price movements, depends on the slope of the demand curve for stocks. When the demand curve slopes downward (that is, demand increases with price decreases), changes in demand will lead to continuous price changes. When the demand curve slopes upward (with demand decreasing as price declines), however, prices may snowball out of control. The trading of insurers relative to all trading activity will determine whether the demand curve slopes upward. Furthermore, their trading may have an effect on overall demand out of all proportion to their size when demand elasticity is less than expected (as will be the case when investors base their decisions on current price changes) or when short-term illiquidity causes insurance sales to overwhelm any buying activity resulting from price drops. Eagle concludes (p. 69) that portfolio insurance trading in October 1987 could have led to a backward-bending demand curve that facilitated a cascade.

According to the SEC (1988: 3.14–3.15), investors' new-found awareness of portfolio insurance programs was combined with continuing uncertainty over the precise extent of these programs' selling demands:

> When puts are purchased, they send a bearish message to the market, with price increases in the put options being translated into price decreases in the component stocks through arbitrage or options marketmakers hedging their short positions. With portfolio insurance, on the other hand, no bearish message is sent to the market even though the investment strategy adopted by the institution is essentially identical. Accordingly, instead of a direct message sent through a put purchase, the market becomes generally aware that there is an increasingly large commitment to sell futures, stocks or both, anytime the stock index price moves downward. The market suffers from limited information that does not permit it to calculate selling interest successfully. The impact of this limited information is to discourage buying activity during market downturns because market professionals cannot determine whether any rebound in the market will be overwhelmed by an avalanche of portfolio insurance futures selling and resultant index arbitrage selling in the stock market.

Thus, as the uncertainty about the extent of portfolio insurance purchases likely contributed to the market's rise in the months preceding the 1987 crash, uncertainty about the extent of the sales mandated by such programs contributed to the market's collapse on the 19th.

Insurance, Arbitrage, and Liquidity

Some advocates of synthetic insurance argued that it would come to be regarded as a source of liquidity. According to Kidder Peabody's Wunsch (1986), for example, "without portfolio insurance, investor preferences are expressed very inaccurately in fits and starts that surprise the markets with liquidity demands that are very expensive. In fact, portfolio insurance trades will probably come to be viewed not as a strain on market liquidity, but as a source of liquidity and compensated accordingly."

Yet the trading demands of synthetic insurance can interact with other trading strategies in such a way as to consume market liquidity faster than it can be supplied. Several incidents prior to the 1987 crash indicated that the market did not possess sufficient liquidity to accommodate the trading needs of insurers. On September 12, 1986, the Dow Jones industrial average (DJIA) fell 120 points on what was then record trading volume, one of the sharpest declines in market history. But futures prices fell even more; all of a sudden, S&P 500 futures were selling at an unprecedented 5-point discount to stock prices. The SEC (1987: 6–11) later suggested that news about economic fundamentals had precipitated the decline and index arbitrage had accelerated it. The SEC (1987: 1.9) found "no evidence that portfolio insurance had reached a level at which it would have played a significant role in the market downturn."

But on January 23, 1987, the market again experienced extreme price volatility. In about one hour, the DJIA fell 115 points on record volume, and the futures discount was extreme. This time, according to the SEC (1987: 28), there was no news to justify the decline. Furthermore, the SEC (1987: 16, 21) noted that some market commentators had raised the specter of a "cascade scenario" driven by the confluence of index arbitrage and synthetic portfolio insurance.

When stock index futures appear to be cheap relative to the underlying stock, arbitragers buy the futures and sell the stock. The sale of stock might push stock prices lower. This, however, would be a signal for synthetic portfolio insurance programs to reduce their stock positions; as almost all such insurance programs relied on futures, this would mean selling futures short. The result might be an even wider futures discount, which would trigger more stock sales by arbitragers. As long as portfolio insurers' short sales of futures had a greater impact than arbitragers' purchases of futures, prices in both markets would continue to spiral downward.[7]

The SEC (1987: 21) suggested then that the likelihood of a cascade scenario would depend on "the design of portfolio insurance programs, the incidence of the 'trigger points' at which the programs generate sell orders, [and] the amount of capital subject to these programs." The SEC interviewed several market participants and echoed their view that the possibility of a cascade scenario was remote.

One counterargument to this cascade scenario was that market forces would resolve the demand for insurance. Price declines would attract value investors. Synthetic portfolio insurance positions would become more expensive to purchase, demand would taper off, and more capital

FIGURE 9.11

The Insurance – Arbitrage Cascade

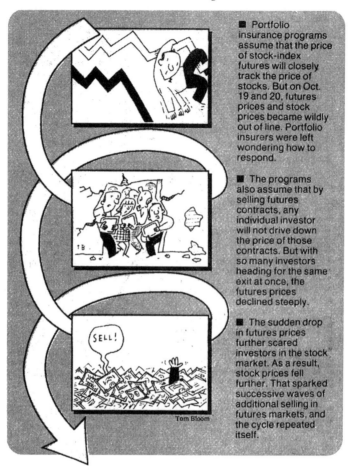

Source: *New York Times*, December 15, 1987, p. D6.

would be made available for index arbitrage and index substitution, which would stabilize futures prices. But we have already noted the problems with assuming that value investors will rush to take the opposite side of portfolio insurance trades. As Gregory Duffee and his colleagues (1992: 36) write: "The lack of information [about the extent of dynamic strategies underway] does not encourage potential buyers . . . and the speed of the price fall induced by dynamic hedging reduces the potential that non-market makers can place stabilizing orders."

A second counterargument to the cascade scenario was that a mature synthetic insurance market would cover a broad range of strategies, with insurance buyers selecting different minimum ending values (or deductibles) and different lengths of coverage (or horizons). The market impact of portfolio insurance would thus be "distributed over a wider range of trading sessions rather than focused at a particular point in time" (SEC 1987: 22–3). But this ignores the fact that all insurance programs utilize a common rule: they buy as prices rise and sell as they fall. A large enough market move will thus trigger all insurers to trade simultaneously, regardless of the specific parameters of their insurance policies.

As we have noted, by the time of the crash virtually all portfolio insurance programs were being conducted using futures, rather than the underlying stocks. According to the Brady Commission (1988: 55), "institutions employing portfolio insurance strategies . . . assumed that it would be infeasible to sell huge volumes of stock on the exchange in short periods of time with only a small price impact. These institutions came to believe that the futures market offered a separate haven of liquidity sufficient to allow them to liquidate huge positions over short periods of time with minimal price displacement."

After the crash, however, the SEC (1988: 3.22) concluded: "Low margins . . . contribute to the illusion of almost unlimited liquidity in the futures market. During a market break, however, that liquidity disappears at a rate geometrically larger than liquidity in the lower leveraged stock market." The Brady Commission (1988: 56) finds that the equity and futures markets during the crash were simply incapable of bearing "the full weight of the estimated $25 billion of selling dictated by portfolio insurance strategies." This volume translates into about four days' worth of average trading volume on the NYSE at the time. According to the Brady Commission (p. 56), "the selling pressure in the futures market washed across to the stock market, both through index arbitrage and indirect portfolio insurance stock sales."

Summary

The trading demands of synthetic portfolio insurance interface with some theories presented in part II to create a picture of why and how the market crashed in October 1987. To begin with, portfolio insurance trading, being noisy, increases uncertainty in the market and discourages potential counterparty traders from acting to offset the effects of insurance trades. Thus insurance trades, being trend-following, can exacerbate any tendencies for prices to move away from fundamental values. In the years leading up to the crash, portfolio insurance may have become a fad that, by encouraging the use of more insurance and increased equity exposure, amplified the market's rise.

The contribution of synthetic insurance to the market's rise before the crash may have been augmented by other investors following the lead of insurers. Because the hidden price of synthetic insurance obscures the extent of the strategy's use, any price increases caused by portfolio insurance trading may be mistaken by other market participants as positive signals for the market's direction. Investors acting on these (mis)signals may be encouraged to maintain or even increase their equity exposures until they begin to become aware of the extent of insured strategies (and the extent to which price increases are unsustainable).

That time came in the week preceding the crash, as market price declines caused insurance programs to unload large futures positions. This may have fed into an insurance–arbitrage cascade scenario, as index arbitragers looking at large futures discounts sold off stock in the underlying market, causing synthetic insurance programs to short more futures in response. With potential buyers sidelined, either by their lowered assessments of stock market values or their unwillingness to step in front of the fast-moving insurance–arbitrage selling train, liquidity vanished. Both stock and futures markets were soon in freefall.

Notes

1 *Intermarket*'s "1987 Portfolio Insurance Directory & Survey."
2 Shiller models the dynamics of this fad in terms of a contagion model, where the "infection rate" measures the speed at which the fad develops.
3 See the ad in, for example, *Pensions & Investment Age* (October 19, 1987: 47).
4 This is supported by Grossman and Zhou's (1996) equilibrium model of market prices in the presence of portfolio insurers.
5 Ten years after the crash, Leland (quoted in Burton 1997: 26) admitted: "If the market had been fully aware that [insurance] selling was based not on information but rather on a reactive strategy, there would have been more liquidity and the price impact would have been much less."
6 Jacklin et al. (1992) present a model of this kind of informational cascade.
7 Perceived arbitrage opportunities are also likely to lead to index substitution – the swapping within an index fund between stock index futures contracts and the underlying stocks. While the primary objective of an index fund is the replication of index returns, some index funds participate in index substitution to enhance returns. When an index futures contract is selling at a discount to its fair value, relative to stock prices, substitutors will buy the index futures and sell the stocks that comprise the index.

10

Synthetic Puts and the 1987 Crash: Evidence

> There were periods when the linkage between stock and futures markets became completely disconnected, leading to a freefall in both markets.
>
> *The Brady Commission, 1988*

Chapter 9 outlined several theories of how synthetic portfolio insurance may have contributed to the crash, including its effects on information aggregation and the portfolio insurance–index arbitrage cascade scenario. But what does the evidence say? In the months following the crash, a number of investigative reports examined the trading data for the crash period. The Securities and Exchange Commission (SEC) and the Brady Commission (the Presidential Task Force), for two, found that the evidence implicated portfolio insurance as a prime culprit.

Before the Crash

In the two weeks preceding the crash itself, the market had declined substantially, with particularly sharp losses on Wednesday, October 14, Thursday, October 15, and Friday, October 16. M. Goldberg and S. Schulmeister (1988) blame the decline on market technicians, noting that a wide variety of commonly used technical trading rules were enormously profitable beginning on October 14, 1987. They suggest that a confluence of technical sell signals caused technicians to dump futures, which contributed to the already prevailing futures discount and fueled a portfolio insurance–index arbitrage cascade. The *Wall Street Journal* (October 16, 1987: 3) notes that futures traders in Chicago believed the late-day sell-off on Thursday the 15th, at least, was set off by portfolio insurers (selling perhaps in response to the market's sharp decline on October 14).

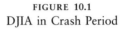

FIGURE 10.1
DJIA in Crash Period

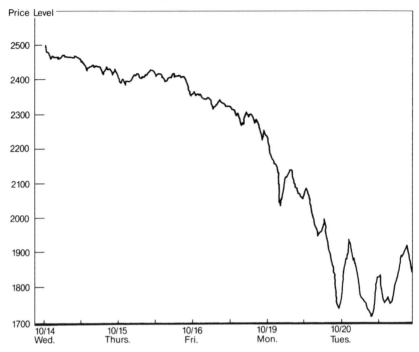

Source: Report of the Presidential Task Force on Market Mechanisms
(Brady Commission), 1988.

In fact, portfolio insurers sold futures equivalent to $530 million, $965 million, and $2.1 billion in stocks on the Wednesday, Thursday, and Friday preceding the crash (SEC 1988: 2.6, 3.9). But the market fell 10 percent in this same period. A typical portfolio insurance strategy calls for stock sales in excess of 20 percent in response to a 10 percent decline in the market. Applied to a very conservatively estimated $60 billion in insured assets, this would have required $12 billion in sales. Less than $4 billion in sales had been completed by the end of the week.

According to the Brady Commission (1988: 29), the market's decline on October 14 through 16 "created a huge overhang of selling pressure – enough to crush the equity markets in the following week. This overhang was concentrated within two categories of reactive sellers, portfolio insurers and a few mutual fund groups, and exacerbated by the actions of a number of aggressive trading-oriented institutions selling in anticipation of further declines."

FIGURE 10.2
The Crash Reports

How Five Studies Viewed The Market Collapse

Securities and Exchange Commission New computer-assisted trading techniques that link the stock and futures markets fueled last October's wild swings in stock prices. The danger of extreme volatility persists, it said. Also found that many market-makers did not do enough to cushion the plunge in prices. The S.E.C. called for curbs on speculation in stock index futures. It recommended bolstering the financial strength of market-makers and encouraging greater disclosure of the identity of big buyers and sellers.

Presidential Task Force on Market Mechanisms Otherwise known as the Brady commission, attributed the market plunge mainly to a handful of major investors using computer-assisted trading techniques. Rather than ban those techniques, it urged greater coordination among stocks and futures exchanges, under one regulatory authority, possibly the Federal Reserve Board. Recommended unification of settlement and clearing mechanisms among stocks, options and futures and comparable margin (or down payment) standards on them. Also urged "circuit-breakers" on stocks to suspend and cool off runaway trading.

New York Stock Exchange

Study by Nicholas deB. Katzenbach, a former Attorney General, blamed speculation in stock index futures and recommended restraints on such trading. Also urged contingency plan for shutting exchanges in emergencies.

General Accounting Office

Repeated breakdowns of computer systems on the New York Stock Exchange aggravated selling on Oct. 19. Faulted Federal regulators for inadequate contingency planning.

Commodity Futures Trading Commission

Regulator of futures exchanges did not conclude that trading in stock index futures was the main problem. Urged better communication between exchanges.

Source: *New York Times*, February 3, 1988, p. 1.

James Gammill and Terry Marsh's (1988) study of open futures interest prior to the crash suggests that frontrunners shorted futures in anticipation of sales by insurers. Both the Brady Commission (1988: 15–30) and the SEC (1988: 3.31–3.32) also document massive stock and futures trading on October 14 through 16 in anticipation of trading by insurers. The Brady Commission (1988: 29) identifies some aggressive trading-oriented institutions (including hedge funds, pension and endowment funds, money management firms, and investment banking houses) that anticipated the insurers:[1]

> These traders could well understand the strategies of the portfolio insurers and mutual funds. They could anticipate the selling those institutions would have to do in reaction to the market's decline. They could also see those institutions falling behind in their selling programs. The situation presented an opportunity for these traders to sell in anticipation of the forced selling by portfolio insurers and mutual funds, with the prospect of repurchasing at lower prices.

Frontrunning of this type can prove extremely destabilizing to markets. As Bradford De Long and his colleagues (1990a) point out, although rational speculation can be stabilizing when the speculators are trading against irrational noise traders, when noise traders use trend-following strategies such as portfolio insurance, rational speculation becomes destabilizing. This occurs because speculators attempt to jump on the bandwagon ahead of the noise traders, fueling the trend-following strategies (De Long et al. 1990b).

The existence of some knowledgeable anticipators trading ahead of the insurers may on the surface appear to contradict our earlier assertion that the unknown magnitude of insurance selling pressure raised market volatility. But only a small number of speculators knew enough to anticipate the huge overhang of portfolio insurance selling pressure. A careful inspection of the *Wall Street Journal* and other publications reveals that the insurance overhang was not common knowledge just prior to the crash. Stock specialists, futures traders, institutional investors, and the public at large had at best only partial information, and could not distinguish portfolio insurance trades from information-based ones. They had no way of knowing that the selling was led by some nimble speculators and the mechanistic insurers.

Frontrunning increases the cost of portfolio insurance. Fred Grauer, chairman of insurance-provider Wells Fargo Investment Advisors, concedes that frontrunning made portfolio insurance more costly to implement during the crash: "To the extent they [frontrunners] can anticipate, they can take the market down before you get there" (*Wall Street Journal*,

January 13, 1988: D1).[2] In fact, by Friday insurers were encountering growing difficulties selling futures economically, and some began to sell stock directly. This was but a precursor to the massive stock selling by insurers to come on October 19 (Brady Commission 1988: 29).

Black Monday

The SEC (1988: A.10) asserts that insurers' hesitancy (or inability) to follow through on their strategies and sell futures as required on Wednesday, October 14 through Friday, October 16 "may have contributed to the last minute dumping of futures and stocks on the 19th and 20th." In one extreme case, a portfolio insurance client was instructed, based on Friday's close, to sell 70 percent of its remaining stocks on Monday. These sales were required even though the client had been selling on Wednesday, Thursday, and Friday (Brady Commission 1988: 29).

Some mutual fund groups were also confronted with an overhang of sell orders. Telephone redemptions made it easy for customers to retreat from equity funds, and on Friday alone net redemptions exceeded $750 million. More redemption requests were made over the weekend (Brady Commission 1988: 29).

During the first half hour of trading on Monday, October 19, a few portfolio insurers sold futures equivalent to about $400 million in stocks. That represented 28 percent of public futures volume (that is, volume exclusive of local market makers' volume).[3] Insurers' direct sell programs in stocks amounted to $250 million at the opening, and sell programs by index arbitragers amounted to another $250 million in stock. A small number of mutual funds also placed some large sell orders for individual issues. One mutual fund (Fidelity Investments) sold about $500 million during the first hour. Institutional sell orders overwhelmed the stock market at the opening (Brady Commission 1988: 30).

The SEC (1988: 3.31–3.32) also finds that some member firms known to be active portfolio insurance vendors or executing brokers traded ahead of their insurance customers. While the SEC finds no evidence of classic frontrunning by these firms, several member firms did sell a substantial amount of futures on the 19th, at the opening (and some also bought at the opening on the 20th). The SEC argues that this proprietary trading may have been based on the many indicators (in addition to a firm's particular customer orders) that the market would open low on the 19th (and would rebound on the 20th). The SEC concludes, however, that because of this proprietary trading, insurance customers sold at lower prices on the 19th (and bought at higher prices on the 20th) than they would have otherwise.[4]

FIGURE 10.3
Program Selling on NYSE, October 19

Millions of shares

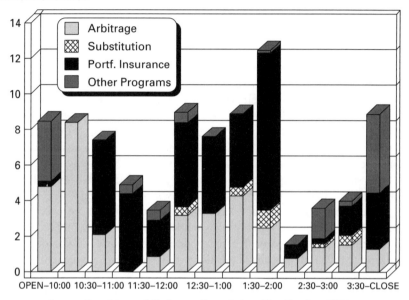

Source: Securities and Exchange Commission, *The October 1987 Market Break*, 1988.

Futures selling by portfolio insurers remained significant throughout the morning. Between 11:40 a.m. and 2:00 p.m., portfolio insurers sold about $1.3 billion in futures, representing about 41 percent of public futures volume (Brady Commission 1988: 36). In addition, portfolio insurers sold approximately $900 million in NYSE stocks. In stocks and futures combined, portfolio insurers had contributed over $3.7 billion in selling pressure by early afternoon.

Program selling pressure from portfolio insurers and arbitragers often hit the NYSE simultaneously. For example, total program selling constituted 61 percent of NYSE volume in S&P 500 stocks from 9:30 to 9:40 a.m., 63.4 percent from 1:10 to 1:20 p.m., and over 60 percent in two intervals from 1:30 to 2:00 p.m. (SEC 1988: 2.15–2.16).

According to the Commodity Futures Trading Commission's (1988: 137) report, the interaction of index arbitrage and portfolio insurance cannot explain the market decline on October 19. Its analysis of intraday trading shows instances when the stock market temporarily reacted to arbitrage selling, but the CFTC dismisses these as evidence of an insurance–arbitrage cascade because it finds that "futures prices were also declining despite offsetting arbitrage purchasing pressure in the futures market"; the CFTC report concludes that "such a situation is more suggestive of a general weakness in the market than a stock market reaction to the selling side of arbitrage transactions." An alternative explanation is that the futures sales by portfolio insurers overwhelmed futures purchases by arbitragers, setting off an insurance–arbitrage cascade.

By 2:00 p.m., in any case, order execution problems had slowed index arbitrage, whereas futures sales by portfolio insurers remained heavy. Nevertheless, even though portfolio insurers were the largest group of sellers, "they remained far behind the hedge ratios dictated by their computer programs" (Brady Commission 1988: III.21–2). Both LOR and Aetna, for example, stepped out of the market before completing the number of sales dictated by their computer programs (McClain 1988: 86). The SEC (1988: xiii) finds that this large portfolio insurance overhang had a significant psychological impact on the markets on Monday, October 19:

> The knowledge by market participants of the existence of active portfolio insurance strategies created . . . a market "overhang" effect in both the futures and stock markets; this resulted in the maintenance of futures discounts that discouraged institutional traders from participating in the stock market on the buy side, specialists from committing capital to maintain fair and orderly markets, and block positioning firms from maintaining normal levels of activity.

In the last hour and a half of trading, insurers sold $660 million in futures. With index arbitrage largely absent from the market, futures fell to a discount of 20 index points (Brady Commission 1988: 36). Portfolio insurers also continued to sell stock directly in program trades. The DJIA sank almost 300 points in the last hour and a quarter of trading.

By the end of trading on October 19, portfolio insurers had sold thirty-nine million shares and index arbitragers another thirty-eight million shares (SEC 1988: 2.15–2.16). According to the Brady Commission (1988: III.21–III.22), futures sales by portfolio insurers on the 19th amounted to 21 percent of total futures volume and 43 percent of public futures volume.

The Brady Commission (1988: 36) finds that much of the selling activity on the 19th was concentrated in the hands of surprisingly few institutional investors:

> Out of total NYSE sales of just under $21 billion, sell programs by three portfolio insurers made up just under $2 billion. Block sales of individual stocks by a few mutual funds accounted for another $900 million. About 90 percent of these sales were executed by one mutual fund group. In the futures market, portfolio insurer sales amounted to the equivalent

FIGURE 10.4
S&P 500 Futures Discounts and Portfolio Insurance Trades on October 19

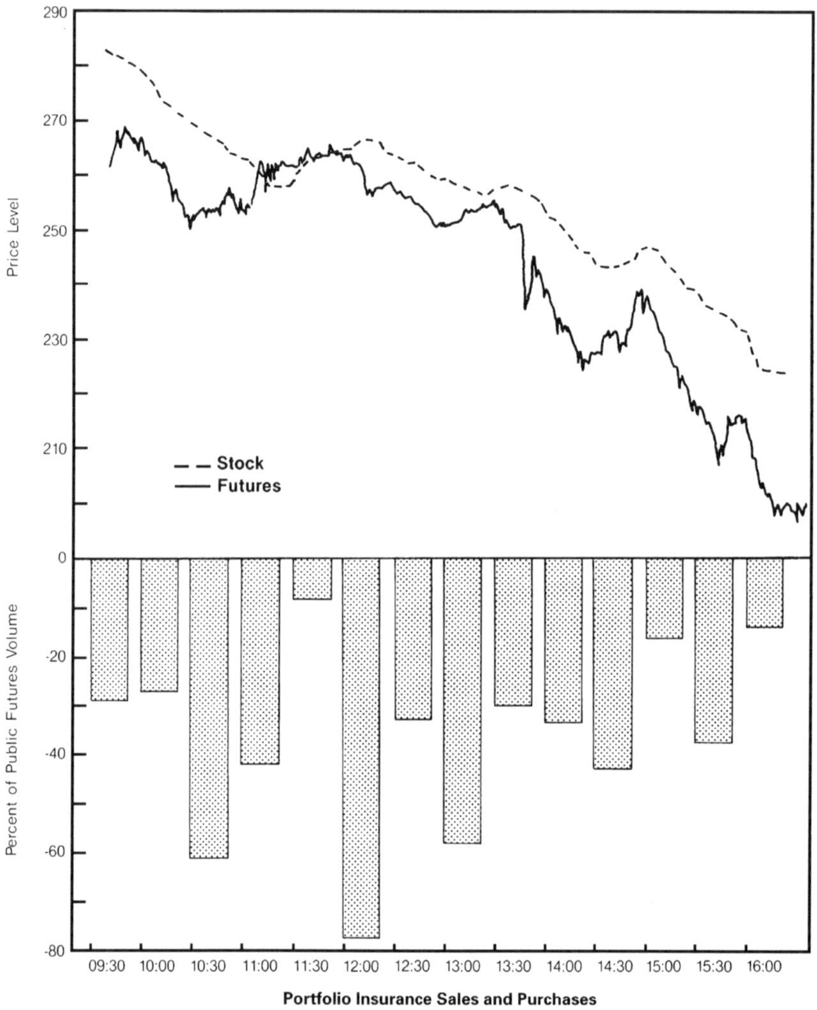

Source: *Report of the Presidential Task Force on Market Mechanisms*
(Brady Commission), 1988.

of $4 billion of stocks, or 34,500 contracts, equal to over 40 percent
of futures volume, exclusive of locals' transactions; $2.8 billion was done
by only three insurers. In the stock and futures markets together, one
portfolio insurer sold stock and futures with underlying values totaling
$1.7 billion. Huge as this selling pressure from portfolio insurers was, it
was a small fraction of the sales dictated by the formulas of their models.

FIGURE 10.5

S&P 500 Futures Discounts and Portfolio Insurance Trades on October 20

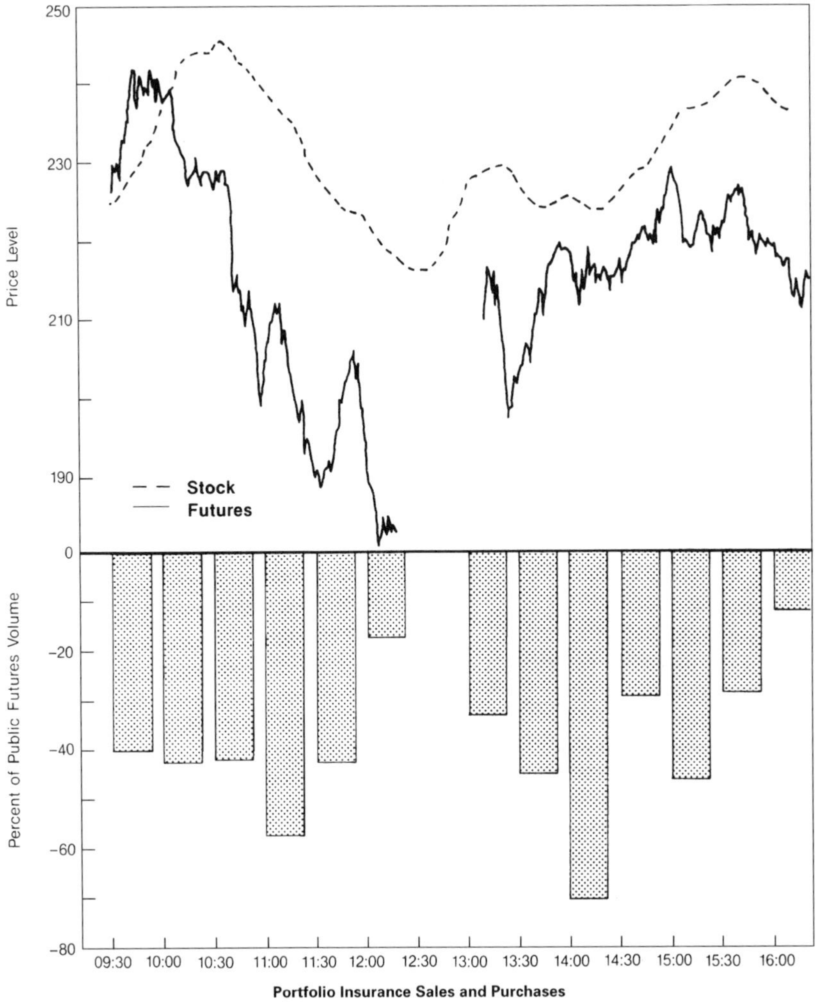

Source: *Report of the Presidential Task Force on Market Mechanisms*
(Brady Commission), 1988.

Roller Coaster Tuesday

Volume on Tuesday, October 20 remained high and price movements re-
sembled a roller coaster ride. S&P 500 futures opened at a substantial
premium to fair value as the market surged upward, but that premium

had reversed to a slight discount by approximately 10 a.m. During this period, portfolio insurance selling accounted for 26 percent of S&P 500 futures volume (SEC 1988: 2.21).

The volume of portfolio insurance trading appears to have been a substantial factor behind futures discounts at several points during the day. Insurance strategies accounted for 25 percent of futures volume between 10:00 and 10:30 a.m., as the discount widened to 16 points, and for more than 34 percent of futures volume during the next hour, as the markets plunged (SEC 1988: 2.21).

The futures contract moved to a discount as wide as 40 points as the market plummeted 27 percent between 10:00 a.m. and 12:15 p.m. (Brady Commission 1988: 40). At its lowest point, the S&P 500 futures price implied a DJIA level of about 1400 (Brady Commission 1988: 57). At this point, the CBOE and CME temporarily halted trading in stock index futures.

According to the SEC (1988: 2.21), "portfolio insurance futures and stock selling played a significant role on October 20th in dampening price recoveries in both markets." By the afternoon, however, several factors converged to offset insurance selling and produce a market rally. These factors included news of pending corporate buybacks of stock, assurances of sources of liquidity for NYSE specialists, the ebbing of stock sales, and the availability of bargain prices. The DJIA closed at 1841, up 102 points for the day, or 5.9 percent, on record volume of 614 million shares (upping the previous day's 604 million shares).

Brady Commission and SEC Views

The Brady Commission (1988: 41–2) finds that several important themes emerge from the crash:

> First, reactive selling by institutions, which followed portfolio insurance strategies and sought to liquidate large fractions of their stock holdings regardless of price, played a prominent role in the market break. By reasonable estimates, the formulas used by portfolio insurers dictated the sale of $20 to $30 billion of equities over this short time span. . . . Second, a few mutual funds sold stock in reaction to redemptions. To the market their behavior looked much like that of the portfolio insurers, that is, selling without primary regard to price. Third, some aggressive trading-oriented investors, seizing the profit opportunity presented by the predictable forced selling by other institutions, contributed to the market break. Fourth, much of the selling pressure was concentrated in the hands of surprisingly few institutions. . . . Fifth, . . . futures and stock market movements were inextricably related. Portfolio insurers sold in the futures

market, forcing prices down. The downward pressure in the futures market was then transmitted to the stock market by index arbitrage and diverted portfolio insurance sales. While index arbitrageurs may not have accounted for a substantial part of total daily volume, they were particularly active during the day at times of substantial price movements. They were not, however, the primary cause of the movements; rather, they were the transmission mechanism for the pressure initiated by other institutions. Finally, there were periods when the linkage between stock and futures markets became completely disconnected, leading to a freefall in both markets.

The SEC (1988: 3.11) concludes that investor perception about fundamentals was the trigger for the market declines during the pre-crash period of October 14 through 16. But it maintains that the market decline was accelerated by portfolio insurance and other futures-based strategies:

The existence of futures on stock indexes and the use of the various strategies involving program trading (i.e., index arbitrage, index substitution and portfolio insurance) were a significant factor in accelerating and exacerbating the declines. For the three critical trading days – October 16, 19, and 20 – we have been able to attribute 6.3 percent, 16.7 percent, and 25.5 percent, respectively, of futures trading to portfolio insurance selling. In response to the resulting real or apparent futures price discounts, index arbitrage and portfolio insurance strategies represented significant percentages of volume on the NYSE in the stocks comprising the S&P 500 on each of these days. Moreover, during certain critical trading periods, index arbitrage or portfolio insurance or both accounted for between 30 and 68 percent of total NYSE volume in the S&P 500 stocks.

The SEC (1988: 3.12) also finds that:

The use of derivative products in program trading strategies had a significant indirect impact on the markets, particularly on October 19, in the form of negative market psychology. . . . Futures trading during the critical periods had a disproportionately negative effect on the market considering the absolute number of contracts or shares sold in arbitrage or portfolio insurance strategies. First, the knowledge by market participants of the existence of active portfolio insurance strategies created a market "overhang" effect in both the futures and stock markets. Institutional traders were able to anticipate significant selling in futures and stocks coming from portfolio insurance. Thus, they refrained from entering the market as buyers and their absence acted as a damper to price rises. More important, however, was the effect on market psychology of the persistent discount that appeared in the S&P 500 futures on October 16 and continued at record levels on October 19 and throughout that week.

The SEC (1988: 3.15) concludes that "portfolio insurance dramatically increases the amount and velocity of trading and permits a group of institutions that manage a relatively small proportion of total pension fund assets to have a substantially disproportionate impact on stock market volatility."

Summary

Synthetic portfolio insurance contributed to the crash in several ways. First, synthetic insurers sold over $3.5 billion in futures in the week preceding the crash. This sell-off was exacerbated by some aggressive traders that attempted to frontrun insurance programs. It also alerted the market to the extent of insured strategies and their imminent selling needs.

Furthermore, sales by insurers on October 14 through 16 amounted to less than a third of the sales that were required by their programs, given the magnitude of the market's decline. Thus the market opened on Monday the 19th with a huge overhang of insurance selling pressure.

Insurers sold 39 million shares on that Monday, and index arbitragers another 38 million shares. Insurers also accounted for 43 percent of public futures volume (exclusive of locals' transactions). Yet, throughout the day, they continued to lag the sales dictated by their programs. The continuing overhang of selling pressure undoubtedly discouraged other investors from stepping in on the buy side of the market. Not until the next afternoon were buyers able finally to turn the market around, after several intensive bouts of selling by insurers had squelched nascent rallies on Tuesday morning.

Despite the preponderance of evidence against synthetic portfolio insurance, the strategy did not lack for defenders, even after the crash. Their arguments in defense of portfolio insurance (and our counterarguments) are presented in the next two chapters.

Notes

1 There was also anticipation of selling by mutual funds because of redemption requests. But mutual fund sales were a much smaller factor than insurance sales (Brady Commission 1988: IV.1, V.18).

2 Grauer also charges (in "What Fred Grauer really said," *Institutional Investor*, February 1988: 17) that brokers traded for their own accounts ahead of their insurance clients, and advocates that "dealers ... be bound [by regulation] not to adversely impact clients' strategies by taking advantage of their intimate knowledge of customers' strategies."

3   Because market makers (locals) both buy and sell intraday, some analysts argue that comparisons are more appropriately made to public futures volume than to total volume (Leland 1988b: 89).

4   In 1988, the NYSE, the Chicago Mercantile Exchange, and the New York Futures Exchange adopted a policy that prohibits members or associates of members from intermarket frontrunning – for example, trading in stock index futures or options on stock index futures in an attempt to capitalize on material, non-public information about program trades in the underlying stock.

11

Alibis I: The US Crash

The buyers who were not there on October 19 were just as responsible for the price decline as the sellers who were there.

Franklin Edwards, 1988b

The evidence presented thus far strongly implicates synthetic portfolio
insurance as a major factor in the crash. Soon after the crash, however,
proponents of portfolio insurance began to present arguments and alibis
that let portfolio insurance off the hook. Among them:

1   The market did not immediately bounce back.
2   Insurers were not the only big sellers.
3   Investors would have sold anyway.
4   Insurance trades were insufficient to cause the crash.
5   Insurance trades were uncorrelated with market moves.

We discuss and reject each of these alibis below.

No Bounce Back

As we noted in chapter 5, the 1987 crash had a minimal economic impact,
despite the dire predictions of economists in the immediate aftermath of
the crash. The market did not recover immediately, however; it took almost
two years for it to regain its precrash peak.

Some see the absence of an immediate bounce back as an exoneration of portfolio insurance. For example, Hayne Leland and Mark
Rubinstein (1988a: 47) observe that "the US market remained within
1.3 percent of its Black Monday close one week after the crash and has
still . . . on April 18, 1988 not significantly rebounded." If the culprit

were portfolio insurance alone, they argue, one "would have expected more of a correction back to pre-crash conditions by now" (Leland and Rubinstein 1988a: 48). Eugene Fama (1989: 77) makes a similar point, and Richard Roll (1988b: 27) notes the lack of rebound in international markets.

But Leland (1988b: 86) argues elsewhere that an immediate rebound should not have been expected, given investor perceptions: "Investors were accustomed to prices correctly reflecting information about future economic prospects. Seeing the large price fall, these investors thought that there was a change in economic fundamentals. . . . Eventually, these investors should realize their misperceptions and increase their investment in the stocks."

Fischer Black (1988: 274) also notes the effect of the crash on investor psychology: "It frightened people. The sharp decline, the high volatility, the mispriced securities, and the congestion caused people to withdraw from the market. This led to a decline in the equilibrium level of the market that was greater than the decline a model would have figured, unless it accounted for the psychological factor."

Yakov Amihud and his colleagues (1990) argue that the crash reduced long-term liquidity. Part of the price decline on October 19, they reason, resulted from insufficient liquidity and intense selling pressure; this was temporary. Another part reflected investors' reassessment of market liquidity; this was more long-lived.

Amihud et al. use bid–ask spreads and market depth (measured by the number of shares in market-makers' bid and ask quotes) to gauge liquidity, with wider spreads and smaller-size quotes indicating more illiquidity. They find that the price declines of individual securities were greater, the more illiquid the securities were. They conclude that, following the crash, investors continued to demand a higher expected return to compensate them for the perceived increase in the illiquidity of stocks.

The SEC (1988: 3.8) also asserts that liquidity problems lingered after the crash, as specialists were reluctant to offset order imbalances in the face of futures discounts or premiums indicative of further selling or buying pressure. Other investors seemed directionless in the aftermath of the astounding, and seemingly meaningless, burst of volatility. According to Linda Sandler, writing in the *Wall Street Journal* (October 20, 1987: 77): "Many money managers say they have few guideposts to the future. Computerized portfolio insurance and trading programs obscure fundamental trends in stock prices, they say."

A shift in investor psychology, coupled with a perceived increase in market illiquidity and security riskiness, could explain why the market failed to rebound as the immediate effects of synthetic portfolio insurance selling waned. In fact, investors fled the market in droves after the

crash. Many individual investors were traumatized by the crash and reduced their equity holdings for the long term (*Barron's*, October 10, 1988).

Institutional investors also retreated from the market. A survey of the
nation's largest pension funds conducted several months after the crash
found that 7.5 percent had made significant asset allocation shifts,
reducing their long-term equity commitments by an average of 8 percent, or an estimated $10.4 billion. Another 10 percent of pension plans
were considering reducing their long-term equity exposure (see Chernoff
1988).

Of course, insured investors also contributed to the post-crash depression in stock prices. When the market was soaring, earlier in 1987, they
had been almost fully invested in stocks. After the crash, they were either
stopped out of stocks or held significantly smaller positions than before.
They could repurchase stocks only by canceling their insurance policies
(and many eventually did).

As the trauma wore off and economic fundamentals continued strong,
investors gradually returned to the market. It should not be surprising,
however, that it took two years for the market to surpass its precrash
highs. Given the dramatic shifts in asset allocation and investor psychology
caused by the crash, it is farfetched to believe that the market would
have rebounded more quickly. Lack of an immediate bounce back thus
does not exonerate portfolio insurance.

Insurers Far From Only Sellers

Obviously, a lot of investors were sellers during the crash. But was selling concentrated in any one group of investors? Barrie Wigmore (1998),
for one, suggests that the withdrawal from the market of foreign and
mutual fund investors had a greater impact than trading by portfolio
insurers.

At the time of the crash, however, there was little mention of excessive selling by non-US investors. The *Wall Street Journal* (October 20,
1987: 1) noted that sales by foreigners on the 19th were modest, certainly "not enough to suggest that they were bailing out completely."
Steve Lohr, in the *New York Times* (October 23, 1987: D1), reported
that, far from fleeing New World markets, "many foreign investors were
focusing on the good that might result: that the plunge might finally scare
Washington into cutting the budget deficit." The SEC (1988: 2.17–2.18)
concluded that selling by foreign investors did not account for a substantial amount of sales on October 19.

Mutual funds did sell substantial amounts of stock, but they also bought
stock. On Monday, October 19, one major mutual fund group (later

FIGURE 11.1

Stock (NYSE) Sales and Purchases by Large Institutional Investors
(millions of dollars)*

	October 15	October 16	October 19	October 20
SELL				
Portfolio insurers	$257	$566	$1,748	$698
Other pension	190	794	875	334
Trading-oriented investors	1,156	1,446	1,751	1,740
Mutual funds	1,419	1,339	2,168	1,726
Other financial	516	959	1,416	1,579
Total	3,538	5,104	7,598	6,077
Index arbitrage (included in above)	717	1,592	1,774	128

	October 15	October 16	October 19	October 20
BUY				
Portfolio insurers	$201	$161	$449	$863
Other pension	368	773	1,481	920
Trading-oriented investors	1,026	1,081	1,316	1,495
Mutual funds	998	1,485	1,947	1,858
Other financial	798	1,221	2,691	2,154
Total	3,391	4,721	7,884	7,290
Index arbitrage (included in above)	407	394	110	32

* Sample does not include: (1) individual investors, (2) institutional accounts with purchases and sales less than $10 million per day and (3) certain sizable broker/dealer trades.

Source: *Report of the Presidential Task Force on Market Mechanisms* (Brady Commission), 1988.

identified as Fidelity Investments) sold $500 million of stock in the first half hour of trading (after having off-loaded about $90 million in London before the open in New York). By the end of the day, Fidelity had sold a total of 25.8 million shares (Brady Commission 1988: IV.1).

Most funds did not do a lot of selling, however. As of the weekend preceding the crash, both Merrill Lynch and Dreyfus reported no significant redemptions (*New York Times*, October 17, 1987: 1). A survey by the Investment Company Institute reveals that only about 2 percent of equity mutual fund shares were redeemed on Friday, October 16 and Monday, October 19. Furthermore, most funds were able to meet

FIGURE 11.2

Futures (CME) Sales and Purchases by Large Traders (millions of dollars)

SELL

	October 14	October 15	October 16	October 19	October 20
Portfolio insurers	$534	$968	$2,123	$4,037	$2,818
Arbitrageurs	$108	$407	$392	$129	$31
Options	$554	$998	$1,399	$898	$635
Locals	$7,325	$7,509	$7,088	$5,479	$2,718
Other pension	$37	$169	$234	$631	$514
Trading-oriented investors	$1,993	$2,050	$3,373	$2,590	$2,765
Foreign	$398	$442	$479	$494	$329
Mutual funds	$46	$3	$11	$19	$40
Other financial	$49	$109	$247	$525	$303
Published total	$16,949	$18,830	$19,640	$18,987	$13,641
Volume accounted for	$11,045	$12,655	$15,347	$14,801	$10,152
Percent accounted for	65.2	67.2	78.1	78.0	74.4
Portfolio insurance: Percent of publicly accounted for volume	14.37	18.80	25.70	43.30	37.91

BUY

	October 14	October 15	October 16	October 19	October 20
Portfolio insurers	$71	$171	$109	$113	$505
Arbitrageurs	$1,313	$717	$1,705	$1,582	$119
Options	$594	$864	$1,254	$915	$544
Locals	$7,301	$7,530	$7,125	$5,682	$2,689
Other pension	$90	$76	$294	$447	$1,070
Trading-oriented investors	$1,494	$2,236	$3,634	$4,510	$4,004
Foreign	$240	$298	$443	$609	$418
Mutual funds	$0	$27	$73	$143	$51
Other financial	$155	$57	$126	$320	$517
Published total	$16,949	$18,830	$19,640	$18,987	$13,641
Volume accounted for	$11,259	$11,976	$14,763	$14,320	$9,915
Percent accounted for	66.4	63.6	75.2	75.4	72.7
Portfolio insurance: Percent of publicly accounted for volume	1.80	3.86	1.43	1.31	6.98

Source: Report of the Presidential Task Force on Market Mechanisms (Brady Commission), 1988.

redemptions from available cash reserves. Fidelity, whose huge Magellan Fund maintained fully invested positions, was the notable exception.

As noted in chapter 10, the Brady Commission (1988: 36) did find selling concentrated in the hands of portfolio insurers, with insurance sales on October 19 accounting for 21 percent of total futures volume and up to 43 percent of volume exclusive of locals' transactions. But Merton Miller and his colleagues (1989: 7), based on their report for the CME, argue that "it is important to keep the portfolio insurance sales in perspective. On the 19th, portfolio insurance sales of futures represented somewhere between 20 and 30 percent of the share equivalent of total sales on the NYSE. The pressure of selling on the NYSE by other investors (mutual funds, security dealers and individual shareholders) was thus three to five times greater than that of the portfolio insurers." Similarly, Franklin Edwards (1988b: 237) states that "the fact that such [portfolio insurance] sales were 20 percent of total futures sales on October 19 . . . suggests that such sales were *not* a dominant feature of the sell-off. Eighty percent of the sales came from other sources!" (See also Malkiel 1988: 10.)

But the unidirectional nature of insurance trading contrasts with the trading practices of other portfolio strategies. Traditional asset allocation methods take a variety of divergent approaches toward gauging the future course of the market. Portfolio insurance strategies are keyed solely to market moves. Unlike traditional allocation methods, portfolio insurance calls consistently for selling during a downturn. The SEC (1988: 3.14) finds that this practice leads to more concentrated selling pressure than that generated by traditional methods.

This is evident in the transaction figures for the crash. According to the Brady Commission's (1988: III–35, 36) survey of large institutional investors, portfolio insurers were the only group whose sales far overwhelmed their purchases in both the stock and futures markets. Index arbitrage selling was concentrated in the stock market, where arbitragers sold sixteen times as much as they bought on the 19th; however, in the futures market, they bought about twelve times as much as they sold. Similarly, futures purchases by mutual funds far outweighed their sales. Even in the stock market, if one excepts Fidelity, mutual funds in the aggregate were net buyers on October 19. In contrast, portfolio insurers not only sold thirty-six times as much as they bought in the futures market, they also sold four times as much as they bought in the stock market (as the sharp discounts in the futures market forced them to sell stock directly in order to reduce their equity exposures).

Furthermore, as we have noted, the amount of insurance-related selling during the crash extended beyond the sales by insured investors themselves. To their sales must be added those of frontrunners selling in anticipation of insurance sales, as well as mutual fund and other investors selling in reaction to insurance-induced price declines.

Estimates of the amount of insured assets at the time of the crash range from $60 billion to $100 billion. This represents 2.0 to 3.5 percent of the US market's capitalization on October 16, 1987.[1] It is hardly surprising that most trading on the 19th came from investors other than insurers. When one considers the intensity of trading by insurers and its influence on other investors' trading decisions, however, it becomes apparent that insurance selling on October 19 had an effect far greater than the relatively small amount of insured assets would imply.

Investors Would Have Sold Anyway

LOR's John O'Brien has argued that, even in "difficult moments, portfolio insurance is better than the 'panic selling' to which big investors might otherwise be driven" (*Wall Street Journal*, October 14, 1986: C6). LOR's Robert Ferguson (1989: 44) takes a similar tack: "One thing is certain. Portfolio insurance attracts investors who sell in down markets. These investors may well have felt less secure without a formal portfolio insurance program. If so, they might have sold even more on October 19."

But pension plans are not generally geared up to sell significant percentages of their equities in one trading day, as insurers did during the crash. Had they not been insured, these pension plans would probably have sold substantially less stock. In fact, among pension plans not utilizing portfolio insurance, only 7 percent sold stock on October 19, while 17 percent were net buyers, and 74 percent did little or no trading (Brady Commission 1988: V.18). By contrast, all insured pension plans would have been required by their insurance programs to sell futures or stocks on the 19th.

Rubinstein (1988: 45–6) in effect admits that portfolio insurance did lead to more selling than would otherwise have occurred during the crash – because investors were overinsured:

> Even before the crash, it seemed that many investors who had attempted to buy portfolio insurance had selected policies containing "too much insurance." . . . After the crash, when many insured investors were completely in cash, and required by the initial policy to remain in cash for some time, these investors showed their true intentions by quickly "reinsuring" and moving to a more balanced position. It was not that these investors did not want insurance; rather, they wanted much less insurance than indicated by their initially stated intentions.

FIGURE 11.3
Actions Taken by Non-Insured Pension Funds During Crash

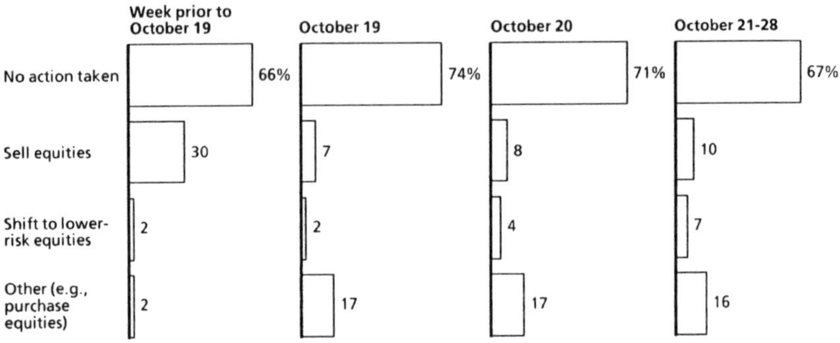

	Week prior to October 19	October 19	October 20	October 21-28
No action taken	66%	74%	71%	67%
Sell equities	30	7	8	10
Shift to lower-risk equities	2	2	4	7
Other (e.g., purchase equities)	2	17	17	16

Source: *Report of the Presidential Task Force on Market Mechanisms*
(Brady Commission), 1988.

While some investors may have decided they needed less insurance, many others decided they did not want any insurance at all. Black (1988: 272) finds that "the most important fact in sorting through the story behind October 19 is the termination of portfolio insurance strategies after the crash." The overpurchase of insurance in the months prior to the crash, spurred no doubt by the vigorous marketing efforts of insurance vendors, caused more stock liquidations than otherwise would have occurred on October 19.

Insurance Sales Insufficient

Leland argues (*New York Times,* January 17, 1988: C1) that insurance sales were too small to account for the crash: "Portfolio insurance selling on October 19 was equal to just two tenths of 1 per cent of the total value of stocks. It is hard for me to believe that such a small amount of selling drove down the market by 20 percent."[2] He asks (Leland 1988b: 84): "Is 15 percent [of total selling] enough to trigger a large fall? There is no easy answer to this question. A natural interpretation would be that it caused 15 percent of the decline."[3]

Leland and Rubinstein (1988a: 49) themselves argue that, when it comes to explaining stock price movements, the market should be treated as much smaller than its actual size: "Most 'investors' have other things on their minds besides the securities markets; they work during the day and spend time with their families in the evening. Most investors don't know what stocks are worth, tacitly leaving this valuation up to a small set of professional investors. But only a subset of these stand ready to make active investment decisions."

If the market should be treated as much smaller than its actual size for the purpose of explaining stock price movements, comparing the amount of portfolio insurance trading with the market's total capitalization is misleading. It is much more relevant to compare the demands for liquidity on the part of portfolio insurers during the crash with the market's available liquidity.

Chapter 9 discussed in some detail the problems that synthetic portfolio insurance may pose for market liquidity. In effect, because a market move of sufficient magnitude will cause all insured investors to trade in the same direction, and because their trades will generally be made much faster and represent a much larger percentage of their portfolios than the potentially counterbalancing trades of, say, value investors, portfolio insurance may demand more liquidity than the market can provide. According to Arnold Kling's (1988) model of the 1987 crash, if 99 percent of investors have very diffuse beliefs regarding possible future returns, but the remaining 1 percent all decide to sell at the same time, prices can fall dramatically, even though the returns expected by the majority of investors have changed little, if at all.

Michael Brennan and Eduardo Schwartz (1989) conclude that even modest levels of portfolio insurance can impose major strains on market liquidity, since the associated trading volume may be large relative to normal levels. They show, for example, that if portfolio insurance represents 5 percent of the market, each 1 percent change in stock prices induces portfolio insurance-related trading equal in value to about 0.1 percent of the value of the market.

On October 19, 1987, the market fell over 20 percent. According to Brennan and Schwartz's estimates, a drop of this magnitude would have called for portfolio insurance trading equivalent to 2 percent of the market. Compare this figure with the average daily turnovers of the NYSE and the S&P 500 futures contract in 1986 – 0.3 percent and 0.5 percent, respectively. Insurers simply required far more liquidity than the system could provide.[4]

Leland himself (1988b: 86) admits that:

> On October 19th, the amount of selling by portfolio insurance alone far overwhelmed the total capital (estimated at $4 billion) of all specialists combined. And of course, there were many other sellers as well. In sum, the short-run supply of liquidity available from market makers was incapable of handling the demands from liquidity traders. This explains why the market could drop more than 20 percent on less than a 1 percent decline in the demand for stocks.

Of course, here Leland looks to pin the crash on the inadequacy of specialist capital, rather than asking why a level of capitalization that had served adequately for so many years suddenly proved inadequate on October 19, 1987.

Similarly, Franklin Edwards (1988b: 238) argues that "the buyers who were not there on October 19 were just as responsible for the price decline as the sellers who were there." But this seems rather like blaming the victim. Imagine trying to locate, under the best of circumstances, buyers for 600 million shares of stock, over three times the average daily volume at the time, and 162,000 futures contracts, twice the average daily volume. Then consider the conditions of the markets during the crash: orders being delayed or lost, markets moving so fast and unpredictably that prices were simply unknown, mechanical failures, and panic.

Based on their analyses of portfolio insurance trading as a percentage of actual trading volume, the Brady Commission (1988) and the SEC (1988) conclude that portfolio insurers played a major role in the crash. Moreover, both the Brady Commission and the SEC find that trades by portfolio insurers alone understate the impact of insurance on the market. Some knowledgeable investors traded in anticipation of the insurers' trades, adding to selling pressure. Rubinstein (1992) himself admits this, asking: "How should we count sales, which although they were not made by portfolio insurers, were nonetheless made in anticipation of sales by insurers?"

Insurance Trades Not Correlated with Market Moves

The Brady Commission (1988) and the SEC (1988), as noted, found a relationship between the timing of portfolio insurance trades and intraday price movements during the crash. Dean Furbush (1989) reports that prices tended to fall at times of above-average portfolio insurance selling on October 16 and 20, but he does not find a significant relationship on the 19th.

The CFTC (1988: viii) finds that "portfolio hedge sales of futures contracts were persistent throughout the day [October 19], but the highs and lows of that activity did not correspond with the periods of greatest weakness or recovery of futures prices." Miller et al. (1989: 7) also dispute the finding of a correspondence between insurance trading and market moves. But they concede that "no reliable methods exist for relating observed price changes in active, competitive markets to the actions of particular sellers or buyers. Hence we chose not to attempt the detailed, almost tick-by-tick account of trading presented in the Brady and SEC Reports."

Instead, Miller et al. (1989: 7) attempt to deflect criticism of portfolio insurance trading by ridiculing the analyses of the Brady Commission and the SEC:

The SEC Report notes that portfolio insurance and index arbitrage, though accounting for no more than 20 percent of S&P 500 volume during the entire day of the 19th, and no more than 40 percent in the fateful 1.00–2.00 p.m. EST hour, did account for "more than 60 percent of S&P 500 stock volume in three ten minute intervals within that hour." (SEC 1988: xiii, fn. 2) But . . . there must surely have been shorter intervals in which portfolio insurance trades approached 100 percent of total market trades!

Ferguson (1989: 44) agrees, terming the SEC's findings the "fallacy of trading density": "There will always be short time intervals during which the designated culprits [portfolio insurers] are responsible for a majority of the selling. After all, as a time interval including a designated culprit's sale approaches zero, the percentage of stock sold by the designated culprit approaches 100."

Based on this logic, one could reason that Muhammad Ali's punches did not defeat Joe Frazier, because analyses of those brief instants when punches were landed are invalid. But if one considers the whole fight, there is a clear relationship between Ali's punches and Frazier's loss.

In any event, there are several reasons why any analyses that focus on the absence or presence of intense trading over finite periods understate portfolio insurance's role in the crash. First, chaotic market conditions resulted in many trade times being incorrectly recorded. Second, the presence of frontrunners selling in anticipation of insurers makes it difficult to locate a portfolio insurance effect (Gammill and Marsh 1988: 38–9). Third, uncompleted portfolio insurance sales acted as a depressant on the market, independent of the price impact of completed insurance sales.

Perhaps most importantly, insurers threw out their rule books during the crash. The SEC (1988: 2.21) finds that, rather than selling after price declines, as their trading rules required, "portfolio insurers appear to have used periods of strength in the futures market . . . to sell some of their 'overhang' of sales." Leland (1988b: 84) uses the fact that insurance sales were made at "times when the stock index was moving in a (relatively) positive direction" as an exoneration of portfolio insurance. But the insurance sales during brief periods of market strength, in contradiction to the strategy's trading rules, merely highlight the infeasibility of dynamic hedging during a market break. They also likely dampened any nascent market rallies.

Summary

The proponents of synthetic portfolio insurance argue that, if insurance had been the main culprit in the crash, the market would have bounced back much sooner than it actually did. But investors, both retail and institutional, fled the market in droves after the crash, because it frightened them. Their asset allocations contained substantially less equity after the crash than before.

Defenders of portfolio insurance also argue that insurers were not the only sellers during the crash, and in any case did not sell enough to account for the dramatic drop in prices on October 19. But portfolio insurers sold more intensively than any other single group of investors. Furthermore, although insurance sales may not have accounted for the majority of futures or stock trades at all times during the crash, constant selling pressure from insurers, combined with that from frontrunners attempting to stay ahead of insurance sales and the repressive effect on buying activity of overhangs of pending insurance sales, overwhelmed the market's ability to provide liquidity.

Finally, the CFTC, among others, argues that portfolio insurance could not have played a major role in the 1987 crash because insurance sales did not coincide with the points of greatest selling pressure. But this ignores the chaotic conditions that prevailed during the crash, when trades were delayed and misrecorded, if they were completed at all. It also ignores the fact that the effects of insurance trading may be distributed over time, with frontrunners selling in anticipation of insurers and uncompleted insurance trades exerting a downward influence on prices. Furthermore, many insurers during the crash exploited temporary price rebounds to execute their sales, contrary to the strategy's rules, dampening any attempts by the market to rally (and hindering attempts to pinpoint insurance's role in the crash!).

Notes

1   Given the $2,813 billion capitalization of the Wilshire 5000.
2   See also Leland and O'Brien (1988: 26) and Leland and Rubinstein (1988a: 49).
3   Later, however, writing with Gerard Gennotte, Leland demonstrated how, if the market is unaware of insurers' trading intentions, insured assets amounting to only 5 percent of the market can set off a market decline of 30 percent (Gennotte and Leland 1990: 1015–17).
4   Brennan and Schwartz (1989) also find that, in a world of "perfect markets," in which the activities of portfolio insurers are fully anticipated, portfolio insurance will have only small effects on market volatility. But perfect market conditions of rational investor expectations, continuously functioning markets, and continual optimization by all investors do not hold in the real world.

12

Alibis II: Across Time and Space

Any plausible theory of market crashes . . . should be able to explain October 28, 1929. . . . This would seem to preclude blaming the 1987 crash solely on instruments and techniques which were not available in 1929.

Hayne Leland, 1987

The overall [worldwide] pattern . . . suggests the presence of some underlying fundamental factor. . . . This would not be the observed empirical pattern, if, for instance, portfolio insurance and program trading in New York and Chicago were the basic triggers of the worldwide crash.

Richard Roll, 1988b

Another school of portfolio insurance defenses argues that synthetic insurance trading could not have been a primary factor in the 1987 crash because it was not a factor at other times when, or in other markets where, crashes occurred. This school offers three basic alibis:

1 Portfolio insurance cannot explain the 1929 crash.
2 Portfolio insurance cannot explain why stocks not in the S&P 500 crashed.
3 Portfolio insurance cannot explain the crashes in non-US markets.

Explaining the 1929 Crash

Hayne Leland (1987: 1–2) asserts that "any plausible theory of market crashes must be able to explain more than just the crash of October 1987. It should be able to explain October 28, 1929, and perhaps other financial 'panics' as well. This would seem to preclude blaming the 1987 crash solely on instruments and techniques which were not available in 1929." Lester Telser (1989: 101–2) and Robert Ferguson (1989: 49) make a similar point.

This line of reasoning would suggest that high-powered rifles should not be considered when analyzing President Kennedy's assassination because such weapons were not available when Julius Caesar was assassinated. But if one focuses on enduring causes and effects, rather than specific instruments, one may find many instances in which history does repeat itself. There are, for example, some striking similarities between the crashes of 1929 and 1987.

Leland (1987: 2) himself suggests one similarity: "While portfolio insurance did not exist in 1929, investors were using hedging techniques (such as 'stop-loss' orders) which are closely related." In fact, an even closer parallel than stop-loss orders exists between the crashes of 1929 and 1987. It turns out that the mechanisms and the impact of portfolio insurance in the 1980s bear a strong resemblance to how margin speculation worked in the 1920s, and how it brought down the stock market in October 1929.[1]

Margin Calls in 1929

Between 1925 and 1928, the market rose over 200 percent. The gain reflected a spurt in new consumer goods (including radios and automobiles), the maturing of the Liberty bonds sold to finance World War I, and a US interest rate kept artificially low to bolster the British pound (Geisst 1997). But margin credit also played a significant role.[2] Margins were unregulated at that time and exhibited considerable variation across brokerage firms. Minimum margins were customarily on the order of 10 to 25 percent; the average effective margin rate was about 50 percent in October 1929.[3] Just as margin investing facilitated the purchase of stocks in 1929, portfolio insurance increased the demand for equities in the 1980s.

While margin credit abetted the market's rise in 1929, the stock sales forced by margin calls exacerbated the ensuing crash.[4] The Securities Exchange Act of 1934 recognized this, empowering the Board of Governors of the Federal Reserve System to regulate margin credit in the hope of preventing subsequent collapses.[5] Just as margin liquidations contributed to the 1929 crash, the forced selling of stock by insurers served to undermine the market in 1987.

The potential selling pressure from portfolio insurers was similar in magnitude to that from margined stockholders in 1929. Just prior to the

1929 crash, NYSE broker loans totaled 9.8 percent of NYSE market capitalization.[6] This figure, however, overstates the amount of stock bought on credit. While most broker loans were made to cover margin loans, some were made for other purposes. Also, not all margin loans were used for security purchases, the securities purchased on margin were not all stocks, and the collateral did not consist solely of stocks, but also included bonds (Brady Commission 1988: VIII.13). Stocks bought on margin collateralized by bonds would have been subject to fewer margin calls than stocks bought on margin collateralized by other stocks. Margin loans thus effectively accounted for less than 9.8 percent of market capitalization at the 1929 market peak.

Just prior to the 1987 crash, insured assets amounted to about 3 percent of the market's total capitalization. Of course, the extent of forced selling that results from a given market decline differs between and across portfolio insurers and margined stockholders, so these percentages are not directly comparable without further analysis.

As noted, the average margin rate was 50 percent in October 1929. With a 10 percent drop in the market, an 11 percent liquidation of assets would be required to restore this margin level.[7] Portfolio insurers facing a similar decline would be forced to sell anywhere from under 10 percent to up to 50 percent of their insured assets, depending on the specifications of their insurance programs. The average sale would constitute 23 percent of assets (Brady Commission 1988: V.17). Of course, not all insurance-mandated sell orders were executed during the 1987 crash; many insurers chose not to (or could not) complete their mandated sell programs. But neither were all required margin liquidations carried out in 1929 (Kindleberger 1986: 106).

While a larger proportion of equities was margined in 1929 than was insured in 1987, the liquidations triggered by a given market decline appear to be greater for insured strategies than for margined strategies. Also, margin calls in 1929 were often met by providing additional collateral rather than by selling stocks, whereas insured investors must sell stocks (or stock index futures) in order to maintain their insurance protection. A market decline may thus have unleashed as much selling pressure from insurers in 1987 as from margin speculators in 1929.[8]

There is, however, a major difference between 1929 and 1987 in how rapidly selling pressure was unleashed as the market decline began. In 1929, brokers generally possessed an unequivocal power to sell out client positions whenever margin was impaired. Margins were recalculated daily, based on closing prices. Beginning on October 19, 1929, each day's decline prompted a new wave of margin calls, culminating in the crash on October 28 and 29. During the 1987 crash, computers could often generate insurance-mandated sell orders in a matter of seconds, rather than days.

In terms of actual trading, margin liquidations totaled at most 25 percent of volume during the 1929 crash (Brady Commission 1988: VIII.13). Net selling by portfolio insurers comprised about 25 percent of total NYSE volume on October 19, 1987.[9] As a percentage of trading volume, liquidations by portfolio insurers in 1987 were as substantial as margin liquidations in 1929. In short, the rapid forced selling by insurers in 1987 may well have played as large a role as margin calls did in 1929. Different instruments, both requiring essentially automated trading in the same direction as the market, led to a similar bloodletting.

Stocks Not in the S&P 500 Crashed

Ferguson (1989: 43) argues that if portfolio insurance was responsible for the crash, "then the decline in S&P 500 stocks (on which the primary futures contract is based) should have exceeded the decline in non-S&P 500 stocks. That there was no unusual difference between S&P index stocks and other stocks suggests that the futures market had no impact whatsoever on the severity of the S&P 500's decline." But the evidence belies Ferguson's claim. In fact, as Marshall Blume and his colleagues (1989) demonstrate, S&P 500 stocks were down a significant 7.4 percent more than non-S&P 500 stocks on October 19.[10]

Furthermore, in a study of the impact of earnings announcements on stock prices during the crash period, Robert Bowen and his colleagues (1989) find a significant difference between NYSE and NASDAQ stocks, with NASDAQ but not NYSE stocks reacting in an expected manner to earnings news during October 19 and 20. They attribute the difference to the impact of portfolio insurance and other program trading, which would have disrupted NYSE but not NASDAQ stocks.

Explaining the International Crash

One of the popular arguments against portfolio insurance as a major causative factor in the 1987 crash rests on the international scope of the debacle. Mark Rubinstein (1988: 42) asserts that "the case that portfolio insurance was a substantial contributor to the market crash is . . . somewhat weakened by the fact that portfolio insurance currently plays a very small role in foreign markets, and yet the crash was international in scope." Merton Miller and his colleagues (1988: 208), in a report for the Chicago Mercantile Exchange, make a similar point: "Price falls as large, and market conditions as chaotic, as those in the US occurred in many countries on the 19th, even in those with no portfolio insurance or index futures markets."

FIGURE 12.1
The International Crash

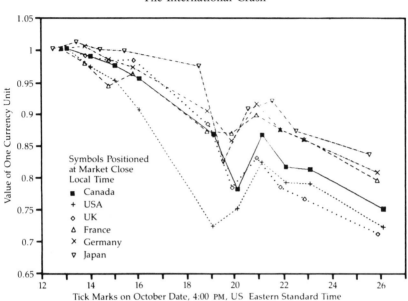

Source: Richard Roll, "The International Crash of October 1987,"
Financial Analysts Journal, September/October 1988, p. 26.

Richard Roll has developed this line of reasoning more extensively than
anyone else. He maintains that the worldwide crash did not originate
in the US market because markets overseas were the first to drop: "Most
of the other markets around the world displayed dramatic declines on
their October 19, foreshadowing the crash in North America." Roll
concedes that "there remains the possibility that other market crashes,
though generally occurring before the major US crash, were in fact precipitated by the relatively modest US decline from October 14 through
16" (Roll 1988b: 22).

But the US decline of 10 percent from Wednesday the 14th through
Friday the 16th was hardly "relatively modest." As we noted earlier,
it was, in fact, the sharpest drop over such a short time period since
the fall of continental Europe in World War II (Mitchell and Netter
1989). Furthermore, a chronological review of worldwide market returns
reveals that non-US markets crashed after, not before, the US. This is
evident from Roll's (1989b) own graphs of daily prices in major markets (although Roll's interpretation differs from ours). From October 1
to October 16, the last trading day before the crash, the US market had
slipped about 12 percent, far more than any non-US market.[11]

On Monday, October 19, the Asian markets, among the first to trade each calendar day, opened to significantly bad news. Friday's sharp sell-off on Wall Street, which came on the heels of two prior down days, had occurred after the Asian markets had closed. Furthermore, military hostilities between the US and Iran were escalating in the Persian Gulf, and US Treasury Secretary Baker threatened, over the weekend, to let the dollar decline in order to combat the Bundesbank's tightening of German interest rates. In the light of the news, it is not surprising that the Asian markets were down on the 19th. Even so, the average Asian market decline from October 1 through 19 was less than the US market decline through its close on the 16th.

The European markets were the next to trade on the 19th, and they fell sharply. Leland and Rubinstein (1988a: 45) highlight the 10 percent drop in London on Monday as setting the stage for the US crash. But the London market had been effectively closed on the previous Friday because of extremely adverse weather conditions (International Stock Exchange 1989: 276). As a result, much of the decline on the 19th in London may be attributable to the previous Friday's decline in the US. Also, US institutional investors (notably Fidelity Investments), wishing to get a jump on the New York opening, sold in European markets early in the day. By the end of the day in Europe, of course, markets there were feeling the effects of the crash in New York. Even so, the average European market decline from October 1 through Monday the 19th, the day of the crash, was less than the US market's decline through the Friday preceding the crash. The rest of the world clearly lagged behind the US market decline through the 19th.

The 22.6 percent US crash on October 19 in turn triggered crashes around the globe. The Asian markets were devastated on the 20th. The Tokyo exchange closed down a record 14.9 percent that Tuesday, despite delayed openings in 95 percent of its stocks and price-limit circuit breakers halting trading in half of its names. The markets in Australia and New Zealand were also off sharply. The European markets, which had witnessed the start of the US crash the previous Monday afternoon, were hit hard on Tuesday, with London experiencing the most extreme drop, off 11.5 percent. While the rest of the world's markets reeled from the US crash the day before, the US market, always the last to trade, rose on October 20, closing up 5.9 percent. All major international markets rose on Wednesday the 21st.

To market observers at the time, the epicenter of the crash certainly seemed to be New York. In London, Nigel Lawson, chancellor of the exchequer, noted: "This began on Wall Street. It has a lot to do with the American market and a lack of confidence in the US" (*New York Times*, October 21, 1987: D16). After the US market bottomed, a London-based analyst reported that "European stock exchanges . . . rebounded strongly from record losses posted earlier in the week as markets continued to follow Wall Street's unprecedented moves" (*Wall Street Journal*, October 22, 1987: 46).

Quoted in the *Wall Street Journal* (October 20, 1987: 50), Ruediger von Rosen, executive vice chairman of West Germany's stock exchanges, blamed the German market crash on a "significant dependence on Wall Street." In the same article, a fund manager in Stockholm noted that "New York can just drag the whole Swedish market lower because of those listings"; most large Swedish firms also trade in the US markets.

Peter J. Morgan, chief economist for Barclays de Zoete Wedd, Tokyo, attributed the Japanese market's collapse to Wall Street: "It's a reaction to New York. It's just coming out of the clear blue sky. There's nothing domestically that would lead to this" (*New York Times*, October 20, 1987: D1). Masaaki Kurokawa, chairman of Nomura Securities International, said "it is evident that major events abroad have always had a hefty impact on the Japanese stock market. October 19 was no exception" (Kurokawa 1988: 4).

Regulatory agencies corroborate the US market's lead. The SEC (1988: 11.8) finds that the US market led Japan and the UK during the crash and concludes that "a cataclysmic market event such as that which occurred on October 19 can be expected to have worldwide repercussions." The International Stock Exchange (1989: 283) concurs, noting that "by the next morning [Tuesday, October 20] perceptions had changed due largely to the dramatic 509 point fall in the Dow Jones Industrial Average Index on the NYSE overnight."

More formal inquiries have also detected a leading role for the US. Using the *Financial Times* indexes of share price movements in twenty-three countries (available only since January 1987), Elisabetta Bertero and Colin Mayer (1990) find that the US market led non-US markets from Friday, October 16 through Wednesday, October 21, falling more than other markets on Friday and recovering ahead on Tuesday.

While the magnitude of price movements in October 1987 was certainly unusual, the fact that the US led the rest of the world was not at all unusual. Cheol Eun and Sangdal Shim (1989) analyze daily returns from nine large markets over the 1979–85 period prior to the crash and find the US to be by far the most influential. While US stock market movements are rapidly transmitted to other markets, no single non-US market can significantly explain US market movements. Furthermore, an analysis of daily returns from twenty-three countries' stock market indexes over the 1986–8 crash period confirms that the US market led most other national markets (Fischer and Palasvirta 1990: 389). Using daily returns from 1985–8, Yasushi Hamao and his colleagues

(1990) also find that US stock price volatility leads volatility in Japan and the UK.

Wen-Ling Lin and his colleagues (1994) take issue with the findings that suggest the transmission of market movements flows only from New York to other markets, and not in the other direction. Examining intraday data from New York and Tokyo over the period from late 1985 through 1989, they find that return and volatility in one market can affect the opening in the other market, with the influence being bidirectional. This may be true in general, but, in the case of the crash of 1987, the chronological evidence clearly indicates transmission from the US to the rest of the world. Even Lin, writing with Takatoshi Ito (undated), finds return spillovers from New York to Tokyo during the crash period.

The Synchronization of World Markets

International market returns have always been somewhat correlated; even in 1929, when the world and its financial markets were presumably far less integrated than they are today, international markets crashed more or less simultaneously.[12] As Roll (1988b: 21) points out, however, the synchronized behavior in October 1987 was unprecedented. In fact, October 1987 was the only month during the period from January 1981 through December 1987 in which all twenty-three international markets he examined moved in the same direction, most falling more than 20 percent.[13] Bertero and Mayer (1990: 1168–71) note that the correlations of various markets' daily returns increased sharply during the crash, and that the highest correlations were observed between countries in consecutive time zones, suggesting a geographic progression of price signals, with the US leading the way.

This unusual synchronization of international market returns leads Roll (1988b: 21–2) to conclude that "an international trigger . . . swamped the usual influences of country-specific events." He suggests that the trigger was some unidentified fundamental factor, and not portfolio insurance: "The overall pattern . . . suggests the presence of some underlying fundamental factor. . . . This would not be the observed empirical pattern, if, for instance, portfolio insurance and program trading in New York and Chicago were the basic triggers of the worldwide crash."

Bertero and Mayer (1990) can also find no significant evidence of a structural element, such as program trading or the existence of stock index futures, affecting international market declines in the crash period. As we have already noted, however, price signals in the US market in the three trading days prior to the crash contributed to the US crash on the 19th. It is likely that these same signals were also transmitted to non-US markets.

Supporting the view that price signals can transmit a crash internationally, Paul Bennett and Jeanette Kelleher (1988) maintain that traders adopt a conditioned response to foreign price changes even when they do not fully understand the underlying cause. In effect, the positive correlation between price movements in international markets can become self-reinforcing. Their analysis reveals that volatility spreads from market to market, and that correlations between markets have generally increased.

Bennett and Kelleher note that the degree to which volatility spread in October 1987 was unusual, even after taking into account the trend toward more integrated international markets. They suggest (p. 26) that "a wave of panicky selling circled the globe, with traders paying an unusually large amount of attention to price developments in foreign markets in the absence of fundamental news sufficient to account for the disruption."[14]

Bertero and Mayer (1990) examine the role of direct international market linkages, including the listing and trading of shares on foreign markets. They hypothesize (p. 1173) that "arbitraging of foreign share prices creates a mechanism by which idiosyncratic news, that would normally only affect domestic markets, is transmitted internationally." They find that correlations are higher between markets with strong interlinkages. But Robert Aderhold and his colleagues (1988), examining such linkages (including cross-border selling and stock trading outside the home market), find that these cannot explain the worldwide crash. Rather, they assert (p. 42): "The principal linkage was most likely an indirect one. . . . In the panicky environment surrounding the crash, market participants interpreted steep price declines in overseas markets as signals of impending declines in their own markets."

Contagion Effects

Mervyn King and Sushil Wadhwani (1990) develop a contagion model of international price transmission that is observationally equivalent to a panic model. They show that rational investors could use price changes in other countries to infer underlying economic fundamentals, even in the absence of news. Given this reliance on price movements, a pricing mistake in one country can be transmitted to other nations. While such contagion effects may not be present in normal market environments, they increase markedly with increases in market volatility.

King and Wadhwani (p. 6) believe "it is difficult to come up with a credible story that links 'fundamentals' to the crash. . . . Moreover it is extremely hard to imagine that any such explanation would be consistent with the uniform decline in equity prices in different countries." But they do find that contagion effects increased in the period during and immediately after the crash and conclude (p. 29) that "the pattern of correlations between markets that is revealed by the data seems easier to reconcile with the contagion model than with a . . . 'fundamentals' model."

Roll (1989: 240) concedes that "a 'contagion' process of the type suggested by King and Wadhwani . . . *would* allow a world-wide crash to begin by a particular news event or even by a market 'mistake' in one country." But he asserts that the same dramatic increase in cross-country correlations during the crash period that would support this hypothesis also supports an alternative theory: that increased volatility during the crash reduced transaction-cost barriers to cross-country arbitrage (see also Neumark et al. 1991).

King and Wadhwani (1990: 31) suggest: "The possibility of contagion means that one cannot assert that, because markets without formal portfolio insurance fell as much as the US market, portfolio insurance could not have been responsible for the crash." In a commentary on Roll, Wadhwani (1989: 256) adds: "It is at least theoretically possible that a US price decline which was exacerbated by portfolio insurance could have been spread to markets without formal portfolio insurance. Of course, in order to make that case, one would still have to find direct evidence that portfolio insurance did contribute to the US price decline."

George Von Furstenberg and Bang Nam Jeon (1989) examine the volatilities of various markets' stock price indexes over the ten months preceding and thirteen months following the crash to determine whether price reactions can be attributed to contagion or to fundamental news of common significance. They find that stock price movements cannot be linked with broad economic fundamentals such as exchange rates, oil prices, or gold prices. They also find that messages between markets tend to be relayed at the level of national market indexes, suggesting that prices respond more to changing opinions about the prospects for stocks in general relative to other assets, than to changes in views about the quality of underlying investments. They conclude that a contagion effect cannot be ruled out.

Relating the work of Von Furstenberg and Nam Jeon to the 1987 market crash, Greg Mankiw (1989: 170) finds that correlations between different countries' markets more than doubled in October. Whether this doubling reflected the globalization of news or the globalization of market psychology, Mankiw argues that the result, according to standard asset pricing models, should have been a doubling in the required rate of return for stock, provided that investors expected the increase to be more than transitory.

King et al. (1994) examine the effects on world markets of both observable variables (including interest rates, exchange rates, the real money supply, and inflation) and other, unobservable variables (whether unobserved fundamentals or psychologically based factors). They find that observable variables can explain only a small portion of the changes in correlations between world markets. They attribute the increase in market correlations at the time of the crash to an increase in the volatility of unobservable factors that affect all stock markets in the same direction. The increase in market correlations may thus be transitory.

Roll (1988b: 30) compares the market declines in nations where computer-directed trading was prevalent with declines in nations where it was not. He finds that declines were greater in those nations without computer-directed trading and concludes that, "taken as a characteristic in isolation, computer-directed trading (for example, portfolio insurance and index arbitrage), if it had any impact at all, actually helped mitigate the market decline." But it is hard to reconcile this statement with his later assertion (1989: 241): "However, no one (including me) argues that the existence of portfolio insurance actually *mitigated* the extent of the crash."

Just because a crash occurred in many countries where portfolio insurance does not exist, such as Mexico and Singapore, does not mean portfolio insurance should be exonerated. The preponderance of the evidence examined suggests that the US market crash precipitated the worldwide crash, and that synthetic portfolio insurance played a major role in the US crash.

Summary

Synthetic portfolio insurance in 1987 performed a role similar to that played by margin speculation in the crash of 1929. Just as margin buying elevated the bull market of the 1920s, portfolio insurance increased the demand for stocks in the 1982–7 period. And, just as the automatic, trend-following stock sales of portfolio insurers exacerbated the 1987 crash, so the trend-following stock sales forced by margin calls accentuated the decline in stock prices in October 1929.

Perhaps the most persistent argument in favor of a benign role for portfolio insurance in the crash rests on the fact that markets around the world fell in October 1987, despite the absence of portfolio insurance programs in markets outside the US. But this viewpoint rests on the assumption that the US market did not lead international markets into the crash. In fact, a great deal of evidence suggests that the 1987 crash was primarily a US event and only secondarily an international one. Declines in non-US markets during October echoed the collapse of the US market. Although synthetic insurance trading may have been limited largely to the US market, its effects were felt around the world.

Notes

1 Mark Rubinstein (1992: 820), too, has drawn a connection between portfolio insurance and earlier strategies with the same underlying mechanisms and the same effects on markets:

> Did you know that a study after the 1946 market crash [reprinted in Miller (1991)] indicated that between 17 percent and 28 percent of the shares sold were sell orders triggered by a mechanically applied formula, even though portfolio insurance hadn't been invented yet? Mechanical trend-following strategies, of which portfolio insurance is but one example, apparently have a long history.

Perhaps a long history, but not apparently an illustrious one.

2 See Federal Reserve System (FRS) (1984: 13–14, 135–40, 165); Galbraith (1988: 18–22, 78); and Kindleberger (1996: 54–8). Note that White (1990) finds that margin credit ballooned because of speculative demand, despite tight monetary policy by the Federal Reserve.

3 For the 10 to 25 percent range, see FRS (1974: 41). For the 50 percent average effective rate, see the Brady Commission (1988: VIII.2) and Galbraith (1988: 32). For a more detailed review of margin practices at the time, see FRS (1984: 45, 85–91).

4 See FRS (1984: 13–14, 135–40, 165) and Galbraith (1988: 36–7, 95, 189). This view is not universally held. See FRS (1984: 157–9) and Miller et al. (1988: 15).

5 See FRS (1984: 46). A study by Hardouvelis (1990a) finds that higher margin requirements are associated with lower stock price volatility. But Hsieh and Miller (1990) find no such evidence, and uncover flaws in Hardouvelis's test design. These findings, however, do not suggest that margin calls play no role in market crashes.

6 NYSE member firm loans were $8.5 billion, compared with NYSE market capitalization of $87.1 billion (see Brady Commission 1988: VIII.13 and FRS 1984: 154–5, fn. 2).

7 Suppose $100 of net worth was levered with a $100 margin loan to purchase a $200 stock portfolio. A 10 percent market drop would reduce the portfolio value to $180 and net worth to $80. A sale of $20 of stock (11 percent of the $180 portfolio) would result in a $160 portfolio and an $80 loan, thereby restoring the 50 percent margin.

Note that in 1933, the NYSE required minimum maintenance margins for the first time. The Securities Exchange Act of 1934 granted authority to the Board of Governors of the Federal Reserve System to set both initial and maintenance margins. The board decided that it would set initial margins and that the exchanges would set maintenance margins, with SEC approval. Initial margins have ranged from 40 to 100 percent, and maintenance margins have been set at 25 percent (FRS 1984: 48, 90). A 10 percent market decline, as in the above example, would not set off a margin call if the maintenance margin was 25 percent. Prior to 1934, however, there was no distinction between initial and maintenance margin rates (FRS 1984: 90).

8 Gennotte and Leland (1994) note that selling forced by margin calls may have led to the 1929 crash, because investors generally were not aware of the motivation for the sales. They believe that forced selling of margined futures positions would have a minimal impact on markets in the 1990s, as open interest in futures is small relative to the total volume of stocks. However, they admit that a decline in the market, leading to a substantial liquidation of futures positions, could have an impact similar to portfolio insurance's impact in 1987.

9 On October 19, 1987, portfolio insurers sold a net $1.3 billion of stock and $3.9 billion of futures. This represented 25 percent of NYSE volume of $21 billion on the 19th (Brady Commission 1988: 43–4, figs 29–32).

10 Blume et al.'s (1989) analysis considers only NYSE-listed stocks, omits those non-S&P 500 stocks smaller than the smallest stock in the S&P 500, and controls for stale prices and the small-firm effect. The return differential significantly narrowed on the morning of Tuesday, October 20.

11 The analysis in this section, as was Roll's, is based on the FT-Actuaries World Indices, compiled by the *Financial Times*, Goldman, Sachs, and Wood MacKenzie in conjunction with the Institute of Actuaries and the Faculty of Actuaries.

12 Kindleberger (1996: 109) makes this point and notes that the likelihood of international markets crashing simultaneously poses problems for investors who seek risk reduction via international diversification.

13 See also Malliaris and Urrutia (1992). For a longer perspective (31 years) on intermarket correlations and correlations during the crash, see Dwyer and Hafer (1988).

14 However, Roll (1989: 223) believes their work suffers from econometric problems.

13

Did Insurance Live Up To Its Name?

Although few insurers missed the minimum return, they were stopped out and forced into cash for the remainder of the life of their policies.

Mark Rubinstein, 1988

Chapter 9 described how portfolio insurance trading can cause an increase in overall market volatility. Essentially, unless there exist sufficient insurance "sellers" ready, willing, and able to buy into the market as prices decline and sell as they rise, insurance buyers' trades will magnify market moves. I have described the consequences of the absence of sufficient trading partners: "If insurers enter the market-place faster than do their partners, the dance becomes one-sided and prices gyrate substantially. The cost of protection rises (as it is primarily based on market volatility), the likelihood of being whipsawed increases, and the chance of a steep descent increases. In this environment, synthetic strategies are more likely to fail" (Jacobs 1987: 79). In contributing to the crash, synthetic portfolio insurance contributed to its own demise.

Crash Conditions

In his own postmortem on the performance of portfolio insurance during the crash, Donald Luskin, senior vice president of Wells Fargo, an LOR licensee, notes:

The severe market decline . . . presented three serious challenges to the effectiveness of portfolio insurance. First, the volatility of the decline was greater than anyone had imagined to be possible. . . . Second, the trading

rules used by some portfolio insurance managers were overwhelmed
by the sheer magnitude and rapidity of the decline. . . . Third, the chaotic
trading conditions . . . led to severe mispricings between stock index
futures and their underlying indexes. . . . Did portfolio insurance pass
the test? Yes, but not with flying colors. (Luskin 1988: 312–13)

Most insurance programs, in fact, did not pass this live stress test, but
rather failed miserably.

Some of the *hourly* stock price moves on October 19–20 were comparable in magnitude to the previous daily record fall of 12.8 percent
on October 28, 1929. The futures markets were no more well behaved.
Before the crash, LOR's Hayne Leland (1986: 33) had asserted that
it was a "myth" that "unexpected high volatility can kill an insurance
program." But the large, and discontinuous, price moves on the 19th
and 20th, along with the resulting chaotic conditions, created major
problems for all insurers.

Mark Rubinstein (1988: 40) himself concedes that it was "probably
impossible" to execute the necessary portfolio insurance trades because
the markets moved so quickly. And when interviewed upon the occasion of the tenth anniversary of the crash (Burton 1997: 24), Leland admitted: "We would have liked to have traded more. But when arbitrageurs
couldn't keep stocks and futures together, futures detached from stock
prices, and by the end were selling at a 10 percent discount. When we
sold, we incurred huge transaction costs." (Note that Leland now shifts
his finger of blame from the market specialists – see chapter 11 – to
arbitragers.)

When the same firm manages the derivatives and the underlying
assets, it can implement hedging in whichever market is most advant-
ageous. Insured S&P 500 index funds, for example, can either hedge
with futures or liquidate stocks. General Motors directed Wells Fargo,
manager of its pension plan's stock index funds, to sell massive quant-
ities of stock on the day of the crash, presumably as part of its portfolio
insurance program. Wells Fargo accordingly sold off over $1 billion in
GM's stock holdings, executing thirteen programs of about $100 mil-
lion each between 10:30 a.m. and 2:00 p.m. W. Gordon Binns, Jr., then
GM's vice president and chief investment funds officer, asserted that this
"wasn't one of those mindlessly computer-driven things" (*Wall Street
Journal*, January 15, 1988: C2). Presumably the judgmental override was
to sell in the stock market, rather than the hopelessly depressed futures
market.

Insurers that had the flexibility to sell in the stock market during
the crash generally fared somewhat better than those confined to the
futures market (see Grannis 1987: 3; Leland 1988b: 82; and Rubinstein

FIGURE 13.1

LOR/Wells Fargo Ad: Hedging with Stock or Futures

Hedged Core strategies

In February Wells Fargo Investment Advisors (WFIA) began managing a unique hedging strategy. This strategy, called Hedged Core^{SM}, allows the pension sponsor to reshape the distribution of return of the S&P 500 Index in a way that works to protect the sponsor from downside risk at a modest cost to upside potential.

Hedged Core, a technique of variable hedging, is implemented with the Wells Fargo Investment Advisors S&P 500 Index Fund and S&P Futures Contracts. The degree of hedging depends on rules derived from the Dynamic Asset Allocation/Fiduciary Hedge Program technology. Because the WFIA S&P 500 Index Fund follows the actual S&P 500 Index within a few basis points per year, crosshedge risk between the futures and the underlying equities is virtually eliminated. Hedged Core, then, offers sponsors a dynamic strategy with the highest level of control. In addition, because futures trading is about one-tenth as costly as equity trading, this highly controlled strategy is carried out at minimum cost.

Frederick L.A. Grauer, Chief Investment Officer of

WFIA describes the Hedged Core strategy as "a perfect complement to the products offered at Wells Fargo Investment Advisors. Hedged Core, like our Index Fund, is a high quality, low cost method of participation in the equity market. The difference is that Hedged Core offers an opportunity to participate in upward movements while diminishing participation in downward movements."

Jeffrey L. Skelton, Chief Research Officer of WFIA, adds: "Hedged Core is here to stay. The payoff patterns offered in the market are limited, while the tastes of investors are as varied as the investors themselves. Hedged Core offers a cheap and reliable method of transforming the payoff patterns offered in the market to those preferred by individual investors and institutions."

WFIA offers dynamic hedging strategies based on the full range of its index products and on the active portfolios of other investment managers. WFIA has committed substantial resources to the development of the Hedged Core technology and the organization necessary to manage these strategies at lowest cost and lowest risk.

WELLS FARGO INVESTMENT ADVISORS
WELLS FARGO BANK, N.A.

Hedged Core is a service mark of Wells Fargo Investment Advisors.

Source: LOR Sponsored Section, Institutional Investor, 1984, p. 5.

1988: 41). Even firms that enjoyed this flexibility, however, found it difficult to hedge properly. According to the Securities and Exchange Commission (SEC 1988: 2.15), for example, GM was able to sell less than half the amount it needed to in order to attain full insurance coverage.

Furthermore, as futures discounts to underlying spot prices became extreme on the 19th, some insurers deliberately deferred futures sales. During the afternoon of October 19, for example, LOR decided to underhedge, gambling that futures prices would snap back (Rubinstein 1988: 39). LOR sold 2,000 S&P 500 futures contacts, equivalent to about $1 billion. But that was less than half the number of contracts needed to establish the theoretically correct hedge.

According to John O'Brien: "At each point during the day, we felt we were making the right decision" (Wall Street Journal, October 28, 1987: C6). After the crash, Rubinstein (1988: 42) defended LOR's decision to underhedge as the correct response to market conditions, saying that, given the high transaction costs on October 19, "a rational implementation of portfolio insurance would have stopped far short of implementing the full hedge." But the very inability to establish protective hedges during the crash proved the invalidity of the tenets of portfolio insurance. Insurance coverage was not available on an as-needed basis, and portfolio values were left unprotected from the very price declines they were insured against.

Also, the market's abrupt decline on Monday, October 19 represented only part of the problem for portfolio insurance. With the market's rebound on the 20th and 21st, the other shoe dropped.

Whipsaws

Prior to the crash, Leland (1986: 33) had asserted that it was a "myth" that "whipsawing can kill an insurance program." Quick price reversals create whipsaws that can prove costly, even fatal, for trend-following strategies like portfolio insurance. Transaction costs can explode (and protection erode) when insurers have to trade against waves of price reversals. They find themselves reducing stock positions right before the market rises, then adding to stock positions right before the market falls.

When market prices are nearly continuous, whipsaws tend to be small and are not unexpected. In effect, they represent gradual payment of the insurance premium (see, for example, T.J. O'Brien 1988: 44). In the crash, however, as Rubinstein (1988: 40) himself conceded after the event, "the volatility that had been expected to occur smoothly over the entire planned life of the policy instead occurred in one day."

The whipsaws of the market during the crash period wreaked havoc on portfolio insurance programs. As stocks were bottoming on October 20, for example, LOR sold futures, belatedly boosting its equity hedge. When the market surged on October 21, however, its accounts were 65 percent hedged, and unable to benefit fully from the rebound. According to Leland: "When the market reversed, clients felt something was beyond recall. They were down from where they had started, yet the hedge was costing them money" (*Wall Street Journal*, October 28, 1987: C6).[1] Leland's whipsaw myth had become a grim reality.

Leland (1988a: 18) argues elsewhere that LOR's clients were able to "avoid much of the whipsaw costs associated with the market reversal on October 20–21" because they were underhedged as the market bounced back. But this ignores the fact that, by being underhedged on October 19, portfolios suffered significantly greater downside damage. Furthermore, the mega-whipsaws that occurred on the 19th through the 21st put the lie to Robert Ferguson's (1986a: 79) assertion, before the crash, that "well-designed portfolio insurance strategies are relatively robust. For the most part, trades of a specific size need not be done on specific dates."

A Retreat

Leland (1984) had said, in the early days of portfolio insurance: "The acid test of an effective insurance program is whether it avoids unpleasant surprises." As we saw in chapter 2, LOR had claimed to offer clients such assurance: "All the implications and expectations of the selected strategy are known in advance. No unhappy surprises" (*Wall Street Journal*, January 4, 1988: B4). After the crash, Rubinstein (1988: 40) conceded that portfolio insurance "did not in many cases perform as expected."

While data on individual insured portfolios' performances are (understandably) hard to come by, the evidence available indicates that insured portfolios performed poorly. The San Diego Gas and Electric pension plan had "borne the brunt" of the market's decline (*Wall Street Journal*, October 28, 1987: 6) The Boston Company had a client with a 5 percent loss limitation that expected to suffer a loss of 8 or 9 percent (Ring 1987b).

LOR's O'Brien (quoted in Ring 1988a: 2) admitted that, for the January 1 through October 19 period, their average account fell 3 or 4 percentage points below its insured floor. He nevertheless claimed that portfolio insurance had been "exonerated" (*New York Times* Business Section, October 2, 1988: 2). Scott Grannis (1987: 3) of LOR concurred, arguing that insurance had provided some downside protection, hence was preferable to being unhedged.

These statements are extremely misleading, however. First, they ignore the fact that portfolio insurance failed to deliver the promised "insurance." Second, they ignore the substantial opportunity costs of being stopped out of the market for the remainder of the insurance program's horizon. Consider the example of a policy that was stopped out during the crash until its termination date in August 1989. The market recovered steadily after the crash, with a new high on August 24, 1989 over 57 percent above the crash low. The insured portfolio would have been shut out of this enormous market rise – a painful whipsaw indeed.

While Rubinstein (1988: 40) claims that "few insurers missed the minimum return," he concedes that "they were stopped out and forced into cash for the remainder of the life of their policies." But since insurance programs were stopped out, they had surely fallen below their minimum floors; the option replication had failed. Ironically, portfolio

FIGURE 13.2
Insurance Fails the Crash Test

Source: *Wall Street Journal*, October 28, 1987, p. 6.
New York Times, October 24, 1987, p. D42.
Pensions & Investment Age, November 16, 1987, p. 3.

FIGURE 13.3
"Stock Averages Reach New Highs"

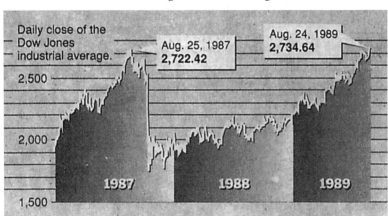

Source: *New York Times*, August 25, 1989, p. 1.

insurance, touted as a vehicle for locking in bull market gains, ended up locking many insurance clients out of subsequent market gains and into their maximum loss limitations instead.

To avoid staying in cash for the remainder of a stopped-out policy's life, insured investors may decide, judgmentally, to override the insurance policy. They may "reinsure" by restarting with a new policy. In other words, they can permit a new loss deductible for a portfolio that has already suffered a loss exceeding its original deductible. This not only nullifies the original policy and the protection it was designed to provide, but exposes the portfolio to further losses.

In the immediate aftermath of the crash, many insurance vendors did revise their approaches. Some vendors suggested that synthetic insurance programs with longer time horizons and/or lower floors would reduce synthetic portfolio insurance's destabilizing effects on the market and improve the reliability of synthetic strategies (Leland 1988a: 17). LOR said they were discontinuing their short-term policies of one year or less and planned to emphasize longer-term policies of three to fifteen years. This would, they claimed, halve the required trading and lessen the impact of insurance trading on market volatility (*New York Times*, November 10, 1987).

Again, however, these changes would effectively reduce the amount of protection provided. If the original policies were appropriately specified, the revised policies would not meet their clients' protection needs. And although the market's capacity to accommodate synthetic insurance trading would initially be less strained with a reduction in the level of protection provided, purchase of enough new insurance policies could lead to another capacity crisis. Furthermore, while the revised policies would initially be less sensitive to market moves (hence require less dynamic trading), policies near their expiration dates would require as much trading as shorter-term policies, with similar ramifications for market volatility and for the successful delivery of the insurance promised.

Some insurance vendors stopped offering the strategy altogether. For example, Aetna had $17 billion in portfolio insurance assets on September 30, 1987 but only $3 billion by December 31, 1987, mostly in strategies using stock, rather than the futures. According to Aetna's Ralph Tate, Aetna urged clients in the futures-based strategies to discontinue their programs, because the futures markets were no longer dependable (Ring 1988a). BEA stopped using $1.4 billion worth of portfolio insurance following the crash; according to BEA Vice President Jeff Geller, he and clients were "totally re-evaluating the strategy" (*New York Times*, October 23, 1987: 42).

Several plan sponsors also terminated their insurance coverage. San Diego Gas and Electric canceled its insurance policy. Manville Corp.

FIGURE 13.4
Portfolio Insurance Drops 66% (millions of dollars under management)

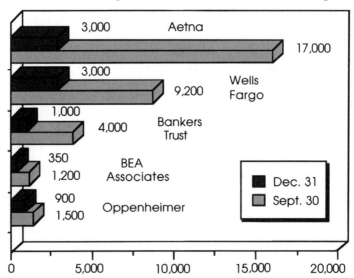

Source: *Pensions & Investment Age*, January 25, 1988, p. 2.

reportedly suspended its $300 million insurance portfolio, which had been scheduled to run another fifteen months (*Wall Street Journal*, October 28, 1987: 6). Burlington Industries switched out of insured equities into all cash, and Duke University and Bayer USA dropped their portfolio insurance in favor of bonds (Ring 1988c: 3). A number of LOR clients placed their portfolio insurance programs "in suspension" (*New York Times*, November 10, 1987).

The Brady Commission (1988: V.17) reports that of the thirteen insured pension funds responding to their survey, two had dropped insurance prior to October 19 and seven more eliminated their programs following the crash. Another survey of fourteen vendors indicates that their insured assets dropped by two-thirds between September 30, 1987 and December 31, 1987, from $37 to $12.6 billion (Ring 1988a).

The decline in insurance strategies was reflected in a simultaneous decline in the volume of S&P 500 futures contracts. Since the advent of exchange-traded futures in 1982, the average daily volume of futures trading had grown steadily, and had doubled between year-end 1985 and early October 1987. The volume dropped off by about half in the wake of the crash. Demand for exchange-traded options soared, however, "primarily because portfolio insurance managers quickly needed to convert futures-based dynamic hedges into options hedges" (Zurack and Hill 1997: 3). Prices for options steepened dramatically on the 19th, as evidenced by the dramatic increase in option implied volatility.[2]

Why It Failed

In the wake of the crash, portfolio insurance vendors blamed the failures of the strategy on higher than expected market volatility, discontinuities or gaps in stock prices, and substantial futures discounts – everything but the strategy itself. Eric Seff (1988: 13) of Chase, a provider of portfolio insurance, claimed that insurance "worked"; in his opinion, it had merely experienced additional costs due to unanticipated high volatility. Rubinstein (1988: 40) contended that the crash proved nothing about insurance that had not already been known: "The dependency of typical portfolio insurance strategies on preconditions of low transactions costs and market continuity should have been well-known to both those marketing the strategy and those using the strategy on their own portfolios. Even the most elementary understanding of the implementation of portfolio insurance would make this obvious."

These equivocations, however, contradict the very assertions that had been used to sell synthetic portfolio insurance in the first place. As we

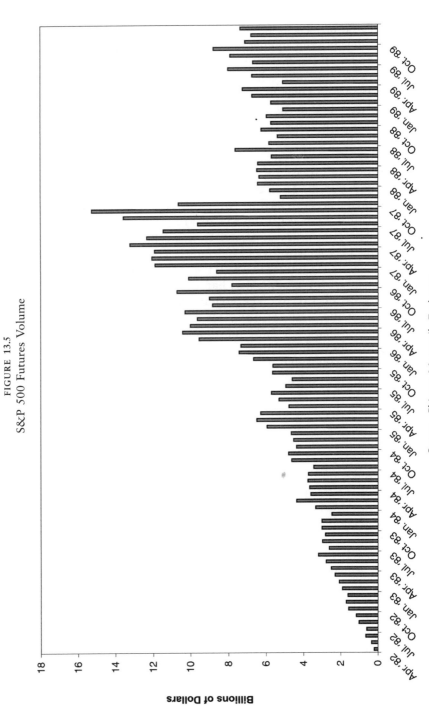

FIGURE 13.5
S&P 500 Futures Volume

Source: Chicago Mercantile Exchange.

FIGURE 13.6
Implied Volatility Soars, October 1987

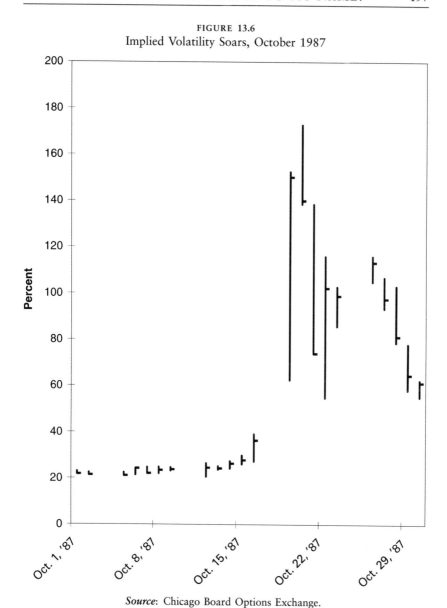

Source: Chicago Board Options Exchange.

saw in part I, dynamic hedging was marketed as the equivalent of a traditional insurance policy. LOR's O'Brien explained: "If we didn't use the term 'portfolio insurance,' people wouldn't know what we meant" (Sloan and Stern 1988: 57). Rubinstein and Leland (1981: 9) maintained

that synthetic insurance was "tantamount to insuring the equity portfolio against losses by paying a fixed premium to an insurance company." Steven Wunsch (1984), at Kidder Peabody, stated that synthetic
insurance assured a floor return, even under "the worst of all worst-case
scenarios."

LOR colleagues Ferguson and Larry Edwards (1985: 2) agreed: "It
doesn't matter that formal insurance policies are not available. The
mathematics of finance provide the answer. . . . The bottom line is that
financial catastrophes can be avoided at a relatively insignificant cost."
In fact, as we saw in chapter 2, many early proponents of portfolio insurance even argued that it would provide, not only protection, but also
better returns than uninsured strategies.

As we also noted in part I, synthetic portfolio insurance, even in
theory, differs markedly from traditional insurance for, say, homes or
automobiles. Aetna Life's Guaranteed Equity Management (GEM)
product, mentioned in chapter 2, was in some ways an exception. It did
provide an insurance company guarantee – at least of meeting a prespecified minimum; GEM did not reimburse for shortfalls on the upside
(see Tate 1988). Of course, this meant that the issuer had to eat any
losses beyond the deductible. GEM was discontinued after the crash.

For synthetic insurance programs other than GEM, there was no third
party obligated to reimburse losses. Rather, all risk was borne by the
"insured" (see Bookstaber and Langsam 1988: 1531). That's because,
as we have noted, synthetic portfolio insurance is really a form of self-
insurance, with coverage "purchased" by selling stocks as they decline.
Joel Bleeke (*Wall Street Journal*, December 11, 1987) likens the idea to
a driver going into a skid and attempting to order automobile insurance
by car phone before crashing.

Furthermore, unlike conventional insurance (or a publicly traded
option), which requires an explicit premium payment up front, synthetic
portfolio insurance is essentially a pay-as-you-go proposition. One can
estimate what the experienced premium of an insurance program will
be, but this estimate is only as good as the insurer's best guess as to
what the volatility of stocks will be over the life of the insurance program. As Leland (1987) admitted after the crash: "Typically, a weighted
average of long-term and recent market volatility have [sic] been used
to analyze the most likely outcomes of alternative protection programs.
. . . This volatility will . . . correctly reflect past (but not necessarily
future!) realized volatility."

As the crash proved, greater than expected volatility can cause
the costs of an insurance program to explode. More critically, the discontinuous price movements characteristic of excessive volatility can
compromise the ability of an insurance program to provide the level of

FIGURE 13.7

Its Vendors Stick Up for Insurance

Sources (in clockwise order): *Pensions & Investment Age*, November 16, 1987, p. 3.
New York Times, January 13, 1988. Photo: Terrence McCarthy.
New York Times, October 2, 1988. Photo: David Guilburt.
Pensions & Investment Age, February 8, 1988, p. 13.

protection promised. After the crash, LOR's Scott Grannis admitted: "What we learned [in October] is that the options market was correct in the price it charged for protection. You pay a premium for the certainty that options give you, whatever form you choose to buy the options in" (Heston 1988: 38). The illusion of a small or negative premium for synthetic insurance simply reflects the uncertainty of its protection.

Perhaps the most critical distinction between portfolio insurance and real insurance, however, lies in the nature of the promise portfolio insurance makes that traditional insurance would never proffer. Conventional insurance pools independent risks, such as homeowners' risks of fire destroying their properties, across many participants (see Brennan and Schwartz 1976: 196 and Leland 1980: 581). But no insurance company purports to be able to insure successfully all homeowners against a common risk, such as the risk of a general decline in real estate values.[3]

Rubinstein (1987: 77) had once asserted: "In the absence of special information, if someone claims a particular strategy is generally superior, here is a simple way to test it: ask what would happen if everyone tried to follow it. This is called the macroconsistency test."[4] But it would seem to be obvious that not all investors can be insured against a general decline in stock prices. All investors can not trade in the same direction at the same time.

Before the crash, LOR's Ferguson (1983: 38) had indicated that synthetic portfolio insurance would appeal to all informed investors (see chapter 2). By this standard, uninsured investors are uninformed. But because everyone can not trade in the same direction at the same time, an insurance strategy actually requires the existence of such "uninformed" investors to work.

The existence of uninsured ("uninformed") investors is not really enough, however. For portfolio insurance relies on the ability to shift the risk of market declines, on demand, from one group of investors to another. This in turn requires the existence of sufficient numbers of insurance sellers who engage in the same mechanical trading as insurance buyers, but in the offsetting direction. Just as for every put buyer, there must be a put seller, for every insured investor who demands to sell a given amount of stock as the market declines there must be an investor demanding to buy that given amount.

October 19, 1987 demonstrates what happens when such investors do not exist. The selling demands of insured investors overwhelm the market, creating just those conditions least conducive to encouraging ordinary (if "uninformed") investors to take on the risks insured investors want to unload. Without willing insurance "sellers," insurance "buyers" are doomed. Unfortunately, they take the market down with them.

Portfolio insurance is thus most likely to fail precisely when it is most needed. As Nobel laureate William Sharpe states it: "We learned in the 1987 market crash that if everyone wants the upside and no one wants the downside, then everyone can't get it" (Burr 1993: 50).

FIGURE 13.8

"Creators not down on dynamic hedging"

Creators not down on dynamic hedging

By Trudy Ring

Hayne Leland and Mark Rubinstein foresee a return to favor for their dynamic hedging strategies, which were so popular before last year's stock market plunge and so maligned after it.

"What you give up by not using (dynamic strategies) is like tying your hands behind your back," Mr. Rubinstein said.

"If anything, the need for risk management has become more acute," Mr. Leland added. "The more volatile markets tend to be, the more pressing is the need for risk management. The mere fact of the crash itself has reinforced the reality that markets move both directions."

The men, both professors in the School of Business Administration at the University of California, Berkeley, gained fame in money management after forming

Leland O'Brien Rubinstein Associates Inc., Los Angeles, with John O'Brien in 1981. Both are directors of the firm, which specializes in dynamic hedging — also known as portfolio insurance — to assure

M. Rubinstein   **H. Leland**

a minimum return on a portfolio by reducing equity exposure as the market declines.

They had been interested in money management since the mid-1970s, when they were doing

Source: Pensions & Investment Age, October 31, 1988, p. 66.

Summary

Synthetic portfolio insurance did not live up to its name. Rather, it proved that it is not insurance under the generally accepted meaning of the term. There is no pool of assets an insurance provider can draw on to reimburse client losses; in fact there is no insurance provider to bear the risk of loss. The insured investors themselves bear that risk, relying on the ability to get into and out of stocks in a timely and cost-effective manner. Whether they can do so, however, depends upon the volatility of the market and, importantly, on the willingness of other investors to accept the downside risk that insured investors want to lay off.

During the crash, transaction costs skyrocketed. Liquidity dried up. The dynamic hedging required by synthetic insurance programs became impossible at almost any price. Insured investors could not unload their stock positions, or could not do so quickly enough to preserve the value of their insured assets and the integrity of their insurance programs. Synthetically insured portfolios fell through their "guaranteed" floors and were shut out of the substantial gains the market produced following the crash.

Portfolio insurance failed just when it was most needed. As we will see, however, that has not deterred investors and investment advisers from continuing to seek the Northwest Passage of no-risk reward.

Notes

1 For a more detailed account of LOR's inability to hedge properly, see the example given in Leland (1988a: 16–7).

2 See chapter 16 for a discussion of option implied volatility.

3 Shiller (1993) proposes a real estate futures instrument to allow homeowners to hedge against declines in the values of their homes. Futures contracts would be based on regional or national real estate market values. While the risk of declining real estate values could thus be shared interregionally or internationally, regional, or national, contracts could not insure all homeowners against a nationwide, or worldwide, decline in real estate values.

4 According to Rubinstein (1987: 77), this test dealt a "bone-crushing knockout punch" to Rendleman and McEnally's (1987a) assertion that all investors would want to follow a logarithmic utility function.

___ Part IV ___

Option Replication Resurrected

Gregory Duffee and his colleagues (1992: 37, 47) suggest that "the realization that portfolio insurance can not work well when everyone is attempting to insure their portfolios led many to abandon dynamic hedging strategies. . . . Such strategies have lost appeal among institutional investors." But, even in the wake of the crash, synthetic portfolio insurance vendors defended its performance, if sometimes halfheartedly. Michael Granito (1987: 73), managing director of the Capital Market Research Group at J.P. Morgan, a large insurance provider, asked:

> Is portfolio insurance dead? Following the October crash, many if not most programs fared better than casual reaction would suggest, and portfolio insurance clients were generally very pleased to have had some form of protection. Nonetheless, it is apparent that a sufficiently discontinuous market can immobilize certain forms of dynamic trading and that such events are more likely than we had thought before.

Other insurance vendors were unabashedly bold in their continued advocacy. For example, LOR's Hayne Leland (1988a: 16) averred that "a long history of both theory and fact suggests that dynamic hedging strategies (of which 'portfolio insurance' is a leading example) can serve a useful role in controlling risk in an intelligent fashion. The events of October 19 contradict neither theory nor fact." Mark Rubinstein maintained that "what you give up by not using [dynamic strategies] is like tying your hands behind your back" (Ring 1988b: 66). Wells Fargo's Donald Luskin (1988: 315) asserted: "Now that the marketplace has had a vivid lesson in the true possible magnitude of risk . . . portfolio insurance is now understood to be more valuable."

Following their words with practice, in 1989 LOR took synthetic portfolio insurance global with the launch of its "Celebration Fund." Aimed exclusively at Japanese institutional investors, the Celebration Fund used a dynamic asset allocation strategy to shift assets between US and Japanese markets, moving into the stronger of the two and out of the weaker one in an effort to achieve the higher return of the US or the Japanese market (less the insurance premium). From November 1989 through January 1990 alone, the strategy shifted some $700 million out of Japanese stocks, allowing participants to dodge the precipitous decline in the Tokyo market. Upside capture was more problematic. Although LOR had claimed the fund should capture 90 percent of the "absolute relative return" of the better performing of the two markets, experience through mid-1990 was more modest – from a shortfall a few percentage points below the average of the two markets when the markets performed similarly to no more than 70 percent of the gain in the better of the two markets when they diverged significantly (*Wall Street Journal*, June 8, 1990: C1). Furthermore, the strategy benefited in this period from ideal circumstances for dynamic asset allocation – sustained and diverging trends in the two markets.

The Celebration Fund raised many now familiar issues. Jeffrey Skelton of Wells Fargo Nikko, manager of the Celebration Fund, noted that commitments to the strategy were well below the $10 billion or more that would constitute a threat to market stability (*Wall Street Journal*, June 8, 1990). However, the fund itself was only one of several publicly available strategies, including synthetic warrants, that effectively constituted a put on the Japanese market. Their possible role in the Nikkei's plunge in 1990 is discussed in chapter 16.

In fact, synthetic portfolio insurance in the decade following the crash was to be replaced by a cornucopia of products and strategies designed to protect investors from market downturns. These included the burgeoning market in over-the-counter (OTC) options, swaps, and warrants, as well as an expanded list of exchange-traded options geared to institutional investors and hybrid products offering retail investors stock participation with a bond-like guarantee of principal. These largely option-based or option-like products have in common with the old synthetic insurance products more than just a similar investment objective. They have an ultimate reliance on the same option-replicating dynamic hedging that destabilized the market in 1987.

Chapter 14 examines the role of dynamic hedging in the significant market declines of 1989, 1991, and 1997. Chapter 15 provides a brief review of the offspring of portfolio insurance – new instruments and strategies that have gained popularity since the 1987 crash. Chapter 16 addresses the risk these new portfolio insurance mechanisms pose for clients, insurance providers, and the markets themselves. Chapter 17 proposes some deep-seated behavioral reasons why investors have found and continue to find portfolio insurance and its ilk so desirable, despite the fact that alternative approaches can provide more reward and confront markets with less disruption.

Chapter 18 shows how option replication and other strategies that require mechanistic trading are affecting real markets today. In the summer and fall of 1998, financial markets in the US and abroad were roiled by the dynamic hedging of option market makers attempting to meet the public's demand for option puts and by the disintegration of the giant hedge fund, Long-Term Capital Management. As we will see, the story of Long-Term Capital Management bears some eerie resemblances to the story of portfolio insurance.

14

Mini-Crashes of 1989, 1991, and 1997

> The market decline on November 15, 1991 appears similar to the declines in October 1989, and October 1987. Institutional money managers had grown concerned over protecting year-to-date gains in their stock portfolios.
>
> *Securities and Exchange Commission, 1991*

As well as attempting to dissect the events of October 1987, the various governmental reports on the crash suggested structural changes that might help to prevent a recurrence of those events. Their recommendations resulted, among other things, in the establishment of a system of circuit breakers designed to restore order to markets in freefall.

In October of 1988, the US stock exchanges set price limits that would halt trading in stocks at times of unusual market stress. Initially, the parameters called for a one-hour halt in trading of stocks on all exchanges if the Dow Jones industrial average (DJIA) fell 250 points below the previous day's close (about 12 percent of its value at that time). A two-hour trading halt would be triggered if, upon reopening, the DJIA fell another 150 points (400 points in total, or about 20 percent, off the previous day's close).

The futures exchanges instituted their own price limits, which were coordinated with those on the stock exchanges. All the futures exchanges called for a trading halt if their index futures contracts fell more than the equivalent of 250 DJIA points; most called for a halt at 100 DJIA-equivalent points. On the Chicago Mercantile Exchange (CME), for example, trading in the S&P 500 futures contract would be suspended for thirty minutes if the contract fell 12 points below the previous day's close. At 30 points down, trading in the contract would be halted for one hour or, if the DJIA had fallen more than 250 points, until at least half the stocks in the S&P 500 index had begun trading again. If the DJIA fell over 400 points, trading in the futures contract would halt for two hours. In addition, the contract was subjected to a daily limit of 50 points up or down, and to a 5-point limit, up or down, on its opening price.

The New York Stock Exchange (NYSE) also passed rules to limit program trading during periods of significant market volatility. The "sidecar" rule comes into effect if the DJIA falls 100 points, or the S&P 500 futures contract drops 12 points, below the previous close. With this rule, program trades are diverted from the exchange's automated DOT system and placed on hold for five minutes while the exchange gives priority to retail trades. The "collar" rule, adopted in 1990, limits arbitrage program trades when the DJIA moves up or down by 50 points from the previous day's close, and stays in effect until the DJIA returns to within 25 points of the previous close; during this limited-trade period, arbitragers must submit limit orders or tick-sensitive orders (buying on a down tick or selling on an up tick).

These circuit breakers were designed to give markets room to breath in periods of intense trading pressure, such as experienced in October 1987. Other measures were taken to address some of the liquidity problems that had become evident in the 1987 crash. In 1987, an investor who had assets in one market could not use them to meet margin requirements in another market. With the market gyrations in October 1987, investors with futures and short option positions, and those who had purchased stock on margin, had to come up with substantial amounts of cash to meet margin requirements. This had the effect of draining even more liquidity from a market that, as we have seen, was already strapped for liquidity. Since the crash, cross-margining agreements have allowed investors to use their end-of-day asset positions in all markets to determine overall margin requirements. When an investor has offsetting positions in more than one market, as is the case with synthetic portfolio insurance, this allowance for cross-margining can reduce cash demands on the investor and thereby increase liquidity in all markets.

Another substantive problem in 1987 was the lack of system capacity. As we saw, on the Monday of the crash numerous issues could not trade because of the inability of exchanges to process orders fast enough. On the following day, the Chicago Board Options Exchange (CBOE) and CME actually closed down for a period in midafternoon because they could not keep up with the volume of trading.

In the years following the crash, all exchanges have stepped up replacement of time-consuming manual processes with automated systems that permit electronic routing and execution of orders. Improvements have also been made to automated dissemination of trade information. Most exchanges now have the capacity to handle at least three times an average day's volume. The major broker-dealers have also upgraded their systems to the point where they now have the capacity to handle about twice their average daily volumes (Lindsey and Pecora 1997: 24).

These system improvements were tested on October 13, 16, and 24, 1989, when the markets experienced severe price volatility and heavy volume reminiscent of the 1987 crash. Below, we describe the 1989 mini-crash, analyzing some of the effects of post-1987 market reforms and changes in institutional trading behavior. We then go on to examine the subsequent mini-crash of November 1991 and the real test of circuit breakers – October 27, 1997.

Friday the 13th, October 1989

After the 1987 crash, the economy continued to grow. The stock market remained stable throughout 1988 and then rose substantially in 1989. On Monday, October 9, the DJIA set a new record high, closing at 2791. On each of the next three days, it lost about 30 points. On Friday the 13th, the DJIA plunged 191 points, or 6.9 percent.

Before 2:30 p.m. on the 13th, the DJIA fell by about 25 points, possibly because of economic indicators released by the government before the opening. Specifically, a rising producer price index and an increase in retail sales were viewed as negative factors for stocks because they implied a delay in any easing of monetary policy by the Federal Reserve.

The steep fall-off in stock prices later that day was triggered by corporate events. At 2:40 p.m., the NYSE specialist in United Airlines (UAL) stock received permission to halt trading pending significant news. By 2:55, newswires were carrying the announcement that financing for the planned takeover of the company was in doubt (SEC 1990b: 19–20), as well as news that a proposal in Congress to cut the capital gains tax rate had been defeated (Kuhn et al. 1991: 139). In the context of an already weakened market for high-yield bonds (CFTC 1990: 16), the UAL news seemed extremely bearish for actual and rumored takeover targets, as well as for stocks in general (SEC 1990b: 19–20).

Prices on both the NYSE and the CME immediately began to fall sharply. By 3:07 p.m., the S&P 500 December futures contract, the most actively traded stock index futures contract, hit its 12-point price limit. This was equivalent to a 92-point drop in the DJIA (which itself was 84 points off the previous day's close) and triggered NYSE sidecars that detoured program trades for five minutes.

Unrestricted trading in the CME's S&P 500 futures contract resumed at 3:30 p.m., and prices proceeded to plunge fairly steadily until the 30-point limit was hit at about 3:45. This limit was equivalent to a 230-point drop in the DJIA, which was actually down by 150 points (SEC

FIGURE 14.1
DJIA on Friday the 13th

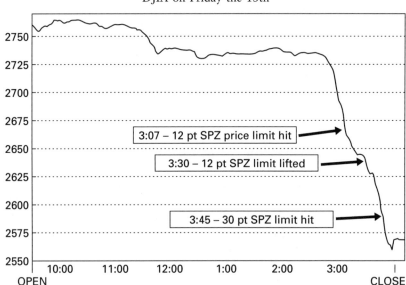

3:07 – 12 pt SPZ price limit hit

3:30 – 12 pt SPZ limit lifted

3:45 – 30 pt SPZ limit hit

Source: Securities and Exchange Commission, *Trading Analysis of October 13 and 16, 1989*, 1990.

1990b: 23). Stock index futures on other exchanges also hit their limits during this period. The Amex and CBOE halted trading in their index option futures after 3:16 and effectively remained closed for the rest of the day (SEC 1990a: 72).

By the time the NYSE closed at 4:00 p.m., the DJIA had fallen 191 points to 2569, the market's second-largest single-day point decline (CFTC 1990: 10–11). Trading in American Airlines and two other airline stocks as well as in UAL had stopped, and neither American nor UAL had reopened by the end of the day. Sell-order imbalances had halted trading in six additional stocks, only one of which had reopened (SEC 1990a: 21–3).

About 87 percent of the DJIA's drop on October 13 occurred in the last ninety minutes before the close on extraordinarily heavy volume. During the last hour alone, 112 million shares were traded on the NYSE, a level approaching the 116.6 million shares traded during the busiest hour of October 19, 1987 (SEC 1990b: 1).

On Monday morning, the 16th, a backlog of sell orders suggested that Friday's market decline would continue. The S&P 500 December futures contract opened 5 points below Friday's close, triggering the CME's opening price limit. However, the price bounced back immediately, and the limit was lifted after just one minute of trading (SEC 1990b: 53). On the NYSE, sell-order imbalances delayed openings in 151 stocks (SEC 1990a: 23), representing nearly 20 percent of the DJIA's price weight and 11 percent of the capitalization of the S&P 500. By the time UAL opened at 11:08 a.m., it had lost $55, or 20 percent of its value, since Friday afternoon (SEC 1990a: 25).

Heavy selling and delayed openings drove the DJIA down more than 60 points in the first hour of trading. After that, however, prices recovered dramatically, following the lead of the stock index futures market (SEC 1990b: 54). The recovery maintained its momentum throughout the day, and the DJIA ended 88 points above its close on Friday, October 13. NYSE trading volume on the 16th was 421.5 million shares, the fourth heaviest on record at the time, exceeded only by October 19, 20, and 21, 1987 (SEC 1990b: 1). More than 225 million shares traded during the first two hours on the 16th, setting a new record for the NYSE (SEC 1990a: 35).

On the Tuesday of the following week, October 24, the DJIA fell 80 points in the first hour of trading. The S&P 500 December futures contract briefly hit the 12-point limit at 10:33 a.m., but recovered almost immediately. Stocks reversed their decline just as rapidly, regaining 40 points in the next half hour and ending the day off just 4 points on total volume of about 239 million shares. The initial sell-off may have been triggered by news after Monday's close that UAL's board wanted to keep the airline independent, once again dashing prospects of a buyout (CFTC 1990: 18, 20, 60–1).

Effect of Circuit Breakers

Despite the fact that the volume of trading on October 13 and 16, 1989 at times rivaled the worst periods of October 19–21, 1987, the NYSE experienced no significant problems with routing orders or other operations (SEC 1990b: 2). In fact, the SEC found that in October 1989, the NYSE, Amex, and some regional exchanges had far fewer problems than in 1987, largely because they had expanded capacity and enhanced their routing and execution systems (SEC 1990a: 4–5).

However, circuit breakers proved less than an unqualified success. Even with the circuit breakers imposed in the futures markets on October 13, for example, futures prices generally fell faster and farther than prices in the underlying spot market (SEC 1990b: 2). The SEC nevertheless notes (p. 5) that the halt in S&P 500 futures trading coincided with a sharp drop-off in the level of program selling on the NYSE and a reduction in the rate of the price decline in stocks from 3:07 to 3:30 p.m. The SEC observed the same effect in the later high-volatility episode on Tuesday, October 24. The SEC concludes that, while a direct causal relationship is difficult to establish, the evidence indicates that no harm was done to the markets by futures price limits (SEC 1990b: 5).

But Betsey Kuhn and her colleagues (1991: 146) calculate several measures of volatility for S&P 500 spot and futures prices in various periods on the 13th and 16th and find "no evidence that price volatility in the cash market fell after the imposition of . . . price limits in the futures market." Furthermore, though circuit breakers virtually eliminated volatility while they were in effect, volatility returned to above-normal levels once trading restrictions were lifted.

The return of volatility after the imposition of circuit breakers leads Kuhn et al. to conclude that volatility, at least in the period studied, reflected the arrival and dissemination of information into the market, rather than the reactions of panicked investors. Merton Miller (1991: 242) points, for example, to the significant role played by the United Airlines news. Henry McMillan (1991), however, adjusts for the effect of the UAL announcement on market prices and finds, even with the adjustment, an unusual number of consecutive price declines between the UAL announcement and the imposition of the first circuit breaker on Friday the 13th.[1]

McMillan detects the presence of a gravitational effect surrounding circuit breakers on October 13, which he attributes to arbitragers, hedgers, and speculators unwinding positions or refraining from taking positions before anticipated trading restrictions kicked in.[2] He also finds an after-effect, with futures prices changing by minimum increments before the imposition of the first circuit breaker at 3:07 p.m., but changing in increments of from ten to twenty times the minimum tick after the resumption of unrestricted trading; in effect, the circuit breakers on Friday the 13th turned an orderly decline into a mad rush to the bottom. McMillan also notes that the weekend of October 14 and 15, which should have acted as a natural circuit breaker, restoring order by the morning of the 16th, did no such thing; instead, it was trading itself that proved the cure for excessive volatility. He concludes that circuit breakers can contribute to price declines, although the evidence on October 16 and 24 suggests that the circuit breakers actually stabilized futures prices on those days.

Furthermore, although the circuit breakers are coordinated by price levels, differences in timing across markets mean that restrictions will not be triggered in all markets simultaneously. According to the CFTC, there is evidence that activating circuit breakers in one market increases volatility in other, unfettered markets (CFTC 1990: 6–7). On October 13, for example, the volatility of Major Market Index (MMI) futures and stocks increased during the nine-minute interval between the S&P 500 contract hitting its 12-point limit and the MMI hitting its own limit (CFTC 1990: 7).

The CFTC estimates that sell program trades accounted for 11 percent of NYSE volume on October 13 and 10 percent on October 16. The bulk of those trades represented index arbitrage, which was carried out at a slightly higher volume than normal. This contrasts with October 1987, when most program sales represented non-arbitrage trades, mainly because of portfolio insurance (CFTC 1990: 28–9).

OTC Puts

As in October 1987, price declines in both the futures and stock markets in October 1989 were exacerbated by market participants attempting to hedge their risk exposures through forced selling, first in futures, then in stocks (SEC 1990b: 25). But in 1987 these sellers were mainly institutions implementing portfolio insurance hedging strategies; in 1989, speculative and professional traders generated the bulk of futures and stock sales.

On October 13, institutions were actually net buyers of futures (SEC 1990b: 4–5). It is possible that institutions would have been heavier sellers if they had had sufficient time to react. The swift and dramatic drop, coming late in the day on the 13th, gave the advantage to market professionals, who have readier access to the exchange floors than institutions (SEC 1990b: 35).

A more important factor, however, was that most institutions were not using synthetic portfolio insurance in October 1989. The SEC (1990b: 34) suggests that "more extensive portfolio insurance programs might have resulted in more sustained selling of futures and stocks by institutions or their money managers on the afternoon of the 13th." But the SEC could not identify any significant futures or stock selling attributable to portfolio insurance strategies on either October 13 or October 16 (SEC 1990b: 6, 34). In fact, earlier in 1989, a survey by the SEC's Division of Market Regulation found that the amount of assets covered by portfolio insurance had declined by 60 to 90 percent from its peak just before the market crash of 1987 (SEC 1990b: June 1989 Memorandum 34, fn. 82).

Synthetic portfolio insurance had lost favor after the 1987 crash in part because of the liquidity problems that prevented institutions from executing their dynamic hedging strategies during the market break (SEC 1990b: 40). But institutions had realized substantial market gains by late 1989, which they wanted to protect without having to liquidate their portfolios. Some institutional money managers had therefore purchased OTC puts to protect their portfolios' values (SEC 1990b: 36).

OTC portfolio puts are privately negotiated options written by broker-dealers and purchased by institutional money managers as tailored protection for their stock portfolios. Their purchase means that the institutions themselves do not need to sell in the stock and futures markets in the event of a market decline. Instead, it is the broker-dealers providing the insurance that need to hedge their positions, frequently through dynamic trading programs (SEC 1990b: 37–8).

Whenever it sells a put (or, indeed, a call) option, an OTC dealer exposes itself to substantial risk. If the value of the underlying portfolio declines below the put's strike, so that the option is exercised, the dealer must pay the option holder the exercise price and receive, in return, a portfolio that is worth less. Now, the dealer will presumably have incorporated this risk exposure into the premium it charged the option buyer. Nevertheless, the risk remains, as it did for synthetic insurers, that volatility will turn out to be greater than expected, hence the price of the underlying portfolio will drop more than expected and the premium charged for the option will fail to cover the loss in portfolio value.

Dealers are generally not speculators; they do not wish to remain exposed to the risk that an option will be exercised against them. They will therefore try to lay off the risk their short option positions expose them to. Ideally, they will be able to close out short option positions by buying exchange-traded options. OTC dealers who have sold customized options, however, may find that the specifications they need to offset their short option positions are not available from exchange-traded options; this would have been especially true in the late 1980s and early 1990s, before the relaxation of position limits in options and the explosive growth of new option instruments (see chapter 15).

Furthermore, options market makers generally do not want to hold net short positions any more than dealers do. They, too, will try to offset short option positions with long option positions. Ultimately, both dealers' and market makers' ability to obtain these long positions, or to obtain them at reasonable cost, depends on the presence of investors willing to bear the risk of short option positions. These speculative sellers take on the risk of uncertain market volatility in the expectation either that volatility will move the market in a direction profitable to them or that volatility will remain within a range in which exercise of the option is unprofitable.

When option dealers (or market makers) cannot buy options to hedge the exposures from the options they have sold, they may have to replicate long option positions synthetically. As we have seen, replicating long option positions requires selling stock (or shorting stock futures) as the market falls and buying stock (or covering short stock futures positions) as the market rises. In other words, it requires the same positive-feedback, trend-following, dynamic hedging that synthetic portfolio insurance relied upon!

In 1989, OTC portfolio puts were a brand new product. They had not been actively used until 1988, but the dollar amount of assets covered by them had grown substantially by October 1989. At least three major broker-dealers had written put coverage for eight institutional money managers. The aggregate value of institutional portfolios protected in this manner was approximately $2 billion (SEC 1990b: 37).

While seemingly small compared with the $60 to $100 billion covered by traditional portfolio insurance in 1987, the portfolio put strategy nevertheless contributed significantly, albeit indirectly, to market behavior on the afternoon of October 13 and again at the opening on October 16. The institutions using portfolio puts as insurance were able to avoid selling in the stock and futures markets. For the broker-dealers that had written the puts, however, it was a different story. The dynamic hedging they used to insulate themselves from the risk their put sales exposed them to required program selling as the market fell.

On October 13, selling pressure on the CME pushed S&P 500 futures prices to discounted levels, which created index arbitrage opportunities. Arbitragers' program trades transferred selling pressure to the stock market. With futures continuing at a discount, however, broker-dealers who had written portfolio puts but had not been able to hedge sufficiently in futures in the early afternoon had to sell stocks in non-arbitrage-related program trades at the end of the day (SEC 1990b: 44).

At 3:49 p.m. on October 13, for example, just before the DJIA reached its low, at nearly 200 points down, three firms hit the floor of the NYSE with a downdraft of program sell orders for two and a half million shares. All three told the SEC that the programs were for hedging transactions. Two of them, accounting for 83 percent of the program volume, attributed the selling directly to portfolio put strategies (SEC 1990b: 44–5).

In sum, OTC portfolio puts did not so much reduce the need to sell into declining markets as they shifted this need from institutional insurers to broker-dealers. Just as portfolio insurers had earlier in the decade, these broker-dealers trusted that the liquidity of the futures market would allow them to hedge their own proprietary risk exposures as needed. And just as portfolio insurers learned in 1987, they found that a hedge that depends on selling during market downturns can be a hazardous proposition.

We have noted that before the markets opened on Monday, October 16, accumulated sell orders indicated that Friday's price declines would continue. Some broker-dealers that were net sellers at the opening told the SEC that those transactions were a continuation of the hedging they had begun late Friday afternoon. On balance, however, broker-dealers were net buyers for the day (SEC 1990b: 63).

Of fifteen large traders identified by the CME as net sellers of more than 100 S&P 500 futures contracts in any ten-minute period from 9:30 to 10:00 a.m. on October 16, only one was an institution. To the SEC, this indicates that portfolio insurance was not a significant factor in the morning sell-off. However, the SEC also warns against drawing conclusions about current portfolio insurance strategies from the events of that day; it maintains that portfolio insurance selling could develop during and contribute to future market declines (SEC 1990b: 59).

As on October 19, 1987, the plunge in stock prices at the October 16, 1989 opening was heavily influenced by concentrated arbitrage sell programs. When they abated, prices on the NYSE began to recover. In 1987, however, arbitrage sell programs were joined by synthetic portfolio insurance sell programs, and the market's partial recovery from the morning sell-off was reversed. On October 16, 1989, without those synthetic insurance programs, buy programs were able to maintain enough momentum to support the recovery (SEC 1990b: 68–9).

We have noted that portfolio puts had largely supplanted synthetic portfolio insurance by 1989. While the use of these puts certainly aggravated selling into the market downturn in the mini-crash of 1989, protective puts probably had less effect than synthetic insurance strategies had in 1987. Of course, it is primarily the difference in the sizes of put coverage in 1989 and synthetic portfolio insurance in 1987 (two billion dollars versus tens of billions) that accounts for the difference in effect.

November 15, 1991

On Friday, November 15, 1991, another severe market decline piqued regulators' interest in derivatives-related program trading and in investment strategies designed to insure portfolio values. On that date, the S&P 500 fell 3.3 percent and the DJIA 3.9 percent. Again, much of the decline came in the afternoon, and again futures contracts at times overshot underlying spot market declines by considerable margins. Unlike Friday the 13th, however, Friday the 15th was a "double-witching hour" – a non-quarterly expiration day for equity options and index options and futures contracts.

The NYSE requires member firms to enter expiration-related market-on-close (MOC) orders before 3:00 p.m. on expiration Fridays. Shortly

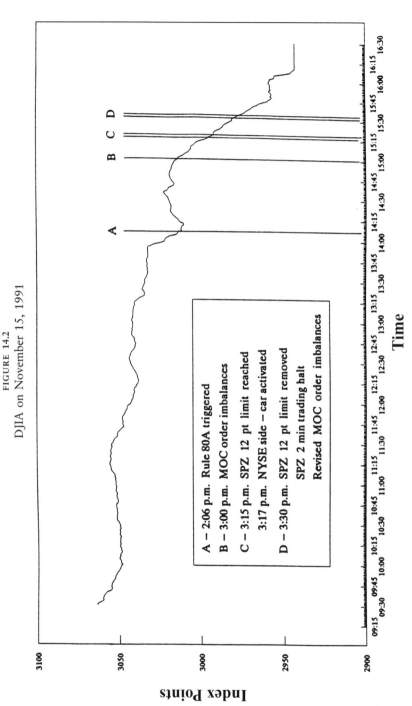

FIGURE 14.2
DJIA on November 15, 1991

A – 2:06 p.m.   Rule 80A triggered
B – 3:00 p.m.   MOC order imbalances
C – 3:15 p.m.   SPZ 12 pt limit reached
       3:17 p.m.   NYSE side – car activated
D – 3:30 p.m.   SPZ 12 pt limit removed
       SPZ 2 min trading halt
       Revised MOC order imbalances

Index Points

Time

Source: Securities and Exchange Commission, "Market Decline on November 15, 1991," 1991.

after 2:00 p.m. on the 15th, the DJIA had fallen 50 points below its previous close, triggering the NYSE's collar rule limiting index arbitrage program trading. The DJIA and the S&P 500 held fairly steady over the next hour, with the DJIA actually gaining a little ground. When unexpectedly large sell-order imbalances became apparent after 3:00 p.m., however, both indexes began to decline sharply. Down 1.6 percent at 3:00, the DJIA was down a full 2.7 percent by 3:30. The S&P 500 also fell, but not by as much as the futures contract on the index.

The CME's December S&P 500 futures contract had started gapping down relative to the underlying spot index before 3:00 p.m. It hit its first 12-point limit at 3:15. Despite the breather, the contract continued to gap down, falling to its low for the day (down 4.7 percent) between 3:15 and 3:30. Following a two-minute trading halt at 3:30, the contract regained substantial ground by 3:45 and ended the day down just 3.6 percent. The S&P 500 spot index stabilized briefly with the recovery in futures prices at 3:45, but continued its sell-off afterward.

The SEC's preliminary study of the mini-break found that less than half the share volume of MOC sell orders was related to the options and futures expirations (SEC 1991: 8–9). The potential for large expiration-related selling nevertheless appears to have pressured market prices on the 15th. The SEC virtually dismisses a number of macroeconomic factors that were offered as possible triggers for the decline (including negative economic news released on that Friday morning, a proposal in Congress to limit the interest rates that could be imposed on credit card debt, and rumors about unrest in the Soviet Union), looking instead to investor behavior and investment trading strategies (SEC 1991: 5).

The SEC (1991: 6) finds, in particular, that: "The market decline on November 15, 1991, at least on its face, appears similar to the declines in October 1989, and, to a lessor [sic] extent, October 1987. In all of these instances, it appears that institutional money managers had grown concerned over protecting year-to-date gains in their stock portfolios." The report goes on to note (p. 7): "In some of our preliminary telephone interviews with traders, it was discovered that some firms may have engaged in dynamically hedging (in options and futures) risks assumed in OTC puts negotiated with institutional money managers."

Testing the Brakes: October 27, 1997

The 250- and 400-point DJIA price limits set in 1988 were never triggered, even though the mini-breaks of 1989 and 1991 tripped a number of other limit alarms. By mid-1996, however, it had become apparent that the price limits set in 1988 were no longer appropriate for a stock

FIGURE 14.3
DJIA on October 27, 1997

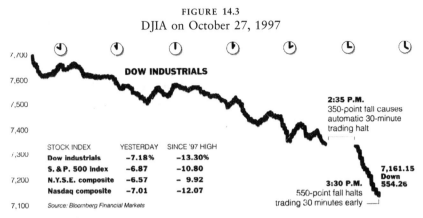

Source: New York Times, October 28, 1997, p. A1.

market that had since quadrupled in value. In July 1996 and January 1997, price limits in stock and stock futures markets were duly relaxed, at least in point terms (although, in percentage terms, they were tighter than the original limits). According to the new limits, the DJIA would have to decline by 350 points from the previous day's close to trigger a half-hour trading halt and by 550 points to trigger a one-hour halt (with similar limits set for futures markets, based on the S&P 500 futures contract).

Both these limits were hit on Monday, October 27, 1997. For the day, the DJIA was off 7 percent, or 554 points (a record point drop), on record NYSE volume – over 685 million shares. But it was a shortened day. Trading was first halted at 2:35 p.m., when the 350-point limit was hit. Although trading resumed at 3:05, it didn't last long. The threat of the second price limit appeared to act like a black hole, sucking prices down. It took less than half an hour for the average to fall another 200 points. The 550-point limit was hit at 3:30, and trading was halted for the day, half an hour before the exchange's usual closing.

On Tuesday, the market rallied. The DJIA rose 4.7 percent – its biggest percentage gain in more than a decade. Volume was a whopping 1.2 billion shares, more than twice the volume seen on October 19, 1987.

So, on the tenth anniversary of the 1987 crash, the market appeared to be repeating the pattern – a steep decline on a Monday followed by a strong rebound on the following day. Were the causes the same? Superficially, October 1997 appears to have little in common with October 1987. Unlike 1987, neither interest rates nor inflation rates were rising (or even perceived to be rising). Furthermore, the US budget deficit was at its lowest ebb since the early 1970s. US economic fundamentals were strong.

In 1997, market "fundamentalists" looked East to explain the market break. Several Asian currencies, particularly Thailand's and Hong Kong's, had been under attack, and the Asian economic miracle seemed to be coming to a close, with booms in Thailand and Indonesia imploding, Hong Kong definitely shaky, and the Japanese economy and stock market continuing to drag on in a sickly state. Fears of how depression in Asia would affect US businesses may well have had something to do with the US market's dive on the 27th. However, it is difficult to construe the bounce back on the 28th as reflective of an overnight change in fundamentals.

Some anecdotal evidence suggests that, again, dynamic hedging was rearing its ugly head. The *New York Times* noted on October 28, 1997 (p. 1) that the previous day's sell-off had been characterized by substantial program selling, which "may indicate use of some strategies known as 'dynamic hedging,' which call for traders to limit losses by selling as prices fall." Large, institutional-size trades continued to fall on the sell side on Tuesday, even as retail investors drove the market up.

The value of OTC options had grown substantially since the 1989 mini-break. By early 1995, according to the Bank for International Settlements (BIS 1996), the notional value of OTC equity index options (both puts and calls) in the US amounted to some $107 billion, out of a worldwide market of $527 billion. Assuming this market grew at the same rate as the listed option market over the 1995–7 period, OTC options on US equity indexes would have reached about $200 billion in notional value by the time of the 1997 market break. The notional principal value of exchange-traded options on US equity indexes totaled about $300 billion by that time (BIS 1998: 70). Of course, these values do not indicate the associated hedging demands. If OTC dealers and option market makers hold relatively balanced positions, long and short, the need to hedge dynamically in underlying markets will not be great. However, the evidence indicates that dealers and market makers were net short option positions in the fall of 1997.

Goldman, Sachs (1988: 27) reports that, on the basis of the volatility in listed options markets and the differences between listed put and call premiums, demand for listed index puts had increased as the market rose through the first three quarters of the year. Demand undoubtedly reflected both investors hedging their stock portfolios and OTC option dealers hedging their option positions. In any case, both dealers and market makers stuck with net short option positions would have had to resort to dynamic hedging in the stock market to hedge their exposures.

The good news was that market mechanisms proved ready for the task (although there was some congestion on Tuesday afternoon in the National Association of Securities Dealers' Automated Quotation System, or NASDAQ). The news on circuit breakers was less sanguine. In particular, besides the astounding drop in stock prices between the impositions of the first and second trading halts on the NYSE, many saw a direct relationship between the implementation of circuit breakers in the New York market and subsequent collapses in overseas markets (with the Hang Seng down the most, over 13 percent, on the following day). According to Robert Glauber of the Kennedy School of Government at Harvard (and executive director of the Brady Commission): "Circuit breakers . . . seem to have stimulated a lot more . . . selling in foreign markets. On balance, they may well have done more harm than good" (*New York Times*, October 28, 1997: 1).

Glauber and others, including SEC Chairman Arthur Levitt and Senators Phil Gramm and Christopher Dodd, immediately pressed for a review of the circuit breaker system (*Wall Street Journal*, October 30, 1997). In 1998, the NYSE adopted new price limits based on predetermined percentage declines in the DJIA; the limits are to be updated every three months. Now a point drop equal to about a 10 percent decline will close the market for one hour if it occurs before 2:00 p.m. and for thirty minutes if it occurs between 2:00 and 2:30; a 10 percent decline after 2:30 will not close the market. A point drop equal to about a 20 percent decline will close the market for two hours if it occurs before 1:00 p.m., for an hour if it occurs between 1:00 and 2:00 p.m., and for the rest of the day if it occurs after 2:00 p.m. In addition, a point drop equal to about 30 percent of the market's level will close the market for the day if it occurs at any time.

Summary

While investors' use of synthetic portfolio insurance dramatically declined as a result of the 1987 crash, market volatility did not disappear; nor did insurance. On October 13, 1989, the DJIA fell by 6.9 percent; on November 15, 1991, it endured a 3.9 percent drop; on October 27, 1997, it declined by more than 7 percent. The use of option-related dynamic hedging links these mini-breaks to the crash of 1987.

While economic news apparently triggered the 1989 mini-crash, regulators put much of the blame for the 1991 market break on trading related to expirations of equity-linked options and futures. In both episodes, and in October 1997, market declines were exacerbated by dynamic hedging related to option replication. While OTC and listed puts require no trading by the investors who have purchased them for insurance, the OTC dealers and option market makers who have sold the puts must hedge dynamically in the futures and underlying stock markets.

A number of factors may have prevented these mini-breaks from turning into full-scale crashes. Circuit breakers, however, appear to have been at best only partly successful. They contributed to price discontinuities on October 13, 1989, and in October 1997 they seem to have increased selling pressure in the US stock market on the 27th and to have fostered panic in overseas markets on the 27th and 28th. The exchanges' efforts to facilitate liquidity do appear to have worked, with expanded operational capacity able to handle record volume in October 1997.

Notably, too, the total amount of assets covered by put options was, reportedly, much smaller than the amount protected by synthetic portfolio insurance in 1987 – $2 billion in 1989, for instance, versus up to $100 billion in 1987. By 1997, however, the value of OTC and exchange-listed options had grown substantially, and it is likely that option sellers' need to hedge via option replication in the underlying market had also grown. The next two chapters take a more detailed look at these options and at some of the other alternatives to synthetic portfolio insurance and examine their potentially unsettling impact on investors and the stock market.

Notes

1 Muthuswamy (1991) argues that McMillan fails to correct his data for certain biases, including the autocorrelation in index prices introduced by thin trading in the constituent stocks and the overstatement of futures price volatility caused by bid-ask bounce in agitated markets.

2 Margulis (1991), in a response to the McMillan article, finds some fault with this explanation of the gravitational effect. He points out that arbitragers would not be loath to hold arbitrage positions over a trading halt. He feels the effect can be better explained by the withdrawal from the market of liquidity-supplying market makers, day traders, and short-term speculators.

15

Sons of Portfolio Insurance

We felt ultimately that demand for hedges would persist.
John O'Brien (Forbes, February 15, 1993)

On the one hand, the crash of 1987 highlighted two major problems with portfolio insurance as carried out by dynamic asset allocation. First, it showed that the strategy of self-insurance upon which synthetic portfolio insurance rests is not insurance in the true sense of the word; the market declined to serve as the guarantor of insured portfolio values. Second, the crash made manifest the latent danger large amounts of insured assets pose for market liquidity and market stability. On the other hand, the crash if anything increased investors' awareness of the potential fragility of the market, and their consequent desire for protection.

The financial community has taken two basic approaches in addressing synthetic portfolio insurance's problems and investors' continuing desire for asset protection. One approach has been to "fix" portfolio insurance itself, generally by means of innovative trading structures. The other approach has been to develop new financial products that can provide the protection portfolio insurance promised while avoiding the pitfalls. This chapter examines some of the trading strategies and investment instruments that have followed in the wake of the failure of portfolio insurance.

Sunshine Trading

Chapters 4 and 9 considered the natural sellers of portfolio insurance, the value investors, market timers, and tactical asset allocators that might take the other side of insurers' trades. When synthetic strategies were first introduced to the financial community, insurance buyers signed up in droves, but no effort was made to sign up offsetting sellers of insurance. Could insurance-induced order imbalances, such as occurred during the 1987 crash, be reduced by a better match between insurance buyers and sellers? Fischer Black and Erol Hakanoglu (1987) proposed a clearinghouse for insurers, which would explicitly match insurance buyers' and sellers' trades.

Not long after the crash, Robert Ferguson and John O'Brien (1988) proposed matching buyers and sellers through instruments called "stabilizing forwards." Portfolio insurers and their counterparties (investors willing to commit to a limit buy order if the market were to decline or to a limit sell order if the market were to rise) would enter into binding agreements to trade stock index futures at prices and in amounts agreed upon in advance, if and when the market reached prespecified levels. These forward contracts would, in effect, presell the trading needs of insurers at prenegotiated prices. If the market experienced a major decline, the insured investor would presumably sell the amount of futures contracts specified in the agreement at the specified price to achieve a given level of portfolio protection. Such protection would not require unannounced dynamic hedging, as the trading required has been prearranged. There would thus be no impact on the market in periods of price declines (or price rises, for that matter).

A more indirect approach would be to advertise traders' intentions, what has become known as "sunshine trading." In the aftermath of the crash, Merton Miller (1991: 137–8) noted that:

> Many observers believe, with some justification, that massive liquidations by portfolio insurers overwhelmed the normal marketmaking capacities of both the New York Stock Exchange and the Chicago index futures and options exchanges. The selling pressure was further intensified, some believe, by the public's inability at the time to distinguish adequately between "informationless" trades by portfolio insurers and those of informed investors.

Miller asserts (p. 158) that preannouncing insurers' stock sales during the crash might have encouraged the prompter participation of buy-side traders.

Michael Brennan and Eduardo Schwartz (1989) have noted that the unexpected volume of trading required by portfolio insurance strategies can have amplified effects on market volatility. Gerard Gennotte and Hayne Leland (1990: 1015–17), writing some time after the crash, demonstrate that insured assets amounting to 5 percent of the market can set off a market decline of 30 percent, if the market is completely unaware of

FIGURE 15.1
"The Guys Who Gave Us Portfolio Insurance"

BUSINESS PEOPLE OF THE YEAR

THE GUYS WHO GAVE US PORTFOLIO INSURANCE

LELAND, O'BRIEN, AND RUBINSTEIN

State, Reed relied on bank credit cards, then in their youth. In 1977 he mailed out 20 million applications, enlisting thousands of deadbeats who failed to pay their bills. When interest rates shot up far beyond what Citicorp was then allowed to charge its card customers, the consumer bank lost $100 million. Reed wasn't chastened by the credit card fiasco, recalls then-President William Spencer: "He's never at a loss for a decision, even if he's wrong." Still, by this time Reed needed all his ace issue. Because of the consumer bank's losses, Wriston cancelled year-end bonuses for all Citicorp employees in 1980. Workers in other divisions were furious at Reed, says Wriston. "The chill around the water cooler was about 50 below."

Reed, who says he doesn't worry much, concedes there were times during the credit card fiasco when he told his wife, Sally, that he might be fired. "I knew it was a disaster," he says. "I figured if I get another job, I'd be paid less. So what. It wouldn't have meant that I was a bad person."

If Wriston's confidence in Reed was wavered, he doesn't admit it. In any case, the boss's faith paid off—big. The consumer bank recovered so smartly that 55% of Citicorp's revenues and 40% of its earnings in 1986. Says Reed, almost modestly: "I have a good sense of where things are going in the long term."

WHERE DO Citicorp and John Reed go from here? For inspiration Reed pores over books on the history of scientific thought, studying, he says, "how ideas evolve, how the really great scientists have a sense of where the breaks are coming." Reed figures Citicorp's breaks will keep coming from sophisticated banking tools reminiscent of ... the spawning of several billion dollars on computers, and Reed wants to do lots more. For example, he would like to expand Quotron, an electronic stock price quotation service the bank bought in 1986, into the business of dispensing advice on, say, portfolio management.

The company's operating style has changed from the back office days, when he says he was "culturally uncouth." Today he claims to be "broader, more tolerant and philosophical." And confident. "If I'm going to make a mistake, it's not likely that I'll be working on the wrong problem," he says. "If I fail, it will be from having too long a reach." ... Only to reach out seven years when people would only back me for four." Reed may scramble his letters, but he has no doubts about this vision for Citicorp.   —Brian O'Reilly

A FEW MONTHS AGO, before the deluge, it seemed like a lot of stock market arcana of interest only to managers of vast sums. Now it is a prime topic of conversation, especially among people eager to fix blame for the day the Dow lost 508 points. Much of that talk has focused on Hayne Leland, John O'Brien, and Mark Rubinstein, the inventors and missionaries of portfolio insurance, a hedging technique that many think made the plunge steeper and deeper than it would have been otherwise.

By 1987, six years after the three men started a company, called LOR (or short), in market their method, fund managers had bought coverage for upwards of $60 billion of assets from LOR and companies under its license to it. In those six years, the years that they had only one dissatisfied major customer—until October 19. On that day their technique failed to do what some of LOR's clients expected. One complainant that his company lost more in a day than it was supposed to in three years. Several suspended their policies. Overall, only about half of that $60 billion remains covered. The recriminations remind us to miss out on the year's recovery. But no matter on the road again.

One thing it really is not is insurance, at least in the conventional sense of a policy that guarantees a certain benefit in case of a covered loss. Instead it is an investment strategy that a client pays a financial management company to carry out. The aim is to make sure that stock portfolios decline by no more than a specified amount over a fixed period—say, 5% over three years.

Originally, portfolio insurance essentially meant hedging a portfolio by adjusting the ratio of stocks to money market instruments as stock prices rise and fall. In a simplified example, if stocks sink 8% in a bad stretch, the insurer switches some of the portfolio to money market instruments, which begin earning interest. He switches enough so that the interest earned will bring the client's assets back up to at least −5% by the end of the contract. When stock prices rise, raising the cushion between the new value of the portfolio and the acceptable minimum, the insurer uses cash to buy more equities.

That is how portfolio insurance worked when Leland, O'Brien, and Rubinstein began selling it. Since 1984, however, they have hedged by selling stock index futures—that is, agreeing to sell a basket of the stocks in the S&P index at the current price on a specified future date. This contract locks in the present value of the portfolio if stocks fall. Index futures helped portfolio insurance take off, partly because they are cheaper, easier, and quicker to buy and sell than stocks are.

HAYNE LELAND, now 46, got the germ of the idea in the mid-1970s, when his brother, an investment manager, lamented that institutional investors had been scared away from the market by the 1974 slump, missing out on the start of the year's recovery. They even finish each other's sentences. Leland is a vigorous promoter of the company and is innovative product; Rubinstein, 43, more modest and self-deprecating, plays an academician's curiosity. As recounts the history of the company, he talks with such enthusiasm about what slowed them as he does of what made things finally come together.

"The selling ingredient turned out to be" O'Brien. For when the two professors ly ventured off campus and tried to sell their product, nothing happened. "We n't really have the time and talent to be ous marketers," says Leland. "I made is to four or five banks. Then I waited them to call me." Finally, in 1980, they made their first big convert—O'Brien.

A native of the Bronx, O'Brien, 50, followed a longer path to the world of finance than Leland and Rubinstein. Like his two partners, he went to college in Cambridge, but down the river at MIT, where he earned a dual degree in engineering and economics. He spent four years in the Air Force and five with the Planning Research Corp., an offshoot of the Rand Corp., whose main projects involved war-gaming and defense against ballistic missiles. He later switched from military risks to investment risks and crossed over to the financial side for good when he was assigned to evaluate Planning Research's pension fund.

EVENTUALLY O'Brien went to work for A.G. Becker, where he analyzed pension fund investments. That led him to visit Berkeley, where he saw a presentation by Leland and Rubinstein. Impressed with the commercial potential of the

idea, O'Brien took it back to Becker, which rejected it as too complicated. So he quit his lucrative haven to become chief executive of Leland O'Brien & Rubinstein in 1981, bringing what the venture sorely needed: the ability to break down complicated ideas into graspable pieces. His easygoing, good-natured manner helped too.

What, then, happened on October 19? Theories conflict, and different things happened to different portfolio insurers. Though no one suggests that portfolio insurance was the sole or even the principal cause of the crash, it may have contributed to the depth and rapidity of the decline. In the wake of the previous week's steep losses, portfolio insurers sold an unusually large number of futures contracts when the Chicago futures exchanges opened on Black Monday. That helped drive futures prices down sharply. Stock prices then followed suit. So portfolio insurers, and others, sold still more futures contracts, reinforcing the downward spiral.

NOT EVERY INSURER was selling futures like crazy, though. Some, including LOR, stopped selling them because a gap appeared between the futures market and the stock market, with stocks trading higher. If the gap reflected a real divergence between the two markets, then selling futures contracts would lock in a value that was too low—significantly lower than what stocks were trading for at the same time. But there was no way of knowing how much of the gap was real and how much reflected a greater time lag in recording trades on the stock exchange than on the futures exchange. In retrospect, insurers who stopped selling futures recognize that they should have continued.

Messrs. Leland, O'Brien, and Rubinstein admit to being chastened by events; they are now busy figuring out what to do next. They insist that the theory underlying portfolio insurance is sound, and they want to make it perform better when markets move quickly. They are also working on a new way of hedging, to be unveiled early in 1988, that O'Brien says won't necessitate going to the stock, futures, or options markets.

O'Brien's reaction has been philosophical. The events of October 19 didn't reduce people's concern with risk," he says wryly. "In every big event there are the seeds of a new order." Perhaps he has been looking out his office window for inspiration—or for a less tangible form of insurance. In big, red neon letters, a sign atop a nearby building says JESUS SAVES.   —Andrew Kupfer

continued

Source: Reprinted from the January 4, 1988 issue of *Fortune* by special permission; copyright 1988, Time Inc. Photo by Hans Neleman.

insurers' trading intentions. If, on the other hand, the market is fully informed of insurers' trading intentions, Gennotte and Leland predict a market drop of only 1 percent. They recommend wider dissemination of information about hedgers' intended actions through the preanouncement of trading requirements.

Steven Wunsch's (1987) proposal for sunshine trading was designed to reduce the destabilizing impact of insurance trading through the advertisement of investors' trading intentions. Under this scheme, insurers voluntarily announce their intentions to trade. In a similar vein, Sanford Grossman (1988a: 295) suggests that insurers be permitted to publicize their trading needs at various market levels.

As insurers are "informationless" traders, they arguably have nothing to lose by revealing their trading plans. And if insurers' trading intentions were fully anticipated, market timers and other sellers of insurance could commit more resources to accommodating their trading needs. Its advocates claim that sunshine trading could stabilize the market by curtailing unanticipated demands for liquidity. They point to the US Treasury auctions as an example of successful prea nounced trading.

Some critics, however, maintain that sunshine trades would attract frontrunners (see Gammill and Marsh 1988: 36). Frontrunners trade in anticipation of large-volume trades that have the potential to change prices; by buying before an expected large purchase, for example, they may be able to reap a profit if the purchase raises prices still higher. As we noted in chapter 10, frontrunners can destabilize markets whe.. they trade before, or in tandem with, trend-following strateξ..s such as synthetic portfolio insurance.

Anat Admati and Paul Pfleiderer (1991) examine sunshine trad..ng in a market with three types of rational traders: liquidity (informationless) traders who preannounce their trades, liquidity traders who do not preannounce, and speculators with varying levels of information about the trades. They find that, when speculators have varying information about the trades, and when their trading entails costs, sunshine trading does encourage speculative traders to enter the mar'-et in times of greater demand for liquidity. The larger the size of the preannounced orders, the higher the proportion of speculators who will enter the market and trade, thereby providing liquidity.

In 1992, Wunsch put his sunshine trading concept into practice with the launch of the Arizona Stock Exchange (AZX). Participants in this electronic market, all institutional investors, log on to the exchange's computer at specified periods during the day. In each period, they reveal their trading intentions, listing the stocks, the numbers of shares, and the prices at which they wish to buy and sell. They can then observe the orders of other participants and reconfigure their own orders as they see fit. At the end of the period, the computer matches as many orders as possible, in what is known as a single-price auction.

Initially, the AZX had one auction each business day. It has currently been cleared to offer four auctions a day, two in the morning and two in the afternoon. Three of these are open to both NASDAQ and exchange-listed stocks, while the fourth is restricted to the OTC stocks. Nevertheless, Wunsch (1997: 2) admits that the AZX remains relatively inactive and illiquid, especially in relation to institutional trading demands; for this, he blames regulatory restrictions.

Sunshine trading, by revealing the demand for insurance and the informationless nature of insurance trades could reduce some of the problems discussed in chapter 9. Investors aware that the trading is coming from insurers would not confuse it with information-motivated trading, hence would not be desirous of trading along with insurers. Investors might even be encouraged to take the other side of the dynamic hedging trades of insurers and other option replicators. Sunshine trading could thus reduce the volatility-amplifying effects of dynamic hedging, which had such a devastating impact on the market in 1987.

To the extent that it reduces market instability, sunshine trading may ameliorate another major problem highlighted by the 1987 market break – the failure of portfolio insurance strategies to protect portfolio values as promised. As we noted in chapter 13, the chaotic conditions during the crash (to which portfolio insurance itself contributed not a little) made it impossible for many portfolio insurers to unload equities in time to prevent substantial violations of their insured floors. The decade since the crash has seen the emergence of a number of new financial instruments and strategies designed to offer more dependable protection of equity portfolio values. Below, we look at some examples of what might be called the "sons of portfolio insurance."

Supershares

LOR's O'Brien (*Forbes*, February 15, 1993: 224) admits that the stock market crash of 1987 and its aftermath was "a very difficult time for our firm. But we felt ultimately that demand for hedges would persist." In 1992, LOR brought to the public exchanges a new product that offered more solid downside protection for insurers and less instability for markets. Building on Nils Hakansson's (1976) concept of a superfund, LOR's "SuperTrust" offered exchange-traded mutual fund shares that could be broken out in several ways according to investors' desires for capital gains, downside protection, or current income.[1]

The idea of divisible equity shares had been marketed previously in the form of Americus Trust units, which were available for some five years beginning in the mid-1980s. Americus Trust units were finite-lived instruments redeemable into shares of the underlying common stock and fully collateralized by common stock held by the trustees. Purchasers of units, however, could choose to convert them into either PRIMEs or SCOREs. PRIMEs offered income in the form of dividends on the underlying stock plus varying degrees of participation in the stock's appreciation over the term of the trust. Provided the underlying share value at termination did not exceed a predetermined Termination Claim value (equivalent to a strike price), PRIME purchasers received a full share of common for each PRIME; if value at termination exceeded the Termination Claim, PRIME purchasers received a fractional share equal to the ratio of the Termination Claim value to the closing price of the common. The total return to PRIME purchasers was thus capped by the value of the Termination Claim. Any capital appreciation above the Termination Claim went to SCORE purchasers; SCORE purchasers in effect held a call on the underlying shares with a strike price equal to the Termination Claim.

Whereas the underlying securities for PRIMEs and SCOREs were the shares of a small number of individual corporations, LOR's "Super-Trust" rested on two broad-based market funds. Shares in the trust, which were fully redeemable, were convertible into two "SuperUnits" traded on the Amex.[2] One unit, the "Index SuperUnit," was based on an S&P 500 index fund; the other, the "Money Market SuperUnit," was based on a money market fund. Each "SuperUnit" had a three-year life and earned the dividend or interest associated with the underlying assets.

Each unit could be divided in turn into two complementary "Super-Shares" that were listed on the CBOE. Complementary shares of a unit could be traded separately or recombined into the unit and sold on the Amex or redeemed. The sum totals of their payoff patterns equaled the total payoffs of the underlying assets, and the shares were fully collateralized by the assets in the funds.

The "SuperTrust" allowed investors to pick and choose between shares in order to emphasize income, equity market opportunity, or equity market protection. For example, the "Index SuperUnit" split into a "Priority SuperShare" and an "Appreciation SuperShare." The former received the dividends earned by the unit plus total capital gains of up to 25 percent of original value. The latter earned the capital gains in excess of 25 percent. "Appreciation SuperShares" were thus the equivalent of a three-year call option on the S&P 500 index, rising in value when the market rose above the strike price (an index appreciation of

FIGURE 15.2
"If You Loved Portfolio Insurance . . ."

If You Loved Portfolio Insurance...

Investment Concern Unveils SuperShares

By GEORGE ANDERS
Staff Reporter of THE WALL STREET JOURNAL

Four New Ways to Play the Market

Here's how the four SuperShares proposed by Leland O'Brien Rubinstein Inc. would perform in different market conditions. The Upside Appreciation one would provide the most leverage in a bull market. The Downside Protection one would do best in a bear market. The other two SuperShares would do best in a flat or slightly rising market; they would fall if stocks slumped, but wouldn't gain past a certain point if stocks rose. The SuperShares would be listed on the New York Stock Exchange. All the returns are over a three-year period.

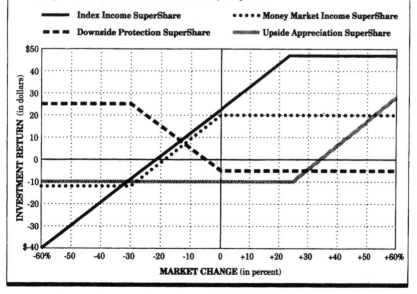

Index Income SuperShare   • • • • Money Market Income SuperShare
- - - Downside Protection SuperShare   Upside Appreciation SuperShare

Source: Wall Street Journal, November 30, 1988, p. C1.

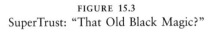

FIGURE 15.3
SuperTrust: "That Old Black Magic?"

That Old Black Magic?
The Portfolio Insurance Crowd's New Idea

Source: *Barron's*, May 15, 1989, p. 62. Cartoon copyright Peter Spacek.

25 percent), but with the possibility of expiring worthless after three years if the index did not appreciate by more than 25 percent.

The "Money Market SuperUnit" broke down into a "Protection Super-Share" and an "Income and Residual SuperShare." The former received the capital value lost by the index unit after three years, if any, up to a maximum of 30 percent. The latter received all interest due the money market unit, plus the residual of its final value after the protection share was paid off. "Protection SuperShares" thus offered downside protection, acting as a three-year put option on the S&P 500 index, and appreciating in value when the market fell below the strike price (the starting value of the index). Of course, this option too could expire worthless, but O'Brien advised in an April 1993 marketing letter that it "could be an important hedging security for your general equity portfolio."

Because they were based on market indexes, "SuperShares" provided a broader vehicle for portfolio management than PRIMEs and SCOREs.

Furthermore, the addition of the money market component introduced an ability to hedge against actual market declines, which SCOREs and PRIMEs alone could not provide.

"SuperShares" also offered advantages over synthetic portfolio insurance. Exchange listing, because it fully reveals prices, hence investor demand, should encourage liquidity. "SuperShare" prices were determined by competing investor demands. Investors desiring protection against market declines would have purchased protection shares; others, looking for exposure to an index fund, would have bought appreciation shares. If the demand for protection rose, say as the result of market pessimism, the cost of the protection shares would also rise. Share prices should thus have revealed fully the demand for and the cost of protection.

Price transparency, exchange listing, and the unit sizes of shares (small enough to appeal to retail investors) should have encouraged the participation of investors willing to provide the liquidity needed by institutional hedgers. This in turn would have made the underlying markets less susceptible to the instability posed by synthetic insurance. Stability would also have been enhanced by the fact that, beyond initial purchase of the shares, no further trading would be required to achieve protection over a given horizon, even in volatile markets.

The ultimate value of LOR's "SuperTrust" for investors desiring to hedge against market declines depended on its success in attracting enough speculative investors and active professional traders to ensure secondary market liquidity. Unfortunately, what "SuperShares" failed to offer was simplicity. In fact, it was claimed (see Schmerken 1991: 46) that the shares were "so complex that many wonder if retail investors will understand them." And, indeed, their initial reception and subsequent performance were less than royal. LOR had planned to launch with $2 billion in initial subscriptions (Star 1992: 38), but ended up settling for only $1 billion in commitments, mainly from large institutional investors. The "SuperTrust" was not renewed after its initial three-year run.[3]

Options Reborn

Publicly traded options offer numerous advantages over the synthetic strategy when it comes to providing protection. They do not require selling stock into a falling market, as portfolio insurance does. Real put options are thus not susceptible to replication failures because of volatile or discontinuous markets.

Insurance through publicly traded options offers another advantage over dynamic trading strategies – trading intentions are not as obscured. The open interest in and the prices of exchange-traded options are publicly available. These data provide an indication of the public's demand for protection and expectation of market volatility. Exchange-traded options may therefore be less destabilizing than dynamic strategies, although, as we will see in the next chapter, even exchange-traded options may increase dynamic hedging.

But synthetic portfolio insurance arose in large part because portfolio protection via publicly traded options faced substantial obstacles. First, exchange-traded options were only available for certain standardized strike prices and expiration dates, and their time horizons were fixed and generally quite short. While an investor could have used a series of publicly traded short-term options to provide protection over the long run, the cost would not be known in advance, as it would depend on market volatility at the times the options were rolled over; the ultimate cost could be substantial.[4]

Second, the maximum position limits imposed by SEC regulation reduced the usefulness of exchange-traded options to large institutional investors. Gary Gastineau (1992: 96) suggests that insurers need not have traded stock and futures during the 1987 crash if they had been permitted to have large positions in listed options: "Long puts or calls would have cut their stock exposure automatically, and given them time to analyze the risk of the market – without the necessity to trade. An efficient option market with no position limits might have attracted portfolio insurance buyers and sellers to a trading and risk management mechanism designed to price and redistribute the impact of market volatility."

The shortcomings of synthetic portfolio insurance and exchange-traded options, made evident by the 1987 crash, opened the door for the development of an array of customized, over-the-counter vehicles to meet institutional investors' hedging and other portfolio management needs. Taking its cue from OTC customized interest rate, currency, and commodity contracts (pioneered in large measure by the Europeans), the US financial services industry has developed and marketed a wide range of OTC equity derivatives. Institutional investors who do not see what they need on the menu of exchange products are increasingly joining the stampede to the over-the-counter market where, it seems, they can achieve just about any desired payoff pattern (or combination of patterns), as long as a counterparty can be found to provide it.

One of the most popular equity products suitable for use in insurance strategies has been the OTC option, discussed in chapter 14. This is a privately negotiated contract between two parties – the option writer (usually an investment bank, bank subsidiary, or broker-dealer) and option buyer (typically a large institutional investor). Because the counterparties design the option to meet their own specific needs, it can be tailored to meet particular exposure and protection requirements and can offer maturities and capacities not available on the listed options markets. So-called "plain vanilla" OTC options may offer customization in the way of the amount or nature of the underlying assets (stock, stock portfolio, or index), the option strike price, the option's maturity, and the exercise style (European or American). Elaborations on the simple option concept are provided by so-called "exotic options," which have payout patterns that differ from the plain vanilla.

Exotic options include average rate options, barrier options, lookback options, and rainbow options. The payoff on an average rate, or "Asian," option depends on the average price of the underlying asset over the specified period. The payoff on barrier options is contingent, not only on the underlying security's price at exercise, but on that security's price achieving or not achieving a specified level before expiration; a "knock-in" option may reach expiration in the money, but nevertheless expire worthless if the underlying security fails to pass a specified barrier over the course of the option's life, whereas a "knock-out" option will become worthless if the underlying security passes a specified barrier.

Both barrier and average rate options are generally less expensive than their more orthodox counterparts because they offer less opportunity of payoff or a more limited payoff. Lookback options, by contrast, are generally more expensive than plain vanilla OTC options because they allow their purchasers to choose the option's strike price on the basis of the underlying asset's prices over the option's life.

Rainbow options are options whose payoffs depend on the prices of at least two different underlying assets, which cannot be valued as if they were options on a single underlying asset. With spread options, for example, payout depends on the difference between the prices of two underlying assets. Basket options are based on the price for a basket of underlying assets. Quanto payouts depend on both underlying prices and underlying ratios; for an option that pays out in another currency, for example, total payout will depend, not only on the performance of the underlying asset, but on the relative performances of the two currencies. Some rainbow options may be more expensive than the plain vanilla variety. A spread option, for example, which pays out as long as relative performance turns out as expected, even if both underlying assets decline (or rise), may be more expensive. A basket option that can take advantage of the diversification and lower volatility of a combination of assets may be less expensive.

OTC options suffer from several disadvantages relative to listed options. In the absence of a secondary market, OTC options are substantially illiquid and more difficult to value. They are also customized instruments, hence generally more expensive (although increasing competition among financial intermediaries has driven down prices of those options with the most common specifications). Finally, because there is no exchange clearinghouse providing a financial guarantee, holders of OTC options face the risk of counterparty default (which will be discussed at length in the next chapter).[5]

Expanding the Listed Option Menu

Spurred by the mushrooming volume (and profits) in OTC markets, the exchanges themselves began in the late 1980s and early 1990s to offer options that were more suitable to institutional investors' needs. Ironically, the Amex introduced three-year, European-style options on the Institutional Index on the morning of October 19, 1987. In early November 1987, the CBOE began trading options on the S&P 500 index with a two-year maturity.

October 1990 witnessed the birth of LEAPS – "Long-term Equity AnticiPation Securities" – two-year puts and calls on a select number of individual securities as well as the S&P 100, the S&P 500, and the MMI. Today index LEAPS, traded most actively on the CBOE and Amex, have maturities of up to six years and cover market sectors such as oil and biotechnology as well as broader-based indexes. However, although volume has picked up, thanks largely to a surge of retail interest, liquidity remains low compared with short-term equity index options (Hunter 1997).

The CBOE announced plans in early 1993 for "flexible options" geared to institutional investors (initial transactions of at least $10 million of notional principal on the S&P 100 or 500). FLEX options, introduced in 1996, allow customization of contracts for the underlying index (S&P 100 or S&P 500), expiration date (up to five years), strike price, exercise style (American, European, or capped European), and settlement value (expiration-day opening, closing, or average price). Position limits on FLEX options were eliminated at the end of 1997. Like other exchange-traded instruments, FLEX options enjoy the credit guarantee of a clearinghouse (the Options Clearing Corporation in this case); price transparency; and an established secondary market (CBOE 1993: 106).

The purchase of puts or calls, whether exchange-traded or OTC, requires payment of a premium up front, whether or not the option is eventually exercised. The fallacious statement made with regard to synthetic portfolio insurance – that it would offer comparable protection at little or no cost – was later heard on behalf of option collars. "Zero-cost" collars became particularly popular in early 1991. Estimates of the total stock value covered by zero-cost collars in that year range as high as $25 billion (*Wall Street Journal*, January 9, 1992: C1).

With a collar, the investor purchases an out-of-the-money index put option and pays for it by selling an out-of-the-money call option. The strike price of the put option serves as the floor for the portfolio's value, while the strike price of the call option represents a cap on the portfolio's value. A well-designed collar may indeed cost nothing at the time of purchase. As with synthetic portfolio insurance, however, its true cost becomes apparent only after the fact. If the market rises beyond the cap, the portfolio will incur an opportunity cost equal to the amount by which the index outperforms the strike price of the call. This may turn out to be a substantial cost to pay for a "zero-cost" collar.

Synthetic Warrants, Swaps, and Guaranteed Equity

In addition to OTC and exchange-listed options, the past decade has witnessed tremendous growth in other vehicles designed to offer option-like payoff opportunities, including synthetic warrants, swaps, and guaranteed equity. These vehicles are naturally suited to investors desiring to speculate on market movements, to attain index-like returns with one instrument, or to achieve otherwise unattainable exposures to certain markets. They can also be used to hedge against downside moves, hence may play a role in certain portfolio insurance strategies.

Warrants

Synthetic warrants are similar to but distinct from both publicly traded and OTC options. Synthetic warrants are options that may trade on public markets, but they are issued by individual corporations, financial institutions, or governments rather than exchanges. Consequently, as with OTC option contracts, the investor must look solely to the issuer for payment, not to an exchange or clearinghouse.

Traditionally, warrants have been issued by individual companies in conjunction with equity or debt issues; they give the investor the right to purchase additional equity or debt at specified prices at some future date and allow the company to lower its funding costs. Such traditional warrants have been particularly popular in sustained bull markets such as the US experienced in the 1920s and Japan in the 1980s. Whereas companies issuing warrants can create additional shares as warrants are exercised, the issuer of synthetic warrants must have the underlying assets on hand or must purchase them to deliver as demand dictates (see also Lindberg 1995).

Broker-dealers have issued synthetic call and put warrants on individual stocks and on indexes. Among the more popular warrants were those issued on the Japanese and other foreign market indexes. In early 1990, the Kingdom of Denmark, Salomon Brothers, and Bankers Trust issued put warrants on the Nikkei index, which were listed on the Amex. These (like LOR's Celebration Fund) offered protection against decline for a portfolio of Japanese stocks, and allowed bets against the Japanese market. Although these products (especially the Nikkei puts) have primarily been used for speculative purposes, some institutions have used warrants to hedge their international portfolios (Hansell 1990: 56 and *Wall Street Journal*, April 9, 1992).

Firms that issue such warrants hedge their exposures by using a number of trading strategies, including dynamic hedging. As Barbara Donnelly and Michael Sesit note in the *Wall Street Journal* (April 17, 1990: C1): "Without these and other strategies to hedge the puts, issuers would have risked losing hundreds of millions of dollars in the recent plunge in Japanese stock prices. The put issuers execute the portfolio insurance strategy primarily by purchasing and selling Nikkei futures contracts on the Osaka and Singapore stock exchanges." Chapter 16 will discuss the impact of such hedging on the Japanese market in the early 1990s.

Swaps

Swaps have gained huge popularity in the interest rate and currency markets. Swaps are contracts between two counterparties to exchange a series of cash flows. A simple example might be an issuer that swaps the fixed-rate interest payments on a new bond issue for floating-rate payments, or dollar-denominated bonds for bonds in other currencies.

With equity swaps, one or both of the flows are linked to the performance of an established equity index or basket of stocks. The investor generally exchanges a fixed or floating interest rate for the dividend and capital appreciation on the stock index. An investor with a stock portfolio, however, can overlay it with an equity swap, paying out the dividends and any capital gains on the stocks in exchange for receipt of a fixed rate of return (see Marshall and Kapner 1993: 129–30).

Bankers Trust initiated the first reported equity swap in 1989 (Marshall and Kapner 1993: 6). They are now a booming business, and to some observers a potentially destabilizing one. Gerald Corrigan, then president of the New York Federal Reserve Bank, suggested that "some of the specific purposes for which swaps are now being used may be quite at odds with an appropriately conservative view of a swap, thereby introducing new elements of risk or distortion into the marketplace" (*New York Times*, February 9, 1992: C1). An example of a less than conservative use of swaps might be a corporation that gains equity exposure by investing in a fixed income instrument and then swapping the fixed income returns for the returns on a stock market index; under accounting rules in effect until June 1999, the fixed income instrument would enter the corporate balance sheet as an asset, but the swap would not have to be reported on the balance sheet, hence would not appear as a liability (Marshall and Kapner 1993: 148).

Furthermore, a dealer that has taken on one side in a swap will probably want to hedge any market exposure incurred. This may be done by entering into a matching swap with another counterparty. But if such an opportunity is unavailable, the dealer may engage in a dynamic hedging strategy in order to lay off its market exposure.

Guaranteed Equity

The early 1980s saw the emergence of "90:10" funds. Ninety percent of the fund would be invested in certificates of deposit (CDs) and the remaining 10 percent in a call option on a stock index. The investor was thus guaranteed the return of at least 90 percent of the initial investment, while the call option offered participation in any stock market advance. Most of these funds languished in the low-volatility, high-return environment that prevailed until mid-1987 (Culligan 1997).

Nevertheless, some banks began offering similar instruments in the mid-1980s. With Chase Manhattan's Market Index Investment, first offered in March 1987, depositors received a guarantee of 100 percent of their initial deposit (backed up, for accounts up to $100,000, by the US Federal Deposit Insurance Corporation). In place of the usual interest rate on bank deposits (averaging 5.4 percent at the time), depositors could choose to receive 75 percent of any gain in the S&P 500; 60 percent of any gain or a 2 percent return, whichever was higher; or the higher of 40 percent of the index return or a 4 percent return. In exchange for the give-up in interest, the depositor received the opportunity to participate in a stock market that had been rising smartly.

The 1987 crash put an end to many of these instruments because their issuers lost so much money on their risk management transactions (Baubonis et al. 1993). (As we will see in chapter 18, volatility also proved a problem for issuers in 1998.) Nevertheless, as we have noted, the crash instilled in investors a renewed appreciation for protection of portfolio value. In the spring of 1993, Citibank began marketing a "stock index insured account," aimed at retail investors, that offered "Stock market returns. Zero risk to principal."[6] Citibank promised returns on a five-year deposit of twice the average monthly increase in the S&P 500 index (*New York Times*, March 23, 1993).

FIGURE 15.4
Merrill Lynch Ad: ". . . have it both ways . . ."

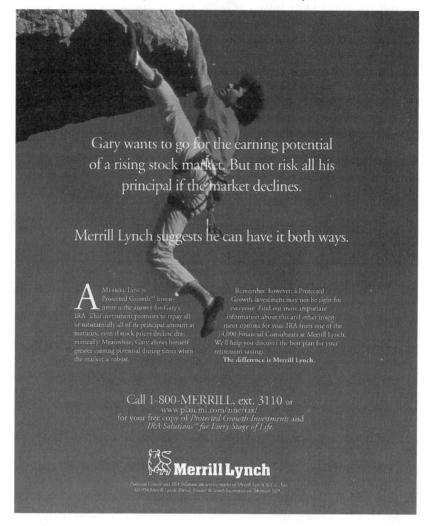

Gary wants to go for the earning potential
of a rising stock market. But not risk all his
principal if the market declines.

Merrill Lynch suggests he can have it both ways.

A Merrill Lynch Protected Growth℠ investment is the answer for Gary's IRA. This investment promises to repay all or substantially all of its principal amount at maturity, even if stock prices decline dramatically. Meanwhile, Gary allows himself greater earning potential during times when the market is robust.

Remember, however, a Protected Growth investment may not be right for everyone. Find out more important information about this and other investment options for your IRA from one of the 14,000 Financial Consultants at Merrill Lynch. We'll help you discover the best plan for your retirement savings. **The difference is Merrill Lynch.**

Call 1-800-MERRILL, ext. 3110 or
www.plan.ml.com/zine/tax/
for your free copy of *Protected Growth Investments* and
IRA Solutions℠ for Every Stage of Life.

Merrill Lynch

Protected Growth and *IRA Solutions* are service marks of Merrill Lynch & Co., Inc.
© 1998 Merrill Lynch, Pierce, Fenner & Smith Incorporated. Member SIPC.

Source: *Smart Money*, April 1998, p. 13.

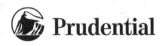

Source: *New York Times*, October 11, 1998, p. BU9.

This is only one example of a myriad of guaranteed equity products sold by banks, broker-dealers, and other financial institutions, primarily to retail investors. Banks have followed Chase's example with equity-linked certificates of deposit that pay little or no interest but give back at maturity the original deposit plus a return linked to the performance of a given equity index. The depositor receives protection of principal (with the added benefit of FDIC insurance) and participation in equity market rises. Broker-dealers and others offer a variety of similar instruments, named variously Equity Participation Notes (EPNs), Stock Upside Notes (SUNs), Structured Upside Participating Equity Receipt (SUPER), and Synthetic High Income Equity Linked Security (SHIELD).

The underlying structure is a CD or bond plus an index call option. Purchase of the call can be funded by the interest forgone by the investor or depositor or, in part, by the sale of an out-of-the-money call option. Selling a call option, however, will place a cap on investors' potential upside capture.

Such instruments offer investors participation in equity returns at a bond-like level of risk, although with a reduced or zero interest rate. As such, they have been described as "stocks with training wheels" (Burchill 1997: 19). Long-term guaranteed equity has really taken off in Europe, where it can often offer investors tax breaks. Estimated sales there total $40 to $100 billion. Guaranteed equity has lagged in the US, where investors apparently feel more comfortable with stock mutual funds or direct stock investment (Payne 1998: S15). Goldman, Sachs (1998) estimates that the notional value of US guaranteed equity in 1997 amounted to only $3 to $5 billion.

Although the ultimate users of guaranteed equity may be primarily retail investors, the issuers and offerers are generally financial intermediaries that rely on OTC broker-dealers to supply them with the index options that provide the equity participation. These option writers in turn may have to engage in dynamic trading to hedge their risk exposures.

Summary

The 1987 crash demonstrated that synthetic portfolio insurance does not work in the face of market illiquidity and price discontinuities and, further, that it can actually destabilize markets, making a collapse more likely. A number of instruments and approaches developed since the crash aim to sidestep the pitfalls of synthetic portfolio insurance while meeting investors' desire for portfolio protection.

Sunshine trading would supposedly reduce market volatility and encourage liquidity by providing an arena in which portfolio insurers preannounce their trading intentions. New option and option-like instruments traded on the public exchanges may go even further toward reducing potential market instability and increasing assurance of portfolio protection. LEAPS and FLEX options, for example, offer the guarantee of the exchange clearinghouse, plus price transparency.

OTC options offer more flexibility for purchasing portfolio insurance than even the newer exchange-traded options, but because these instruments are privately negotiated contracts, there is no clearinghouse to guarantee them. Furthermore, although an insured investor that buys an OTC put will not have to sell into a falling market (or buy into a rising market) to establish the desired level of protection, the broker-dealer or other financial intermediary that has issued the option may have to engage in trend-following dynamic trading in order to hedge the exposures it has taken on. As with synthetic insurance, the extent of such dynamic trading will not be revealed to the market.

The next chapter focuses on the risks options may pose for their buyers and their sellers, as well as for the overall market.

Notes

1 For a brief introduction to "SuperShares" see an early discussion by Anders in the *Wall Street Journal* (October 30, 1988) or, as the LOR product was being approved by the SEC, a piece by Schmerken (1991).

2 Open-end mutual funds are prohibited from selling at prices that differ from net asset value by the Investment Company Act of 1940. This bars them from trading on an exchange, although their shares are redeemable. Closed-end funds may be listed on an exchange, but they cannot offer or sell redeemable shares.

3 In 1994, it was reported (*Pensions & Investments*, May 2, 1994: 1) that LOR had sold its binomial tree option pricing technology to BARRA to obtain cash to underwrite expansion of the "SuperTrust" into Europe and to fund management of overlay hedged portfolios.

4 See Heston (1988); Hill and Wood (1988); and Choie and Novomestky (1989).

5 The OTC market has been moving toward more formal arrangements, such as the CME Swaps Collateral Depository and the CBOT's Hybrid Instrument Transactions Service (HITS). Such quasi-clearinghouses, dealing primarily with swaps, function mainly as collateral depositories, providing services such as marking positions to market and bilateral netting, but not guaranteeing contracts.

6 See the ad in, for example, the *New York Times* (April 14, 1993: A22).

16

The Enduring Risks of Synthetic Options

Continued rapid growth of derivatives contracts at the pace of
the past several years would begin to raise the mania flag. Even
in a global financial marketplace there must exist a finite limit to
shiftable risk.

Jerry Jordan, 1995

As a method of hedging against declines in portfolio value, exchange-
traded and OTC options offer several advantages over synthetic portfolio insurance as implemented with dynamic hedging in the stock and
stock futures markets. First and foremost, these option instruments are
binding contracts, rather than trading strategies implemented as circumstances demand and allow. The option holder is thus assured the purchased level of protection – as long as the option issuer remains solvent.

Second, the purchaser pays the price of protection up front. Unlike
synthetic portfolio insurance, where the cost will reflect the volatility
experienced over the life of the insurance strategy, option prices are set,
either by competition in the listed option markets or by issuers of OTC
options, to reflect the volatility expected over the life of the option.
Whereas portfolio insurers using dynamic hedging take on the risk that
volatility may be greater than expected, purchasers of options shift this
risk to the option seller.

Third, to the extent that it requires less trading of underlying assets
and to the extent that the demand for and the cost of protection are
more transparent, portfolio insurance undertaken with options may
pose less of a threat to market stability than portfolio insurance undertaken via dynamic hedging in the stock and stock futures markets. Whether
these conditions hold remains a moot point. There are at least two major
reasons for concern.

One concern is that information about privately negotiated OTC
options is not readily available. For corporate reporting purposes, most

derivatives contracts are considered off-balance-sheet, hence not included in financial statements, except perhaps in a footnote.[1] And despite the fact that trading volume and price are a matter of public record for exchange-listed options, interpretation of these data may not be so straightforward.

A second concern is the nature of the hedging undertaken by dealers selling OTC options and by market makers on option exchanges. In particular, an option issuer or market maker may have to resort to dynamic hedging in the stock and stock futures markets in order to control the risks it has assumed. John O'Brien notes that these option sellers are "usually . . . doing what suppliers of portfolio insurance were doing before 1987" (*Wall Street & Technology*, July 1993: 30).

Unlike the "pea" in the notorious shell game perpetrated on unsuspecting tourists in the Big City, the risk covered by options is not so easily made to disappear.

Risks to Buyers

For exchange-listed options, the exchange clearing corporation serves as guarantor of the contract. With risk of default diversified across all exchange members, and margin payments required of option sellers, there is little likelihood that an option purchaser will be unable to exercise the option because of counterparty insolvency. With OTC equity options, however, the counterparty is no longer an exchange, but rather the individual issuer (generally a securities dealer). While it may remain unlikely that any one firm will default over the life of any given contract, there is obviously a greater possibility of default for an individual firm than for the amalgam of firms constituting an exchange.

For the investor that has only a single counterparty contract, there is an ever present danger of that counterparty defaulting. The credit quality of one's counterparties is thus of prime concern for investors purchasing OTC options. At the same time, Wall Street firms suffered a steady deterioration in credit quality in the 1980s, as measured by Moody's and Standard & Poor's ratings. Declining credit ratings hampered firms' ability to attract customers in the lucrative area of OTC derivatives (including equity options, but most especially the much larger markets in interest rate and currency swaps and options).

Some firms sought to ameliorate this problem by setting up Special Purpose Vehicles (SPVs), independent subsidiaries designed to deal only in OTC derivatives. SPVs are run by their own managers and directors, separate from those of the parent company, and are subject to special operating and accounting safeguards and ongoing independent audits.

Most importantly, their levels of capitalization are high enough to justify superior credit ratings. Goldman Sachs Financial Products International, Merrill Lynch Derivative Products, and Salomon Swapco have all obtained triple-A credit ratings. Thus buyers of OTC options can feel reasonably comfortable that their options will be honored, provided they monitor the credit ratings of their counterparties and seek to purchase options only from entities with superior ratings.

One substantial risk any purchaser of portfolio protection via OTC options surely runs, however, is that of overpaying for a level of protection that could be obtained at cheaper cost either from other OTC dealers or from exchange-traded instruments. Unfortunately, an OTC option purchaser may find its attempts at comparison shopping thwarted. OTC options are essentially proprietary vehicles tailored to the needs of individual customers. Prices are not publicly quoted and, even if they were, noncomparability across different options would make price comparisons difficult.

Issuers themselves price the options "according to sophisticated theoretical financial models, which rely heavily on the ability to decompose complex contracts into such simpler components as [listed] options, futures, forwards, etc., for which the information necessary for valuation is widely available in the prices observed in the organized securities markets" (Tinic 1995: 356). In general, the price they charge will reflect their expected cost of hedging the risk they have taken on (see Neuhaus and Kusuda 1997). Issuers may be able to hedge relatively cheaply if they can find offsetting, exchange-traded contracts with a liquid market. In that case, the premium they charge the purchaser will cover the theoretical value of the option (via Black–Scholes or other pricing formula) plus the cost to them of purchasing the offsetting options, plus a mark-up reflecting the issuer's profit.

But the cost of an OTC option can balloon if the dealer feels it can not find economically priced options to hedge the risk of the option it has sold. In that case, the dealer will have to rely on dynamic hedging in the stock and stock futures markets. The cost to the option buyer will then include, in addition to the option's theoretical value and a profit margin, surcharges to cover the issuer's expected transaction costs for the dynamic hedge and to compensate the issuer for possible changes in the underlying asset's volatility over the course of the option's life and for possible hedging errors.

Henrik Neuhaus and Yasuo Kusuda (1997) estimate that OTC issuers may charge from 6.5 percent to 35 percent over the theoretical option price, depending upon the difficulty they face in hedging the option sold. Barry Schachter (1992) notes that one issuer he examined sold OTC options at price levels 45 percent above their theoretical values. In other words, the customer was being charged almost one and a half times what it should cost the issuer to replicate an option position affording the specified level of protection. In many cases, then, the cost of an OTC option may bear little relationship to any underlying theoretical price, Black–Scholes or otherwise.

In fact, it is a matter of substantial conjecture just how much listed option prices themselves conform to Black–Scholes theory. No less an authority than Fischer Black (1989a: 67) has said:

> The Black–Scholes formula . . . depends on at least 10 unrealistic assumptions. Making the assumptions more realistic hasn't produced a formula that works better across a wide range of circumstances.

One of the more obvious disparities between modeled and actual listed option prices is the so-called volatility smile. Black–Scholes allows one to estimate the volatility of the underlying market by plugging in known market prices for options, their strike prices, and their expiration dates. According to Black–Scholes, the volatility implied by this exercise in inference should be invariant to the precise relationship between option strike prices and the value of the underlying asset. That is, implied volatility should be the same whether an option is in, at, or out of the money.

In the real world, however, the volatilities implied by the prices of options on the same underlying asset, with the same maturity, but differing strike prices trace a crooked, rather than a straight, line. For options on foreign exchange, for example, implied volatility generally rises as the underlying asset moves away from the option strike price, with implied volatility rising for either in- or out-of-the-money options, forming a smile pattern. Equity index options display more of a grimace or smirk, with the implied volatility obtained from put options significantly greater than that obtained from call options, and rising, the further out of the money the put option.

Mark Rubinstein, addressing the American Finance Association as its president in 1994 (Hayne Leland was to assume the post in 1997), attributed the grimace to the 1987 crash. In his view, it was a form of "crash-o-phobia" reflecting a heightened probability of outlier-type price changes. Jens Carsten Jackwerth and Rubinstein (1996: 1630) find that "the probability of a 3 (or a 4) standard deviation decline [in the S&P index] is 10 times more likely after the crash than before." Klaus Toft and Brian Prucyk (1997) find evidence of a relationship between the volatility smirk and firms' leverage ratios.

Rubinstein and Jackwerth (1997) use observed prices for options on the S&P 500 index to derive a distribution of the probabilities investors attach to possible future outcomes. This distribution shows a much higher probability assigned to large negative outcomes than one would expect. Rubinstein and Jackwerth then use a modified binomial tree process (discussed in appendix C) to find the process by which implied volatility must evolve in order to be consistent with this distribution. They find that the implied volatilities of at-the-money options vary inversely with the underlying asset's price. That is, a decline in the underlying stock index is associated with an increase in implied volatility.

Rubinstein and Jackwerth discuss several possible reasons for this finding. A fall in stock price, for example, might increase a firm's leverage, hence the volatility of its stock (à la Toft and Prucyk). Rubinstein and Jackwerth, however, feel this rationale is lacking inasmuch as leverage effects should be strongest at the individual stock level, whereas the volatility smirk is much more pronounced for index options than for individual stock options. Alternatively, they propose a correlation effect, whereby declining asset prices lead to reduced diversification, hence increased risk; a wealth effect, whereby investors become more risk-averse as their wealth declines with decreasing equity prices; and a risk effect, whereby exogenous factors increase market risk, leading investors to demand higher expected returns. They conclude (p. 30) that "the high prices of out-of-the-money puts may be the result of mispricing that a normally efficient market fails to correct. For some reason, enough capital may not be mobilized to sell these types of options."

Rubinstein and Jackwerth do not consider the possible impact on option prices (hence implied volatility) of option-replication trading. The volatility smirk may reflect a positive feedback channel at work between the supply of and demand for protected strategies in the form of index options. As investor demand for put options increases, option issuers and exchange market makers will be stuck with short put option positions. They will try to hedge their short option exposures by purchasing listed index options. This demand will place more upward pressure on put option prices.

As listed options become more costly, option issuers and market makers will resort to more dynamic hedging in underlying markets. This hedging will exacerbate price movements in the underlying market, just as synthetic portfolio insurance did in the 1980s. Not only will the hedgers' own buying and selling move markets but, again, it will induce other investors, unaware of the informationless nature of hedgers' trades, to buy and sell (or to refrain from selling and buying). And, given that investors are innately risk-averse, hedging trades are likely to have a larger impact in a falling market than in a rising market (hence the inverse relationship between implied volatility and asset price level).[2]

As Sanford Grossman and Zhongquan Zhou (1996: 1401) describe it: "The volatility of the risky asset price process is determined by the demand for option-like payoffs. It is as if the risky asset is the 'derivative' security, and the options are the 'underlying' security."[3] This is hardly a world in which Black–Scholes theoretical option prices can be expected to hold.

Attempts to develop option models that better reflect the actual behavior of option prices, including refinements of Black–Scholes, binomial tree and lattice approximations, and Monte Carlo simulations, constitute one of the hotter areas in finance today.[4] It is not our purpose to go into these in detail, but rather to draw the reader's attention to their implication: option pricing is not a simple matter of plugging the right numbers into the right equations. The right equations (and the right numbers, for that matter) remain, to a nontrivial extent, matters of conjecture.

Risks to Dealers

OTC option issuers face their own versions of the risks confronted by the option purchaser. Furthermore, their risk-control task is complicated manyfold by the number and the variety of contracts they may be engaged in. As we have noted, the value of OTC equity instruments is dwarfed by that of interest and exchange rate vehicles (including swaps, options, swaptions, and forwards). The dealer selling OTC equity options designed to reduce the risk of one corporation's pension fund may also be intermediating an interest rate swap to reduce the cost of financing another's capital, and an exchange rate forward to reduce the risk of yet another's foreign operations or supplies.

While the volume and diversity of its counterparties necessarily make assessment of credit risk a more complex task for a dealer than for the typical end-user, they also afford the benefit of a diversified book of business. The typical dealer will be less susceptible to sustained damage from a default by any one of its multiple counterparties than will the end user with a limited number of counterparties. Furthermore, the dealer is more likely to be able to benefit by netting arrangements, whereby contracts with any given counterparty are pooled so that positively and negatively valued contracts offset each other. With netting, a counterparty cannot choose to default on those contracts under which it owes the dealer while continuing to collect on contracts under which the dealer owes.

Dealers of OTC contracts also generally apply a number of formal boundaries in order to control credit risk. These include limitations on exposures to individual counterparties and on aggregate exposures to given credit rating categories and to given countries of counterparty origin (Behof 1993). Dealers, like end-users, will require that their counterparties have relatively high credit ratings. Vijay Bhasin (1995) finds that the average credit quality of derivatives users is significantly better than that of all firms with senior debt ratings. He also finds, however, that the gap between the credit quality of derivatives users and the average rating of all firms has narrowed over time.

Bhasin does not look at contract specifications, which may contain requirements that mitigate the increase in credit risk. Dealers may require posting of collateral or periodically mark contracts to market in order to offset perceived increases in default risk due to counterparty credit quality or the nature of the contract. The International Monetary Fund's (IMF's) 1993 survey of banks issuing interest and exchange rate derivatives found that they were beginning to mark contracts to market and require periodic margin payments to offset the increased risk of their longer-term contracts. It also found that securities dealers charged higher premiums, in the form of wider bid–asked spreads, when dealing with riskier counterparties.

Derivatives themselves may reduce the probability of a counterparty default. As Ludger Hentschel and Clifford Smith, Jr. (1995) point out, there are two necessary conditions for default: (1) the counterparty owes a payment on its derivatives and (2) the counterparty is insolvent. They argue that, to the extent the derivatives are used to hedge (and not for speculation), the probability of counterparty insolvency will be reduced.

Credit exposure for dealers may also be ameliorated by the nature of the relationship between macroeconomic factors and the value of derivatives contracts (although this relationship may also serve to heighten exposure). As John Hull (1989) argues in regard to interest and exchange rate swaps, if bankruptcy becomes more likely when interest rates rise, the exposure of interest rate swap portfolios may be stabilizing insofar as the counterparty paying fixed and receiving floating generally has the higher credit risk. Gregory Duffee (1994), however, finds that, historically, default is more likely in periods of falling, rather than rising rates, so that credit risk is increased for the counterparty paying fixed.

The task of assessing exposure to credit risk is nevertheless a difficult one for dealers (as well as end-users), inasmuch as it involves not only estimating counterparty default probabilities over often multiyear horizons, but also estimating the potential behavior of the derivatives over changing economic environments. Shortcomings in available models as well as unavoidable errors in forecasting model inputs make valuation of derivatives far from an exact science. Standard & Poor's *Credit Week* (November 1992) notes: "In general, the models and the systems' capability for tracking credit exposure are in a catch-up mode, and have experienced difficulty keeping up with the growth of the business." The chore is further complicated by the now seemingly ubiquitous use of derivatives: "Participation in derivatives markets can cause firms to become connected through complicated transactions in ways that are not easily understood, making the evaluation of counterparty risk extremely difficult" (IMF 1993: 28).

While dealers do not face credit risk exposure from their short option positions (as the option premium has been paid up front), they may face substantial market risk exposure from changes in the options' values in response to changes in underlying markets. In selling a put on an equity portfolio, for example, a dealer or market maker places itself at risk of a market decline that will force it to purchase the portfolio at above-market prices, just as a dealer that enters into a swap to pay a counterparty a fixed interest rate in exchange for receiving a floating rate is at risk of a decline in interest rates leaving it with a negative cash flow. Sale of a call, conversely, places the dealer at risk of a market rise that will force it to sell the portfolio at below-market prices.

As we have seen above, the dealer will charge a price for an option that reflects the costs the dealer expects to incur in hedging the risks associated with holding the short option position. The price may be lower if the dealer can buy listed options to offset its short position than if the dealer thinks it will have to replicate the option by dynamic hedging in the stock and stock futures markets.

The dealer's pricing problem is essentially a mirror image of the buyer's pricing problem; whereas the buyer risks paying too much for the option, the selling dealer risks charging too little. Furthermore, for both, determination of the correct price rests on the same basic set of inevitably flawed option pricing formulas. Model and estimation errors, however, may prove more crucial for the dealer than for the option buyer.

This is certainly true if the dealer has to hedge dynamically in the stock and stock futures markets in order to replicate a desired long option position. As we have seen, this involves taking positions in stock futures or stock, plus cash, and trading in line with the dictates of an option pricing formula. The replicating stock-cash hedge will equal the delta of the option. Delta represents the option's price sensitivity to small changes in the underlying asset's price (see appendix B).

An option's delta does not remain constant as the price of the underlying asset changes. Rather, it rises as the underlying asset's price rises and falls as the underlying asset's price falls. The replicating portfolio must thus buy the underlying asset as its price increases and sell as its price declines. This is the mechanistic, trend-following trading that synthetic portfolio insurers engage in.

The change in an option's delta for a given change in the underlying asset's price is termed the option's gamma. The higher the option's gamma, the more the replicating portfolio will have to trade to maintain the correct delta as the underlying asset's price changes. Of course, Black–Scholes assumes that trading is continuous, and costless, so that one will always be able to trade at the time, at the price, and in the amount required to keep up with the option's changing delta. As we know, or should certainly know after October 1987, this is not always possible.

If prices jump up or down, as they did during the 1987 market crash, dynamic hedging may fail to replicate the option. In this case, the replicating portfolio may not deliver the protection it was designed to provide; a gap between the proper hedge for the option the dealer has sold and the actual hedge the dealer has been able to create will leave the dealer exposed. Note that the same is not true for the option buyer. Once the buyer has purchased the option, the option will provide the level of protection or equity market participation anticipated, even if underlying market prices are discontinuous.

The option buyer is also protected against unexpected changes in volatility over the life of the option. An option's potential value, hence its price, generally increases as the volatility of the underlying asset increases, and decreases as the underlying asset's volatility decreases. This occurs because higher (lower) volatility brings a higher (lower) probability of the option ending up in the money. An option price's sensitivity to the underlying asset's volatility is termed its vega.

A change in the underlying asset's volatility after the option is purchased, however, has no impact on the option buyer. The option buyer will not have to pay more if volatility increases; nor will the buyer receive a refund if volatility decreases. Furthermore, the option buyer will not have to trade more options in order to maintain the original level of protection or participation.

In contrast, the cost of an option-replication program can increase (decrease) relative to the level anticipated at the outset of the program if the volatility of the underlying asset increases (decreases) unexpectedly. This is because a change in volatility can require more or less trading, and associated costs, than were anticipated at the outset. This may cause the outcome of a dynamic hedging program to diverge from that of the option it was supposed to replicate.

Moreover, the very act of dynamic hedging can increase the cost of dynamic hedging by increasing the underlying asset's volatility. As Rudiger Frey and Alexander Stremme (1997: 351) argue, "when carried out on a large scale, dynamic hedging is most likely to perturb the very stochastic law it is based upon." That is, the very act of dynamic hedging can increase the cost of dynamic hedging, because it increases the underlying asset's volatility. Frey and Stremme find that, in order to insulate itself from the positive feedback effects of dynamic hedging, an option replication program may have to overhedge; that is, a program designed to replicate a put option might have to take a smaller stock position than the option-replication formula would indicate.[5]

Because prices in underlying markets are not continuous, because their volatilities are not constant, and because replicating portfolios cannot be continuously and costlessly rebalanced, option replication really requires the use of other options; only other options can fully match the unique characteristics of options. These defining characteristics include the option's gamma (the change in the option's delta for a given change in the underlying asset's price) and its vega (the option's price sensitivity to changes in the underlying asset's volatility).

For these reasons, and because of cost considerations, dealers (and options market makers) often prefer to use listed options to hedge their exposures. Hedging with listed options presents its own problems, however. For example, the option positions used for hedging must be altered to reflect changes in the dealer's or market maker's net exposure over time. Short-term options must be rolled over as time passes. The need for discrete rebalancing introduces the virtual certainty of hedging errors, leaving the dealer or market maker open to the same dangers of market gaps and hidden costs that threaten dynamic hedging strategies.

Furthermore, the listed market is not always so accommodating. As we noted in chapter 14, the listed market may not provide the contract specifications needed to offset a customized OTC option. Furthermore, demand for listed index options, particularly as vehicles for portfolio protection, can exceed the natural supply of sellers.[6] An uncovered short option position is essentially a speculative bet on the market's volatility; it entails the risk of substantial loss (even unlimited loss, in the case of call positions) if the market moves against the bet. Thus dealers, and exchange market makers, too, may find they cannot obtain the listed options necessary to form complete hedges, or cannot obtain them at an economical price.

Fortunately, the risk control needs of derivatives dealers and of option exchange market makers may be streamlined when viewed in the context of an overall portfolio. Dealers, for example, generally break down all their transactions into their constituent cash flow components and aggregate these to arrive at an approximation of the residual market exposure of their derivatives portfolios. According to the Group of Thirty (1993: 43):

Dealers . . . typically manage the market risks of their derivatives activity on the basis of the net or residual exposure of the overall portfolio. A dealer's portfolio will contain many offsetting positions, which substantially reduce the overall risk of the portfolio, leaving a much smaller residual risk to be hedged.

The type of automatic self-hedging that reduces market exposure, however, is more likely to be found with currency and interest rate derivatives than with equity derivatives. Either side of a currency or interest rate swap, for instance, may be used to reduce risk, depending upon the nature of the user's cash inflows and outflows. A UK company exporting to the US and a US company exporting to the UK might be natural counterparties in a swap of US dollars for pounds sterling. There is thus likely to be a natural interest in either side of the swap from companies seeking to hedge their particular market exposures. For the dealer, then, payments to (or from) one counterparty are mirrored by payments from (or to) the other; its own market exposure is eliminated.

Dealers may find equity derivatives, particularly equity options, more problematic than currency or interest rate instruments, despite the fact that they are likely to make up a much smaller portion of their business.[7] This is because, as we have noted, the sell side of an option trade is essentially a speculative position. The dealer's ability to offset option positions thus depends upon the presence of traders willing to take on speculative risk.

Furthermore, the assets underlying equity derivatives are considerably more volatile than those underlying interest rate and currency derivatives. Benjamin Weston, managing director of Credit Suisse Financial Products, notes:

If the underlying volatility of interest rates is a 1 and forex is a 2, then equity is about a 4. We manage our business on the basis of market-crash conditions, assuming that things can move 10 to 15 percent in a single day. (Hansell 1990: 59)

It may be harder to find speculators to take on the risk inherent in equity options than the lesser risk involved in rate-based options. Dealers may thus tend to find themselves with net short option positions, which have to be hedged.

Calculating Risk

Firms have at their fingertips numerous new tools designed to manage the risks of their derivatives positions. Many firms estimate the market risk of their derivatives positions by estimating Value at Risk (VAR). VAR is an estimate of the largest likely loss that will occur with a certain (prespecified) frequency. VAR estimates rely on models of the probability distribution of returns and their volatility, and often take into explicit account the possibility of price jumps.

VAR estimates are, of course, only as solid as the models and variables used to derive them. Objections have been raised on several grounds. Richard Bookstaber (1997) argues that VAR generally uses average risk and return distributions and typical market correlations, thereby ignoring two critical factors. First, events that lie outside the norm, although unlikely statistically, can have very real effects on portfolios if they do occur. Second, correlations between assets' returns tend to increase in periods of market stress, as international stock market correlations did during the 1987 crash. As Bookstaber (p. 105) puts it: "Large market moves are contagious." Hedges that were good enough under normal market conditions can fail during crises. Alternatives, or supplements, to VAR include scenario analysis, which studies the effects on asset values of different market environments, and stress tests, which examine returns under worst-case conditions.

Under new rules promulgated by the Securities and Exchange Commission (SEC), registered corporations must disclose (outside their financial statements) information about the risk of their derivatives positions, using either a tabular presentation, a sensitivity analysis, or a Value at Risk calculation. They must also disclose qualitative information about their primary derivatives risk exposures, explain how these risk exposures are managed, and expand their footnote disclosure of the methods used to account for derivatives.[8] Mark Anson (1996) faults the SEC for its failure to consider derivatives within the context of the total investment portfolio, but lauds (p. 309) its emphasis on disclosing the assumptions underlying the selected risk models: "It is important not to accept these models as accurate black boxes, but rather to understand the implications of the models if the underlying assumptions are wrong."

In truth, however, the risks of OTC derivatives are difficult to track and control. Their management requires complex mathematics and computer-based valuation and trading techniques. Operations are thus susceptible to computer and communications software breakdowns (Abken 1994: 10). In an ironic twist to the story of portfolio insurance, in early 1993 O'Brien and his colleagues at LOR began selling a software product that audits the "black boxes" that drive derivatives trading strategies.

Finally, it is important to note that some of the largest, most publicized losses suffered by derivatives dealers have involved neither credit nor market risk but, rather, human frailty. At Barings bank, a single trader in the Singapore office lost $1.3 billion trading in futures on the Japanese market; the losses led to the collapse of the over 200-year-old company in 1995. Within the year, it was disclosed that a single trader at Daiwa bank in New York lost an estimated $1.1 billion over an eleven-year period. These disasters were enabled by the fact that the trader in each case was in charge of both the trading desk and the back-office operations that oversaw the trading operations. In the opinion of Hentschel and Smith (1995), it is such agency risks, including inappropriate incentives for traders, that pose the greatest problem for derivatives dealers and market stability.

Risks to Markets

Even before Barings and Daiwa, a number of well publicized failures had heightened concerns about the potentially destabilizing effects of derivatives. The German industrial giant Metallgesellschaft lost $1.3 billion on oil futures and swaps in 1993. Procter & Gamble lost $157 million on swaps in 1994.[9] Also in 1994, Orange County, California, went bankrupt because of swap-like deals in interest rates.[10]

Concerns about the safety of derivatives led a number of governmental and quasi-governmental groups (including the Commodity Futures Trading Commission, the International Monetary Fund, and the Group of Thirty) to undertake studies and convene conferences. The focus of many of these inquiries was on the possibility that, given the linkages created by derivatives themselves, difficulties at one derivatives user or dealer, or in one market, could lead to widespread systemic failure. According to the IMF (1993: 30):

> The tendency for derivatives to create arbitrage opportunities and to strengthen the linkages between markets has increased the possibility that disruptions or increased uncertainty in these markets might spread over into other derivatives markets and into the cash markets more readily than in the past.

John Marshall (1995: 309), executive director of the International Association of Financial Engineers, argues to the contrary:

> The reality . . . is that the derivatives markets have weathered a major stock market collapse, a sharp rise in interest rates, several currency crises, and the failures of several major financial institutions – all without anything remotely resembling a systemic crisis. My own view, after much study and

contemplation, is that derivatives are not a source of significant systemic risk. Precisely the opposite. They are a prophylactic, a preventative for systemic risk. Through widespread use of derivatives for risk management purposes, individual firms, industries, and indeed the integrity of the system as a whole is increasingly insulated from the vagaries of the market.

Merton Miller (1997: 21) also dismisses derivatives-related systemic risk:

> [Systemic collapse] can happen, of course, but it's most unlikely. The major derivatives dealers are all big banks. The big banks of this world . . . are all very heavily capitalized, highly diversified in their portfolios, thanks in part to derivatives, incidentally, and constantly monitoring their aggregate risk exposure.

As for the concerns of regulators, Miller (1997: 35) states: "I wish they [regulators] would stop crying and tell us what *exactly* is bothering them."

Peter Abken (1994: 5) cites the differential between revenues and losses on derivatives trading ($35.9 billion in trading revenues over the ten years through 1993, versus cumulative losses of $19 million) and notes that no commercial bank had failed as the result of derivatives trading (although Barings bank was soon to do so). According to the CFTC Symposium on OTC Derivatives Markets and Their Regulation (1993a: 5):

> when insolvent financial institutions have been wound up in the last few years, including DFC New Zealand, Bank of New England, British & Commonwealth Bank, and Drexel Burnham, the derivatives activities were either transferred or closed out reasonably quickly. In fact, the derivatives books were closed out more rapidly and in a more orderly fashion than the firms' other traditional assets and liabilities could be liquidated.

Myron Scholes (1996) admits, on the one hand, that derivatives trading can lead to losses stemming from model risk and illiquidity in hedging vehicles, as well as from unanticipated changes in the legal and regulatory environments. On the other hand, he argues, model risk and illiquidity are not unique to derivatives markets. He feels the fear of a system-wide collapse from the use of derivatives is largely unwarranted, given the diversity of contract offerings and specifications. Similar arguments, of course, were made on behalf of portfolio insurance (see chapter 9).

Franklin Edwards (1995) of the Center for the Study of Futures Markets at Columbia University suggests that concern about the threat of derivatives rests on four characteristics – the magnitude of dealer counterparty credit risk, concentration of OTC activity among a few dealers, extensive linkages between dealers and between dealers and markets, and a lack of regulation of non-bank dealers. He notes that the US General Accounting Office has found that dealers' net credit exposure is less than 1 percent of the notional value of outstanding derivatives contracts; that the top eight US dealers (seven banks, one security firm) account for only 33 percent of the worldwide notional value of derivatives held by dealers; that market linkages should increase liquidity and cushion local disturbances; and that nonbank dealers are well capitalized and, unlike banks, not beneficiaries of government deposit insurance, hence not a potential threat to government and taxpayer finances. Robert Easton (CEO of the Commodities Corporation) further notes (in CFTC 1993a) that derivatives market participants are sophisticated investors, as recognized in the Futures Trading Practices Act of 1992.

The threat posed to the overall economy by the possible insolvency of a few derivatives dealers, however, may be secondary to the threat posed by derivatives-related trading to underlying markets. Already several incidents have signaled cause for concern. In 1994, for example, OTC dealers aggressively sold call options on European bonds as that market rose, hedging themselves by buying bonds; when prices turned down, dealers sold bonds, adding to the considerable selling pressure from speculators who had bought bonds on margin, in many cases with funds received from selling puts. A dealer at one European bank described the result:

> People sold in the [bond] market until prices got pushed too far, then in the bond-futures markets, then in the swap market. And then they started trying to hedge in other instruments – like selling German bonds to hedge losses in Italian bonds – until all the markets were rolling along in the same black hole. (*Wall Street Journal*, March 17, 1994: C1)

Equity markets may be at even greater risk than bond markets, given their much higher volatility and the potentially greater mismatch between buyers and sellers of risk-reducing equity derivatives. There have already been some episodes of exaggerated market volatility resulting from the "sons" of portfolio insurance. As we saw in chapter 14, dealers that had sold portfolio puts and were forced to hedge their own positions by selling futures accentuated the market decline in 1989. Similarly, in 1991, "some firms may have engaged in dynamically hedging . . . risks assumed in OTC puts negotiated with institutional money managers" (SEC 1991: 7).

The Japanese market decline of the early 1990s has been linked to writers of Nikkei put warrants. It is probable that this slow and drawn-out crash was exacerbated by program selling in the index futures market (Hansell 1990: 56). Barbara Donnelly and Michael Sesit report in the *Wall Street Journal* (April 17, 1990) that: "While the Nikkei put warrants weren't the cause of the Tokyo stock market's drop, . . . the computerized hedging programs backing them exacerbated the decline once it started and added to the market's volatility."

Equity derivatives can exert buying as well as selling pressure. Many of the "zero-cost" collars bought in early 1991 had proved to be expensive by the end of the year when the market soared through many investors' established caps. This may have caused an additional market rise as stocks that had been called away were bought back. A number of traders described the way the market received an extra kick upward as reminiscent of portfolio insurance (see *Wall Street Journal*, January 9, 1992).

More recently, demand for option-related strategies in both Europe and the US seems to have increased risks for both dealers and equity markets. In Europe, for example, dealers selling long-term call options have been strained by the demand from financial service companies, which purchase the calls in order to repackage them as guaranteed products for sale to retail investors. According to Richard Irving (1998: S1): "There are nagging worries that the sensitivity of equity markets to event risk, and the sheer size of some [dealers'] inventories, effectively force dealers to trade on the margin of what might be currently perceived to be prudent in terms of risk control."

Data from Goldman, Sachs (1998) indicate that the US dealer community, too, was increasingly short options by the fall of 1997; as investor demand for protective hedges rose with the equity market throughout the year, dealers sold more and more options. Hedging these short volatility positions would have required trend-following dynamic trading in the stock and stock futures markets. When economic and monetary woes in Asia triggered market downturns in the US in October 1997, selling by these hedgers undoubtedly contributed to the market's decline.

The new derivatives such as OTC portfolio puts may thus pose problems for equity markets similar to those posed by synthetic insurance strategies. The extent of this danger will depend in part upon the size of the demand for insurance and the willingness of market participants to supply that demand. Here again we can detect unhappy correspondences to synthetic portfolio insurance.

First, the explosive growth in equity and other derivatives suggests to some a fad element similar to that detectable in the growth of synthetic insurance in the 1980s. Jerry Jordan (1995: 434), president and CEO of the Federal Reserve Bank of Cleveland, notes:

> The explosive growth of OTC derivatives contracts conceivably could be classified as a temporary mania, particularly from the point of view of

those whose mismanagement has produced spectacular losses. With hindsight, marginal private cost was apparently seriously underestimated. Continued rapid growth of derivatives contracts at the pace of the past several years would begin to raise the mania flag. Even in a global financial marketplace there must exist a finite limit to shiftable risk.

As with synthetic insurance, faddish pursuit of equity risk control via listed and OTC options and other instruments may lead to unwarranted dismissal of the inherent risks of stock investment and encourage higher than warranted commitments to stock. As demand for stock pushes prices away from fair valuations, prices become more susceptible to correction.

Whether a major correction will pose a significant threat to equity markets may depend upon the hedging designs of option traders. If a decline in overall market prices forces a substantial amount of selling in underlying stock and stock futures markets, liquidity problems may result. Illiquidity may be exacerbated if, as with synthetic portfolio insurance, uncertainty about the identity and extent of hedging sales diminishes the willingness of value investors, speculators, and others to take the buy side in declining markets:

> A paucity of reliable price information is viewed as potentially increasing liquidity strains because market-makers or other market users may be unwilling to commit capital to transactions without such data. The effects of price opacity upon liquidity may be particularly significant in the markets for highly customized, "exotic" instruments or for instruments of longer maturities due to the unavailability of a meaningful exchange transaction price as a reference price. (CFTC 1993b: 116)

The price transparency of exchange-traded options may help to reduce liquidity problems by revealing the demand for protective option strategies and the possible extent of related hedging. As Miller (1992: 9) asserts: "With exchange-traded puts, the bearishness in portfolio insurance would make its presence known immediately in the market prices and implicit volatility of the puts." Interpreting such information is not always easy, however, even for informed market participants. Options market maker Allen Jan Baird (1993: 136) notes:

> Following broker order flows and strike open interest is sometimes an arduous and protracted affair in which perfection is impossible. The trader may expect some modest success in pits where he or she can generally observe most of the trading during the day. The chances for success are less in larger pits or under conditions of screen (upstairs) trading.

And, of course, there is always the question of hedges that are undertaken, not with listed options, but with the underlying securities or futures contracts.

When the source of hedging trades is obscured, liquidity may dry up. In the absence of willing trading partners, OTC dealers are particularly vulnerable to loss. Of course, losses on short equity option positions may be offset by gains on other derivatives positions. And even a default by a single dealer is unlikely to cause the systemic collapse feared by regulators if, as Hentschel and Smith (1995: 116) contend, "defaults on derivatives contracts are approximately independent across dealers and over time."

As Jordan (1995: 440) points out, however: "The risk levels of all financial contracts are interdependent in that they jointly depend on the state of the aggregate economy." Derivatives and dynamic strategies such as portfolio insurance may transfer risk, but they cannot eliminate it. The ability to transfer risk is finite. Strategies that presume otherwise are fated to fail, if not sooner then later.

Furthermore, their failure can spell trouble for investors generally. According to Nicholas Brady (1998: 4), former chair of the Brady Commission that investigated the 1987 crash:

> Arguments abound about how derivatives and dynamic hedging decrease transaction costs and increase the depth of markets. But carried to extremes they are not worth what they cost. Derivatives and dynamic hedging are fine until sentiment turns one-sided. Then, when the sellers of puts and the buyers of contracts hit the sidelines, all the pessimism that exists in these markets is pushed back on the stock exchanges and increases volatility.

Summary

Exchange-traded and OTC options have several advantages over synthetic portfolio insurance conducted via dynamic hedging. First, option buyers have a guarantee (backed, in the case of publicly traded options, by the exchange clearinghouse) that the purchased level of protection will be there if needed. Second, option buyers pay for this protection in advance; its price does not change with subsequent volatility in the underlying asset. Third, they do not have to sell into falling markets or buy into rising markets.

What is true for option buyers, however, is not necessarily true for option sellers. Option sellers expose themselves to market risk. Unless an option seller wants to maintain a speculative posture, it will have to hedge its short option positions by buying offsetting listed options or by option replication – dynamic hedging – in the stock and stock futures markets. Dynamic hedging exposes the option seller to the same problems that confronted institutional investors using synthetic portfolio insurance, including the shortcomings of available option pricing models. Of greater concern, the dynamic hedging undertaken to replicate option positions is likely to be the same kind of trend-following, positive feedback trading that proved so disastrous for the equity market in the 1980s.

Faddish pursuit of portfolio protection via puts, calls, and other derivatives strategies may lead to unwarranted dismissal of the risks inherent in stock investing. At the same time, extensive use of dynamic hedging by dealers attempting to control option-related market exposures (especially given the lack of information about the volume of such hedging) may create the same liquidity problems that proved so catastrophic in 1987.

In such an environment, the possibility increases that major derivatives users or issuers may face insolvency. And today, with the linkages that derivatives have forged between firms and markets, the problems may not be confined to a few firms, or even to the stock market alone.

Notes

1   The Financial Accounting Standards Board's Statement No. 133 requires companies to report the fair market value of derivatives contracts on corporate balance sheets, starting in June 1999; gains or losses on derivatives used for hedging may be matched with losses or gains from marking to fair value the underlying hedged position. With a perfect hedge, then, there will be no impact on net income. See McConnell et al. (1998). A March 1996 US Department of Labor letter asked pension plan fiduciaries to estimate plan exposures to potential derivatives losses. The letter stresses the use of simulation models to estimate exposure. It also takes a total-portfolio perspective, looking at derivatives' contributions to the risk and return of the overall plan's portfolio.

2   The sudden appearance of the smile/smirk following the 1987 crash may reflect the emergence of the true premium for protection, which became apparent once investors started using real options instead of synthetic options.

3   See also Platen and Schweizer (1998). Basak (1995), by contrast, finds that the presence of portfolio insurers leads to a decrease in volatility. Basak's conclusions are doubtful, however, because he uses several unrealistic assumptions. For example, he allows for discontinuous price jumps, but constrains those jumps to occur at a predetermined time. Also, the model allows for infinite interest rates. Because of this, the study contains an internal inconsistency. For although it states that volatility is reduced, it also states (pp. 1060–1), paradoxically, that "the prehorizon . . . market . . . increases in price in the presence of portfolio insurance. As soon as the portfolio insurance matures, . . . the asset prices jump down discontinuously." In view of this statement, Grossman and Zhou (1996) dismiss Basak's results.

4   See, for example, Jarrow (1995). Attempts to improve upon Black–Scholes by improving the model's assumed stochastic process have met with little success to date. Rubinstein and Jackwerth (1997) test Black–Scholes, jump diffusion models (which accommodate price jumps in the underlying asset), constant elasticity of variance diffusion models, implied binomial trees, stochastic volatility models, and various naive models against real option prices and find that, for the post-1987 period, all but the implied binomial trees and the stochastic volatility and naive models performed very poorly. A naive model assuming future implied volatilities would remain the same as current implied volatilities of options with the same strike price performed best. See also Derman and Zou (1997).

5   New instruments introduced in the US and Europe could reduce uncertainty in hedging volatility. The German stock exchange just introduced a futures instrument, the VOLAX, based on the implied volatility of a three-month, at-the-money German index option. In the US, Salomon Smith Barney introduced OTC volatility swaps, whereby the investor can contract with Salomon, which then buys or sells an option portfolio, delta hedges it, and pays the customer any positive difference or collects any negative difference.

6   Corporations have begun to take advantage of the thirst for options by issuing options on their own stock. The option premiums result in tax-free income for them, and that income can be substantial. The *New York Times* (November 22, 1998: C1) notes that technology companies, with their high operating costs, are particularly active in issuing puts, and that Microsoft's income from put premiums accounted for 13.4 percent of its net income.

7   According to estimates from the Bank for International Settlements (BIS 1996), in 1995 OTC equity derivatives (including options, swaps, and forwards) had a notional value worldwide of about $630 billion, versus a notional value of over $47 trillion for all OTC derivatives.

8   SEC Item 305(a), Item 305(b), and Rule 4.08(n).

9   See Smith (1997) for a review of the Procter & Gamble case.

10 Orange County had engaged in extensive reverse repurchase agreements, whereby it sold securities to a dealer with the promise to repurchase them at a later date; proceeds from the sale were used to buy more securities. See Miller and Ross (1997) and Jorion (1997). Miller and Ross argue that the county should not have declared bankruptcy, as its monthly interest income exceeded the monthly cost of the reverse repurchase agreements in December 1994. Furthermore, Miller and Ross show that, had the portfolio not been liquidated, its unrealized losses would have been eliminated by March 1996. Jorion, however, points out that the bankruptcy filing was justified in that the county's total liabilities greatly exceeded its assets. Jorion also notes that the improved performance of the portfolio from December 1994 to early 1996 reflected an entirely unexpected decline in interest rates; he finds (p. 64) that Miller and Ross's "evidence that the portfolio would have recovered its losses is based on hindsight. Nobody could have foretold with certainty that rates were going to drop precipitously. . . ."

17

Living with Investment Risk

An investor . . . who computed the value of her portfolio every day would find investing in stocks very unattractive, since stock prices fall almost as often as they rise on a daily basis. . . . On the other hand, a modern . . . Rip Van Winkle . . . should sleep soundly in the knowledge that over a 20-year period, stocks have never declined in real value.

Jeremy Siegel and Richard Thaler, 1997

The promotion of synthetic portfolio insurance strategies seduced investors with the promise of eliminating the risk of losses while preserving the opportunity for gains. Investors could enjoy all the benefits of stock investing without having to suffer any of the risks. It would be the best of all possible worlds.

The events of October 1987 dashed the promises of portfolio insurance. Those who had insured found they were not protected against discontinuous gap-downs in stock prices, which decimated their portfolios' values. The precise costs of insurance became even more evident to stopped-out insurers as prices rebounded after the crash.

To add insult to injury, much of the blame for the crash could be laid at the feet of portfolio insurance itself. Synthetic insurance undoubtedly contributed to the virtually uninterrupted run-up in prices between 1982 and mid-1987, while insurance sales mandated by market declines in the week preceding the crash set off an avalanche of selling pressure on Monday, October 19.

The 1987 crash revealed that the hidden costs of synthetic portfolio insurance, borne by both insured investors and the markets generally, can outweigh any promised benefits. New insurance instruments and techniques, including exchange-traded and OTC options, may be able to reduce the costs to insured investors of falling below a given floor, but they have not eliminated the potential costs to market stability. OTC dealers and options exchange market makers engage in the same type of destabilizing, trend-following trading that synthetic portfolio insurance relied

FIGURE 17.1

LOR Ad: "Reward, risk and the challenge of increasing one without increasing the other."

LOR Ad: "Reward, risk and Saving Intermarket, September 1987, pp. 32–3.

on. And as investors found out in October 1989, November 1991, and October 1997, their dynamic hedging can bring markets down just as fast as portfolio insurance did in October 1987.

There must be a better way.

Predicting Market Moves

Synthetic portfolio insurance is inherently insightless and foresightless. It effectively presumes that market prices will evolve in a random manner, hence makes no attempt to anticipate their movement. But what if markets are not entirely random? Then an investor may be able to gain insights into the future movement of prices. Such an investor will have the edge over a portfolio insurer with no insight.

Part II presented several theories and some evidence indicating that security prices may be predictable. Return patterns such as those associated with Wall Street analysts' earnings estimates, investor overoptimism, and calendar turning points suggest that security prices can be successfully forecast. In particular, certain patterns of stock price reversals suggest that periods of above-average returns will be followed by periods of below-average returns, and vice versa. That is, stock returns tend to revert to their long-run averages over time.

If stock returns are inclined to mean-revert, investors may have a hope of successfully predicting broad market moves (Samuelson 1989). Investors able to forecast mean reversion patterns can exploit them, selling before prices trend downward and buying before they trend upward. By contrast, a synthetically insured investor will always be trading behind the trend, and losing ground to the insightful investor.

The period leading up to and including the 1987 crash proved to be a particularly ripe one for tactical asset allocators. Tactical asset allocators withdraw from stocks when prices rise above what they deem to be fair value and buy stocks when prices fall below. The distinctive upward price trend in the years before the crash, exaggerated in no small measure by synthetic portfolio insurance, provided tactical asset allocators with a perfect opportunity to sell stocks, at a profit, to portfolio insurers (and other trend-following investors). By the time the crash occurred, many tactical asset allocators were out of the stock market and invested in cash and bonds (Philips et al. 1996).

In the aftermath of the crash, investors fled synthetic portfolio insurance, while tactical asset allocation gained many new adherents. Perhaps not surprisingly, given the increased competition among tactical asset allocators and the diminution of their natural other side – portfolio insurers exaggerating market trends – the performance of tactical asset allocators dropped off considerably. In 1988 and 1989, tactical asset allocators, still underweighting stocks, missed out as the S&P 500 gained upwards of 20 percent per year (Philips et al. 1996: 63, 58).

No one ever said market timing was easy. In fact, many would say it is virtually impossible.[1] It does not necessarily follow, however, that investors will be better off if they insure their risky asset positions against unpredictable market declines.

A Long-Run Perspective

Traditionally, investors have attempted to pursue stock market rewards while dampening their exposure to market volatility by combining investments in stocks with investments in other assets, such as bonds, whose returns are less than perfectly correlated with stock returns. Appropriate asset diversification reduces the risk associated with the return on any single asset class and enhances the menu of risk-return tradeoffs. An investor will choose from among the available combinations of assets the mix that maximizes expected return at the desired level of risk-taking. This is portfolio *theory*, as distinct from portfolio *insurance*.

The investor who chooses such a strategy is effectively assuming that expectations about the relevant assets, whether based on a simple extrapolation of prior data or on forecasts of market behavior, will play out over the investment horizon. Whether or not this turns out to be the case may depend, in part, on the length of the horizon. There exist both theory and historical evidence to suggest that the risk of holding stock can be expected to decrease as the investment horizon lengthens.

For example, if market movements are random (as synthetic portfolio insurance supposes), the principle of time diversification may apply. Time diversification is analogous to stock diversification. Just as holding many stocks with uncorrelated returns is less risky than holding a single stock, holding stocks over a long period of time is less risky than holding stocks for a single short period. Over time, years with disappointing performances will be offset by years with good performances, so the risk of ending up with a loss on stock investments decreases as the investment horizon lengthens (see Thorley 1995). Random-walk enthusiast Burton Malkiel thus asserts: "Long term investors can and should ignore short-term market swings. They should stay in the market no matter what the volatility" (*New York Times*, June 15, 1990).[2]

Investors can also benefit from taking a long-term view if markets are not random, but are mean-reverting. We discussed above the case for market timing when stock returns are mean-reverting. But investors with no timing skills, or no desire to exercise them, can take advantage of mean reversion by investing for the long term.

Mean reversion, like time diversification, suggests that the risk of holding stock will decrease as the investment horizon lengthens.[3] In a market characterized by mean reversion, an investor holding stock over the long run can expect to see losses incurred during periodic market declines offset by gains in subsequent advances.[4]

The historical evidence suggests that the risk of sustaining losses on an investment in stocks decreases as the investment period lengthens. On the basis of inflation-adjusted, annualized rates of return over the 1871–1993 period, for example, Charles Jones and Jack Wilson (1995) calculate that, over all investment periods of fifteen years or longer, the probability that an investment in stocks will lose value is less than 10 percent; over one-year horizons, the probability increases to almost 36 percent.

A Premium for Patience

Investors hold stock because it offers a higher expected return than alternative investments over the long term. Jeremy Siegel (1992b: 28), on the basis of inflation-adjusted, annualized compound returns over the 1926–90 period, finds that NYSE stocks outperformed Treasury bills by 5.9 percentage points.[5]

Furthermore, just as the theories discussed above would indicate, an investor's likelihood of earning the so-called "equity risk premium" increases as the investment horizon lengthens. Siegel finds that, over the 1802–1990 period, stocks outperformed short-term bonds 57.7 percent of the time on a yearly basis but 88.8 percent of the time over thirty-year horizons. Over horizons of twenty years or longer since 1871, stocks have underperformed short-term bonds only once.[6]

The equity risk premium has generally been regarded as a compensation to investors for the additional risk of holding stocks as opposed to "less risky" investments such as government bonds or Treasury bills. One problem with this long-held theory is that, as we have discussed above, the risk of holding stocks may be in part a function of the investment horizon. Over reasonably long investment horizons, stocks just don't seem that risky.[7]

Peter Bernstein (1997) suggests that measurement of asset returns is biased because valuation levels change between starting and ending dates. Over the past 200 years, he finds sixty-three periods of roughly thirty-five years each in which equity valuation levels (as measured by dividend yields or price-earnings ratios) were the same on starting and ending dates and sixty-three periods of roughly forty-three years each in which bond valuation levels (as measured by yields) were the same. Over these "like-valuation" periods, equities averaged a real annual return of 5.7 percent with a standard deviation of 1.1 percent, whereas bonds averaged a real annual return of 2.7 percent with a standard deviation of 2.1 percent. Bernstein concludes (p. 27): "Stocks are fundamentally less risky than bonds, not only because their returns have been consistently higher than those of bonds over the long run but also because less uncertainty surrounds the long-term return investors can expect on the basis of past history."

In fact, Rajnish Mehra and Edward Prescott (1985) find that the observed differential between the (high) equity returns and (low) Treasury bill returns over the 1889–1978 period is inexplicable unless one assumes that investors have levels of risk aversion well in excess of (in fact, some thirty times) the level generally assumed for the average investor. Mehra and Prescott term this seeming anomaly the "equity premium puzzle."

Researchers have come up with various theories in attempting to solve this puzzle. George Constantinides (1990) proposes that, once investors become accustomed to a certain level of consumption, they become extremely averse to losses that could threaten their lifestyles. According to Constantinides, this "habit formation" leads investors to demand higher returns for bearing the risk of stock investments, which explains the equity premium. Shlomo Benartzi and Richard Thaler (1995: 78) counter that most stock investments are made by pension and endowment funds and wealthy individuals, whose spending levels are little affected by short-term fluctuations in stock prices.

Benartzi and Thaler argue that the equity premium puzzle is a behavioral anomaly whose solution lies in two concepts from the psychology of decision-making. First, the well-known prospect theory of behavioral economists Daniel Kahneman and Amos Tversky (1979) implies that investors are more averse to losses below a given reference level (such as their current level of wealth) than they are desirous of gains above that level. Second, the theory of mental accounting (Kahneman and Tversky 1984; Thaler 1985) implies that investors can draw contradictory conclusions from essentially identical pieces of information because of the way in which they assign information and experiences to their mental books of account. These two cognitive errors, according to Benartzi and Thaler, create myopic loss aversion.

Investors suffering from myopic loss aversion combine heightened aversion to loss with a tendency to assign the subperiods within their investment horizons to mental accounts distinct from their overall horizons. They tend to evaluate their stock portfolios frequently and to place more emphasis on avoiding losses over the short-term performance review periods than on pursuing gains over the entire horizon. Benartzi and Thaler (1995) find that the observed equity premium is consistent with the behavior of loss-myopic investors who evaluate their portfolios annually.[8] According to Siegel and Thaler (1997: 197):

> When investors have loss averse preferences, their attitude toward risk depends crucially on the time horizon over which returns are evaluated. For example, an investor with these preferences who computed the value of her portfolio every day would find investing in stocks very unattractive, since stock prices fall almost as often as they rise on a daily basis, and losses are psychologically doubled. Consider, on the other hand, a modern version of Rip Van Winkle, who, knowing he is about to go to sleep for 20 years, makes one final phone call to his broker. Rip should sleep soundly in the knowledge that over a 20-year period, stocks have never declined in real value.

In effect, the theory of myopic loss aversion implies that the (unreasonably) short-term outlook of most investors results in a larger equity premium that can be earned by patient investors taking a long-term view. Of course, finding the conviction to take a long-term outlook may not be easy, especially in this age of instant communications, with real-time stock quotes and continuous portfolio performance measurement.

Portfolio insurance exploits investors' tendency toward myopia. Early insurance vendors, for example, focused on the reporting mandates of the Financial Accounting Standards Board's Statement No. 87, which require that any shortfall between pension plan assets and liabilities be reported as a liability on the corporate balance sheet. They touted portfolio insurance as a means of protecting plan surplus and thereby decreasing the potential for short-term volatility in firms' reported earnings.[9]

Accounting statement effects are primarily cosmetic, however.[10] They should not dictate investment policy. As Gordon Binns, then head of the pension plan at General Motors, noted in 1987: "Plan sponsors should not suboptimally manage plan assets to achieve bookkeeping goals. . . . It's more costly to plan sponsors in the long run to do something suboptimally from an investment standpoint" (Givant 1987: 16). Investment policy should focus on the primary goal of meeting current and anticipated pension liabilities, given the plan's expectations of return and appetite for risk.

The coordination of the plan's management of its assets with its management of liabilities is essential (see, for example, Kingsland 1982). In some cases, this may dictate a short-term framework. For defined contribution plans, for example, where participants bear the risk of loss directly, some participants will be nearing retirement, and their investment horizons will necessarily be shorter. Also, bankrupt companies may not be able to afford the risk of loss, hence may find short-term insurance inviting. When Manville Corp. adopted portfolio insurance in 1986, for example, it was in bankruptcy as a result of claims filed against it by workers and others sickened with asbestosis. Manville reportedly planned to use its pension plan's surplus to pay for litigation (Donnelly 1986: 139). For plans adopting a "going-concern," rather than a "plan-termination," philosophy, however, the long-term nature of liabilities should generally dictate a long-term approach to investing plan assets (Jacobs 1983b and Ambachtsheer 1987).

The historical evidence suggests that stock prices have provided returns above those available from alternative investments for investors able and willing to bear stocks' short-term fluctuations. Can investors count on a similar performance from stocks in the future? Siegel (1992b) cautions that the relatively high returns to US equity were certainly not expectable at the start of his study period, 1802, or even later in the 1870s, when Argentina outstripped the US as an international economic powerhouse.

William Goetzmann and Philippe Jorion (1996) detect an element of survivorship bias in the US equity premium. While US stocks have appreciated at an inflation-adjusted annual rate of some 5 percent since the 1920s, other countries' stock markets, more prone to political upheaval, war, and financial crisis, eked out a median, inflation-adjusted appreciation rate of only about 1.5 percent per year. In other words, the experience of the US stock market over the past 200 years cannot automatically be extrapolated to other markets or future times.[11] Siegel (1998b: 20), however, finds that German stocks offered a real return nearly equal to that of US equity over the 1939–60 period, despite the devastating effects of the war years.

History makes a case for holding equities over the long term, while prudence makes a case for diversifying investments across several asset classes. Over the long term, neither the historical evidence nor investment prudence is supportive of portfolio insurance. Portfolio insurance is, rather, likely to prove not only superfluous but costly over the long term. The cost it imposes in terms of erosion of return potential will outweigh its promised benefit of risk reduction.

Summary

For every long-term problem, there's a short-term solution, and it's almost always wrong. Portfolio insurance is a short-term solution that is likely to prove a costly mistake for investors that can afford to take a long-term view. The historical evidence indicates that short-term losses in stock value have been more than offset by gains over the long term. It also indicates that, over longer-term horizons, stocks have almost always offered a premium over the returns available from alternative investments in bonds or bills. Unless circumstances dictate otherwise, prudent investors will be better off eschewing short-term strategies such as portfolio insurance and relying on diversification both over time and across assets to maximize return and minimize risk.

Notes

1 See Sharpe (1975) and Jeffrey (1984).
2 Time diversification is not supported by all researchers. See, for example, Bodie et al. (1993: 239). According to Bodie (1995), a portfolio's risk should be measured by the cost of insuring against portfolio value falling below a certain benchmark. By this standard, the risk of stock increases with horizon. Merrill and Thorley (1996) counter that insurance premiums should be compared on a per annum, per dollar insured basis, which indicates that stock becomes less risky as horizon increases. Van Eaton and Conover (1997) find both Bodie and Merrill and Thorley guilty of generalizing from very specific option instruments; they argue that equity risk in the long term can not be separated from the investor's preferences for risk and reward. They (1998) model asset allocation under mean-variance utility and find that a decreasing allocation to risky assets at longer horizons is a special case, not a general result. Bierman (1997) maintains that comparisons between investment horizons must consider the expected reward differentials, as well as the risk of the investment earning less than the target amount over the given horizon. Levy and Cohen (1998) consider the whole distribution of returns and find that the attractiveness of risky assets increases with horizon. Kritzman (1994) summarizes some of the arguments for and against time diversification.
   Samuelson (1994) questions whether one can conclude, based upon the limited sample afforded by the one and only available history of the stock market, that returns are independent over time, hence that time diversification exists.
3 Brennan et al. (1997) compare the optimal portfolio of a long-term investor with that of a short-term investor and find that investors with long horizons should hold a larger proportion of risky assets (stocks and bonds) than investors with short horizons, because mean reversion in bond and stock returns reduces the risk of these assets in the long run.
4 A long-term investor can experience a "paper loss," whereas an insured investor that is stopped out, as many were by the 1987 crash, will experience a very real loss.
5 Similarly, Ibbotson Associates (1997) data show that the S&P 500 offered a compound annual growth rate of 10.7 percent over the 1926–96 period,

versus 3.7 percent for Treasury bills, 5.1 percent for long-term government bonds, and 5.2 percent for intermediate-term governments. The standard deviation of stock returns over the 1926–96 period was 20.3 percent, versus 3.3 percent for T-bills.

6 Ibbotson Associates (1997) data for the 1926–96 period indicate that stocks outperformed all alternatives (long-term corporate bonds, long and intermediate-term government bonds, and T-bills) in 45 of the 71 one-year periods, in 52 of the 62 overlapping ten-year periods, and in all 52 of the overlapping 20-year periods.

7 Furthermore, mean reversion in stock prices would suggest that even less of a premium would be required to hold stocks. See Campbell (1996).

8 Benartzi and Thaler (1996) report on some experiments that provide preliminary support for their theory of myopic loss aversion. See also Thaler et al. (1997).

9 For a technical discussion of FASB #87, see Revsine (1989). For the view that plan surplus should be protected in some way, especially in light of FASB #87, see Somes and Zurack (1987); Bookstaber and Gold (1988); and Rosenberg (1993).

10 There may be indirect effects on a firm's outstanding contracts specified in terms of reported accounting numbers. An effort should be made to renegotiate such contracts.

11 Laurence Siegel (1997) suggests that mean reversion, hence time diversification, is a statistical illusion created by survivorship bias.

18

Late Developments: Awful August 1998 and the Long-Term Capital Fallout

> Securitized markets and the interwoven linkages of international markets will expedite the flight of capital whenever prospects appear to deteriorate.
>
> *Henry Kaufman, 1994*

On April 20, 1998, the *Wall Street Journal* noted (p. C1) that "Friday's record closes leave large stocks trading at or beyond history's most extreme limits of valuation." Interest rates were low. Inflation remained contained. For the first time in thirty years, the US faced a healthy budget surplus. And investors still seemed to be riding high on the profits of the electronic revolution. The rewards of the New Era of unfettered global markets and permanent sustainable economic growth seemed to be at hand. But investors had yet to meet the summer of their discontent.

On July 17, the Dow Jones industrial average hit 9337.97. This would turn out to be a peak. The tide began to turn in the following week. On the 23rd, the DJIA fell 2.15 percent – over 195 points – with Federal Reserve Board Chairman Alan Greenspan warning Congress that stock price levels were too high. This pushed the average below 9,000 for the first time since June 30. On July 30, the *Wall Street Journal* (p. C1) announced that "the bear market is here," noting that although the DJIA was down only 4.5 percent from its mid-summer peak, the average New York Stock Exchange (NYSE) issue was down over 24 percent from its 52-week high, and the average NASDAQ stock was down a whopping 35 percent.

On August 4, the DJIA closed down nearly 300 points, off 3.4 percent. The *New York Times* (August 5, 1998: A1) cited investors' fears of slower US economic growth, reflecting the impacts on US exports of the economic slump in Asia and the strength of the US dollar. The *Wall Street Journal* (August 5, 1998: C1) pointed to investor psychology, with concerns over continuing weakness in Asia, particularly Japan, overwhelming a US environment characterized by low interest and inflation rates, high employment, and steady, though moderated, growth. Fear continued to pervade the market as the Dow fell over 1 percent on both August 11 and August 13.

On August 17, another kind of bear raised its head, with the Russian government announcing a defacto devaluation of the ruble and a 90-day moratorium on repayment of $40 billion in corporate and bank debt to foreign creditors. The US stock market nevertheless staged a strong rally, rising close to 1.8 percent on the day. The *Wall Street Journal* (August 18, 1998: C1) notes that the rally began, coincidentally or not, just as President Clinton began his testimony before the grand jury investigating his relationship with White House intern Monica Lewinsky.

Still recovering from Thailand's devaluation of July 1997 (which had signaled the beginnings of the Asian crisis that hit US equity markets in October of that year), currency markets were sent into a spin by the Russian default. Funds were sucked out of Russia and other commodity-producing countries, including Canada, Mexico, Brazil, and Venezuela, as well as Japan and Hong Kong, and plunked down on the US dollar. The flight to safety soon spread to equity markets, with international investors dumping emerging market stocks first (*Wall Street Journal*, August 27, 1998: C1). The first real shock waves hit the major markets on August 27, with the DJIA falling nearly 4.2 percent, Tokyo down 3 percent to a six-year low, London off over 3 percent, Canada down 6 percent, and Brazil 10 percent.

On Monday, August 31, the DJIA really approached bear territory. A fall of 512 points, or 6.4 percent, left it down 19.3 percent from its July peak, and below the level at which it had started the year. The day's decline brought the DJIA's loss for the month to 15.1 percent, making it the 11th-worst month in its history. Smaller stocks, caught in a seemingly chronic pattern, did even worse. The NASDAQ fell 8.5 percent on that Monday, with high-flyers Amazon.com off 21 percent and Yahoo 17 percent.

As in 1987, non-US markets followed suit. In the West, Mexican stocks fell 5.1 percent and Canadian and Brazilian stocks 4.1 percent. In Asia, Hong Kong fell 2.9 percent on September 1. European markets opened down on the 1st, but soon recovered on a remarkable comeback in US securities. Following a by-now well-established pattern, the DJIA followed its worst day of the year with one of its best, rallying to close up 3.8 percent on the largest volume ever.

FIGURE 18.1
1998: A Dramatic Drop (and Rise)

DJIA Closing Prices

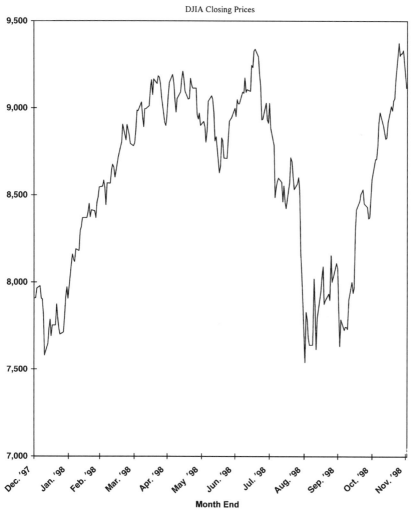

Month End

Behind the Price Moves

The market turmoil of the summer of 1998 obviously unfolded against a turbulent economic backdrop, at least on the global scene. The Russian crisis crystallized a more free-floating anxiety over the economic malaise in Asia generally. The seeming unwillingness of the Japanese government to come to terms with its own leadership role in the area, including its resistance, in the face of huge budget deficits, to underwriting some form of fiscal stimulus (*Wall Street Journal*, July 24, 1998: A1), darkened hopes for an economic recovery in the region. By mid-August, the markets of Hong Kong, Malaysia, and Singapore had fallen by 33 to 45 percent for the year.

Continuing weakness in Asia meant lower demand for the commodity exports that many emerging economies depended on. The effects were most pronounced in Russia, whose market had fallen over 70 percent from the beginning of the year to the time of the ruble devaluation, but were also seen in Mexico (down 32 percent) and Argentina (30 percent). In the US market, oils and banks were among the worst hit in the market slide of August 4, reflecting the downturn in commodity prices and concerns about bank loans to emerging markets.

In general, however, the US market decline came in spite of positive economic fundamentals. Interest rates, rises in which had preceded all but one bear market in the postwar period, were now low. Inflation was well in hand. Corporate earnings, although slowing, were still growing on average. Furthermore, the stock market overall had supposedly already experienced the worst of the Asian flu, most notably in October of 1997, and had had a year to react to possible repercussions.

The US economy appeared to be fairly well insulated from the immediate effects of much of the global turmoil. Russia accounted for only 1 percent of US exports. Even US bank loans to emerging markets were small, at least compared with the exposure of European banks. They totaled just $117 billion, or 1.5 percent of the country's gross domestic product, versus the $426 billion lent by European banks, which constituted 7 percent of European GDP (*Wall Street Journal*, October 7, 1998: A18).

In fact, US markets had provided something of a refuge for international investors fleeing Asian markets. In the last half of 1997, non-US investors had been putting their money into US equities at an annual rate of about $100 billion, quadrupling previous rates. By the first quarter of 1998, that rate had steepened to $125 billion (*New York Times*, September 9, 1998: C6). But non-US investors' flight to safety may have been mirrored by US investors' intramarket actions.

One of the most notable characteristics of the US equity market in 1998 was its duplex nature. As Byron Wien, investment strategist at Morgan Stanley Dean Witter, had pointed out in the *Wall Street Journal* (July 27, 1998: C1), the price-earnings multiples on large-cap stocks were at "extraordinary levels" by mid-year, comparable to the Nifty Fifty stocks of the 1970s. At the same time, smaller-cap companies had been lagging markedly, with small-cap averages peaking in April, well before the DJIA's July peak. And in most of the significant market declines over the summer, the smaller-stock averages had fallen harder than the large-cap DJIA.

This internal flight to safety seems to have been driven in part by individual investors. The *Wall Street Journal* (August 31, 1998: A1) reported that four of the ten largest mutual funds experienced net outflows for the month; only three enjoyed net inflows, and those were of modest size. Overall, mutual fund investors pulled almost $5 billion out of funds during the month (*Wall Street Journal*, September 5, 1998: C3). Georgeson & Co. reported that trading at retail-dominated brokerage firms suggested that individual investors had begun selling after the market's July 17 peak, sold aggressively on the August 4 downturn, and had vacillated since (*Wall Street Journal*, August 31, 1998: A1).

Some larger investors sought safety in more sophisticated measures than simply selling stock. They bought options. The *Wall Street Journal* (July 29, 1998: C22) noted that demand for exchange-listed put options had been picking up. On August 4, the day of the DJIA's 3.4 percent slide, listed index puts became a "hot commodity" (*Wall Street Journal*, August 5, 1998: C28). There was a "frenzy" of index put buying on the 11th (*Wall Street Journal*, August 12, 1998: C13). And on Friday, August 22, index put purchases were characterized as "extremely extreme" (*Wall Street Journal*, August 25, 1998: C16). By the 27th, according to the *Wall Street Journal* (C12), demand for defensive puts had slowed as institutional investors had their hedges in place.

After the DJIA's 4 percent decline on the 27th, however, some investors obviously felt they weren't hedged enough. With implied volatility levels not seen since the mini-crash of October 1997, and index put prices at a level that discouraged buying, many money managers were using individual security options to hedge (*Wall Street Journal*, August 28, 1998: C13). The market's 512-point decline on the 31st sent index option implied volatility to October 1987 levels and premiums skyrocketing. By late Monday, the premium for S&P 500 puts had soared to 7 percent of the index's value (*Wall Street Journal*, September 2, 1998: C19). Despite the elevated price, exceptionally heavy volume on the Chicago Board Options Exchange was causing computer problems by the end of the day (*New York Times*, September 1, 1998: C7).

With demand for index puts at record levels, option market makers and other sellers of protective options were undoubtedly hedging in stock and stock futures markets. Indeed, the *New York Times* (September 2, 1998: C1) reported that a record number of investors had bought listed put options in August, and that S&P 500 futures trading on the Thursday and Friday preceding the August 31 mini-crash had reached record volumes. On the 31st itself, traders noted heavy futures selling and, during the afternoon especially, computerized program trading by institutions, including mutual funds (*Wall Street Journal*, September 1, 1998: C1).

The *New York Times* (September 1, 1998: C7) noted another source of selling pressure on the 31st – index arbitrage trades activated by hedge fund sales of stock index futures. Hedge funds are largely unregulated private investment partnerships limited to well-heeled, "sophisticated" investors. The popularity of these investment vehicles had grown in the 1990s with the growth in capital market values and, no doubt, the explosion in Wall Street compensation. At the end of 1997, there were about 4,500 US domestic and offshore hedge funds with about $300 billion in capital (*New York Times*, October 1, 1998: C1).

August proved a particularly tough time for hedge funds. Many of them had invested heavily in emerging markets, sometimes leveraging their capital with borrowing. The collapse of the ruble and the Russian bond market, and the ensuing flight of investors from other emerging markets, spelled disaster for many of their strategies. According to Julian Robertson, head of Tiger Management, one of the largest such funds, with about $20 billion in assets under management, hedge funds suffered their worst losses in more than a decade in August of 1998; Tiger Management itself lost $600 million in Russian debt investments (*New York Times*, October 13, 1998: C9). Soros Fund Management (with about $13 billion under management) reportedly lost $2 billion on similar positions (*Wall Street Journal*, August 28, 1998: A1).

But the big loser of the month was Long-Term Capital Management (LTC). Its August loss of $1.8 billion amounted to a full 44 percent of its capital. The bulk of the loss derived from global market movements against the firm's arbitrage trades (*Wall Street Journal*, September 24, 1998: A1).

Long-Term Capital: A Hedge Fund in Need of a Hedge

Greenwich, Connecticut-based Long-Term Capital (LTC), headed by former Salomon Brothers bond trading guru John W. Meriwether, had enjoyed hefty returns since its launch in 1994. It had also reaped enormous riches for its managing partners, who collected 25 percent of gross profits, as well as a 2 percent management fee. The partners included Eric Rosenfeld and Lawrence Hilibrand, who had worked under Meriwether at Salomon, and David W. Mullins, Jr., a former vice chair of the Federal Reserve Board who had served, while a professor at Harvard, as the associate director of the Brady Commission that examined the 1987 market crash.

FIGURE 18.2
LTC Partners

From left, David W. Mullins Jr., Myron S. Scholes and Robert C. Merton, three of the
partners in Long-Term Capital Management. Undreamed of rates of return have suddenly
turned into nightmarish losses.

Source: *New York Times*, September 25, 1998, p. C5.
Mullins photo: Paul Hosefros/NYT Pictures.
Scholes photo: Reuters/Lou Dematteis/Archive Photos.
Merton photo: Reuters/Jim Bourg/Archive Photos.

Two of LTC's partners were particularly notable, especially after they
won the Nobel Prize in 1997. Robert Merton had taught Hilibrand,
Mullins, and Rosenfeld while a professor at MIT, and Rosenfeld and
Meriwether had brought him in as a consultant to Salomon Brothers
in the 1980s. Merton in turn had helped to woo Myron Scholes to
Salomon as an adviser to the bond arbitrage group. Merton and Scholes
joined Meriwether as founding partners of LTC in 1994.

Merton and Scholes, of course, were renowned for their work on
option pricing; their theories on derivatives pricing formed the basis for
the complicated computer models that ran LTC's arbitrage strategies.
As noted in chapter 1, a no-arbitrage condition underlies the option-
replicating portfolios used by portfolio insurers and, more broadly, by
option sellers desiring to hedge their risk. The no-arbitrage condition
holds that an option's value and the value of a replicating portfolio should
be equal; otherwise, arbitragers can take advantage of the differential
and earn riskless returns by buying the relatively cheap alternative and
selling the relatively expensive one. It is precisely such deviations, or mispricings, that stock index arbitragers seek to take advantage of. In 1987,
of course, the effects of their arbitrage trading interacted with portfolio
insurance trading to worsen the market crash on October 19.

LTC was involved in several different types of arbitrage strategies in various asset markets around the world. Basically, the strategies involved going long riskier assets and short safer assets, with the expectation of profiting from the spreads between interest rates and from the price gains to be made should spreads converge. LTC's long positions reportedly included Danish mortgages, US mortgage-backed securities, and Russian and Italian bonds (*New York Times*, September 30, 1998: C1), while it had large short positions in US government bonds (*Wall Street Journal*, September 22, 1998: A1), British government bonds (*Barron's*, October 5, 1998: MW5), and German government bonds (*New York Times*, September 25, 1998: C1).

The firm was also arbitraging selected US equity issues. According to a Securities and Exchange Commission (SEC) filing, as of June 30, 1998, LTC had invested almost $440 million in the shares of 76 companies. Its strategies included risk arbitrage, which involves purchasing the stock of takeover candidates, with the expectation of a price rise on completion of the merger, and selling short the stock of would-be purchasers, with the expectation of a price decline. A report in the *New York Times* (September 30, 1998: C1) suggested that LTC was one of the largest risk arbitrage players on the Street, with up to $1 billion in takeover stocks and related derivatives.

Arbitrage-based strategies are theoretically low risk compared with more straightforward investment strategies. Consider, for example, an investor who holds a portfolio of long bond positions. This investor has effectively placed a bet on the direction in which interest rates will move; if rates decline, the portfolio will rise in value, but if rates increase, the portfolio's value will fall. Now consider an investor who has both long and short bond positions – say, long positions in high-yield junk bonds and short positions in lower-yield Treasury securities. If interest rates in general rise or fall, the price changes of the securities held long should be approximately offset by the price changes of the securities sold short. The investor's profit, and risk, depend only on the relative values of the two positions.

LTC had informed its investors in October 1994 that the probability of a loss of 20 percent or more was only one in a hundred; the firm "always maintained that its financial technologies and its meticulously constructed hedges gave the fund a conservative risk profile" (Loomis 1998: 114). This low-risk profile, along with Meriwether's reputation as "a bond trader with a Midas touch" (*New York Times*, September 27, 1998: A1) and the firm's brace of future Nobelists, proved a magnet for investors.

Meriwether had, by mid-1994, raised over a billion dollars in equity from outside investors, on top of the $100 million anted up by the firm's original ten general partners. Merrill Lynch executives, including Chairman David Komansky, had invested $22 million through Merrill Lynch deferred compensation plans. PaineWebber Chairman Donald Marron had put up $10 million. Executives at McKinsey & Co. and Bear Stearns, as well as Sanford Weill, co-chief executive at Citigroup, apparently ponied up the $10 million entry fee. Institutional investors included Continental Insurance of New York ($10 million), Dresdner Bank of Germany ($145 million), Sumitomo Bank of Japan ($100 million), the Italian central bank ($100 million), Prudential Life Corp. ($5.43 million), Bank Julius Baer of Switzerland, Republic Bank of New York, St. Johns University endowment fund, and the University of Pittsburgh.[1]

One of the problems with low risk, however, is that it generally makes for low returns. LTC's solution to this conundrum was to leverage up, through borrowing, so small margins on trades would be magnified into large profits. Again, the supposed low risk of the fund's investments, and the key partners' reputations (not to mention their connections), had Wall Street lenders raiding their piggy banks.[2]

Leverage is hardly unknown (although not universal) in the hedge fund world. In many cases, however, it is limited, either by regulations such as the Federal Reserve Board's Regulation T, which prevents equity investors from being leveraged up by more than two to one, or by concerns over risk. Soros Fund Management and Tiger Management, for example, reportedly have leverage ratios of about four to one (*New York Times*, October 15, 1998: C6), perhaps because they engage in more directional trading, which is perceived as riskier than arbitrage.

In 1996, LTC reportedly had a leverage ratio of thirty to one (Loomis 1998), but leverage had apparently fallen off in 1997. At the end of that year, LTC paid back many of its investors (the lucky ones, as it turned out, although they didn't think so at the time). According to a person identified by the *Wall Street Journal* (September 28, 1998: A3) as "close to the fund," the firm had done so in order to "jack up the leverage on the fund." The return of clients' capital took the fund down from about $7 billion to $4.7 billion (*New York Times*, September 27, 1998: 28), $1.5 billion of which belonged to fund principals; with $125 billion in assets and the new, lower capital base, LTC had a leverage ratio of about twenty-five to one (Loomis 1998: 114).

But this ratio does not take into account derivatives positions, which are not included on the balance sheet. Derivatives allowed LTC to leverage up even more than it could have by relying on borrowing alone. LTC held derivatives positions, including equity and interest rate swaps, with a notional value of $1.25 trillion at the end of August. According to Merton Miller (1997: 35), notional values "are just bookkeeping conventions, not serious money." Yet its huge derivatives exposures did cost LTC serious money when markets moved against them.

Some of the derivatives positions appeared to be more directional in nature than LTC's usual relative-value trades. For example, the fund appears to have placed a large bet on the direction of volatility, having sold several billions of dollars of options on European equity markets (*Barron's*, October 5, 1998: MW5). LTC partners had also purchased a large call option on the value of their own firm. In 1997, the partners paid the Union Bank of Switzerland (UBS) some $300 million for a warrant that gave them the right to purchase from UBS a fixed number of LTC shares in seven years' time. The deal allowed the partners to transform expected short-term capital gains into long-term gains taxable at a lower rate. UBS in turn got the opportunity to invest in a hot hedge fund; it reportedly purchased $800 million worth of the fund's shares to hedge its exposure on the warrant, and invested an additional $266 million in the hedge fund.[3]

At first, leverage worked well for LTC. The fund's returns went from 20 percent (partial-year 1994) to over 40 percent in each year 1995 and 1996, before declining to 17 percent in 1997. Return volatility was low, too, as had been expected. But, as Nobel laureate and Stanford University finance professor William Sharpe noted (after the LTC bailout), something was amiss with this picture: "Most of academic finance is teaching that you can't earn 40 percent a year without some risk of losing a lot of money" (*Wall Street Journal*, November 16, 1998: A19). As it turned out, LTC's leverage, which had magnified its returns in 1994, 1995, 1996, and 1997, ended up magnifying the fund's risk in 1998, and magnifying the risk of world financial markets as well.

As chapter 8 noted with regard to stock index arbitrage, arbitrage should not be destabilizing. LTC-type arbitrage, unlike portfolio insurance, is not trend-following. In fact, it stabilizes markets to the extent that it narrows perceived mispricings. With arbitrage positions as heavily leveraged as LTC's, however, even relatively minor discrepancies between expectations and actual outcomes can force trading that threatens market stability.

If mispricings grow, counter to the arbitrager's bets, losses mount. Fresh infusions of capital are needed to meet margin calls. If the capital cannot be found, positions must be unwound. When the strategies constitute a large enough fraction of the market (and are mirrored by the actions of other investment organizations, including other hedge funds and investment banks), instantaneous unwinding can devour market liquidity. Arbitrage can then become destabilizing.

With the collapse of emerging market debt and the severe declines in global equity markets in August 1998, LTC's bets imploded; the prices of its long positions tanked and the prices of its short positions skyrocketed. Similar positions at other hedge funds and Wall Street banks and brokers suffered a similar fate. Goldman, Sachs and Chase Manhattan, as well as hedge fund managers George Soros and Leon Cooperman, suffered substantial losses in Russian bonds. Travelers and Salomon Brothers, like LTC, lost as the spreads between European interest rates widened instead of converging toward the Euro (*Wall Street Journal*, September 22, 1998: A1).

By mid-August, with its losses mounting, LTC was scrambling for additional sources of capital. In late August, LTC approached George Soros, Julian Robertson, and Warren Buffett, as well as some of the investors who had been cashed out in 1997, but was rebuffed (Loomis 1998: 114). Other sources of capital did not materialize (not surprisingly, as many of these potential sources were already hurting from their own LTC-like positions). LTC began unwinding some of its more liquid positions in order to maintain its core arbitrage trades, many of which involved illiquid, customized OTC derivatives.

The *Wall Street Journal* noted (August 24, 1998: C1) that many hedge funds were selling off their liquid assets, including stocks and high-yield bonds, to cover losses on leveraged investments in Russia and other emerging markets. On August 31, according to the *New York Times* (September 1, 1998: C7), heavy selling of stock index futures by hedge funds motivated index arbitragers to sell in the underlying equity market, contributing to the market's slide.

A Frenzied Fall

On September 1, the DJIA rallied to close up 3.8 percent on its largest volume ever. But the bounce back that Tuesday was to turn out to be more prescient in terms of volatility than market direction. With reports of Russia-related losses at major US investment banks and hedge funds, including LTC, the DJIA fell slightly on Wednesday and ended the week off 5.1 percent. The market recovered sharply on the following Tuesday, September 8 (following the Labor Day holiday on Monday), closing up almost 5 percent.

On the 10th, however, the DJIA fell 3.2 percent, on heavy selling by US investors offsetting losses in foreign markets and foreign investors pulling out of US equity in confusion over the Clinton situation (*Wall Street Journal*, September 11, 1998: C1). The option market was truly getting out of hand, with premiums surging and money managers paying top dollar for index puts (*Wall Street Journal*, September 11, 1998: C15). With a dearth of option sellers, option premiums were too expensive

FIGURE 18.3
Implied Volatility, 1998

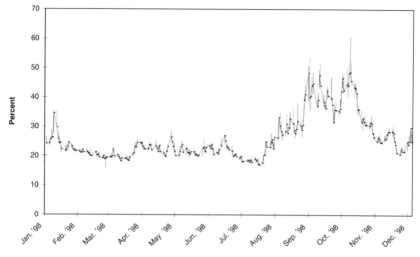

Source: Chicago Board Options Exchange.

for market makers trying to hedge their net short positions; many were trying to hedge dynamically in the underlying stock and stock index futures markets. By one estimate, option market makers were net short $27 billion in stock index futures as of September 11 (*Wall Street Journal*, September 14, 1998: C4).

According to an options trader quoted in the *Wall Street Journal* (September 16, 1998: B18B), the "market gets more and more volatile because you end up trading stock against the options." On September 8, as the market rose, there had been a flurry of buying by investors covering short positions (*New York Times*, September 9, 1998: C1). On the 10th, as the market fell, trading in S&P 500 futures was "insane" (*Wall Street Journal*, September 11, 1998: C1). Option hedgers were getting whipsawed by a market that was rising over 3 percent, then falling over 3 percent in the same week, partly as a result of their own trading.

Paul Stevens, president of the Options Clearing Corporation (the clearinghouse owned by the US options exchanges) indicated that some market makers were suffering "big time" (*Wall Street Journal*, September 16, 1998: B18B). Options traders found the environment more painful than the 1987 crash. According to Steven Sears (*Wall Street Journal*, September 16, 1988: B18B), "this market has been likened to a long, slow bleed; 1987 was just a quick hanging."

The equity market's extreme volatility sharpened investors' thirst for safety and liquidity. As investors continued to transfer funds from riskier assets to safer havens, LTC's spreads, and its problems, deepened. At the end of August, following its monthly loss of $1.8 billion, LTC had had a capital base of about $2.3 billion, still supporting balance sheet assets of about $125 billion – a leverage ratio of over 50 to one (*Wall Street Journal*, September 25, 1998: A1). By mid-September, LTC's capital base had fallen to just $600 million (with the insiders' stake down to about $200 million), and balance sheet assets had shrunk to $100 billion. The fund's leverage was thus over 150 to one (*New York Times*, September 26, 1998: C1).

On Wednesday morning, September 23, following meetings over the weekend, senior officers of 16 banks and brokerage firms met at the Federal Reserve Bank's New York headquarters to put together a deal for LTC. Of the firms represented, including Merrill Lynch, UBS, J.P. Morgan, Morgan Stanley Dean Witter, Travelers, and Goldman, Sachs, many had invested in or lent money to LTC; some were also on the other side of derivatives trades with the fund. Virtually all stood to lose should LTC collapse. It nevertheless took the offices of the Fed, in the person of New York FRB president William McDonough, to forge the coalition that would come to LTC's rescue.

As the meeting at the New York Fed was getting under way, another offer for LTC materialized. According to Loomis (1998), Warren Buffett's Berkshire Hathaway (allied with American International Group, an insurance company, and Goldman, Sachs) offered $250 million for the fund's assets, with the promise of adding $3.75 billion in capital on completion of the deal, but demanded a commitment from Meriwether by 12:30 that afternoon. Meriwether rejected the offer, averring that he could not meet Buffett's time demands. A more pertinent concern may have been the lower take and the absence of a role for Meriwether in the post-takeover management.

At the end of the day, Meriwether did accept the offer that came from fourteen of the institutions present in the New York Fed's offices – $3.6 billion dollars in exchange for 90 percent of LTC's assets. This left the old investors with about $400 million, including the principals' share of about $130 million – less than one-tenth of its value at the beginning of the year. The old management team was to remain in place under an oversight committee representing the new investors.

The rescue of LTC lifted the curtain on its secretive workings. LTC and other hedge funds, as private investment partnerships, do not face the extensive disclosure requirements of public investment funds. This lack of transparency became a problem for the market generally as the extent of the firm's leverage, and of its involvement with equity strategies, became known in the wake of the bailout.

Even to many of LTC's lenders and investors, the magnitude of the fund's problems was revealed only as the bailout unfolded. David Komansky later suggested that each lender had not known the extent of the fund's borrowing from other sources because finding out would have violated laws against collusion (*New York Times*, October 23, 1998: C22). The Fed admitted that it did not become aware of the full measure of LTC's debt until September 20, when the fund's would-be rescuers first met, despite the fact that it had been looking into its banks' exposures to the hedge fund since early September (*New York Times*, October 23, 1998: C22).

If LTC's problems came as such a surprise to these interested parties, imagine its impact on investors generally. On Thursday, September 24, the day following the bailout, the DJIA fell almost 1.9 percent. William Sullivan, Morgan Stanley Dean Witter chief money market economist, noted in the *Wall Street Journal* (September 25, 1998: C1) that "the awareness that exposure [to LTC] was extensive, and larger than many expected, helped spark a renewed flight to quality. . . ." Helping the truth sink in was the coincident announcement by UBS of a $720 million loss for the third quarter, much of it related to the bank's LTC investment.

Inasmuch as the bailout gave investors some idea of the amount of trading that might be required to unwind LTC's positions, and the positions of other funds and investment institutions holding similar portfolios, it is not surprising that the bailout failed to quell the US equity market's volatility. This remained at the highest levels since the 1987 crash. In part, of course, the volatility reflected the same problems that had helped to bring LTC so close to collapse. But it also reflected the effects of the bailout itself, including investors' awareness of a new source of risk – the overhang of arbitrage positions that would have to be unwound. This motivated some speculators' attempts to frontrun arbitrage trades and it most certainly discouraged many investors from entering the market to buy the positions arbitragers had to lay off.

LTC was itself contributing to selling pressure. At around the time of the bailout, LTC was unwinding some of its risk-arbitrage trades. It reportedly sold half a million shares of American Bankers Insurance, for example, at prices substantially below the projected takeover price (*Wall Street Journal*, September 29, 1998: C1). The fund had also bailed out on MCI earlier in the month, only days before its acquisition by Worldcom (*New York Times*, September 30, 1998: C1). One bank later blamed trading by LTC, perhaps related to its option positions, for 30 percent of the volatility in the French stock index, the CAC-40, during the year (*New York Times*, October 23, 1998: C22).

FIGURE 18.4

Spread Between High-Yield Bonds and Treasuries

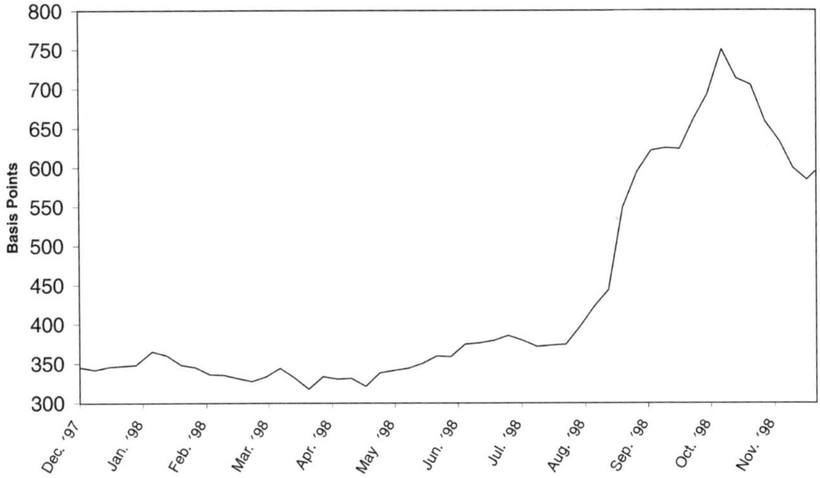

Source: Bear Stearns Global High Yield Research.

On Thursday, October 1, the DJIA fell 2.7 percent, concurrent with Merrill Lynch's announcement that it had a $1.4 billion exposure to LTC, including derivatives positions. In the following week, the Dow moved in a 450-point trading range. Since September, the DJIA had whipsawed between 7,400 and 8,200, with intraday swings averaging 240 points. The options market had moved from crisis to panic. Investors were buying index puts at prices that would have required a market decline of 15 percent in order for the puts to pay for themselves (*Wall Street Journal*, October 9, 1998: C11).[4]

The problems that had led to (and were exacerbated by) LTC's troubles were felt perhaps most acutely in other markets, however. In the week following the bailout, the yield on 30-year Treasuries fell below 5 percent for the first time in 30 years, as investors in search of safety and liquidity drove its price up (*Wall Street Journal*, October 5, 1998: C1). At the same time, investors fearing the eventual liquidation of LTC's huge arbitrage portfolio shunned high-yield bonds, emerging market debt, and mortgage-backed securities.

From the beginning of August to mid-October, the premium investors demanded to hold high-yield, high-risk bonds jumped from 375 to 750 basis points. This doubling came despite any change in actual default rates (*Wall Street Journal*, October 7, 1998: A18). According to *Barron's* (October 5, 1998: MW5), bond markets were "paralyzed" by the LTC overhang.

In addition, US banks and brokerage firms, with exposures to LTC and other hedge funds, and with their own proprietary trading desks reeling from similar strategies, were retreating from global bond markets. In the third quarter of 1998, the average emerging market bond fell over 27 percent. In August and September, there were virtually no new issues by an emerging market government or company (*Wall Street Journal*, October 7, 1998: A19).

The market for US commercial mortgage-backed securities, in which LTC held substantial positions, was also collapsing. The spread between 10-year commercial mortgage-backed securities and 10-year Treasuries had risen from 80 basis points in June to 110 basis points at the end of August. Despite a brief rally on September 24, sparked by the relief that LTC would be able at least to defer liquidations (*Wall Street Journal*, September 25, 1998: C1), the spread continued to widen, from 135 to 155 basis points, between the bailout on September 23 and October 4 (*Wall Street Journal*, October 5, 1998: C1).

Rising rates led the largest US buyer of the riskiest bonds backed by commercial mortgages (Criimi Mae Inc.) to file for bankruptcy on October 5. Problems were showing up in underlying markets as lenders faced increasing difficulty in laying off their risks by securitizing loans. In the absence of the protection afforded by securitization, lenders were asking for higher and higher collateral from potential buyers – up to 25 percent of the loan, versus the 5 percent that had prevailed in midsummer. Despite tight supply and growing demand, commercial real estate prices fell 15 to 20 percent between mid-August and the beginning of October, primarily because potential buyers simply could not find the financing (*Wall Street Journal*, October 5, 1998: A19).

By mid-October, several Wall Street firms, including Merrill Lynch and Bankers Trust, were backing away from commitments they had made in the summer to finance pending mergers; most involved high-yield debt (*Wall Street Journal*, October 16, 1998: A3). The IPO market was drying up, too. Mutual funds heavily invested in initial public offerings were suffering double-digit losses, after hefty double-digit gains in the mid-1990s (*Wall Street Journal*, October 5, 1998: C2). By early October, the number of companies going public had declined to its lowest level in seven years (*Wall Street Journal*, October 7, 1998: A1). One of the victims was Goldman, Sachs, which announced on September 28 that it was postponing its public offering; earlier in the year, analysts had estimated that the Goldman IPO could amount to the biggest ever, close to $30 billion (*New York Times*, June 16, 1998: C4).

As Greg Ip (*Wall Street Journal*, October 7, 1988: A18) pointed out, the lack of liquidity in capital markets posed a particular threat to the US economy because of the significant shift in US lending and borrowing practices in the last twenty years. Corporations had become more reliant on capital markets and less reliant on traditional banks. According to Franklin Edwards and Frederic Mishkin (1995), commercial banks had provided 35 percent of funds to nonfinancial borrowers in 1974, but only 22 percent in 1994. The growth of money market funds and commercial paper and high-yield bond markets, the increased securitization of assets (allowing nonbank institutions to lay off the risk of lending), and the increased quality and availability of financial information (making it easier for firms to raise funds through stock issuance), significantly reduced the edge commercial banks had held in obtaining and lending funds.[5]

Noted Wall Street economist Henry Kaufman had observed in 1994 that this change in financial structure was compounded by the growth in the importance of individual investors at the expense of institutions, the increasing "Americanization" of global markets, and the emergence of "high-octane" portfolio managers ranging across all markets and all countries. As a result, the world's economies were more susceptible to excesses in both credit creation and credit withdrawal. Kaufman warned that this was likely to increase volatility in financial markets. And, with traditional sources of credit losing ground to the capital markets, "restraint will come more from unprecedented asset price variation and less from squeezes on short-term credit availability or cost" (Kaufman 1994: 11).

This, of course, was precisely what was happening as the US economy entered the fourth quarter of 1998 – a credit crunch as the capital markets seized up, despite low interest rates and healthy reserves at commercial banks. Fearing the effects on the economy should such a squeeze continue, the Fed was moved to cut interest rates by a quarter point on October 15. This cut came as a surprise to the market, as the Fed had just announced a quarter-point reduction on September 29. The DJIA responded with a strong rally, closing up 4.15 percent, with financial firms' shares, which had been down as much as 50 to 60 percent from their peak prices, leading the way. The DJIA ended up in October at 8592, its highest level since August 25; it proceeded to climb back over the 9000 mark by late November.

Despite the recovery in the DJIA, the easing of volatility, and the return of the option markets to relative sanity in the latter half of October, repercussions from the woes of summer and the hedge fund fiasco were still to be felt. LTC continued to hemorrhage. In the two weeks after its bailout, the fund had reportedly lost $200 to $300 million on investments (*New York Times*, October 10, 1998: C2), partly because the dollar's plunge against the yen on October 7 had required covering short yen positions at a loss.[6] The *Wall Street Journal* announced on

October 28 (p. C1) that LTC was looking for more funding, and laying off about 20 percent of its employees, while rebuffing a renewed offer from Warren Buffett to buy the fund at a deeply discounted price (*Wall Street Journal*, October 27, 1998: C13).

The carnage extended beyond LTC. The chairman and several other executives at UBS resigned. Merrill Lynch laid off 3,400 employees, and demoted its worldwide risk manager. On October 22, Nomura Securities announced that it had lost $1.7 billion in the first half of the year, largely owing to positions in US mortgage-backed securities. The same day, Bankers Trust reported a loss of $488 million, primarily because of emerging market and high-yield debt, and probable layoffs.

On October 14, BankAmerica had announced a 50 percent drop in earnings for the quarter, with a $370 million charge relating to its investment in the hedge fund D.E. Shaw. Shaw, founded by a former Columbia University computer professor, had leveraged up a $1 billion investment from BankAmerica into a $20 billion bond arbitrage portfolio similar to LTC's. David Shaw blamed his fund's losses on the price distortions caused by the asset liquidations of distressed firms.

By mid-December 1998, LTC was reporting a profit of $400 million, but facing an SEC inquiry into its August fund-raising activities (in particular, its disclosures to potential investors). The SEC and the President's Working Group on Financial Markets had opened investigations of hedge fund activities in general. And the Commodity Futures Trading Commission, despite opposition from the SEC, the Fed, and Congress, was pressing forward in its efforts to expand regulation of derivatives.

Controversy over the Fed's role in the LTC bailout continues. Fed Chairman Alan Greenspan, testifying before Congress on October 1, had pointed to the dangers that the collapse of LTC might have posed for economic growth. According to Greenspan (*New York Times*, October 2, 1998: C3):

> Had the failure of L.T.C.M. triggered the seizing up of markets, substantial damage could have been inflicted on many market participants, including some not directly involved with the firm, and could have potentially impaired the economies of many nations, including our own. . . . The consequences of a fire sale triggered by cross-default clauses, should L.T.C.M. fail on some of its obligations, risked a severe drying up of market liquidity.

It was not only the size of LTC's derivatives positions and loan arrangements, but their complexity that posed such a threat to financial markets generally. As many as 75 financial institutions were involved with LTC as lenders or as counterparties to its derivatives trades. And many of LTC's paired trades were split up between different institutions, contrary to common practice. That is, when financing arbitrage trades, lending institutions ordinarily demand to be in on both legs of the trade; if they have lent the arbitrager money to purchase the long leg of the trade, they would also like to handle the short sale on the other leg. In this way, they have offsetting positions that cushion their own potential losses if the borrower should drop out of the picture. With its clout, however, LTC had been able to shop around for the best deals, leaving one counterparty holding one leg of a trade and another counterparty the other (*New York Times*, December 6, 1998: BU12).

With the cross-default clauses noted by Greenspan, a default by LTC on any one of its contracts would have caused across-the-board defaults on all its contracts. LTC's counterparties would have been left scrambling to find replacements for their one-sided trades. Furthermore, the collateral LTC had deposited with counterparties was likely to prove little comfort if they were all attempting to liquidate at the same time, sending prices plummeting. The Fed obviously felt that the potential for disruption in many markets worldwide justified its intervention.

Others continue to feel strongly that the Fed's role in the bailout created more problems than it solved. As Paul Volcker, the former, inflation-fighting, chairman of the Federal Reserve Board, asks: "Why should the weight of the Federal Government be brought to bear to help out a private investor?" (*New York Times*, December 6, 1998: BU13). To many, any potential market disruptions that the Fed's intervention may have prevented are outweighed by the shadow of moral hazard the LTC bailout has left behind. If the LTC example encourages financial institutions in the future to take on unreasonable amounts of risk and leverage with the expectation of being rescued by the government in the event of failure, the damage to financial markets may be greater than anything contemplated in 1998.

Déjà Vu

The financial crises of 1998, as exemplified in the story of LTC's near-demise, bring to mind some vivid, often ironic, similarities to portfolio insurance and the financial crises of 1987. Not least of the ironic connections is, of course, the presence of Myron Scholes and Robert Merton. In the foreground as partners of LTC, these two Nobel laureates played dominant background roles in portfolio insurance as the creators, with the late Fischer Black, of the option replication model that underlay the strategy. But less obvious, and more profound, links between portfolio insurance and LTC are to be found in the way both debacles played out, allowing a small number of operators with substantial positions to become significant threats to the stability of global markets.

Portfolio insurance vendors, with a marketing blitz based on the seeming ability of sophisticated finance theory to remove risk from equity investing, were able to attract enough capital from institutional investors to amass a US equity market stake amounting to $100 billion. LTC relied on complicated financial mathematics to devise strategies that also promised low-risk returns, which attracted investors and enough lenders to leverage LTC's capital into a $100 billion portfolio. LTC was also able to draw on the extraordinary marginability of its derivatives contracts (some $1.25 trillion in notional value) to magnify its theoretically low-risk returns into large profits.

LTC, like portfolio insurers, fell prey to the illusion of liquidity. Portfolio insurers believed investors generally would stand ready to underwrite their insurance policies by buying when portfolio insurers needed to sell. The crash of 1987 disabused them of this notion. LTC believed that investors or lenders would be perennially available to underwrite its positions, even as gains turned into ever increasing losses. As Andrei Shleifer and Robert Vishny (1997) have pointed out, however, the type of uninformed, noise trading that creates opportunities for arbitragers also creates uncertainty. Investors' and lenders' willingness to support arbitrage activities is limited; and it is likely to become more and more limited as arbitrage mispricings, and the uncertainty underlying them, increase.

In the absence of infusions of capital, LTC had to unwind its positions. Here, the lack of transparency in LTC's positions had an effect on markets similar to the effect that the lack of transparency in portfolio insurers' trades had in October 1987. The magnitude of LTC's positions came as a shock to market participants, just as the amount of equity assets covered by portfolio insurance had shocked most investors. This in turn discouraged investors from entering the market to provide the other side of the required trades.

LTC, like portfolio insurance, demanded more liquidity than the markets could provide. At this point, LTC's trading activity became as disruptive to markets as portfolio insurance trading had been in 1987. It also contributed to LTC's losses by moving prices against the fund's own positions, just as the pressure created by portfolio insurance selling sent insured portfolios through their floors.

The margin calls on LTC's positions effectively stopped out the strategies (or would have, had the Fed not intervened). The market's abrupt decline in 1987, of course, stopped out portfolio insurance strategies, leaving many insured portfolios fully in cash and unable to participate in the market's subsequent rise. Ironically, LTC's strategies may have become unviable, in practice, just at their moment of greatest promise; as spreads widened, discouraging further support from lenders and investors, so too did the potential profit, provided spreads eventually reverted to longer-term norms.

Had LTC not been bailed out, the immediate liquidation of its highly leveraged bond, equity, and derivatives positions may have had effects, particularly on the bond market, rivaling the effects on the equity market of the forced liquidations of insured stocks in 1987 and margined stocks in 1929. Given the links between LTC and investment and commercial banks, and between its positions in different asset markets and different countries' markets, the systemic risk much talked about in connection with the growth of derivatives markets may have become a reality. As it was, LTC's activities contributed to a panic in credit markets that threatened markets and economies worldwide. It may be, as the CFTC (1993a: 5) asserted, that the unwinding of insolvent institutions' derivatives books in the late 1980s and early 1990s had not disrupted markets (see chapter 16); in 1998, with the tremendous growth in derivatives and with large numbers of financial institutions with hundreds of billions of dollars in similar positions, this was no longer the case.

The events of 1998, as those of 1987, remind us how intractable markets can be. Both LTC and portfolio insurers apparently felt they had the key to risk-free (or near-riskless) returns. But markets, bond, stock, or currency, cannot be completely solved, like a tough problem in mathematics, by virtue of sheer brainpower and academic expertise. Markets have a way of confounding such solutions precisely because they are comprised not of computers, but of human beings subject to behavior outside the realm of mathematics.

Summary

In 1998, as in 1987, fear invaded the world's capital markets, turning on their heads theories of pricing efficiency and strategies based on rational investors and rational prices. Very real economic events chased investors out of Russia, but investors were soon fleeing first other emerging markets, then any markets, emerging or developed, that stood between them and safety and liquidity.

As in 1987, investment and trading strategies that seemed to offer investors a haven from risk ended up adding to risk, their own and investors' generally. Ever-increasing demand for equity put protection from August into October 1998 forced option market makers to trade dynamically in stock and stock index futures in order to hedge their net short positions; their trading increased market volatility generally and amplified the whipsaws that cut into their own dynamic hedges. Ever-increasing margin calls, combined with the drying up of liquidity in an ever more panicky market, forced the Long-Term Capital hedge fund to begin unwinding its arbitrage positions; its trading activities added to market volatility and moved prices against its own strategies.

The federally strong-armed rescue of LTC may have prevented the fund's problems from developing into a global systemic risk problem, but it could not prevent a severe capital-market-induced credit contraction that threatened economic growth. Now regulators will investigate hedge funds, and derivatives, and leverage. While new regulations may ameliorate the problems caused by unfettered leverage and untransparent derivatives contracts, they will not eliminate the potential for financial panic. That risk will remain as long as investors are human.

Notes

1 Sources of amounts of funds raised: for Merrill Lynch executives, *Wall Street Journal* (October 5, 1998: A3); all others, the *New York Times* (October 23, 1998: C22).

2 In 1995 and 1997, four LTC partners took out personal loans totaling over $42 million to increase their stakes in the fund.

3 Shirreff (1998) points out that this "call" worked more like a "put" for the LTC partners that purchased it, owing to the provisions of the warrant. UBS could not sell the LTC shares it had purchased to hedge the warrant, but could only convert them into a loan for which LTC would pay Libor plus 50 basis points. If LTC did poorly, it got a loan at well under market rates; if UBS converted, and LTC performance subsequently picked up, UBS would not be able to hedge its upside exposure by buying more shares.

4 The volatility, and the consequent increase in option premiums, was proving to be a problem for guaranteed equity products. By October 1998, for example, insurance companies selling equity-index annuity products in the US had been forced to cut investors' equity participation rates (from 50 to 35 percent in one case) because of the sharp increase in their hedging costs (*Wall Street Journal*, December 7, 1998: C1).

5 Commercial banks, to maintain adequate profit levels, have moved into riskier areas of lending, including commercial real estate and leveraged buy-outs, and derivatives activities (Edwards and Mishkin 1995). The *Wall Street Journal* (September 29, 1998: C1) reported that commercial banks' derivatives activities have continued to grow, with the total face value of all derivatives sold by US commercial banks jumping 21 percent in the second quarter of 1998 from the year earlier, to $28.2 trillion. Growth has come at the expense of increased risk, with sales to below-investment-grade clients increasing.

6 Tiger Management, with a large short position in Japanese yen, lost $2 billion on October 7, and ended the month down $3.4 billion, or 17 percent, on the year (*Wall Street Journal*, November 2, 1998: A3).

Epilogue

In 1997, on the occasion of the tenth anniversary of the 1987 crash, newspapers worldwide took a look back to review what had happened then and to ask (superstitiously, perhaps, but as it would turn out also presciently) what it bode for contemporary markets. What was most notable about these reviews was – despite the reports of the Brady Commission and the Securities and Exchange Commission, despite the intervening years of research debunking fundamentals as the prime cause of the crash, and despite the evidence from the market disruptions of 1989 and 1991 – the extent of their emphasis on fundamentals.

The *New York Times* (August 24, 1997) pointed to the worsening economy between October 1986 and October 1987, and to higher interest rates, a confused monetary policy, defaults on Brazilian loans, and a ballooning trade deficit. The *Wall Street Journal* stressed, variously, rising interest rates (August 25, 1997) and a looming trade war (October 17, 1997). *Barron's* (October 20, 1997) noted the fears of a weakening dollar, and consequent inflationary pressures. The *Sunday Times* of London (October 19, 1997) looked at high price-earnings ratios, low dividends yields, and creeping interest rates.

It is easy to see why so many market observers view the crash in fundamental terms. For sophisticated investors who believe in the informational efficiency of markets, a fundamental explanation is virtually a sin qua non; efficient markets just don't drop like they did on October 19, 1987 for no good reason. For the lay person, fundamentals provide a handy and readable trail map for navigating the market, a readily understood, if often spurious, cause-and-effect way of seeing things.

It is true that fundamentals provide the underlying structure for the pricing of financial assets. Fundamentals exert a gravitational pull on market prices, so that an overvalued market tends to recede and an undervalued one rise – eventually. And some bits of fundamental news undoubtedly triggered the crash in 1987. But fundamentals did not cause the crash, and there is simply no hard, empirical evidence to indicate that they did.

Fundamentals are particularly wanting when it comes to explaining why the market dropped almost 23 percent on Monday the 19th, only to rise by almost 6 percent the next day, all without discernible long-term economic effects. It would take quite a sea change in fundamentals to account for such a reversal.

Yet the pattern of a sudden downdraft followed by a quick recovery is certainly not unprecedented in US equity markets. Nor was the 1987 crash its last manifestation. Indeed, one lesson of the 1987 crash that has been learned, according to the press, is that market corrections are buying opportunities. David Shulman of Salomon Brothers notes of the 1987 crash: "The No. 1 lesson was that you should buy when Wall Street has a one day sale" (*New York Times*, October 19, 1997, section 3, p. 1).

In this century, the equity markets of the 1920s provide an example not dissimilar to the experience of the 1980s. In the 1920s, margin buying fed a huge market run-up. As speculation inflated share prices, margined investors flush with additional collateral borrowed more and bought more, driving prices up further. When prices began to decline, however, margin calls forced investors to liquidate stock, taking the market down. After the crash of October 1929, the market had begun to rally back before misguided policy efforts and bank failures in the 1930s sent it into a tailspin.

Margin buying and margin calls automate their own trend-reinforcing trading, what has been called "pyramiding" and "depyramiding." In the 1980s, the automated, trend-following trades of synthetic portfolio insurance had much the same effect on markets. By the early fall of 1987, portfolio insurance vendors had sold what amounted to a massive synthetic put on the entire stock market. Portfolio insurance strategies covered up to $100 billion in equity assets, or 3 percent of the market's capitalization at the time.

Institutional investors were drawn to portfolio insurance because it appealed to their basic instincts – their very human fear of loss and desire for gain. It offered them a way to lock in the substantial profits the equity market had made since 1982. It also promised a guaranteed floor return. This apparent safety net in turn seemed to grant investors the leeway to increase their expected returns by increasing their risky equity exposures. Increased return, reduced risk, and, with no payment of an option premium up front, all for free!

Portfolio insurance thus attracted investors who bought more equity than they otherwise would have, or at least sold less. Furthermore, as market prices continued to rise during the mid-1980s, the dynamic hedging programs of these investors dictated that they buy more. Other investors, unaware that these trades were mechanistic and information-less, and mistakenly believing they contained information about funda-mentals, were encouraged to add to the buying pressure by trading in the same direction as the insurers or, alternatively, were discouraged from moderating the effects of insurers by selling out of the market, in effect taking the other side of insurers' trades. Underlying prices rose more than they otherwise would have, exceeding the levels supportable by fundamentals.

The higher prices rose above fundamental values, the more fragile the market became. By the autumn of 1987, even slightly bad news would have triggered a price decline. The same dynamic hedging rules that re-quired buying on the way up, however, required selling on the way down. Some particularly savvy investors, who had guessed the identity and extent of these trades, attempted to frontrun the insurers, taking prices down before the insurers could get off their dynamic trades. Other, less know-ing, investors undoubtedly mistook the insurers' trades for more bad news, and sold with them (or declined to buy from them). As the effects of insurers' dynamic hedging were amplified as the market rose, they now snowballed as the market fell.

By demanding more instant liquidity than the market was able, or willing, to provide, dynamic hedging created a liquidity crisis. As the concentrated selling by insurance programs caused market prices to gap down, the very viability of insurance strategies became problematic. Dynamic hedging requires continuous prices. When prices gap down, hedging trades may not be able to be executed at prices that ensure pre-servation of the portfolio's minimum floor. In 1987, dynamic hedging failed to offer the protection portfolio insurance had promised.

Although the Brady and SEC reports on the 1987 crash emphasized portfolio insurance as a primary culprit, few took notice. Even ten years after the crash, only a handful of the commentaries discussed synthetic insurance. In some cases, it was mentioned only to be exonerated. Nobel laureate and University of Chicago Professor Merton Miller (1997: 10), although he admitted that "portfolio insurance . . . can be shown, as a matter of theory, to be potentially destabilizing," was nevertheless adamant in excusing it from taking the brunt of the blame for the 1987 crash.

Miller and others, including his fellow Nobel laureate Myron Scholes, argue that one cannot blame a strategy that accounted for only a fifth to a quarter of total sales on October 19 (see Burr 1997b). The fact that insurers were responsible for only a fraction of total sales on the 19th, however, cannot exonerate their dynamic hedging. Insured equities amounted to only about 3 percent of the market's capitalization at the time, so it's hardly surprising that the bulk of sales on the day of the crash came from investors holding the remaining 97 percent. Nevertheless, insurers were the only group of large institutional traders whose sales far overwhelmed their purchases in both the stock and the futures markets.

Furthermore, the volume of selling required by insurers' hedging programs was three to four times a normal day's volume; the volume of selling actually accomplished by insurers amounted to an entire average day's worth of trading volume. Portfolio insurers' sales turned a market correction into a liquidity crisis, and into the worst single-day loss in US market history. That 23 percent decline in turn trampled on the guarantees of most synthetic insurance programs. But while investors deserted synthetic insurance in droves in the wake of the crash, they have flocked to other protective strategies that require the same potentially destabilizing dynamic hedging.

Portfolio insurance is option replication; it aimed to provide for institutional-size portfolios the protection that would have been provided by listed portfolio put options, had they been available. The very same trend-following, dynamic hedging undertaken by portfolio insurers in the 1980s is today undertaken by investors insuring their portfolios directly, by options exchange market makers hedging net short option positions, and by option dealers attempting to control the risk they are exposed to from their sale of over-the-counter puts and calls.

Ironically, the tenth anniversary of the 1987 crash coincided with the announcement that the Nobel Prize in Economic Sciences was being awarded to Myron Scholes and Robert Merton for their work on theoretical option pricing. Yet virtually none of the retrospectives on the crash noted the connections between Black–Scholes option pricing, portfolio insurance in the 1980s, and the dynamic hedging of option replicators today. Several, however, pointed to the exchanges' post-1987 installation of circuit breakers, sidecars, and improved computer and trading capacity.

Despite improvements to market capacity and circuit breakers designed to mitigate the effects of panicked selling, dynamic hedging associated with option replication has brought the market down again and again since the 1987 crash, most notably in October 1989, November 1991, October 1997, and August 1998. These episodes, together with the 1987 crash itself and precursor events in September 1986 and January 1987, cohere in a pattern characteristic of US equity markets in the 1980s and 1990s, one of broad trending behavior interrupted by infrequent but large downdrafts followed by fairly rapid recoveries. This is consistent, not with fundamentals, but with a market subject to mechanistic, trading-rule-induced breaks.

The likelihood of further such episodes would seem to be greater, rather than less, with the growth in the market for OTC options. According to the Bank for International Settlements (BIS 1996), OTC equity and stock index options outstanding as of the end of March 1995 had a notional value worldwide of about $527 billion; $107 billion of this represented contracts on US stocks. Between year-end 1994 and March 1998, the notional values of exchange-traded equity index options went from $240 billion worldwide and $140 billion US to about $625 billion and $400 billion, respectively (BIS 1997 and 1998). Assuming the OTC market has grown at about the same rate (and extrapolation of the trends would indicate it has grown a great deal faster), the notional value of OTC equity options would amount to about $1.5 trillion worldwide and $300 billion in the US.

How much option replication is associated with OTC markets of this size? And what of the hedging demands of exchange market makers? One worrisome indication from the listed option market is how quickly demand for put protection increases with an unexpected increase in market volatility. This was evident in August and September of 1998. It was also evident in 1997, when the notional value of US exchange-traded stock index options more than doubled between September and December (BIS 1998), undoubtedly as the result of demand in the wake of the October market correction. Such abrupt spikes in demand force market makers to resort to even more dynamic hedging, which further amplifies market volatility and makes their own hedges problematic.

Are option hedging demands great enough to pose a threat to market stability? Given the current state of disclosure, especially regarding OTC option markets, it's difficult to say. But if history is any guide, it tells us that a level of trend-following dynamic hedging that may seem very small in relation to the overall market can have outsized effects.

The 1998 Long-Term Capital Management crisis demonstrates that other trading strategies can be equally destabilizing to markets. When adverse market moves forced LTC to unwind its "low-risk" arbitrage positions, the result was the same trend-following, destabilizing trading that option replication requires.

But LTC also exemplifies the danger posed by the explosive growth in derivatives markets over the past decade. It is unlikely that LTC could have posed such a threat to market stability, for example, had it not been able, via derivatives, to leverage a few billion dollars in capital into hundreds of billions of dollars in asset positions. Furthermore, because of the network of links its derivatives positions forged between different asset markets and different countries' markets, the collapse of LTC threatened the collapse of financial systems worldwide. In light of this experience, perhaps Merton Miller (1997: 147) will reconsider his view that "Neither economics generally nor finance in particular . . . offer much support for [the] notion of a leverage-induced 'bankruptcy multiplier' or a contagion effect."

Derivatives are most frequently touted for their ability to reduce risk. These instruments, and the strategies that exploit them, have undoubtedly contributed to economic growth by fostering liquidity and the creation of capital. They have also often fostered the illusion of a safe haven offering seemingly unlimited investment returns with virtually no risk. In truth, derivatives-related strategies often entail or lead to trading demands that can add to, rather than mitigate, overall market instability. Their effects, furthermore, are magnified by the tremendous amount of leverage derivatives allow and by the intricate connections they form between different markets and countries.

Given human nature, many investors are probably unable to resist the allure of strategies that promise both increased returns and reduced risk. Investors should thus fasten their seatbelts for more bumpy rides ahead. The good news is that investors who can afford to persevere, buying and holding equities in a diversified asset portfolio, can expect to win out in the long run.

Appendix A
The Early Debate

A Memo

January 17, 1983
To: [Prudential Insurance Company of America]
From: Bruce Jacobs, Pension Asset Management Group
Re: Portfolio Insulation

Recently, a few financial institutions and consulting organizations have started to market a "portfolio insulation" technique which claims to "protect" asset values. Leland, O'Brien, and Rubinstein (LOR) were the first to package and market an insulation product and have since been emulated by Kidder Peabody and Wilshire. While these competitors employ the same basic methodology, their products have been alternately branded "Dynamic Asset Allocation," "Protective Portfolio Management," and "Portfolio Risk Control."

Portfolio insulation techniques utilize the concept of a "protective put." A "put" is an option to sell a stock at a specified price, the strike price, over a given period of time. A put purchased on a security in conjunction with a long position in that security affords downside protection. For the cost of the put, referred to as the "premium," the investor's capital can be protected, hence the term "protective put." If the security's price falls, the put can be "exercised," i.e., the security can be sold at the strike price. If the security appreciates, the gains accrue to the investor less the premium paid for the put.

Theoretically, an entire portfolio can be protected through the purchase of puts on each security in the portfolio. However, puts are not available for all securities. In addition, the cost associated with protecting the investment in each security would be far costlier than protecting the capital invested in the portfolio as a whole. This cost problem arises because the premium paid for a put is directly related to the volatility of the protected asset. The volatility of a portfolio of securities, however, is significantly less than the average volatility of the component securities. Thus the put premium for an entire portfolio would be substantially less than the sum of the put premiums across all underlying securities.

It has been recently recognized in the financial literature that a protective put can be synthetically created for any portfolio of securities. The methodology dichotomizes the total portfolio into two segments – an actively managed portfolio and a cash-equivalents portfolio. The actively managed portfolio can be an all equity, all debt, or a balanced portfolio.

The initial portfolio position would consist of both a cash-equivalent portion and an actively managed portion. The cash-equivalent portion is in a sense a buffer to limit the extent of losses. If the actively managed portfolio falls in value, a portion would be liquidated and invested in cash equivalents. Asset value declines require a more conservative posturing to protect remaining capital. Conversely, cash equivalents would be traded for investments in the actively traded portfolio if it appreciates in value. Asset value appreciation permits a riskier posturing since the appreciation provides a larger buffer above the protected value. The premium is paid implicitly and is represented by the opportunity costs of the hedge position in cash equivalents.

Portfolio insulation is not intended as a market timing technique. There is no attempt to forecast returns, but rather trading is precipitated by past returns. The trades between the actively managed portion and the cash-equivalents portion of the portfolio are activated by recent performance.

The portfolio insulation technique protects asset values for any time period specified by the client, usually a calendar year. Since the chosen horizon bears no relationship to the duration of the liabilities, it is arbitrary. The client may be comforted by limiting losses year-by-year. However, the implicit premium on the synthetic put, represented by the opportunity costs of the hedge, will hinder longer-term performance. While simulations of the portfolio insulation technique using the last decade as a sample period show favorable performance, this period was characterized by poor equity performance. Any methodology that would have had large cash positions would have performed favorably.

If the actively managed segment of the portfolio is a "balanced" portfolio, the portfolio insulation technique would trade a vertical slice of the balanced portfolio for cash when the balanced portfolio fell in value, and conversely, would trade cash for a vertical purchase of the balanced portfolio when the balanced portfolio rose in value. The asset mix of a balanced portfolio is appropriately determined by an efficient frontier analysis, which determines the mix of assets that maximizes expected return for any chosen level of risk. Trades between the balanced port-folio and the cash portfolio, required by the portfolio insulation technique, would alter the mix of assets and thereby be a violation of the long-run efficient frontier assumptions in order to reach a short-term goal of protecting asset values, alternatively stated as "assuring" returns, for an arbitrarily chosen time period. Short-run returns could be assured only by moving off the efficient frontier.

Compared to a traditionally managed portfolio, the trades required by the portfolio insulation technique would increase transaction costs, including both commissions and market impact costs. The insulation technique also requires that the actively managed portfolio consist of highly liquid securities. In fact, if the value of the actively traded port-folio falls significantly, the entire active segment will have to be liquid-ated. In this case, the portfolio would consist of cash equivalents until the beginning of the next performance period. Such asset categories as real estate, for example, may not be readily liquidated.

There are also potential slippages in the system so that the protected amount may not be fully protected. For example, since execution prices may differ from the price at the time of the sell signal, the entire portfolio value may fall below the protected amount. In addition, since the expected volatility of the actively managed portion determines the magnitude of the implicit premium on the synthetic put and thus the appropriate hedge, the technique may fail if the volatility of the actively managed portion is mis-specified.

On a more theoretical note, since the portfolio insulation technique trades cash for the actively traded portfolio when values appreciate, and conversely, trades the actively traded fund for cash when values fall, there is an implicit assumption that the investor's utility for wealth dis-plays decreasing risk aversion (increasing risk tolerance). An individual displaying decreasing risk aversion will commit an increasing (decreas-ing) proportion of his wealth to risky assets as his wealth rises (falls). The evidence in the financial literature is more supportive of the notion of constant proportional risk aversion, i.e., independent of wealth level, an individual will commit the same proportion of wealth to risky assets. That chosen proportion is of course unique to the individual.

Also, from a macro perspective, if a large number of investors utilized the portfolio insulation technique, price movements would tend to snow-ball. Price rises (falls) would be followed by purchases (sales) which would lead to further price appreciation (depreciation). Market prices would not be efficient and it would pay to not use portfolio insulation, since the resulting over- or under-valuation would represent opportun-ities for savvy investors.

A final criticism is that while it may be possible to assure nominal returns, after-inflation or real returns cannot be assured. While the plan sponsor may feel comfort in protecting nominal values for a chosen time period, purchasing power will remain unprotected. Since the plan sponsor's liabilities are real and not nominal in their nature, there is little comfort in assuring nominal returns, especially when the cost is a longer-run return sacrifice.

INNOVATIVE PORTFOLIO INSURANCE TECHNIQUES

THE LATEST DEVELOPMENTS IN "DYNAMIC HEDGING"

TWENTY INDUSTRY LEADERS WILL TELL YOU HOW TO:

- PROTECT AGAINST PORTFOLIO DECLINE
- REDUCE PORTFOLIO VOLATILITY
- LOCK IN GAINS WITHOUT LOCKING OUT POTENTIAL
- GUARANTEE MINIMUM RATE OF RETURN
- SAFELY EXPLOIT ARBITRAGE & SYNTHETIC INSTRUMENTS
- EXTEND YOUR INVESTMENT HORIZONS
- ELIMINATE CASH TRADING BY USING FUTURES

KEYNOTE SPEAKERS:

Fischer Black	Stephen A. Ross
Goldman, Sachs & Co.	Yale University

NEW YORK CITY
June 10 & 11, 1986
Omni Park Central Hotel

 Institute for International Research

DAY ONE

8.00 *Registration — Coffee/Tea*

9.00 **CHAIRMAN'S OPENING REMARKS**
Michael R. Granito, Managing Director
J. P. Morgan Investment Management, Inc.

9.10 **INTRODUCTION TO DYNAMIC HEDGING**
☐ What is Dynamic Asset Allocation? (Dynamic Hedging)
☐ What Does it Do?
☐ How Does it Work?
☐ Why Does it Work?
☐ Portfolio Insurance and Options
☐ Arbitrage Analysis
☐ Path Independent Strategies
☐ Future Applications
Hayne E. Leland, Director
Leland O'Brien Rubinstein Associates Inc., and
Professor of Finance, University of California
Berkeley

Keynote Speaker
9.50 **AN OVERVIEW OF PORTFOLIO INSURANCE**
☐ Alternative Methods for Providing Portfolio Insurance
☐ Costs & Benefits
☐ Who Should Buy Insurance?
☐ Who Should Sell Insurance?
Fischer Black, Vice President
Trading & Arbitrage
Goldman, Sachs & Co.

10.20 *Mid-Morning Coffee/Tea*

10.50 **HOW DYNAMIC HEDGING REVOLUTIONIZES INVESTMENT MANAGEMENT**
☐ There's No Such Thing as a Long Term Investor
☐ Dynamic Hedging as a Substitute for Bonds
☐ "Underwriting" New Markets & Investment Styles
☐ Managerial Implications of Using Futures
Douglas A. Love
Vice President & Director of Research
BEA Associates, Inc.

11.25 **THE DECISION TO USE PORTFOLIO INSURANCE: A PANEL OF CORPORATE PLAN SPONSORS**
☐ What Business Purpose is Served by the Corporation's Dynamic Hedging Program?
☐ How Should the Corporation Analyze Costs & Benefits?
☐ Should the Corporation Purchase or Sell Portfolio Insurance?
☐ What is the Right Time Horizon?
☐ Potential Problems & Possible Solutions
☐ Results to Date
Walter T. Dec, Director
Portfolio Strategy, Research &
Specialized Investments
General Motors Corporation

Robert L. Whalen, CFA Director
Investment Technology
CIGNA Investment Management Company
Richard T. Tyner, Vice President
Investments & Investor Relations
J. P. Stevens & Co., Inc.
Gerald W. Bialka, Assistant Treasurer
The Mead Corporation

12.45 *Luncheon for Delegates & Speakers*

2.15 **DYNAMIC HEDGING FOR CAPITAL PRESERVATION: LOCKING IN PORTFOLIO GAINS**
☐ Asset Allocation for a Four-Year Bull Market
☐ Locking in Gains Without Locking Out Potential
☐ Aggressive Management Program for the Conservative Investor
☐ Creating Variable Beta and Variable Duration Portfolios
☐ Overcoming the Active/Passive Management Dilemma
☐ Molding Portfolio Returns to Meet Multi-Dimensional Investment Objectives
Richard M. Bookstaber, Vice President
Morgan Stanley & Co.

2.45 **THE PUBLIC PENSION FUND & DYNAMIC HEDGING**
☐ Advantages/Disadvantages
☐ Applications in the Public Sector
☐ How Does Dynamic Hedging Impact Asset Allocation Decisions?
☐ The Use of Dynamic Hedging as a Risk Modifier
Howard J. France, Executive Director
State Investment Agency
Maryland Retirement & Pension System

3.15 *Mid-Afternoon Coffee/Tea*

3.35 **ACTUARIAL IMPLICATIONS OF INSURED PORTFOLIOS**
☐ The Current Environment: Is Portfolio Insurance Right for the Times?
  • Overfunded Pension Plans
  • The Growth of Flexible Compensation
  • New Accounting Rules
☐ Implications for Investment Strategy: Many Ways to Rome
  • Dynamic Hedging, Synthetic Instruments, Diversification, Immunization
  • Actuarial Assumptions and Implications
William A. Dreher, Managing Director
William A. Dreher & Associates
Harry Allen, Vice President
Towers, Perin, Foster & Crosby

4.35 **IMMUNIZED PORTFOLIOS & DYNAMIC ASSET ALLOCATION**
☐ The Role of Immunized Portfolios
  • Cash Contributions & Withdrawals
☐ Single & Multi Risky Asset Situations
Oldrich A. Vasicek, Senior Research Consultant
Gifford Fong Associates

5.15 **CLOSE OF DAY ONE**

DAY TWO

00 A GENERAL FRAMEWORK FOR DYNAMIC HEDGING STRATEGIES
- The Linear Investment Rule
- Attractive Characteristics of Linear Rules
- Perpetual Strategies
- Relationship to Portfolio Insurance
- Investor Horizons
- Examples of Linear Investment Rules

Michael R. Granito, Managing Director
J. P. Morgan Investment Management, Inc.

Keynote Speaker

45 DYNAMIC HEDGING: CHALLENGES & PITFALLS
- The Effect of Transaction Costs
- Long Run Hedging
- Market Disruptions
- Measuring the Real Risk
- Hedging the Whole Portfolio
- Problems in Forecasting Input Data

Stephen A. Ross, Adrian C. Israel Professor of International Trade & Finance
Yale School of Organization & Management

•5 Mid-Morning Coffee/Tea

•5 A PUBLIC DEBATE ON DYNAMIC HEDGING
- Whose Interest Does Portfolio Insurance Serve: Sponsors or Plan Beneficiaries?
- What is the Long-Run Impact of Portfolio Insurance?
- The Implications of Accounting Rule Changes
- Should Corporations be Buyers or Sellers of Portfolio Insurance?

John W. O'Brien, Chairman & CEO
Leland O'Brien Rubinstein Associates Inc.

Bruce I. Jacobs, Ph.D., Managing Director
Eagle Rock Asset Management, an affiliate of The Prudential Asset Management Group

Moderator: Michael R. Granito
Managing Director
J. P. Morgan Investment Management, Inc.

0 MULTIPLE RISKY ASSET STRATEGIES: THE MANY DIMENSIONS OF RISK
- Defining Pension Risk
- Insuring the Liability Portfolio
- The Practical Problems
  - Separating the Pension Risk Elements
  - Elemental Insurance
  - The Whole is Cheaper than the Sum of the Parts

Jeremy Gold, Vice President
Morgan Stanley & Co.

12.30 *Luncheon for Delegates & Speakers*

1.45 A NEW APPROACH TO PORTFOLIO INSURANCE: PROCESS-FREE INVESTMENT RULES THAT AVOID COMPLEX MODELS & ASSUMPTIONS
- Problems with Traditional Methods
- Valuation Models & Parameter Estimates
- Introduction to Process-Free Methods
- Simple Investment Rules
- Perpetual Return Formula
- Attractive Risk/Return Balance

John C. Cox, Professor
Sloan School of Management
Massachusetts Institute of Technology

2.15 IMPLEMENTING DYNAMIC HEDGING STRATEGIES
- What Hedging Instrument(s) Should Be Used
- Futures
- Options
- Stocks
- Bonds
- What Trading Techniques Should Be Used

R. Steven Wunsch, Vice President
Kidder Peabody & Co. Incorporated

2.55 *Mid-Afternoon Coffee/Tea*

3.15 EQUITY ENHANCED DEDICATION
- Using Dynamic Asset Allocation Technology
  - Combining the Security of Dedicated Portfolios With the Higher Expected Returns of Equities
- Like Pure Dedication — EED Starts With a Specification of Plan Liabilities
- The Plan Gains Exposure to Market Upside & Assures Realization of the Specified Minimum Outcome
- Initial Asset Mix & Subsequent Changes in Mix
- Allocation Shifts through the Futures Market

Ralph S. Tate, Vice President
Common Stock Department
Aetna Life & Casualty Company

3.45 FUTURES TRADING & MANAGING DYNAMIC ASSET ALLOCATION
- Minimize Transaction Costs
- Avoid Interfering With Manager
- Exploit Arbitrage
- Synthetic Instruments
- Alternative Contracts Create Opportunities

Jeffrey Geller, Vice President
Options & Futures Manager
BEA Associates, Inc.

4.15 CLOSE OF DAY TWO

Appendix B
Option Basics

This appendix reviews the basics of option pricing. The mathematics is not essential to an understanding of the exposition in the text.

Here we describe the two basic option contracts, puts and calls, and their properties. We look at how these options may be valued, how they relate to one another, and how an option's value changes with changes in its underlying parameters. Appendix C explains how an option can be replicated by a position in the underlying stock and a risk-free asset.

Defining Options

A call option is a contract in which the option buyer purchases the right to buy an underlying asset from the option seller at a predetermined price in a predetermined time frame. A put option is a contract in which the option buyer purchases the right to sell an underlying asset to the option seller at a predetermined price in a predetermined time frame. We will focus here on options where the underlying asset is a common stock or a stock index.

For both calls and puts, the predetermined price of the underlying asset is called the strike, or exercise, price. The nature of the predetermined time frame depends upon whether the option is a European-style or an American-style option. A European-style option can be exercised only on the expiration date. An American-style option can be exercised at any time up to and including its stated expiration date. The following discussion will focus on European-style options in the interest of simplicity.

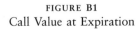

FIGURE B1
Call Value at Expiration

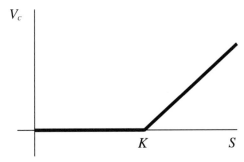

The buyer of a call has purchased the right to buy the underlying stock at the stated strike price, K, on the stated expiration date. If, on that date, the asset's market price, S, exceeds the option's strike price, K, the option buyer will exercise the call, as its value will equal the positive difference $S - K$. If, on that date, the stock's market price is at or below the option's strike price, the option buyer will have no incentive to exercise the call; it will expire worthless. Note that the value of the call is theoretically unlimited on the upside, as the stock's price may attain any value above zero; however, the value of the option is never negative, because the buyer always has the choice of not exercising.

The value of a call option at expiration, V_c, is thus:

$$V_c = \begin{cases} S - K & \text{if } S > K, \text{ or} \\ 0 & \text{if } S \leq K. \end{cases}$$

This may be written more compactly as

$$V_c = \max\{S - K, 0\}.$$

Figure B1 depicts this graphically.

The value of a put option at expiration is the obverse of the value of a call option. If the option's strike price, K, is higher than the underlying stock's market price, S, the put buyer can purchase the underlying stock and turn it over to the put option's seller in exchange for the (higher) option strike price. The value of the put in this case is $K - S$. If the strike price is at or lower than the stock's market price, the option buyer will have no incentive to exercise the put; it will

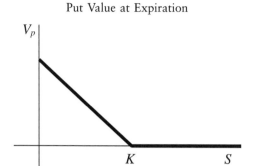

FIGURE B2
Put Value at Expiration

expire worthless. For the put, then, the maximum value would be K, achieved if the stock price falls to zero, and the minimum value would, again, be zero, as the put holder has the choice of not exercising if exercise would result in a negative value.

The value of the put at expiration is expressed mathematically as:

$$V_p = \max\{K - S, 0\}.$$

This value is depicted graphically in figure B2.

A call (put) option whose strike price is below (above) the underlying stock's price is said to be "in the money." A call (put) option whose strike price is above (below) the underlying stock's price is "out of the money." When an option's strike price matches the price of the underlying stock, the option is "at the money."

Option Prices via Black–Scholes

The value of an option at expiration depends simply on the type of option (put or call), the option's strike price, and the market price of the underlying stock. But at what price would an investor be willing to buy an option, or sell an option, before expiration? One can see that, at any time prior to expiration, the value, hence the price, of the option will be related to the probability of the stock's price being above or below the known option strike price.

The current stock price is known. One can make some assumptions about how that price may evolve between the present and the date of the option's expiration. In their seminal pricing model, Fischer Black and Myron Scholes (1973) made a fairly standard assumption about the stochastic process underlying stock price movements. They assumed the stock's return is a normally distributed random variable with a constant mean and a constant variance.

Black and Scholes, however, had a unique insight that greatly simplified the problem of valuing options. They realized that, because the option's price was dependent upon how the stock's price moved, the option price and the price of the underlying stock are very closely correlated. As stock price moves up, the price of a call on the stock moves up and the price of a put on the stock moves down. In theory, one could sell a certain number of calls or buy a certain number of puts against a long stock position, so that the movements of the option price would exactly offset the movements of the underlying stock price. Such a portfolio would be effectively risk-free, and must therefore earn the risk-free rate of return.

Contextualizing the option pricing problem in a risk-free world allowed for a more general solution of the problem because it allowed substitution of the risk-free rate for the stock's rate of return. Previous attempts to value options had required investor risk preferences as inputs. But investor risk preferences do not come into play in setting the risk-free return. One can thus assume any general risk preference, including risk neutrality. And if all investors are risk-neutral, the expected return on all securities is the risk-free rate.

The solution that Black and Scholes obtained for the price, V_c, of a European call option is

$$V_c = N(d_1)S - N(d_2)Ke^{-r\tau}$$

where r is the risk-free rate of return, τ is the time to expiration and, as before, S is the price of the underlying stock and K the option's strike price. The function $N(\cdot)$ is the standard cumulative normal distribution function for the variables d_1 and d_2:

$$d_1 = \frac{\log(S/K) + (r + \sigma^2/2)\tau}{\sigma\sqrt{\tau}},$$

$$d_2 = \frac{\log(S/K) + (r - \sigma^2/2)\tau}{\sigma\sqrt{\tau}},$$

where σ is the standard deviation of the stock's return. The expression $N(d_1)S$ may be thought of as a variable that equals the stock's price at expiration if that price is higher than the option strike price or equals zero otherwise. $N(d_2)$ describes the probability of the option being exercised, so $N(d_2)K$ is the strike price times the probability of its being paid. The term $e^{-r\tau}$ indicates discounting at the continuously compounded risk-free rate over the time until expiration.

The Black–Scholes price of a put option is:

$$V_p = -N(-d_1)S + N(-d_2)Ke^{-r\tau}.$$

This can be derived from put–call parity. That is, a European put and a European call on the same underlying stock, with the same time to expiration and the same strike price, must be related in the following manner:

$$V_c + Ke^{-r\tau} = V_p + S.$$

To see this, note that the quantity on the left-hand side of the equation is the value of a portfolio consisting of the call option plus an amount of cash equal to $Ke^{-r\tau}$. The value of the call option at expiration is $\max\{S - K, 0\}$, and the cash earns interest at the risk-free rate so that its value at the option's expiration is K. The value of the overall portfolio at expiration is thus $\max\{S - K, 0\} + K = \max\{S, K\}$. Now note that the quantity on the right-hand side of the equation is the value of a second portfolio consisting of the put option and one share of the stock. The value of this portfolio at the option's expiration will be $\max\{K - S, 0\} + S = \max\{K, S\}$. As the two portfolios have the same values, their prices must be the same, and the equation must be satisfied. Put–call parity enables one to create puts from calls, or calls from puts. For example, put options can be created from call options, cash, and shares sold short in proportions dictated by put–call parity.

Note that the Black–Scholes formula makes a number of simplifying assumptions. In addition to assuming a constant mean and constant variance for the return of the underlying stock, for example, it also assumes a constant interest rate over the life of the option, and assumes away transaction costs, taxes, and dividends. On the plus side, however, it requires only five inputs – the current stock price, the option's exercise price, the volatility of the underlying stock, the interest rate, and the time to expiration of the option. Four of these are directly observable. Furthermore, they make sense.

It stands to reason, for example, that the relationship between the option's strike price and the current stock price will affect the option's value, hence its price. As the payoff (if any) on a call equals $S - K$, its value, hence its price, may be expected to increase as the underlying stock price increases, other things equal. (Conversely, its price will be lower, the higher the option's strike price.) As the payoff (if any) on a put equals

FIGURE B3
Call Price

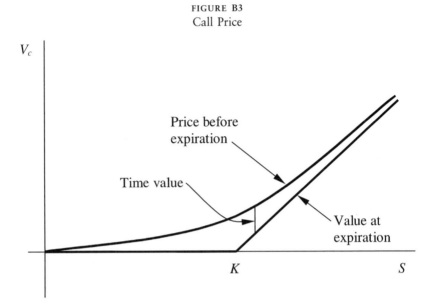

$K - S$, its price may be expected to decline as the underlying stock price increases (and to increase as the option's strike price increases).

Figures B3 and B4 illustrate the Black–Scholes prices of a call and a put, respectively, over a range of stock prices (other variables held constant). Note that the call price increases (and the put price declines) as stock price increases. Viewed in terms of each option's strike price, K, the option price increases as stock price movements place the option in the money and declines as stock price movements take the option out of the money.

Figures B3 and B4 also plot each option's value at expiration (sometimes called the intrinsic value). The difference between the option's price before expiration and its intrinsic value is the time value of the option. The value of the option before expiration almost always exceeds the option's intrinsic value. As long as there remains some time to expiration, there is the potential for the stock price to move in a way favorable to the option's value.

This potential (hence time value) is greatest when the option is near the money (that is, when the stock price is close to the option's strike price). The further out of the money the option is, the less chance there is for it to become valuable by expiration, whatever the time remaining. The further in the money the option is, the smaller will be the

FIGURE B4
Put Price

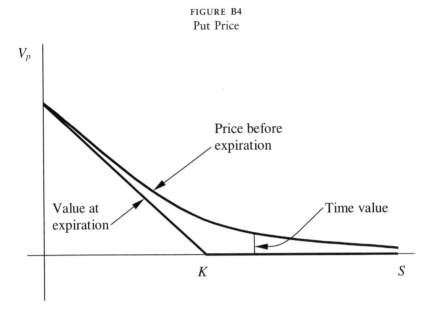

V_p

Price before
expiration

Value at
expiration

Time value

K S

proportional benefit of any additional favorable stock price movements in the time remaining to expiration. As the above discussion suggests, an option's price will decline toward its intrinsic value as its expiration approaches, all else equal, and this time decay will be most pronounced when the option is near the money.

Volatility may be seen to have a similar effect on option value. That is, the lower the volatility of the underlying stock, other things equal, the lower the price of an option on that stock may be expected to be. This relationship, like that between time and option value, reflects the potential for favorable stock price movements. The more volatile the underlying stock, the greater the likelihood of the stock price moving in a manner favorable to the option holder.

Finally, the effect of the risk-free rate on option value may be illuminated if we view the rate as a rough measure of the relative worth of holding an option versus a position in the underlying stock. If we view a call as a substitute for a long stock position, it should be apparent that, the higher the risk-free rate, the more attractive the call becomes, as using cash to purchase stock outright would entail a larger sacrifice in risk-free return. The converse is true for a put. Viewing a put as a substitute for a short stock position, it is apparent that a higher risk-free rate will reduce the attractiveness of the put.

Grecian Formulas

A set of partial derivatives – often called "the greeks" – gives precise measures of how option price changes with changes in the option pricing parameters. For example, the change in an option's price, V, with a change in the price of the underlying asset, S, is defined as delta, Δ:

$$\Delta = \frac{\partial V}{\partial S}.$$

In terms of the Black–Scholes formula, the delta of a call option is:

$$\Delta_c = N(d_1).$$

Similarly, applying the definition to the Black–Scholes formula for the price of a put option (or, alternatively, using put–call parity), one obtains for the delta of a put option:

$$\Delta_p = N(d_1) - 1.$$

Delta equals the slope of the option's price curve with respect to changes in the price of the underlying stock. From figures B3 and B4, one can see that the slope of the curve changes as stock price changes. For calls, delta increases as stock price rises and declines as stock price falls. As stock price climbs, and the option moves deeper and deeper into the money, the slope of the price curve approaches one, indicating that the option price is moving almost one-for-one with the stock price. As stock price falls, and the call moves further out of the money, the slope of the price curve flattens, approaching zero. As the likelihood of the option ever being exercised decreases, the option behaves less and less like the underlying stock. The put delta behaves similarly, but as put delta declines as stock price rises and increases as stock price falls, it is negative.

An option's delta can be conceptualized in terms of the shares underlying the option. A standard stock option contract represents one hundred shares. But when the option's delta is 0.5, the option behaves approximately as if it represented fifty shares; for a given move in the stock price, the option price will move half as much. An out-of-the-money option with a delta of 0.3 will behave as if it represented thirty shares, and an in-the-money option with a delta of 0.6 will behave as if it represented sixty shares.

Delta is extremely useful because it is the starting point for constructing option hedges. Consider a put option with a delta of −0.5. With a given decrease in the underlying stock price, the put option's price will tend to increase by half as much. An investor who holds the stock and wishes to insure against declines in its price will, then, have to buy two puts for every hundred shares of stock owned when the put's delta is at −0.5.

Option exchange market makers, option dealers, and others with large option positions may want to hedge in the other direction − taking positions in the underlying stock in order to protect against adverse movements in option prices. Consider a dealer that has sold calls with a delta of 0.5. A given increase in the underlying stock price will tend to increase the call price by half as much. So if the stock price increases by $1.00, the call price increases by half that much ($0.5 \times \$1.00 = \$0.50$), producing a loss of $50 for the call option seller ($\$0.50 \times 100$ shares = $50). The option seller could have hedged against this loss by buying fifty shares of stock at the outset; in that case, the $1.00 per share increase in the price of the stock would have provided a profit of $50 − exactly offsetting the loss on the option.

A portfolio is perfectly delta hedged when the ratio of the number of shares held long to the number of call options sold, or the ratio of the number of shares sold short to the number of put options sold, is equal to the absolute value of Δ. For this reason, Δ is sometimes called the hedge ratio. (Note that this is the type of riskless portfolio that Black and Scholes constructed for deriving their pricing formula.) A hedge based on a given value of delta, however, will not remain riskless over large changes in the underlying stock price. In fact, a delta hedge will be riskless only for very small changes in the underlying stock price.

As is apparent from looking at figures B3 and B4, delta changes as the underlying stock price changes because, as we have noted, the slope of the option price curve changes as the option moves into and out of the money. This rate of change of delta with respect to the underlying asset price is called gamma. Specifically:

$$\Gamma = \frac{\partial \Delta}{\partial S} = \frac{\partial^2 V}{\partial S^2}.$$

Gamma is a measure of the curvature of the option price curve. It is greatest for options that are near the money. The curve straightens out to become more linear as the option moves further into or further out of the money.

Gamma is a measure of how sensitive the option's delta is to changes in the underlying stock's price. The higher an option's gamma, the more its delta changes with a given change in the underlying stock price. A change in the option's delta, however, will in turn require a change in the ratio of the option to the underlying stock if a stock-plus-option combination is to maintain a riskless posture.

Theoretically, one can maintain a riskless hedge, even for a high-gamma option, by continuously rebalancing portfolio positions. In practice, however, one cannot trade continuously. Even in the absence of transaction costs, continuous trading is precluded because prices tend to gap, either between market closings and openings or under crash conditions such as those experienced on October 19, 1987.

Changes in volatility introduce another complicating factor. Black–Scholes assumes that the volatility of the stock remains constant over the option's life. This condition may not be met, however. And if the volatility of the underlying stock changes, the price of the option will change. A change in the option's price with respect to a change in the volatility of the underlying asset is measured as kappa or, as it is more often called, vega (although Vega is a star in the constellation Lyra, and not a Greek letter!). Specifically:

$$\kappa = \frac{\partial V}{\partial \sigma}.$$

An increase in volatility makes both put and call options more valuable, increasing their price. A decline in volatility makes both put and call options less valuable, reducing their price. Changes in volatility will usually require rebalancing to maintain riskless hedges.

Perhaps we should note here that rebalancing would not be that much of a problem, provided there were no transaction costs and it could be done continuously (two assumptions of Black–Scholes). Transaction costs make rebalancing expensive. Discontinuity makes exact rebalancing impossible.

The last two greeks, theta and rho, measure the variations of the option's price with respect to changes in time and the risk-free rate, respectively. They are:

$$\Theta = \frac{\partial V}{\partial t},$$

and

$$\rho = \frac{\partial V}{\partial r}.$$

Theta and rho are not as influential as delta, gamma, and vega. In addition to the effects discussed in the previous section, we might note that rho's influence declines as the time to expiration gets shorter. There is not much one can do about the passage of time except to be aware of its possible effects on the value of the option or option portfolio.

Appendix C
Option Replication

This appendix discusses how an option on a stock can be replicated by a portfolio consisting of the stock and a risk-free asset. This is first demonstrated in the context of the Black–Scholes formula and then using the binomial model. As the text notes, and as we will demonstrate here more rigorously, proper replication of a long put position (or, indeed, a long call position) requires constant adjustments to the proportions of the portfolio held in the stock and the risky asset. In particular, replication of a long call or put position requires trend-following dynamic trading – buying stock in response to price rises and selling in response to declines.

Portfolio Insurance via Black–Scholes

As we discussed in appendix B, Fischer Black and Myron Scholes (1973) showed that one can price a put option as follows:

$$V_p = -N(-d_1)S + N(-d_2)Ke^{-r\tau}.$$

Note that a portfolio consisting of $N(-d_1)$ shares of the underlying stock sold short at price S, together with an investment of $N(-d_2)Ke^{-r\tau}$ in a risk-free asset, would have a value equal to the value of the put. This equivalence between a put option and positions in the underlying stock and the risk-free asset can be used in theory to insure a portfolio.

Say, for example, that you have one share of a stock and want to ensure that the value of your investment does not fall below K. You could buy a put option on the stock with a strike price of K. Alternatively, given the equivalence just discussed, you could adjust your position such that you hold $1 - N(-d_1) = N(d_1)$ shares of underlying stock and an amount $N(-d_2)Ke^{-rt}$ in the risk-free asset. This defines a portfolio that can be regarded as one share held long plus a synthetic put comprising $N(-d_1)$ shares sold short and an investment of $N(-d_2)Ke^{-rt}$ in the risk-free asset.

More generally, to find the time-varying capital allocation that replicates an insured portfolio, let the total capital W be allocated to an *equivalent* of x shares of stock at price S and x synthetic puts with strike price K.[1] That is $W = (S + V_p)x$. Using the Black–Scholes formula for the put price together with the relationship between $N(d_1)$ and $N(-d_1)$ gives

$$W = N(d_1)Sx + N(-d_2)Ke^{-rt}x.$$

This is equivalent to a portfolio consisting of $N(d_1)x$ *actual* shares and an investment of $N(-d_2)Ke^{-rt}x$ in the risk-free asset. Thus, to replicate the insured portfolio, out of the total capital of $N(d_1)Sx + N(-d_2)Ke^{-rt}x$, the investor would maintain $N(d_1)Sx$ dollars invested in the stock. That is, the investor would maintain a proportion

$$\omega = \frac{SN(d_1)}{SN(d_1) + N(-d_2)Ke^{-rt}}$$

in the stock and a proportion $1 - \omega$ in the risk-free asset. Note, however, that the relative proportions need to be changed as the stock price changes and as the time to expiration becomes shorter.

In particular, portfolio insurance demands trend-following trading. Using the Black–Scholes formula for the price of the put in the above expression for ω, it can be shown that

$$\omega = \frac{N(d_1)}{1 + V_p/S}.$$

As the stock price S increases, $N(d_1)$ increases, so the numerator increases. Simultaneously, the denominator decreases because the put value decreases as S increases. The value of ω therefore increases with S. The proportional increase in the portfolio's stock position exceeds the amount that would be accounted for by a mere increase in the stock's value. Therefore, one needs to commit a larger fraction of capital to the stock as the stock's price rises. This is trend-following trading.

Example of Proportion Invested in Stock

Suppose an investor wishes to invest in shares that are currently trading at $100 each. Suppose also that the investor wants to use portfolio insurance theory to be assured that, at the end of one year, the investment in each of the shares will not be worth less than $95. Assume that the return on the risk-free asset is 5 percent per year and the standard deviation of the logarithm of the stock's returns is 25 percent per year. What proportion of the investor's capital must initially be invested in shares?

To solve this problem, first compute the values of d_1 and d_2 as follows:

$$d_1 = \frac{\ln(S/K) + (r + \sigma^2/2)\tau}{\sigma\sqrt{\tau}}$$

$$= \frac{\ln(100/95) + (0.05 + (0.25)^2/2) \times 1}{0.25\sqrt{1}} = 0.5302$$

$$d_2 = \frac{\ln(S/K) + (r - \sigma^2/2)\tau}{\sigma\sqrt{\tau}}$$

$$= \frac{\ln(100/95) + (0.05 - (0.25)^2/2) \times 1}{0.25\sqrt{1}} = 0.2802$$

Then, using statistical tables, find the corresponding cumulative normal distribution functions:

$$N(+d_1) = 0.7020$$

$$N(-d_2) = 0.3897$$

and, finally, compute ω as follows:

$$\omega = \frac{SN(d_1)}{SN(d_1) + N(-d_2)Ke^{-r\tau}}$$

$$= \frac{100 \times 0.7020}{100 \times 0.7020 + 0.3897 \times 95 \times e^{-0.05}} = 0.666$$

Thus 66.6 percent of the investor's initial capital must be invested in stocks and the remaining 33.4 percent must be invested in the risk-free asset. Observe that, if the investor's initial capital was $10,000, the required proportion in stocks corresponds to the investor owning 66.6 shares.

Example of Rebalancing

Suppose that one month has passed since the beginning of the period in which the investor initiated the portfolio insurance program of the example above, and the price of the shares has increased to $105. How should the investor rebalance the portfolio?

To solve this problem, proceed as above, using the new stock price, $S = 105$, and the new time to expiration, $\tau = 11/12$, to give

$$d_1 = 0.7293, \; N(+d_1) = 0.7671$$
$$d_2 = 0.4899, \; N(-d_2) = 0.3121$$

so that

$$\omega = 0.740.$$

That is, 74 percent of the investor's capital must be invested in the stocks.

Compare this example with the first. Note that, just before rebalancing, the investor's capital would have grown to $10,347 [66.6 × 105 + 3,340 × exp(0.05/12)]. The proportion of the capital then held in shares would have risen to 67.6 percent [66.6 × 105/10,347]. In order to achieve the new required proportion of 74 percent in stocks, the investor must rebalance the portfolio by buying still more shares.

Put Replication via Binomial Modeling

Another way of viewing option replication is through the binomial model pioneered by William Sharpe (1978) and developed further by John Cox, Stephen Ross, and Mark Rubinstein (1979). The binomial model provides a more intuitive view of option pricing than Black–Scholes.

The binomial model begins by assuming that a stock's price can either rise or fall. At the beginning of a period, for example, the stock's price is S. At the end of the period, the stock price has either gone up to S_u or fallen down to S_d. The stock's behavior is depicted graphically in figure C1.

Suppose an investor holds this stock and wishes to ensure that the investment does not lose value over the period. The investor could buy a put option on the stock with a strike price K equal to S. Whether the stock price rises or falls, the investor finishes out the period with an investment equal to at least K. Alternatively, the investor can replicate

FIGURE C1
Single-Period Stock Price Lattice

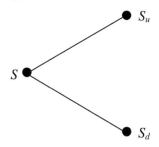

the put option by constructing a portfolio of the underlying asset plus a risk-free asset.

Let the put replicating portfolio consist of N shares of the stock and $B invested in the risk-free asset. Over the period, the value of the risk-free investment will rise to $(1 + r)B = RB$, where r is the risk-free rate, and R is one plus the risk-free rate. The value of the replicating portfolio will thus be $NS_u + RB$ if the stock price rises, or $NS_d + RB$ if the stock price falls.

Let the value of the put option be P_u if the stock price rises and P_d if the stock price falls. Equating the put option's value to the replicating portfolio's value under the two conditions for the stock price gives the following two equations:

$$P_u = NS_u + RB,$$
$$P_d = NS_d + RB.$$

This can be readily solved for the required number of shares and the dollar investment in the risk-free asset. The results are

$$N = \frac{P_u - P_d}{S_u - S_d},$$

and

$$B = \frac{1}{R} \frac{P_d S_u - P_u S_d}{S_u - S_d}.$$

Consider as an example a stock currently priced at $10, which in the next period could either rise to $12 or fall to $8. A put option on this stock with a strike price of \$10 will, at the end of the period, have a value of $P_u = \max\{10 - 12, 0\} = \$0$ if the stock price rises or $P_d = \max\{10 - 8, 0\} = \$2$ if the stock price falls.

Replicating this put would require investment in the underlying stock and the risk-free asset. Assume the risk-free rate over the period is 5 percent, so $R = 1.05$. Substituting these values into the equations above gives:

$$N = \frac{0 - 2}{12 - 8} = -\frac{1}{2},$$

and

$$B = \frac{1}{1.05}\frac{2 \times 12 - 0}{12 - 8} = \frac{6}{1.05} = 5.71.$$

The portfolio that replicates the put consists of one-half share sold short and \$5.71 invested in the risk-free asset.

If the stock price rises, the value of this replicating portfolio will be:

$$P_u = NS_u + RB = (-\tfrac{1}{2}) \times 12 + 1.05 \times \frac{6}{1.05} = 0.$$

This exactly equals the put's value if the stock price rises. If the stock price falls, the value of the replicating portfolio will be:

$$P_d = NS_d + RB = (-\tfrac{1}{2}) \times 8 + 1.05 \times \frac{6}{1.05} = 2.$$

Just as the put has a value of \$2 if the stock price falls, so too does the replicating portfolio. The behavior of the replicating portfolio is indistinguishable from that of the put option.

Note that the value of the replicating portfolio is independent of the probability of the stock price's increasing or decreasing. Whether the probability of an increase in the stock price is 1 percent or 99 percent, the replicating portfolio remains unchanged. Because the model assumes only two outcomes, the replicating portfolio, with its two free parameters, matches the option perfectly.

Note also that the replicating portfolio is independent of the underlying asset's expected return. At first, this may seem counterintuitive. However, it is consistent with the replicating portfolio's independence from the probabilities of future asset prices. The replicating portfolio assumes no foresight and depends only on past changes in asset prices.

Because the replicating portfolio delivers exactly the same payoff as the put option, it must cost exactly the same as the put option; if it did not, an arbitrage opportunity would exist. If the put option were less expensive than the replicating portfolio, one could buy the put, sell the replicating portfolio, and make a riskless profit. If the put option were more expensive than the replicating portfolio, one could sell the put, buy the replicating portfolio, and make a riskless profit.

This no-arbitrage principle is commonly used to find the price of the option. In particular, the (currently unknown) cost of the option must equal the cost of the replicating portfolio, which is $NS + B$. Using the equations derived above for N and B gives:

$$P = \frac{1}{R}\left[\frac{SR - S_d}{S_u - S_d}P_u + \frac{S_u - SR}{S_u - S_d}P_d\right].$$

To simplify this expression, define the quantity

$$q = \frac{SR - S_d}{S_u - S_d}.$$

More commonly, if $S_u = uS$ and $S_d = dS$, where u is a number greater than one and d is a positive number less than one, define q as:

$$q = \frac{R - d}{u - d}.$$

It can be shown that this quantity must have a value between zero and one and can therefore be regarded as a probability. That is, q can be regarded as an artificial probability under which the stock price rises, and $1 - q$ as an artificial probability under which the price falls. Using these probabilities, the put price

$$P = \frac{1}{R}\left[qP_u + (1 - q)P_d\right]$$

can be regarded as the expected value of the put payoff (under the artificial probability measure q), discounted at the risk-free rate. The probability q is known as the risk-neutral probability. Again, the assumption of risk neutrality simplifies the analysis significantly by reducing the expected return of all securities to the risk-free rate.

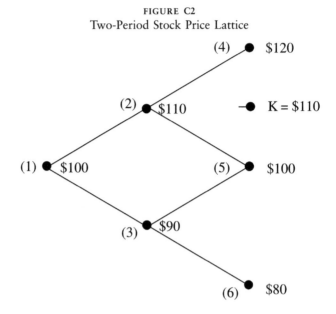

FIGURE C2
Two-Period Stock Price Lattice

A Two-Period Example

Consider now a strategy to replicate a put option over two periods. Assume the stock's current price is $100. In the first period, its price could rise to $110 or fall to $90. From $110, the stock's price over the second period could rise further to $120 or fall back to $100. From $90, the stock's price over the second period could rise back to $100 or fall further to $80. The lattice in figure C2 illustrates the possible stock price movements.

Assume the risk-free rate is 5 percent in each period, and that an investor wishes to replicate a put with a strike price of $110. To find the appropriate strategy, one begins at the expiration date and works backward. The reason is simple: the value of the put in each state is known at that time.

Thus, in the state labeled (6) in figure C2, the option's value P_6 is:

$$P_6 = \max\{K - S_6, 0\} = \max\{110 - 80, 0\} = \$30,$$

where K is the option's strike price and S_6 is the price of the stock in state (6). Similarly, in the other terminal states, the option's value is

$$P_5 = \max\{110 - 100, 0\} = \$10,$$

and

$$P_4 = \max\{110 - 120, 0\} = \$0.$$

Given the option's possible values (or, equivalently, the replicating portfolio's possible values) at the time of expiration, one can compute the portfolio positions in the penultimate states. Specifically, from state (3), two state transitions are possible: either the stock moves to state (5) or it moves to state (6). For state (3), then, the investor needs to find the number of shares N_3 and the amount B_3 to be invested in the risk-free asset so that the resulting portfolio's value will replicate the put option's value, regardless of whether state (5) or state (6) occurs. If state (5) occurs, the value of the portfolio becomes $N_3 S_5 + R B_3$, which must equal the value P_5 already computed for that state. Thus:

$$N_3 S_5 + R B_3 = P_5.$$

Similarly, if state (6) occurs, the equation to be satisfied is:

$$N_3 S_6 + R B_3 = P_6.$$

Solving these two equations for N_3 and B_3 gives:

$$N_3 = \frac{P_5 - P_6}{S_5 - S_6} = \frac{10 - 30}{100 - 80} = -1,$$

$$B_3 = \frac{1}{R} \frac{P_6 S_5 - P_5 S_6}{S_5 - S_6} = \frac{1}{1.05} \frac{30 \times 100 - 10 \times 80}{100 - 80} = \$104.76.$$

Thus, in state (3), the strategy calls for the short sale of one share and an investment of \$104.76 in the risk-free asset. The portfolio value in this state is therefore:

$$P_3 = N_3 S_3 + B_3 = (-1) \times 90 + 104.76 = \$14.76.$$

Applying exactly the same procedure to state (2) gives the following:

$$N_2 = \frac{P_4 - P_5}{S_4 - S_5} = \frac{0 - 10}{120 - 100} = -\frac{1}{2},$$

$$B_2 = \frac{1}{R} \frac{P_5 S_4 - P_4 S_5}{S_4 - S_5} = \frac{1}{1.05} \frac{10 \times 120 - 0 \times 100}{120 - 100} = \$57.14,$$

$$P_2 = N_2 S_2 + B_2 = (-\tfrac{1}{2}) \times 110 + 57.14 = \$2.14.$$

Finally, with the portfolio values known in states (3) and (2), it is possible to move back to the initial state, state (1). Analogous to the above discussion, moving from state (1) to state (2) requires $N_1 S_2 + R B_1 = P_2$, and moving from state (1) to (3) requires $N_1 S_3 + R B_1 = P_3$. The solutions are:

$$N_1 = \frac{P_2 - P_3}{S_2 - S_3} = \frac{2.14 - 14.76}{110 - 90} = -0.631,$$

$$B_1 = \frac{1}{R} \frac{P_3 S_2 - P_2 S_3}{S_2 - S_3} = \frac{1}{1.05} \frac{14.76 \times 110 - 2.14 \times 90}{110 - 90} = \$68.14,$$

$$P_1 = N_1 S_1 + B_1 = (-0.631) \times 100 + 68.14 = \$5.04.$$

The trading strategy is now completely known, and can be summarized as follows:

State (1): With an initial outlay of $5.04, sell 0.631 shares short, and use the proceeds of the short sale together with the initial outlay to invest $68.14 in the risk-free asset.

State (2): If the stock price rises from state (1) to enter state (2), withdraw cash from the risk-free asset (leaving $57.14 there), and use the cash to cover some of the short sale (leaving 0.5 shares short).

State (3): If the stock price falls from state (1) to enter state (3), sell more of the stock short (leaving exactly one share short) and use the proceeds of the short sale to invest more in the risk-free asset (leaving $104.76 there).

This strategy will ensure that the final value of the portfolio (regardless of whether state (4), (5), or (6) occurs) will exactly equal the value of the put option.

An interesting feature of the trading strategy is that shares are sold following a stock price decline and bought following a stock price rise. Furthermore, dynamic replication of a long call position will require similar trend-following trading.

Multiperiod Option Replication

To derive a dynamic option replication strategy, it is necessary, first, to choose a stock pricing model. We will continue to use the binomial

FIGURE C3
Four-Period Stock Price Lattice

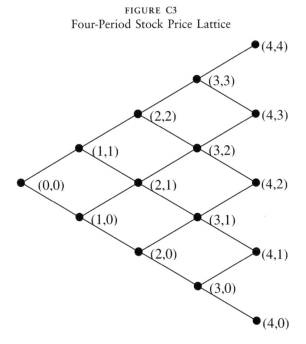

pricing model, in which the stock's price can either move up by a factor u or move down by a factor d. Figure C3 is a graphical representation, showing a lattice in which each node represents a possible state for the stock.

Each node has a label of the form (t, k) where t represents the total number of moves since the starting time and k is the total number of up moves made in the same time. If, in a total of t periods, the stock price moves up k times, it must move down $t - k$ times. Thus, assuming that the price is initially S_0, a general expression for the stock price in state (t, k) is:

$$S_t^k = u^k d^{t-k} S_0.$$

Given this information, it is possible to compute the value of an option – either a put or a call – at expiration. For example, if the option is a put option with strike price K that expires after T periods, its value if the stock has made k up moves is:

$$P_T^k = \max\{K - S_T^k, 0\} = \max\{K - u^k d^{T-k} S_0, 0\}.$$

These known values provide a set of boundary conditions that can be used to solve recursively back through time to find the required option-replication strategy. The strategy consists of a set of shares and a risk-free investment amount to be held in each possible state. This defines the trading required. A general form of the recursion will now be derived.

Assume that the stock is currently in state (t, k). The stock can only reach one of two states in the next period. These are states $(t + 1, k)$ and $(t + 1, k + 1)$. Since we are working recursively back from the expiration date, the option values (or, equivalently, the replicating portfolio values P_{t+1}^k and P_{t+1}^{k+1}) in the two possible future states are known.

The dynamic trader must choose the number N_t^k of shares to hold and the number B_t^k of dollars to invest in the risk-free asset just before moving out of state (t, k). These choices must ensure that the portfolio value at time $t + 1$ is equal to P_{t+1}^k if the stock price falls to state $(t + 1, k)$, or P_{t+1}^{k+1} if the stock price rises to state $(t + 1, k + 1)$. If R equals one plus the risk-free rate, then the value of the portfolio on falling to state $(t + 1, k)$ is $N_t^k S_{t+1}^k + RB_t^k$, and the value on rising to state $(t + 1, k + 1)$ is $N_t^k S_{t+1}^{k+1} + RB_t^k$. Thus the trader must solve the following set of simultaneous linear equations:

$$N_t^k S_{t+1}^k + RB_t^k = P_{t+1}^k,$$

$$N_t^k S_{t+1}^{k+1} + RB_t^k = P_{t+1}^{k+1}.$$

The solution is:

$$N_t^k = \frac{P_{t+1}^{k+1} - P_{t+1}^k}{S_{t+1}^{k+1} - S_{t+1}^k} = \frac{1}{S_t^k} \frac{P_{t+1}^{k+1} - P_{t+1}^k}{u - d},$$

$$B_t^k = \frac{1}{R} \frac{uP_{t+1}^k - dP_{t+1}^{k+1}}{u - d}.$$

Given this known number of shares and risk-free investment, the value of the portfolio in state (t, k) is:

$$P_t^k = N_t^k S_t^k + B_t^k.$$

All the information necessary to follow the dynamic trading strategy is now available, and is stated in the algorithm given in figure C4.

FIGURE C4

Algorithm for Deriving Dynamic Trading Strategy

Input S_0, R, T, K, u, and d.

```
/* Compute possible terminal stock prices and option values. */
for k from 0 to T do
{
```

$$S_T^k = u^k d^{T-k} S_0;$$

```
    if (call)  
```
$$P_T^k = \max\{S_T^k - K, 0\};$$
```
    else  
```
$$P_T^k = \max\{K - S_T^k, 0\};$$
```
}
```

```
/* Compute values recursively backwards through time. */
for t from T-1 down to 0 do
{
    /* Work on each possible state at the current time. */
    for k from 0 to t do
    {
        /* Compute stock price. */
```
$$S_t^k = u^k d^{t-k} S_0;$$

```
        /* Compute required number of shares. */
```
$$N_t^k = \frac{1}{S_t^k} \frac{P_{t+1}^{k+1} - P_{t+1}^k}{u - d};$$

```
        /* Compute required investment in risk-free asset. */
```
$$B_t^k = \frac{1}{R} \frac{u P_{t+1}^k - d P_{t+1}^{k+1}}{u - d};$$

```
        /* Compute portfolio value. */
```
$$P_t^k = N_t^k S_t^k + B_t^k;$$
```
    }
}
```

Note

1   Depending on the insurer's particular requirements, actual implementation may be more complicated; for instance, one may need to synthesize put options with time-varying strike prices.

Appendix D
Synthetic Options versus
Static-Allocation Portfolios

The potential returns on a static-allocation portfolio are bounded by the returns to its constituent assets. Consider, as an example, an investor with a one-year horizon and $1 million that can be invested in the S&P 500 (the risky asset) or a one-year Treasury bill (the riskless asset). Assume the riskless return on the T-bill is 5 percent and that the expected return on the S&P 500 over the same period is 11 percent.[1] However, assume the returns on the S&P 500 have a standard deviation of 15 percent and are distributed along the statistically normal bell-shaped curve. In this case, the index's return can be expected to range between 26 percent and −4 percent most (two-thirds) of the time.

A very risk-averse investor may choose to place the entire $1 million in T-bills, earning the 5 percent return, for a portfolio value of $1.05 million at the end of one year. There is no risk the portfolio will lose ground against its initial value, at least in nominal terms (that is, ignoring inflation). However, given the S&P 500's expected return of 11 percent, there is a risk that the T-bill portfolio will significantly underperform the stock index.

At the other extreme, a very risk-tolerant investor who does not want to give up any of the upside potential of equity may place the entire $1 million in the S&P 500. If the index performs as expected, the portfolio will earn 11 percent and end up being worth $1.11 million. There is a 50 percent chance the index will do even better, returning more than 11 percent. It is equally likely, however (given a normal return distribution), that the portfolio will fall short of the expected 11 percent return. The investor thus risks winding up with a portfolio that is worth less than the alternative T-bill portfolio or even less than its own starting value.

An initial investment that combines cash (in the form of T-bills) with stock will have an expected return somewhere between the T-bill return and the expected stock return. A 50/50 stock/cash allocation would result, given our parameters, in an expected return of 8.0 percent. If the market ended up with a 26 percent return, the portfolio would return 15.5 percent; and if it ended up with a −4 percent return, the portfolio would return 0.5 percent. The 50/50 allocation would thus ensure a portfolio return of at least 0.5 percent most of the time.[2] Ensuring a higher minimum return would entail a higher allocation to cash and a lower allocation to stock. In that case, of course, the portfolio would have a lower expected return.

A static mix of the risky and riskless assets will be a "chance-constrained" portfolio; given the statistical parameters of the assets, one can combine them in such a way as to constrain the likelihood that the overall portfolio return will fall below a certain desired minimum. If a harder floor is needed, it might be obtained by using a publicly traded put option. In the absence of a real option having the desired strike price (floor) and expiration (horizon), one can be synthesized by dynamically rebalancing the portfolio between stock and cash as conditions change over the investment horizon, buying stock as the market rises and selling as the market falls. The rebalancing is done in accordance with option valuation theory, with the parameters of the option pricing model (stock price and volatility, risk-free rate, option strike price, and expiration date) being replaced, in our example, by the S&P 500 price level and volatility, the T-bill rate, and the investor's desired minimum return and investment horizon. (Appendix C gives a quantitative description of this.)

Notes

1   Expected return is positively related to asset risk because investors demand extra return for bearing added risk.
2   Most of the time in this case is five-sixths of the time. Remember, the market return is expected to range between −4 and 26 percent two-thirds of the time (within one standard deviation of its expected return). There is a one-sixth chance that the return will fall below −4 percent (the left-hand tail of the normal distribution) and a one-sixth chance that it will be above 26 percent (the right-hand tail). Thus there is a one-sixth chance that a portfolio allocated 50/50 between the market and the 5 percent T-bill will produce a return less than 0.5 percent. It can be shown that there is about a one-twenty-fifth chance that this static-mix portfolio will produce a return below −5 percent.

Glossary

Actuarial rate An estimate of the rate of return on investments or the discount rate determined statistically by pension fund actuaries.

Agency costs Costs that arise as a result of differing incentives between principals (such as the shareholders of a company) and the agents who act on their behalf (in this case, the company executives).

American option An option that can be exercised at any time on or before its expiration date.

Amex The American Stock Exchange.

Arbitrage Trading that takes advantage of contemporaneous price discrepancies between the same asset in different markets (wheat in Kansas City versus wheat in Chicago, for example) or between asset surrogates (a stock and an option on the stock, for example) in the same or different markets.

Arbitrage bounds The range of price discrepancies within which arbitrage is not profitable, given trading costs, taxes, and other applicable expenses.

Arbitrage pricing theory A model of asset pricing that maintains that a set of factors (such as fundamentals like interest rates, inflation, and economic activity) can explain the behavior of asset portfolios and the expected returns of the constituent assets.

At the money The state of an option when the underlying asset's price equals (or approximates) the option's strike price.

Autocorrelation Correlation between observations of the same variable ordered in time or space; a non-zero autocorrelation implies that past information about a series may be useful in predicting the future behavior of the series. *See* Correlation.

Basis point   One one-hundredth of 1 percent.

Behavioral finance   A branch of finance that seeks to understand how psychology affects financial decision-making.

Beta   A measure of risk indicating the expected return response of a stock or stock portfolio relative to movements in a given market index. A portfolio with a beta of 1.5 measured relative to the S&P 500 index, for example, would tend to go up or down by 1.5 percent in value if the market value of the S&P 500 goes up or down by 1 percent.

Bid–ask spread   The difference at a given time between the price at which sellers are prepared to sell and the price at which buyers are prepared to buy.

Bond arbitrage   A form of risky arbitrage that attempts to profit from perceived mispricings between various fixed income instruments by taking offsetting long and short positions.

Brady Commission   The commission appointed by President Reagan to investigate the market crash of October 1987; chaired by Nicholas F. Brady, then chairman of Dillon, Read & Company and later Secretary of the Treasury under President George Bush.

Bubble   In markets, a price increase created by speculative buying, typically followed by an abrupt price collapse. *See* Speculator.

Bubble premium   A return premium over and above the usual expected return for an asset in the presence of a speculative bubble; it compensates speculators for the risk of a bubble bursting.

CAC-40   Compagnie des Agents de Change 40 index; index of 40 blue-chip stocks traded on the Paris stock exchange.

Call option   An option that grants the owner the right to buy a certain security at a specified price within a specified period of time.

Cap   A maximum value, or ceiling, for a security, or its return, specified in a contract or offered by an option position. *See also* Floor.

Capital asset pricing model   A model of asset prices in which the expected return on an asset in excess of the risk-free rate is expressed in terms of the expected return on the market as a whole (in excess of the risk-free rate) and that asset's beta. *See* Beta.

CBOE   Chicago Board Options Exchange; the largest US exchange for trading stock options, including index options on the S&P 100 and S&P 500.

CBOT   Chicago Board of Trade; one of the main US exchanges for trading in futures, including contracts on grains and US Treasury bonds and notes, and DJIA futures and options on DJIA futures.

CFTC   Commodity Futures Trading Commission, the US federal regulatory agency that oversees US markets for futures and options on futures.

Chaos theory A mathematical description of nonlinear dynamic systems that are deterministic but produce results that appear to be random; such systems are characterized by irregular periodicity, sensitivity to initial conditions, and lack of predictability.

Circuit breakers A system of trading restrictions and halts on stock and futures exchanges, usually triggered by substantial price movements.

Clearinghouse A corporation affiliated with a stock, futures, or options exchange that clears, settles, oversees, and guarantees trades.

CME Chicago Mercantile Exchange, one of the main US exchanges for trading in futures, including agricultural products and S&P 500 futures and options on S&P 500 futures.

Collar A combination of option positions on an underlying asset that sets a floor for the minimum value and a cap on the maximum value.

Constant-mix (static) strategy A strategy that calls for holding a constant mix of assets (such as 60 percent stocks/40 percent bonds), rebalanced periodically.

Contagion The "infectious" transmittal of price movements from one financial market to another.

Contrarian An investor or investment strategy that selects out-of-favor securities.

Convergence trade A trade that takes offsetting positions in two or more related assets with the expectation of profiting from the eventual convergence of the assets' prices.

Correlation A mathematical measure of the relationship between variables.

Correlation coefficient A measure of the strength of the relationship between variables or series, ranging between +1 and −1. A positive (negative) correlation coefficient implies a direct (inverse) relationship between the variables; a correlation coefficient of zero implies no relationship.

CPPI Constant Proportion Portfolio Insurance.

Credit rating A formal estimate of an enterprise's likelihood of defaulting on debt payments, as established by credit rating agencies.

Credit risk The risk of loss stemming from a default or deterioration in the financial condition of a counterparty.

Dealer A financial intermediary, especially in OTC markets, that primarily trades as a principal (buying for and selling from its own account) with other entities.

Deductible The amount of loss an insured party agrees to be exposed to before insurance coverage begins to provide protection. In general, the larger the deductible, the lower the cost of the insurance policy.

Delta In option terminology, the change in an option's price in response to a change in the price of the underlying asset.

Derivative A financial instrument whose value is contingent on the value of an underlying security; for example, a futures contract or an option on a stock, stock index, or commodity.

Discontinuity A significant difference between the prices of a security or a market index from one trade to the next.

Discount rate The rate used to convert future cash flows into a current dollar value.

Diversification Distribution of investments across a variety of individual assets, asset classes, and/or international markets so as to reduce overall investment portfolio risk relative to average return.

Dividend yield Annual dividends per share divided by price per share.

DJIA Dow Jones industrial average; a popular index of thirty blue-chip US stocks.

DOT/SuperDOT Designated Order Turnaround System, the New York Stock Exchange's automated system for transmitting orders to the specialist.

Dynamic asset allocation *See* Dynamic hedging.

Dynamic hedging Process of synthesizing an option-like payoff pattern by trading in the underlying asset or derivatives on the underlying asset. *See* Option replication.

Efficient frontier The set of portfolios whose defining characteristic is that each portfolio has the highest expected return for the level of expected risk or, alternatively, the lowest expected risk for the level of expected return.

Efficient market A market in which security prices fully and instantaneously reflect all available information.

Equilibrium A condition of stability in which the demand for and supply of an asset are in balance.

Equity premium The expected return on equities in excess of the return on the risk-free asset. *See* Risk premium.

Equity swap An OTC derivatives contract between two counterparties that exchange payments, at least one of which is based on the performance of an underlying stock or stock index; generally, one counterparty pays a fixed stream of cash flows and receives in return payments that vary according to the performance of a given stock or stock index.

European option An option that can be exercised only on its expiration date.

Exercise price *See* Strike price.

Expected return The return that a security is anticipated to provide over a given holding period; generally determined by a mathematical model.

Expected utility The level of satisfaction that an investor anticipates when making an economic decision, the ultimate resolution of which is unknown.

Expiration date   The date beyond which an option may no longer be exercised.

Fad   A behavioral phenomenon in which a practice is followed with exaggerated interest, which tends to wane over time.

Fair price   The price at which a security should trade in an efficient market.

Feedback traders   Investors who trade on the basis of price changes, rather than fundamentals. *See* Negative feedback trading; Positive feedback trading.

Fixed income instruments   Debt instruments paying a known interest rate.

Floor   A minimum value for a security, or for its return, specified in a contract or offered by an option position. *See also* Cap.

Frontrunning   Buying or selling in advance of the anticipated actions of other investors.

FT-SE 100   The *Financial Times* stock exchange index of the 100 largest-capitalization UK stocks.

Fundamentals   Economic, industry, or company-related information that may affect a firm's profitability.

Futures contract   An agreement to exchange a specified asset (commodity, financial instrument, index) for a specified price at a specified future date.

Gamma   In option terminology, the change in an option's delta in response to a change in the price of the underlying asset.

GAO   US General Accounting Office.

Guaranteed Equity   A type of investment that offers to guarantee most or all of initial capital plus offers participation in any gains to a specified stock index.

Hedge   An asset position used to offset the risk of another asset position.

Hedge ratio   The ratio of the size of a position in hedging instruments to the size of the position being hedged.

Implied volatility   The volatility of an underlying stock or stock index inferred from the prices of options on the stock or stock index and an option pricing formula.

Index arbitrage   Arbitrage activity between stock index futures and underlying stocks, designed to profit from violations of the normal relationship between the two markets. *See* Arbitrage.

Informational cascade   A price collapse that occurs when investors who have been basing their bullish investment decisions on the prior actions of other investors begin to act on their own bearish private information.

Informationless trade   A trade motivated not by fundamentals, but by liquidity needs, portfolio rebalancing, or dynamic hedging.

Interest rate swap   An OTC derivatives contract between two counter-parties that exchange payments based on underlying interest rates; generally, one counterparty pays a fixed stream of cash flows and receives in return payments that vary with changes in a given interest rate, such as Libor.

In the money   The state of an option if it has intrinsic value. A call is in the money when the price of the underlying asset is higher than the strike price; a put is in the money when the price of the underlying asset is lower than the strike price.

Investment policy   Specification of the investor's long-term objectives, constraints, and requirements, including identification of the typical asset allocation.

Leverage   The use of borrowed funds or derivatives to increase exposure to an asset's price changes beyond the limits of one's own capital.

Libor   London interbank offered rate; the interest rate that banks in London offer on short-term, interbank Eurodollar deposits – it is used as the standard for short-term (up to one year) rates in international markets.

Limit order   An order to buy (sell) a security at or below (above) a specified price.

Liquidity   A market's ability to absorb a sizable informationless trade without substantial impact on the traded security's price.

Long   The ownership position established by purchasing a financial asset or instrument. *See also* Short.

Margin   The amount of funds a broker-dealer requires as collateral for security or derivatives positions.

Margin call   A demand by a broker-dealer for more collateral from a margined customer to cover adverse moves in the customer's position.

Market capitalization   The market value of a publicly traded company's common stock, determined by multiplying share price by the number of shares outstanding.

Market depth   A measure of a security's or market's liquidity. *See* Liquidity.

Market maker   A dealer in options or other financial assets who maintains an inventory of securities and stands ready to buy and sell on demand.

Market risk   Exposure to potential losses arising from changes in a market price or return.

Market timing   The practice of attempting to predict the relative returns of different asset classes for investment purposes.

Mean reversion   A tendency of a series (of security returns, say) to revert to a long-term average over time. With mean reversion, a period of above-average security returns tends to be followed by a period of below-average returns, and vice versa.

MMI The Major Market Index, a price-weighted index of twenty blue-chip US stocks; its performance is similar to the DJIA's. Index options on the MMI are traded on the Amex.

Moral hazard A situation created when an event (say, purchase of insurance, anticipated government intervention, looming bankruptcy) creates an incentive to take unwarranted risks.

Myopic loss aversion A psychological tendency of investors to focus on losses over the short term rather than returns over the longer term.

NASDAQ National Association of Securities Dealers Automated Quotations System, an electronic marketplace for OTC stocks.

Near the money The state of an option when the underlying asset's price is close to the option's strike price.

Negative feedback trading Trading on the basis of and in the opposite direction to current market price changes (for example, buying as market prices fall); inherently stabilizing. *See also* Positive feedback trading.

Nikkei 225 An index of 225 stocks traded on the Tokyo Stock Exchange.

Noise trading Trading on the basis of noise rather than fundamentals. Noise includes sentiment, price changes, and other traders' behavior.

Nonstationarity A condition in which the mean and variance of a process are not independent of time.

Notional value The nominal face amount used to calculate swap payments. In an interest rate swap, for example, the rates are multiplied by the notional amounts to determine counterparty obligations.

NYSE New York Stock Exchange.

Open interest The number of futures or listed option contracts outstanding at a given time.

Opportunity cost The benefit forgone by not pursuing a course of action.

Optimality A condition of best satisfying the preferences expressed by an individual's utility function. *See* Expected utility.

Option A financial instrument that conveys the right (but not the obligation) to buy or sell an underlying asset at a specified price (the strike price) at or before a specified future date (the expiration date).

Option premium The amount of money an option buyer pays for an option.

Option replication The process of duplicating an option's payoff pattern by taking and trading positions in the underlying asset or in derivatives on the underlying asset. *See* Dynamic hedging.

Option writing The act of establishing a short option position by selling an option. *See* Short.

OTC The over-the-counter market for securities and instruments not traded on an organized exchange.

Outlier   An observation that is far removed in value from most of the observations from the same sample.

Out of the money   The state of an option if it has no intrinsic value. A call is out of the money when the price of the underlying asset is lower than the strike price; a put is out of the money when the price of the underlying asset is higher than the strike price.

Overreaction   In investing, a psychologic tendency of investors to overreact to news by buying or selling more than is warranted by the fundamental information contained in the news.

Path-dependent   A property of an investment strategy whose outcome is dependent on the particular price path(s) taken by the underlying asset(s), and not just the price(s) at the end of the path(s).

Path-independent   A property of an investment strategy whose outcome is dependent only on the price(s) of the underlying asset(s) at the end of the investment horizon.

Portfolio insurance   A synthetic protective put strategy, in which the underlying (insured) asset is typically a portfolio of stocks, often a stock index. *See* Protective put.

Portfolio turnover   The lesser of portfolio purchases or sales divided by the portfolio's market value.

Positive feedback trading   Trading on the basis of and in the direction of current market price changes (for example, selling as market prices fall); inherently destabilizing. *See also* Negative feedback trading.

Price-earnings ratio (P/E)   The ratio of a company's share price to the company's earnings per share.

Program trading   The use of computers to deliver simultaneous orders for a large number of securities; used to facilitate strategies such as index arbitrage.

Protective put   An asset position combined with a put option on that asset.

Public futures volume   The volume of futures trading exclusive of trading by dealers for their own accounts.

Put–call parity   A pricing relationship between puts and calls with the same expiration date and strike price written on the same underlying asset.

Put option   An option that grants the purchaser the right to sell a security at a specified price within a specified period of time.

Random walk   A theory describing the way in which stock prices behave, which holds that price movements are uncorrelated, so future prices cannot be predicted from current or past prices.

Rational expectations   A theory explaining the way (security) prices are determined; it holds that investors use all pertinent information and always make consistent, rational choices.

Rebalancing   The act of realigning the weightings of assets in a portfolio in order to achieve an investment goal.

Relative value trade   A trade that takes offsetting positions in two or more related assets with the expectation of profiting from relative price movements.

Return distribution   The arrangement according to their frequency of occurrence of historical or anticipated returns to an asset over a given period (a year, say).

Rho   In option terminology, the change in an option's price in response to a change in the risk-free interest rate.

Risk arbitrage   A form of risky arbitrage that attempts to profit from merger and acquisition situations, generally by taking a long position in the target company's stock (or related derivatives) and a short position in the acquiring company's stock (or related derivatives).

Risk aversion/tolerance   A measure of the willingness of an investor to accept additional risk as a tradeoff for additional expected return. The more risk-averse (risk-tolerant) the investor, the larger (smaller) the incremental return demanded for a given increase in the level of risk assumed.

Risk-free (riskless) asset   An asset that offers a certain return, bearing no credit risk; generally proxied by US government Treasury bills.

Risk-free (riskless) return   The return on a risk-free asset.

Risk premium   The expected return on an asset in excess of the return on the risk-free asset, which provides compensation for bearing risk.

SEC   Securities and Exchange Commission, the federal regulatory agency that oversees the US markets for securities and options on securities.

Securitized markets   Markets for loans and other non-traded instruments that have been converted into securities (such as the market for mortgage-backed securities) in order to increase liquidity and reduce issuing costs.

Sell short   To sell a borrowed security or financial instrument.

Serial correlation   *See* Autocorrelation.

Settlement   Completion of the exchange of assets or funds between the parties to a trade.

Short   A position incurring rights and obligations opposite to the characteristics of another investor's asset position. *See also* Long.

Shut out   The condition occurring when a synthetic portfolio insurance strategy is stopped out and cannot benefit from a subsequent increase in the value of the risky asset. *See* Stop out.

Simulation   A technique that uses historical or probabilistic data and quantitative models to determine the likely outcomes of an investment program over a given historical or hypothetical environment.

Skewness A measure of the lack of symmetry of a distribution. Negative skewness in a return distribution indicates a longer tail extending toward lower values; positive skewness indicates a longer tail extending toward higher values.

S&P 100 Standard & Poor's market capitalization-weighted index of 100 of the most commonly held stocks.

S&P 500 Standard & Poor's market capitalization-weighted index of 500 of the most commonly held stocks.

Specialist A dealer of exchange-listed equities who stands ready to buy and sell on demand and is obligated to maintain orderly markets.

Speculator One who takes a short-term position in an asset with the expectation of profiting from anticipated favorable changes when the position is unwound.

Spot market The market in which transactions in securities or commodities are settled currently, rather than at some future date; the market underlying a derivatives contract.

Spot price The price in spot markets.

Stale price The last recorded price of a security that has not traded recently.

Standard deviation A statistical measure of the dispersion of the observations in a series about their average value; calculated as the square root of variance.

Stochastic process The probabilistic (random) process by which a variable (such as an asset's price) evolves over time.

Stock index A weighted average price of a collection of stocks used to represent a given market.

Stock index futures A futures contract on an underlying stock index.

Stock index futures options An option on a futures contract on an underlying stock index.

Stock index option An option on an underlying stock index.

Stop-loss order An order to sell a particular security if its price drops to or below a specified level.

Stop out A mandatory complete withdrawal from an underlying risky asset when an insured portfolio falls below the insurance floor. *See* Shut out.

Strike price The price specified in an option contract at which an option holder can buy or sell the underlying asset. Also known as the exercise price.

Sunshine trading A strategy whereby the intention to trade a specified security, in a given amount, at a specified price, is announced in advance to attract counterparties.

Swap A private agreement between two counterparties to exchange future streams of payments.

Synthetic option   An option-like instrument created by trading in the underlying asset or derivatives on the underlying asset.

Synthetic portfolio insurance   *See* Portfolio insurance.

Systematic risk   That portion of an asset's total risk that is attributable to sources of variability common to all assets in the same class. Systematic risk is measured by beta. *See* Beta.

Systemic risk   Risk to the overall financial system stemming from problems at one or a few financial institutions.

Tactical asset allocation (TAA)   An investment strategy calling for deliberate short-term departures from a long-term asset mix in order to increase returns.

Technical analysis   Analysis of the past patterns of security prices in an attempt to forecast future prices.

Theta   In option terminology, the change in an option's price in response to a change in the time to expiration of the option.

Trading halt   A temporary halt in trading occasioned by regulated price-limit restrictions, order imbalances, news dissemination, etc.

Transaction costs   The costs of executing a trade, including brokerage commissions plus any market impact cost of the trade and any opportunity cost of not being able to execute in a timely fashion.

Transparency   The availability of accurate and timely information on asset positions, their prices, and trading volume.

Treasury bill   A government debt issue with a maturity of one year or less.

Value investing   An investment strategy that favors assets that are undervalued by some measure, such as, in the case of stocks, low price-to-earnings ratio or high dividend yield.

Variance   The sum of the squared deviations of the observations in a series about their average value, divided by the number of observations.

Vega   In option terminology, the change in an option's price in response to a change in the volatility of the underlying asset.

Volatility   The degree to which the price of a security or the value of a portfolio fluctuates over time, usually measured statistically by standard deviation or variance.

Warrant   An option to buy or sell an underlying asset at a specified price at a specified time, issued by corporations, financial institutions, or governments, rather than by exchanges, generally for periods in excess of a year.

Whipsaw   A sharp price movement in one direction followed quickly by a sharp price reversal.

Yield   The income generated by an asset over a given period (typically a year) as a percentage of the asset's price.

Bibliography

Abken, P.A. 1988: Discrete option replication with transactions costs: an analysis of hedging errors. Atlanta, GA: Federal Reserve Bank of Atlanta.

Abken, P.A. 1994: Over-the-counter financial derivatives: risky business? *Federal Reserve Bank of Atlanta Economic Review*, March/April.

Aderhold, R., Cumming, C. and Harwood, A. 1988: International linkages among equities markets and the October 1987 market break. *Federal Reserve Bank of New York Quarterly Review*, 13 (2), 34–46.

Admati, A.R. and Pfleiderer, P. 1991: Sunshine trading and financial market equilibrium. *Review of Financial Studies*, 4 (3), 443–81.

Aiyagari, S.R. 1988: Economic fluctuations without shocks to fundamentals: or does the stock market dance to its own music? *Federal Reserve Bank of Minneapolis Quarterly Review*, 88 (1), 8–24.

Allen, F. and Gorton, G. 1993: Churning bubbles. *Review of Economic Studies*, 60 (4), 813–36.

Ambachtsheer, K.P. 1987: Pension fund asset allocation: in defense of a 60/40 equity/debt asset mix. *Financial Analysts Journal*, 43 (5), 14–24.

Amihud, Y., Mendelson, H. and Wood, R.A. 1990: Liquidity and the 1987 stock market crash. *Journal of Portfolio Management*, 16 (3), 65–9.

Anderson, R. and Tutuncu, M. 1988: The simple price dynamics of portfolio insurance and program trading. New York: Center for the Study of Futures Markets, Columbia University.

Anson, M.J.P. 1996: Recent corporate and pension plan initiatives in derivatives risk management. *Journal of Financial Engineering*, 5 (4), 303–15.

Antoniou, A. and Garrett, I. 1993: To what extent did stock index futures contribute to the October 1987 stock market crash? *Economic Journal*, 103 (421), 1444–61.

Arbel, A., Carvell, S. and Postnieks, E. 1988: The smart crash of October 19th. *Harvard Business Review*, 66 (3), 124–38.

Arrow, K.J. 1982: Risk perception in psychology and economics. *Economic Inquiry*, 20 (1), 1–8.

Baird, A.J. 1993: *Option Market Making: Trading and Risk Analysis for the Financial and Commodity Option Markets*. New York: John Wiley & Sons.

Bak, P. and Chen, K. 1991: Self-organized criticality. *Scientific American*, January.

Bank for International Settlements. 1996: Central bank survey of foreign exchange and derivatives market activity. Basle: BIS, May.

Bank for International Settlements. 1997: International banking and financial market developments. Basle: BIS, August.

Bank for International Settlements. 1998: International banking and fiinancial market developments. Basle: BIS, August.

Barclay, M.J., Litzenberger, R.H. and Warner, J.B. 1990: Private information, trading volume, and stock-return variances. *Review of Financial Studies*, 3 (2), 233–53.

Barro, R.J. 1989: The stock market and the macroeconomy: implications of the October 1987 crash. In R.J. Barro et al. (eds), *Black Monday and the Future of Financial Markets*, 83–94. Homewood, IL: Mid-America Institute for Public Policy Research and Dow Jones-Irwin.

Barro, R.J. 1990: The stock market and investment. *Review of Financial Studies*, 3 (1), 115–31.

Basak, S. 1995: A general equilibrium model of portfolio insurance. *Review of Financial Studies*, 8 (4), 1059–90.

Bassett, G., France, V. and Pliska, S. 1991: Kalman filter estimation for valuing nontrading securities, with applications to the MMI cash-futures spread on October 19 and 20, 1987. *Review of Quantitative Finance and Accounting*, I, 135–51.

Bates, D.S. 1991: The crash of '87: was it expected? The evidence from options markets. *Journal of Finance*, 46 (3), 1009–44.

Baubonis, C., Gastineau, G. and Purcell, D. 1993: The banker's guide to equity-linked certificates of deposit. *Journal of Derivatives*, 1 (2), 87–95.

Becketti, S. and Roberts, D. 1990: Will increased regulation of stock index futures reduce stock market volatility? *Economic Review*, November/December, 33–46.

Behof, J.P. 1993: Reducing credit risk in over-the-counter derivatives. *Federal Reserve Bank of Chicago Economic Perspectives*, 17 (1), 21–31.

Benartzi, S. and Thaler, R.H. 1995: Myopic loss aversion and the equity premium puzzle. *Quarterly Journal of Economics*, February, 73–92.

Benartzi, S. and Thaler, R.H. 1996: Risk aversion or myopia? The fallacy of small numbers and its implications for retirement savings. Chicago: University of Chicago.

Bennett, P. and Kelleher, J. 1988: The international transmission of stock price disruption in October 1987. *Federal Reserve Bank of New York Quarterly Review*, 13 (2), 17–33.

Benninga, S. and Blume, M.E. 1985: On the optimality of portfolio insurance. *Journal of Finance*, 40 (5), 1341–52.

Bernstein, P.L. 1992: *Capital Ideas: the improbable origins of modern Wall Street.* New York: Free Press.

Bernstein, P.L. 1997: What rate of return can you reasonably expect . . . or what can the long run tell us about the short run? *Financial Analysts Journal*, 53 (2), 20–8.

Bertero, E. and Mayer, C. 1990: Structure and performance: global inter-dependence of stock markets around the crash of October 1987. *European Economic Review*, 34 (6), 1155–80.

Bessembinder, H. and Seguin, P.J. 1992: Futures-trading activity and stock price volatility. *Journal of Finance*, 47 (5), 2015–34.

Bhasin, V. 1995: On the credit risk of OTC derivative users. Washington, D.C.: Federal Reserve Board Finance & Economics Discussion Series 95–50, November 1.

Bierman, H. Jr. 1997: Portfolio allocation and the investment horizon. *Journal of Portfolio Management*, Summer, 51–5.

Bikhchandani, S., Hirshleifer, D. and Welch, I. 1992: A theory of fads, fashion, custom and cultural change as informational cascades. *Journal of Political Economy*, 100 (5), 992–1026.

Bikhchandani, S., Hirshleifer, D. and Welch, I. 1998: Learning from the behavior of others: conformity, fads, and informational cascades. *Journal of Economic Perspectives*, 12 (3), 151–70.

Bird, R., Dennis, D. and Tippett, M. 1988: A stop-loss approach to portfolio insurance. *Journal of Portfolio Management*, Fall, 35–40.

Black, F. 1986: Noise. *Journal of Finance*, 41 (3), 529–43.

Black, F. 1988: An equilibrium model of the crash. In *NBER Macroeconomics Annual*, 269–75. Cambridge, MA: MIT Press.

Black, F. 1989a: How to use the holes in Black–Scholes. *Journal of Applied Corporate Finance*, Winter.

Black, F. 1989b: How we came up with the option formula. *Journal of Portfolio Management*, Winter, 4–8.

Black, F. and Hakanoglu, E. 1987: Simplifying portfolio insurance for the seller. New York: Goldman Sachs Portfolio Strategy.

Black, F. and Jones, R. 1987: Simplifying portfolio insurance. *Journal of Portfolio Management*, 14 (1), 48–51.

Black, F. and Perold, A.F. 1992: Theory of constant proportion portfolio insurance. *Journal of Economic Dynamics and Control*, 16 (3/4), 403–26.

Black, F. and Rouhani, R. 1987: Constant proportion portfolio insurance and the synthetic put option: a comparison. New York: Goldman Sachs Portfolio Strategy.

Black, F. and Rouhani, R. 1988: Constant proportion portfolio insurance: volatility and the soft floor strategy. New York: Goldman Sachs Portfolio Strategy.

Black, F. and Scholes, M.S. 1973: The pricing of options and corporate liabilities. *Journal of Political Economy*, 81 (3), 637–54.

Blanchard, O.J. and Watson, M. 1982: Bubbles, rational expectations, and financial markets. In P. Wachtel (ed.), *Crises in the Economic and Financial Structure*, 295–315. Lexington, MA: Lexington Books.

Blume, M.E., MacKinlay, A.C. and Terker, B. 1989: Order imbalances and stock price movements on October 19 and 20, 1987. *Journal of Finance*, 44 (4), 827–48.

Bodie, Z. 1995: On the risk of stocks in the long run. *Financial Analysts Journal*, 51 (3), 18–22.

Bodie, Z., Kane, A. and Marcus, A.J. 1993: *Investments*, 2nd edn. Homewood, IL: Irwin.

Bookstaber, R. 1997: Global risk management: are we missing the point? *Journal of Portfolio Management*, Spring, 102–7.

Bookstaber, R.M. and Clarke, R. 1985: Problems in evaluating the performance of portfolios with options. *Financial Analysts Journal*, 41 (1), 48–62.

Bookstaber, R.M. and Gold, J. 1988: In search of the liability asset. *Financial Analysts Journal*, 44 (1), 70–80.

Bookstaber, R.M. and Langsam, J.A. 1988: Portfolio insurance trading rules. *Journal of Futures Markets*, 8 (1), 15–31.

Borger, D. 1988: Opportunities for long-term investors. *Financial Analysts Journal*, 44 (2), 74–6.

Bowen, R.M., Johnson, M.F. and Shevlin, T. 1989: Informational efficiency and the information content of earnings during the market crash of October 1987. *Journal of Accounting and Economics*, 11 (2/3), 225–54.

Brady, N. 1998: The crash, the problems exposed, and the remedies. In R.E. Litan and A.M. Santomero (eds), *Brookings-Wharton Papers on Financial Services*, 1–4. Washington, D.C.: Brookings Institution Press.

Brady Commission. 1988: *Report of the Presidential Task Force on Market Mechanisms*. Washington, D.C.: Government Printing Office.

Brennan, M.J. and Schwartz, E.S. 1976: The pricing of equity-linked life insurance policies with an asset value guarantee. *Journal of Financial Economics*, 3 (3), 195–213.

Brennan, M.J. and Schwartz, E.S. 1979: Alternative investment strategies for the issues of equity linked life insurance policies with an asset value guarantee. *Journal of Business*, 52 (1), 63–94.

Brennan, M.J. and Schwartz, E.S. 1988: Time-invariant portfolio insurance strategies. *Journal of Finance*, 43 (2), 283–99.

Brennan, M.J. and Schwartz, E.S. 1989: Portfolio insurance and financial market equilibrium. *Journal of Business*, 62 (4), 455–76.

Brennan, M.J., Schwartz, E.S. and Lagnado, R. 1997: Strategic asset allocation. *Journal of Economic Dynamics and Control*, 21 (June), 1377–1403.

Brennan, M.J. and Solanki, R. 1981: Optimal portfolio insurance. *Journal of Financial and Quantitative Analysis*, 16 (3), 279–300.

Brock, W.A., Hsieh, D.A. and LeBaron, B. 1992: *Nonlinear Dynamics, Chaos, and Instability: statistical theory and economic evidence*. Cambridge, MA: MIT Press.

Brorsen, B.W. 1991: Futures trading, transaction costs, and stock market volatility. *Journal of Futures Markets*, 11 (2), 153–63.

Burchill, A. 1997: Guaranteed products sweep Europe. *Pensions & Investments*, October 13.

Burr, B. 1993: Derivatives hard on fund managers. *Pensions & Investments*, November 1.

Burr, B. 1997a. Jacobs blames portfolio insurance. *Pensions & Investments*, September 29.

Burr, B. 1997b: Nobel-winning strategy criticized. *Pensions & Investments*, December 8.

Burton, J. 1997: The man who made the stock market gasp. *Asset Management*, November/December, 21–8.

Camerer, C. 1989: Bubbles and fads in asset prices: a review of theory and evidence. *Journal of Economic Surveys*, 3 (1), 3–41.

Campbell, J.Y. 1996: Understanding risk and return. *Journal of Political Economy*, 104 (2), 298–345.

Campbell, J.Y. and Kyle, A.S. 1993: Smart money, noise trading and stock price behavior. *Review of Economic Studies*, 60 (1), 1–34.

Cecchetti, S.G., Lam, P-K. and Mark, N.C. 1990: Mean reversion with equilibrium asset prices. *American Economic Review*, 80 (3), 398–418.

Chan, K. 1992: A further analysis of the lead-lag relationship between the cash market and the stock index futures market. *Review of Financial Studies*, 5 (1), 123–52.

Chan, K.C. 1988: On the contrarian investment strategy. *Journal of Business*, 61 (2), 147–64.

Chen, N-F., Roll, R. and Ross, S.A. 1986: Economic forces and the stock market. *Journal of Business*, 59 (3), 383–403.

Chernoff, J. 1988: Equity market exodus. *Pensions & Investment Age*, February 8.

Chicago Board Options Exchange (CBOE). 1993: A marriage between exchange-traded and OTC derivatives: the CBOE's FLEX options. *Journal of Derivatives*, 1 (1), 105–7.

Choie, K.S. and Novomestky, F. 1989: Replication of long-term with short-term options. *Journal of Portfolio Management*, 15 (2), 17–9.

Chopra, N., Lakonishok, J. and Ritter, J.R. 1992: Measuring abnormal performance: do stocks overreact? *Journal of Financial Economics*, 31 (2), 235–68.

Chowdhury, M. and Lin, J-C. 1993: Fads and the crash of '87. *Financial Review*, 28 (3), 385–401.

Clarke, R.G. 1991: Stochastic-dominance tests of portfolio insurance strategies. *Advances in Futures and Options Research*, 5, 185–202.

Commodity Futures Trading Commission (CFTC). 1988: *Final Report on Stock Index Futures and Cash Market Activity During October 1987*. Washington, D.C.: Divisions of Economic Analysis and Trading and Markets, CFTC.

Commodity Futures Trading Commission (CFTC). 1990: *Report on Stock Index Futures and Cash Market Activity During October 1989*. Washington, D.C.: Division of Economic Analysis, CFTC.

Commodity Futures Trading Commission (CFTC). 1993a: *CFTC Symposium on OTC Derivatives Markets and Their Regulation*. Washington, D.C.: Division of Economic Analysis, CFTC, October 27.

Commodity Futures Trading Commission (CFTC). 1993b: *OTC Derivatives Markets and Their Regulation.* Washington, D.C.: Division of Economic Analysis, CFTC, October.

Constantinides, G.M. 1988: Portfolio insurance: optimal investment for a class of path-dependent utility functions. Chicago: University of Chicago.

Constantinides, G.M. 1990: Habit formation: a resolution of the equity premium puzzle. *Journal of Political Economy*, 98 (3), 519–43.

Cox, J.C. and Leland, H.E. 1982: On dynamic investment strategies. In *Proceedings of a Seminar on the Analysis of Security Prices.* Chicago: University of Chicago.

Cox, J.C., Ross, S. and Rubinstein, M. 1979: Option pricing: a simplified approach. *Journal of Financial Economics*, 7 (October), 229–64.

Cox, J.C. and Rubinstein, M. 1985: *Options Markets.* Englewood Cliffs, NJ: Prentice-Hall.

Creedy, J. and Martin, V.L. 1994: A model of the distribution of prices. In J. Creedy and V.L. Martin (eds), *Chaos and Non-Linear Models in Economics, Theory and Applications*, 100–10. Brookfield, VT: Edward Elgar Publishing Company.

Culligan, A. 1997: Providing and packaging retail products. In *Equity Derivatives: applications in risk management and investment*, 159–78. London: Risk Publications.

Cutler, D.M., Poterba, J.M. and Summers, L.H. 1989: What moves stock prices? *Journal of Portfolio Management*, 15 (3), 4–12.

Cutler, D.M., Poterba, J.M. and Summers, L.H. 1990: Speculative dynamics and the role of feedback traders. *American Economic Review*, 80 (2), 63–8.

Cutler, D.M., Poterba, J.M. and Summers, L.H. 1991: Speculative dynamics. *Review of Economic Studies*, 58 (195), 529–46.

Damadoran, A. 1990: Index futures and stock market volatility. *Review of Futures Markets*, 9 (2), 443–57.

Darrat, A.F. and Rahman, S. 1995: Has futures trading activity caused stock price volatility? *Journal of Futures Markets*, 15 (5), 537–57.

De Bondt, W.F.M. and Thaler, R.H. 1985: Does the stock market overreact? *Journal of Finance*, 40 (3), 793–805.

De Bondt, W.F.M. and Thaler, R.H. 1987: Further evidence on investor overreaction and stock market seasonality. *Journal of Finance*, 42 (3), 557–81.

De Bondt, W.F.M. and Thaler, R.H. 1990: Do security analysts overreact? *American Economic Review*, 80 (2), 52–7.

De Long, J.B., Shleifer, A., Summers, L.H. and Waldmann, R.J. 1990a: Noise trader risk in financial markets. *Journal of Political Economy*, 98 (4), 703–38.

De Long, J.B., Shleifer, A., Summers, L.H. and Waldmann, R.J. 1990b: Positive feedback investment strategies and destabilizing rational speculation. *Journal of Finance*, 45 (2), 379–95.

De Long, J.B., Shleifer, A., Summers, L.H. and Waldmann, R.J. 1991: The survival of noise traders in financial markets. *Journal of Business*, 64 (1), 1–20.

Derman, E. and Zou, J. 1997: Predicting the response of implied volatility to large index moves: an October 1997 S&P 500 case study. New York: Goldman Sachs Quantitative Strategies Research Notes, November.

Diamond, D.W. and Verrecchia, R.E. 1981: Information aggregation in a noisy rational expectations economy. *Journal of Financial Economics*, 9 (3), 221–35.

Donaldson, R.G. and Uhlig, H. 1993: The impact of large portfolio insurers on asset prices. *Journal of Finance*, 48 (5), 1943–55.

Donnelly, B. 1986: Is portfolio insurance all it's cracked up to be? *Institutional Investor*, November.

Dorf, R.C. and Bishop, R.H. 1994: *Modern Control Systems*. Reading, MA: Addison-Wesley.

Dreher, W.A. 1986: Actuarial implications of insured portfolios. In *Innovative Portfolio Insurance Techniques: the latest developments in "dynamic hedging"* (videotape). New York: Institute for International Research.

Dreman, D.N. and Berry, M.A. 1995a: Analyst forecasting errors and their implications for security analysis. *Financial Analysts Journal*, 51 (3), 30–41.

Dreman, D.N. and Berry, M.A. 1995b: Overreaction, underreaction, and the low-P/E effect. *Financial Analysts Journal*, 51 (4), 21–30.

Duffee, G.R. 1994: On measuring credit risk of derivatives instruments. Washington, D.C.: Federal Reserve Board Finance & Economics Discussion Series 94–27, September.

Duffee, G.R., Kupiec, P.H. and White, A.P. 1992: A primer on program trading and stock price volatility: a survey of the issues and the evidence. *Research in Financial Services*, 4, 21–49.

Dwyer, G.P. Jr. and Hafer, R.W. 1988: Are national stock markets linked? *Federal Reserve Bank of St. Louis Review*, 70 (6), 3–14.

Dwyer, G.P. Jr. and Hafer, R.W. 1990: Do fundamentals, bubbles, or neither determine stock prices? Some international evidence. In G.P. Dwyer Jr. and R.W. Hafer (eds), *The Stock Market: bubbles, volatility, and chaos*, 31–68. Norwell, MA: Kluwer Academic Publishers.

Dybvig, P.H. 1988: Inefficient dynamic portfolio strategies or how to throw away a million dollars in the stock market. *Review of Financial Studies*, 1 (1), 67–88.

Eagle, D. 1994: The equivalence of the cascading scenario and the backward-bending demand curve theory of the 1987 stock market crash. *Quarterly Journal of Business and Economics*, 33 (4), 60–73.

Edwards, F.R. 1988a: Does futures trading increase stock market volatility? *Financial Analysts Journal*, 44 (1), 63–9.

Edwards, F.R. 1988b: Studies of the 1987 stock market crash: review and appraisal. *Journal of Financial Services Research*, 1 (3), 231–52.

Edwards, F.R. 1995: Off-exchange derivatives markets and financial fragility. *Journal of Financial Services Research*, 9 (3), 259–90.

Edwards, F.R. and Mishkin, F.S. 1995: The decline of traditional banking: Implications for financial stability and regulatory policy. *Federal Reserve Bank of New York Economic Policy Review*, July, 27–45.

Ellis, J. 1994: Non-linearities and chaos in exchange rates. In J. Creedy and V.L. Martin (eds), *Chaos and Non-Linear Models in Economics, Theory and Applications*, 187–95. Brookfield, VT: Edward Elgar Publishing Company.

Etzioni, E.S. 1986: Rebalance disciplines for portfolio insurance. *Journal of Portfolio Management*, 13 (1), 59–62.

Eun, C.S. and Shim, S. 1989: International transmission of stock market movements. *Journal of Financial and Quantitative Analysis*, 24 (2), 241–56.

Fabozzi, F.J., Ma, C.K., Chittenden, W.T. and Pace, R.D. 1995: Predicting intraday price reversals. *Journal of Portfolio Management*, 21 (2), 42–53.

Falloon, W. 1984: The invisible hedge. *Intermarket*, October.

Fama, E.F. 1970: Efficient capital markets: a review of theory and empirical work. *Journal of Finance*, 25 (2), 383–417.

Fama, E.F. 1981: Stock returns, real activity, inflation, and money. *American Economic Review*, 71 (4), 545–65.

Fama, E.F. 1989: Perspectives on October 1987, or what did we learn from the crash? In R.J. Barro et al. (eds), *Black Monday and the Future of Financial Markets*, 71–82. Homewood, IL: Mid-America Institute for Public Policy Research and Dow Jones-Irwin.

Fama, E.F. 1991: Efficient capital markets: II. *Journal of Finance*, 46 (5), 1575–617.

Fama, E.F. and French, K.R. 1988a: Dividend yields and expected stock returns. *Journal of Financial Economics*, 22 (1), 3–25.

Fama, E.F. and French, K.R. 1988b: Permanent and temporary components of stock prices. *Journal of Political Economy*, 96 (2), 246–73.

Fama, E.F. and French, K.R. 1989: Business conditions and expected returns on stocks and bonds. *Journal of Financial Economics*, 25 (1), 23–49.

Federal Reserve System (FRS), Staff of the Board of Governors. 1974: *The Federal Reserve System*. Washington, D.C.: FRS.

Federal Reserve System (FRS), Staff of the Board of Governors. 1984: *A Review and Evaluation of Federal Margin Regulation*. Washington, D.C.: FRS.

Ferguson, R. 1983: Two approaches to asset allocation. *Pensions & Investment Age*, September 19.

Ferguson, R. 1986a: An open letter. *Financial Analysts Journal*, 42 (5), 78–80.

Ferguson, R. 1986b: How to beat the S&P 500 (without losing sleep). *Financial Analysts Journal*, 42 (2), 37–46.

Ferguson, R. 1987: A comparison of the mean-variance and long-term return characteristics of three investment strategies. *Financial Analysts Journal*, 43 (4), 55–66.

Ferguson, R. 1988: The author replies. *Financial Analysts Journal*, 44 (2), 76–7.

Ferguson, R. 1989: On crashes. *Financial Analysts Journal*, 45 (2), 42–52.

Ferguson, R. and Edwards, L. 1985: General characteristics of "portfolio insurance" as provided by fiduciary hedge programs. Los Angeles: Leland O'Brien Rubinstein Associates.

Ferguson, R. and O'Brien, J. 1988: Stabilizing forwards: for a more stable market. *Journal of Portfolio Management*, 14 (4), 4.

Finnerty, J.E. and Park, H.Y. 1987: Stock index futures: does the tail wag the dog? *Financial Analysts Journal*, 43 (2), 57–61.

Fischer, K.P. and Palasvirta, A.P. 1990: High road to a global marketplace: the international transmission of stock market fluctuations. *Financial Review*, 25 (3), 371–94.

Fong, H.G. and Vasicek, O.A. 1989: Forecast-free international asset allocation. *Financial Analysts Journal*, 45 (2), 29–33.

Franklin, G.F., Powell, J.D. and Abbas, E-N. 1994: *Feedback Control of Dynamic Systems*. Reading, MA: Addison-Wesley.

French, K.R. 1988: Crash-testing the efficient market hypothesis. In *NBER Macroeconomics Annual*, 277–85. Cambridge, MA: MIT Press.

French, K.R., and Roll, R. 1986: Stock return variances: the arrival of information and the reaction of traders. *Journal of Financial Economics*, 17 (1), 5–26.

Frey, R. and Stremme, A. 1997: Market volatility and feedback effects from dynamic hedging. *Mathematical Finance*, 7 (4), 351–74.

Friedman, D. and Aoki, M. 1992: Inefficient information aggregation as a source of asset price bubbles. *Bulletin of Economic Research*, 44 (4), 251–80.

Friend, I. and Blume, M.E. 1975: The demand for risky assets. *American Economic Review*, 65, 900–22.

Froot, K.A. and Perold, A.F. 1995: New trading practices and short-run market efficiency. *Journal of Futures Markets*, 15 (7), 731–65.

Froot, K.A., Scharfstein, D.S. and Stein, J.C. 1992: Herd on the street: informational inefficiencies in a market with short-term speculation. *Journal of Finance*, 47 (4), 1461–84.

Furbush, D. 1989: Program trading and price movements: evidence from the October 1987 market crash. *Financial Management*, 18 (3), 68–83.

Galbraith, J.K. 1988: *The Great Crash: 1929*. New York: Houghton Mifflin.

Gamlin, J. 1986: Pension funds changing attitudes towards futures. *Futures*, August.

Gammill, J.F. Jr. and Marsh, T.A. 1988: Trading activity and price behavior in the stock and stock index futures markets in October 1987. *Journal of Economic Perspectives*, 2 (3), 24–44.

Garber, P.D. 1990: Who put the mania in the tulipmania? In E.N. White (ed.), *Crashes and Panics: the lessons from history*, 3–32. Homewood, IL: Dow Jones-Irwin.

Garcia, C.B. and Gould, F.J. 1987: An empirical study of portfolio insurance. *Financial Analysts Journal*, 43 (4), 44–54.

Gastineau, G.L. 1988: *The Options Manual*, 3rd edn, 305–17. New York: McGraw-Hill.

Gastineau, G.L. 1992: Option position and exercise limits: time for a radical change. *Journal of Portfolio Management*, 19 (1), 92–6.

Gatto, M.A., Geske, R., Litzenberger, R.H. and Sosin, H. 1980: Mutual fund insurance. *Journal of Financial Economics*, 8 (3), 283–317.

Geisst, C.R. 1997: *Wall Street: a history*. New York: Oxford University Press.

General Accounting Office (GAO). 1988: *Preliminary Observations on the October 1987 Crash* (Financial Markets GAO/GGD 88–38). Washington, D.C.: GAO.

Gennotte, G. and Leland, H.E. 1990: Market liquidity, hedging and crashes. *American Economic Review*, 80 (5), 999–1021.

Gennotte, G. and Leland, H.E. 1994: Low margins, derivative securities, and volatility. *Review of Futures Markets*, 13 (3), 709–42.

Gilster, John E. Jr. 1997: Option pricing theory: is "risk-free" hedging feasible? *Financial Management*, 26 (1), 91–105.

Givant, M. 1987: FASB 87 shouldn't deter investing. *Pensions & Investment Age*, February 9.

Gleick, J. 1987: *Chaos: making a new science*. New York: Viking.

Goetzmann, W.N. and Jorion, P. 1996: A century of global stock markets. New Haven, CT: Yale School of Management.

Goldberg, M. and Schulmeister, S. 1988: Technical analysis and stock market efficiency. New York: New York University.

Goldman Sachs Equity Derivatives Research. 1998: Global derivatives: 1997 review – 1998 issues. New York: Goldman Sachs, January.

Gould, F.J. 1988: Stock index futures: the arbitrage cycle and portfolio insurance. *Financial Analysts Journal*, 44 (1), 48–62.

Graham, B. 1974: The decade 1965–1974: its significance for financial analysts. In *The Renaissance of Value*. Charlottesville, VA: Financial Analysts Research Foundation.

Granito, M.R. 1987: Is portfolio insurance dead? *Money Management Forum* (Institutional Investor Inc.), December.

Grannis, S. 1987: Viewpoint on portfolio insurance: it proved its worth. *Pensions & Investment Age*, November 16.

Grannis, S. 1988: Applications of dynamic strategies. In D. Luskin (ed.), *Portfolio Insurance: a guide to dynamic hedging*, 49–57. New York: John Wiley.

Grant, J.L. 1990: Stock return volatility during the crash of 1987. *Journal of Portfolio Management*, 16 (2), 69–71.

Greenebaum, Mary. 1982: A strategy for limiting portfolio losses. *Fortune*, June 14.

Greenwald, B.C. and Stein, J.C. 1991: Transactional risk, market crashes, and the role of circuit breakers. *Journal of Business*, 64 (4), 443–62.

Grossman, S.J. 1988a: An analysis of the implications for stock and futures price volatility of program trading and dynamic hedging strategies. *Journal of Business*, 61 (3), 275–98.

Grossman, S.J. 1988b: Insurance seen and unseen: the impact on markets. *Journal of Portfolio Management*, 14 (4), 5–8.

Grossman, S.J. 1988c: Program trading and market volatility: a report on inter-day relationships. *Financial Analysts Journal*, 44 (4), 18–28.

Grossman, S.J. and Miller, M.H. 1988: Liquidity and market structure. *Journal of Finance*, 43 (3), 617–37.

Grossman, S.J. and Vila, J-L. 1992. Optimal dynamic trading with leverage constraints. *Journal of Financial and Quantitative Analysis*, 27 (2), 151–68.

Grossman, S.J. and Zhou, Z. 1996: Equilibrium analysis of portfolio insurance. *Journal of Finance*, 51 (4).

Group of Thirty. 1993: *Derivatives: practices and principals*. Washington, D.C.: Global Derivatives Study Group, Group of Thirty.

Hakanoglu, E., Kopprasch, R. and Roman, E. 1989. Constant proportion portfolio insurance for fixed-income investment. *Journal of Portfolio Management*, 15 (4), 58–66.

Hakansson, N.H. 1970: Optimal investment and consumption strategies under risk for a class of utility functions. *Econometrica*, 38 (5), 587–607.

Hakansson, N.H. 1974: Convergence to isoelastic utility and policy in multiperiod portfolio choice. *Journal of Financial Economics*, 1 (3), 201–24.

Hakansson, N.H. 1976: The purchasing power fund: a new kind of financial intermediary. *Financial Analysts Journal*, 32 (6), 49–59.

Hamao, Y., Masulis, R.W. and Ng, V. 1990: Correlations in price changes and volatility across international stock markets. *Review of Financial Studies*, 3 (2), 281–307.

Hansell, S. 1990: Is the world ready for synthetic equity? *Institutional Investor*, August.

Hardouvelis, G.A. 1988: Evidence on stock market speculative bubbles: Japan, the United States, and Great Britain. *Federal Reserve Bank of New York Quarterly Review*, 13 (2), 4–16.

Hardouvelis, G.A. 1990a: Margin requirements, volatility, and the transitory component of stock prices. *American Economic Review*, 80 (4), 736–62.

Hardouvelis, G.A. 1990b: Stock market bubbles before the crash of 1987. New York: Columbia University.

Harris, L. 1989a: S&P 500 cash stock price volatilities. *Journal of Finance*, 44 (5), 1155–75.

Harris, L. 1989b: The October 1987 S&P 500 stock-futures basis. *Journal of Finance*, 44 (1), 77–99.

Harris, L. 1990: Commentary. In G.P. Dwyer Jr. and R.W. Hafer (eds), *The Stock Market: bubbles, volatility, and chaos*, 171–4. Norwell, MA: Kluwer Academic Publishers.

Hentschel, L. and Smith, C.W. Jr. 1995: Controlling risk in derivatives markets. *Journal of Financial Engineering*, 4 (2), 101–25.

Heston, J.C. 1988: New options strategies rising out of portfolio insurance ashes. *Futures*, June.

Hill, J.M., Jain, A. and Wood, R.A. 1988: Insurance: volatility risk and futures mispricing. *Journal of Portfolio Management*, 14 (2), 23–9.

Hill, J.M. and Jones, F.J. 1988: Equity trading, program trading, portfolio insurance, computer trading and all that. *Financial Analysts Journal*, 44 (4), 29–38.

Hill, J.M. and Wood, R.A. 1988: Option replication: alternative approaches. New York: Kidder Peabody Financial Futures Department.

Hsieh, D. 1991: Chaos and nonlinear dynamics: application to financial markets. *Journal of Finance*, 46 (5), 1839–77.

Hsieh, D.A. and Miller, M.H. 1990: Margin regulation and stock market volatility. *Journal of Finance*, 45 (1), 3–29.

Huberts, L.C. and Fuller, R.J. 1995: Predictability bias in the US equity market. *Financial Analysts Journal*, 51 (2), 12–28.

Hull, J. 1989: Assessing credit risk in a financial institution's off-balance-sheet commitments. *Journal of Financial and Quantitative Analysis*, 24 (4), 489–501.

Hunter, R. 1997: Index LEAPS pick up speed. *Derivatives Strategy*, July–August, 8–11.

Ibbotson Associates. 1997: *Stocks, Bonds, Bills, and Inflation 1997 Yearbook*. Chicago: Ibbotson Associates.

Ingersoll, J.E., Jr. 1989: Option pricing theory. In M. Milgate and P. Newman (eds), *The New Palgrave Finance*, 213–18. New York: W.W. Norton.

International Monetary Fund (IMF). 1993: *International Capital Markets/Part II. Systemic Issues in International Finance*. Washington, D.C.: IMF, August.

International Stock Exchange. 1989: Report of the International Stock Exchange of Great Britain. In R.J. Barro et al. (eds), *Black Monday and the Future of Financial Markets*, 269–340. Homewood, IL: Mid-America Institute for Public Policy Research and Dow Jones-Irwin.

Irving, R. 1998: Growing pains. *Risk*, February.

Ito, T. and Lin, W-L. Undated: Price volatility and volume spillovers between the Tokyo and New York stock markets. Madison, WI: University of Wisconsin.

Jacklin, C.J., Kleidon, A.W. and Pfleiderer, P. 1992: Underestimation of portfolio insurance and the crash of October 1987. *Review of Financial Studies*, 5 (1), 35–63.

Jackwerth, J.C. and Rubinstein, M. 1996: Recovering probability distributions from option prices. *Journal of Finance*, 51 (5), 1611–31.

Jacobs, B.I. 1983a: Jacobs responds. *Pensions & Investment Age*, November 14.

Jacobs, B.I. 1983b: Long-term asset mix policy guidelines for pension asset management clients. Newark, NJ: Prudential Asset Management.

Jacobs, B.I. 1983c: The portfolio insurance puzzle. *Pensions & Investment Age*, August 22.

Jacobs, B.I. 1984: Is portfolio insurance appropriate for the long-term investor? Newark, NJ: Prudential Asset Management.

Jacobs, B.I. 1986: A public debate on dynamic hedging. In *Innovative Portfolio Insurance Techniques: the latest developments in "dynamic hedging"* (videotape). New York: Institute for International Research.

Jacobs, B.I. 1987: Viewpoint on portfolio insurance: It's prone to failure. *Pensions & Investment Age*, November 16.

Jacobs, B.I. 1997a: Crash showed danger of "insured" assets. *Pensions & Investments*, October 13.

Jacobs, B.I. 1997b: The darker side of options pricing theory. *Pensions & Investments*, November 24.

Jacobs, B.I. 1998a: Option replication and the market's fragility. *Pensions & Investments*, June 15.

Jacobs, B.I. 1998b: Long-Term Capital's short-term memory. *Pensions & Investments*, October 5.

Jacobs, B.I. 1998c: Options can destabilize (letter). *Pensions & Investments*, January 26.

Jacobs, B.I. 1998d: Option pricing theory and its unintended consequences. *Journal of Investing*, 7 (1).

Jacobs, B.I. 1999: When seemingly infallible arbitrage strategies fail. *Journal of Investing*, 8 (1).

Jacobs, B.I. and Levy, K.N. 1988a: Calendar anomalies: abnormal returns at calendar turning points. *Financial Analysts Journal*, 44 (6), 28–39.

Jacobs, B.I. and Levy, K.N. 1988b: Disentangling equity return regularities: new insights and investment opportunities. *Financial Analysts Journal*, 44 (3), 18–43.

Jacobs, B.I. and Levy, K.N. 1988c: On the value of "value." *Financial Analysts Journal*, 44 (4), 47–62.

Jacobs, B.I. and Levy, K.N. 1989a: Forecasting the size effect. *Financial Analysts Journal*, 45 (3), 38–54.

Jacobs, B.I. and Levy, K.N. 1989b: The complexity of the stock market. *Journal of Portfolio Management*, Fall.

Jacobs, B.I. and Levy, K.N. 1996: 20 myths about long-short. *Financial Analysts Journal*, 52 (5).

Jacobs, B.I. and Levy, K.N. 1997: The long and short on long-short. *Journal of Investing*, 6 (1), 73–86.

Jacobs, B.I., Levy, K.N. and Krask, M.C. 1997: Earnings estimates, predictor specification, and measurement error. *Journal of Investing*, Summer, 29–46.

Jarrow, R. 1995: Introduction to implied smiles. In R. Jarrow (ed.), *Over the Rainbow: developments in exotic options and complex swaps*. London: Risk Publications.

Jarrow, R. 1997: Review of John E. Gilster, Jr. – "option pricing theory: is 'risk-free' hedging feasible?" *Financial Management*, 26 (1), 106–8.

Jeffrey, R.H. 1984: The failings of stock market timing. *Harvard Business Review*, July/August.

Jegadeesh, N. and Titman, S. 1993: Returns to buying winners and selling losers: implications for stock market efficiency. *Journal of Finance*, 48 (1), 65–91.

Jones, C.P. and Wilson, J.W. 1995: Probabilities associated with common stock returns. *Journal of Portfolio Management*, Fall, 21–32.

Jordan, J.L. 1995: Supervision of derivatives instruments. *Journal of Financial Services Research*, 9 (3), 433–44.

Jorion, P. 1997: Lessons from the Orange County bankruptcy. *Journal of Derivatives*, Summer, 61–6.

Kahneman, D. and Tversky, A. 1979: Prospect theory: an analysis of decision under risk. *Econometrica*, 47 (2), 263–92.

Kahneman, D. and Tversky, A. 1984: Choices, values, and frames. *American Psychologist*, 34, 341–50.

Katzenbach, N. 1987: *An Overview of Program Trading and its Impact on Current Market Practices*. New York: New York Stock Exchange.

Kaufman, H. 1994: Structural changes in the financial markets: economic and policy significance. *Federal Reserve Bank of Kansas City Economic Review*, Second Quarter, 5–15.

Kawaller, I.G., Koch, P.D. and Koch, T.W. 1987: The temporal price relationship between S&P 500 futures and the S&P 500 index. *Journal of Finance*, 42 (5), 1309–29.

Keynes, J.M. 1936: *The General Theory of Employment, Interest, and Money* (1964 reprint). New York: Harcourt Brace.

Kim, G-R. and Markowitz, H.M. 1989: Investment rules, margin and market volatility. *Journal of Portfolio Management*, 16 (1), 45–52.

Kim, M.J., Nelson, C.R. and Startz, R. 1991: Mean reversion in stock prices? A reappraisal of the empirical evidence. *Review of Economic Studies*, 58 (195), 515–28.

Kindleberger, C.P. 1986: *The World in Depression, 1929–1939*. Berkeley and Los Angeles: University of California Press.

Kindleberger, C.P. 1996: *Manias, Panics, and Crashes: a history of financial crises*, 3rd edn. New York: Wiley.

King, M.A. and Wadhwani, S. 1990: Transmission of volatility between stock markets. *Review of Financial Studies*, 3 (1), 5–33.

King, M.A., Sentana, E. and Wadhwani, S. 1994: Volatility and links between national stock markets. *Econometrica*, 62 (4), 901–33.

Kingsland, L. 1982: Protecting the financial condition of a pension plan using simulation analysis. *Journal of Finance*, 37 (2), 577–84.

Kleidon, A.W. 1988: Discussion. *Journal of Finance*, 43 (3), 656–60.

Kleidon, A.W. 1992: Arbitrage, nontrading, and stale prices: October 1987. *Journal of Business*, 65 (4), 483–507.

Kleidon, A.W. and Whaley, R.E. 1992: One market? Stocks, futures and options during October 1987. *Journal of Finance*, 47 (3), 851–77.

Kling, A. 1988: How many rational investors does it take to screw in a light bulb? A theory of fragile equilibria in asset markets. Washington, D.C.: Federal Home Loan Mortgage Corporation, January.

Kritzman, M. 1994: What practitioners need to know . . . about time diversification. *Financial Analysts Journal*, 50 (1), 14–8.

Kuhn, B.A., Kuserk, G.J. and Locke, P. 1991: Do circuit breakers moderate volatility? Evidence from October 1989. *Review of Futures Markets*, 10 (1), 136–75.

Kupiec, P.H. 1993: Do stock prices exhibit volatility, frequently deviate from fundamental values, and generally behave inefficiently? *Financial Markets, Institutions, and Instruments* (Salomon Center, New York University), 2 (1), 1–60.

Kurokawa, M. 1988: Speech to the Brookings Institution, March 8.

Kurz, M. 1997: Asset prices with rational beliefs. In M. Kurz (ed.), *Endogenous Economic Fluctuations: studies in the theory of rational beliefs. Studies in Economic Theory*. New York: Springer Publishing.

Latane, H.A. 1959: Criteria for choice among risky ventures. *Journal of Political Economy*, 67, 144–55.

Lee, C.M.C., Shleifer, A. and Thaler, R.H. 1991: Investor sentiment and the closed-end fund puzzle. *Journal of Finance*, 46 (1), 75–109.

Lee, I.H. Undated. Market crashes and information avalanches. Southampton, UK: University of Southampton.

Leland, H.E. 1971: On turnpike portfolios. In G. Szego and K. Shell (eds), *Mathematical Methods in Investment and Finance, Proceedings of an International Symposium*. Venice, Italy.

Leland, H.E. 1980: Who should buy portfolio insurance? *Journal of Finance*, 35 (2), 581–94.

Leland, H.E. 1984: Portfolio insurance performance, 1928–1983. Los Angeles: Leland O'Brien Rubinstein Associates.

Leland, H.E. 1985: Option pricing and replication with transaction costs. *Journal of Finance*, 40 (5), 1283–301.

Leland, H.E. 1986: Ten myths about portfolio insurance. *Intermarket*, January.

Leland, H.E. 1987: On the stock market crash and portfolio insurance. Berkeley, CA: University of California.

Leland, H.E. 1988a: Dynamic asset allocation: after the crash. *Investment Management Review*, January/February.

Leland, H.E. 1988b: Portfolio insurance and October 19th. *California Management Review*, 30 (4), 80–9.

Leland, H.E. and O'Brien, J. 1985: Equity enhanced dedication: an alternative to bond dedication. Los Angeles: Leland O'Brien Rubinstein Associates.

Leland, H.E. and O'Brien, J. 1988: Maligned or malign? Its inventors make the case for portfolio insurance. *Barron's*, March 21.

Leland, H.E. and Rubinstein, M. 1988a: Comments on the market crash: six months after. *Journal of Economic Perspectives*, 2 (3), 45–50.

Leland, H.E. and Rubinstein, M. 1988b: The evolution of portfolio insurance. In D. Luskin (ed.), *Portfolio Insurance: a guide to dynamic hedging*, 3–10. New York, NY: John Wiley.

Lerner, R.S., Mahlmann, K., Mielke, J.R., Newmark, S.B., Sheehan, R.C., Woodbridge, J.D. and Figlewski, S. 1987: Panel discussion by industry experts on recent market events. *Review of Futures Markets*, 6 (3), 433–71.

Levy, H. and Cohen, A. 1998: On the risk of stocks in the long run: revisited. *Derivatives Quarterly*, Spring, 60–9.

Lin, W-L., Engle, R.F. and Ito, T. 1994: Do bulls and bears move across borders? International transmission of stock returns and volatility. *Review of Financial Studies*, 7 (3), 507–35.

Lindberg, T.J. 1995: Synthetic warrants. In J.C. Francis et al. (eds), *The Handbook of Equity Derivatives*, 263–84. Chicago: Irwin.

Lindsey, R.R. and Pecora, A.P. 1997: 10 Years After: regulatory developments in the securities markets since the 1987 market break. Washington, D.C.: Securities and Exchange Commission.

Liversidge, J. 1976: *Everyday Life in the Roman Empire*. New York: G.P. Putnam's Sons.

Lo, A.W. and MacKinlay, A.C. 1988: Stock market prices do not follow random walks: evidence from a simple specification test. *Review of Financial Studies*, 1 (1), 41–66.

Loomis, C.J. 1998: A house built on sand. *Fortune*, October 26, 111–18.

Luskin, D. 1988: *Portfolio Insurance: a guide to dynamic hedging*. New York, NY: John Wiley.

Maberly, E.D., Allen, D.S. and Gilbert, R.F. 1989: Stock index futures and cash market volatility. *Financial Analysts Journal*, 45 (6), 75–7.

MacKay, C. 1932: *Memoirs of Extraordinary Delusions and the Madness of Crowds*. Boston, MA: L.C. Page.

MacKinlay, A.C. and Ramaswamy, K. 1988: Index-futures arbitrage and the behavior of stock index futures prices. *Review of Financial Studies*, 1 (2), 137–58.

Malkiel, B. 1988: The Brady Commission report: a critique. *Journal of Portfolio Management*, 14 (4), 9–13.

Malliaris, A.G. and Urrutia, J.L. 1992: The international crash of October 1987: causality tests. *Journal of Financial and Quantitative Analysis* 27 (3), 353–64.

Mandelbrot, B.B. 1983: *The Fractal Geometry of Nature*. New York: W.H. Freeman.

Mankiw, N.G. 1989: Comments and discussion. *Brookings Papers on Economic Activity*, 1, 168–71.

Margrabe, W. 1978: The value of an option to exchange one asset for another. *Journal of Finance*, 33 (1), 177–86.

Margulis, A.S. Jr. 1991: Commentary. *Review of Futures Markets*, 10 (2), 279–81.

Markowitz, H.M. 1952: Portfolio selection. *Journal of Finance*, 7 (1), 77–91.

Markowitz, H.M. 1959: *Portfolio Selection: efficient diversification of investment*. 1st edn, New York: John Wiley & Sons; 2nd edn 1991, Cambridge, MA: Blackwell.

Markowitz, H.M. 1990: *Mean-Variance Analysis in Portfolio Choice and Capital Markets*, 42–68. Cambridge, MA: Blackwell.

Marshall, J.F. 1995: Derivatives and risk management. *Journal of Financial Engineering*, 4 (3), 307–13.

Marshall, J.F. and Kapner, K.R. 1993: *The Swaps Market*, 2nd edn. Miami, FL: Kolb Publishing.

Martin, V.L. and Sawyer, K. 1994: Statistical techniques for modelling non-linearities. In J. Creedy and V.L. Martin (eds), *Chaos and Non-Linear Models in Economics, Theory and Applications*, 113–34. Brookfield, VT: Edward Elgar Publishing Co.

McClain, D. 1988: *Apocalypse on Wall Street*, 76–100. Homewood, IL: Dow Jones–Irwin.

McConnell, P., Pegg, J. and Zion, D. 1998: Derivatives and hedging: the FASB's solution. New York: Bear Stearns Accounting Issues, February 5.

McMillan, H. 1991: Circuit breakers in the S&P 500 futures market: their effect on volatility and price discovery in October 1989. *Review of Futures Markets*, 10 (2), 248–74.

Mehra, R. and Prescott, E.C. 1985: The equity premium: a puzzle. *Journal of Monetary Economics*, 15, 145–61.

Merrick, J.J. Jr. 1988: Portfolio insurance with stock index futures. *Journal of Futures Markets*, 8 (4), 441–55.

Merrick, J.J. Jr. 1990: *Financial Futures Markets: structure, pricing and practice*, 199–216. New York: Ballinger Division, Harper & Row.

Merrill, C. and Thorley, S. 1996: Time diversification: perspectives from option theory. *Financial Analysts Journal*, 52 (3), 13–9.

Merton, R.C. 1971: Optimum consumption and portfolio rules in a continuous-time model. *Journal of Economic Theory*, 3 (4), 373–413.

Merton, R.C. 1973: Theory of rational option pricing. *Bell Journal of Economics and Management Science*, Spring, 141–83.

Merton, R.C. 1981: On market timing and investment performance: an equilibrium theory of value for market forecasts. *Journal of Business*, 54 (3), 363–406.

Miller, E.M. 1990: Divergence of opinion, short selling, and the role of the marginal investor. In F.J. Fabozzi (ed.), *Managing Institutional Assets*, 143–83. New York: Harper & Row-Ballinger.

Miller, M.H. 1991: *Financial Innovations and Market Volatility*. Cambridge, MA: Blackwell Publishers.

Miller, M.H. 1992: Financial innovation: achievements and prospects. *Journal of Applied Corporate Finance*, 4 (4), 4–11.

Miller, M.H. 1997: *Merton Miller on Derivatives*. New York: John Wiley & Sons.

Miller, M.H., Malkiel, B., Scholes, M.S. and Hawke, J.D. Jr. 1988: *Final Report of the Committee of Inquiry Appointed by the Chicago Mercantile Exchange to Examine the Events Surrounding October 19, 1987*. Chicago: Chicago Mercantile Exchange.

Miller, M.H., Malkiel, B., Scholes, M.S. and Hawke, J.D. Jr. 1989: Stock index futures and the crash of '87. *Journal of Applied Corporate Finance*, 1 (4), 6–17.

Miller, M.H. and Ross, D.J. 1997: The Orange County bankruptcy and its aftermath: some new evidence. *Journal of Derivatives*, Summer, 51–60.

Mitchell, M.L. and Netter, J.M. 1989: Triggering the 1987 stock market crash: anti-takeover provisions in the proposed House Ways and Means tax bill? *Journal of Financial Economics*, 24 (1), 37–68.

Moriarty, E.J., Gordon, J.D., Kuserk, G. and Wang, G.H.K. 1990: Statistical analysis of price and basis behavior: October 12–26, 1987, S&P 500 futures and cash. In G.P. Dwyer Jr. and R.W. Hafer (eds), *The Stock Market: bubbles, volatility, and chaos*, 141–69. Norwell, MA: Kluwer Academic Publishers.

Mossin, J. 1968: Optimal multiperiod portfolio policies. *Journal of Business*, 41 (2), 215–29.

Mullins, M. Undated: Meltdown Monday or meltdown money: consequences of the causes of a stock market crash. London: London School of Economics Financial Markets Group.

Muthuswamy, J. 1991: Commentary. *Review of Futures Markets*, 10 (2), 275–8.

Naik, V. and Lee, M. 1990: General equilibrium pricing of options on the market portfolio with discontinuous returns. *Review of Financial Studies*, 3 (4), 493–521.

Neal, R. 1993: Is program trading destabilizing? *Journal of Derivatives*, 1 (2), 64–77.

Neuhaus, H. and Kusuda, Y. 1997: Pricing and hedging equity options. In *Equity Derivatives: applications in risk management and investment*, 199–222. London: Risk Publications.

Neumark, D., Tinsley, P.A. and Tosini, S. 1991: After-hours stock prices and post-crash hangovers. *Journal of Finance*, 46 (1), 159–78.

O'Brien, J.W. 1982: Dynamic hedging: a new "option." *Pensions & Investment Age*, March 15.

O'Brien, J.W. 1983: Research questioned. *Pensions & Investment Age*, September 19.

O'Brien, T.J. 1988: Portfolio insurance mechanics. *Journal of Portfolio Management*, 14 (3), 40–7.

Payne, B. 1998: Delivery guaranteed. *Risk*, February, S12–S15.

Peek, J. and Rosengren, E.S. 1988: The stock market and economic activity. *Federal Reserve Bank of New England Economic Review*, 88 (3), 39–50.

Pericli, A. and Koutmos, G. 1997: Index futures and options and stock market volatility. *Journal of Futures Markets*, 17 (8), 957–74.

Perold, A.F. 1986: Constant proportion portfolio insurance. Cambridge, MA: Harvard Business School.

Perold, A.F. and Sharpe, W.F. 1988: Dynamic strategies for asset allocation. *Financial Analysts Journal*, 44 (1), 16–27.

Peters, E.E. 1991: *Chaos and Order in the Capital Markets: a new view of cycles, prices, and market volatility*. New York: John Wiley.

Phillips, T.K., Rogers, G.T. and Capaldi, R.E. 1996: Tactical asset allocation: 1977–1994. *Journal of Portfolio Management*, Fall, 57–64.

Platen, E. and Schweizer, M. 1998: On feedback effects from hedging derivatives. *Mathematical Finance*, 8 (1), 67–84.

Poterba, J.M. and Summers, L.H. 1988: Mean reversion in stock prices: evidence and implications. *Journal of Financial Economics*, 22 (1), 27–59.

Reddy, G. 1987: A new approach to asset allocation for endowments. In *The Challenges of Investing for Endowment Funds*, 45–50. Charlottesville, VA: Institute of Chartered Financial Analysts.

Regan, P.J. 1993: Analyst, analyze thyself! *Financial Analysts Journal*, 49 (4), 10–2.

Rendleman, R.J. Jr. and McEnally, R.W. 1987a: Assessing the costs of portfolio insurance. *Financial Analysts Journal*, 43 (3), 27–37.

Rendleman, R.J. Jr. and McEnally, R.W. 1987b: The authors reply. *Financial Analysts Journal*, 43 (6), 78–80.

Rendleman, R.J. Jr. and O'Brien, T.J. 1990: The effects of volatility misestimation on option-replication portfolio insurance. *Financial Analysts Journal*, 46 (3), 61–70.

Renshaw, E. 1988: The crash of October 19 in retrospect. *Market Chronicle*, October 27.

Revsine, L. 1989: Understanding Financial Accounting Standard 87. *Financial Analysts Journal*, 45 (1), 61–8.

Ring, T. 1986a: FASB #87 may boost hedging. *Pensions & Investment Age*, February 3.

Ring, T. 1986b: Portfolio insurance is gaining exposure. *Pensions & Investment Age*, December 8.

Ring, T. 1986c. Portfolio insurance's merits spur debate. *Pensions & Investment Age*, July 7.

Ring, T. 1987a: 18 funds put dynamic hedging to use. *Pensions & Investment Age*, January 26.

Ring, T. 1987b: Bloom off portfolio insurance. *Pensions & Investment Age*, November 2.

Ring, T. 1987c: High hedging costs surprise funds. *Pensions & Investment Age*, March 23.

Ring, T. 1988a: 66 percent drop in portfolio insurance. *Pensions & Investment Age*, January 25.

Ring, T. 1988b: Creators not down on dynamic hedging. *Pensions & Investment Age*, October 31.

Ring, T. 1988c: Risks hedged in new ways. *Pensions & Investment Age*, April 18.

Ritchken, P. 1985: Enhancing mean-variance analysis with options. *Journal of Portfolio Management*, 11 (3), 67–71.

Roll, R. 1988a: R-squared. *Journal of Finance*, 43 (3), 541–66.

Roll, R. 1988b: The international crash of October 1987. *Financial Analysts Journal*, 44 (5), 19–35.

Roll, R. 1989: Price volatility, international market links, and their implications for regulatory policies. *Journal of Financial Services Research*, 3 (2/3), 211–46.

Rosenberg, H. 1993: Beware the shrinking pension surplus. *Institutional Investor*, January.

Rubinstein, M. 1985: Alternative paths to portfolio insurance. *Financial Analysts Journal*, 41 (4), 42–52.

Rubinstein, M. 1987: No "best" strategy for portfolio insurance. *Financial Analysts Journal*, 43 (6), 77–8.

Rubinstein, M. 1988: Portfolio insurance and the market crash. *Financial Analysts Journal*, 44 (1), 38–47.

Rubinstein, M. 1991: Continuously rebalanced investment strategies. *Journal of Portfolio Management*, Fall, 78–81.

Rubinstein, M. 1992: Book review of M.H. Miller, Financial Innovations and Market Volatility. *Journal of Finance*, 47 (2), 819–23.

Rubinstein, M. 1994: Presidential address: implied binomial trees. *Journal of Finance*, 49 (3), 771–818.

Rubinstein, M. and Jackwerth, J. 1997: Recovering probabilities and risk aversion from options prices and realized returns. Berkeley, CA: University of California, September 26.

Rubinstein, M. and Leland, H.E. 1981: Replicating options with positions in stock and cash. *Financial Analysts Journal*, 37 (4), 63–72.

Ruelle, D. 1991: *Chance and Chaos*. Princeton, NJ: Princeton University Press.

Runkle, D.E. 1988: Why no crunch from the crash? *Federal Reserve Bank of Minneapolis Quarterly Review*, 88 (1), 2–7.

Samuelson, P.A. 1989: The judgment of economic science on rational portfolio management: indexing, timing, and long-horizon effects. *Journal of Portfolio Management*, Fall, 4–12.

Samuelson, P. A. 1994: The long-term case for equities. *Journal of Portfolio Management*, Fall, 15–24.

Santoni, G.J. 1987: The great bull markets 1924–29 and 1982–87: speculative bubbles or economic fundamentals? *Federal Reserve Bank of St. Louis Review*, 69 (9), 16–30.

Santoni, G.J. and Dwyer, G.P. Jr. 1990: Bubbles or fundamentals: new evidence from the great bull markets. In E.N. White (ed.), *Crashes and Panics: the lessons from history*, 188–210. Homewood, IL: Dow Jones-Irwin.

Schachter, B. 1992: Breaking up is hard to do: the risks in the financial engineering of customized options. *Journal of Financial Engineering*, 1 (2), 133–49.

Scharfstein, D. and Stein, J.C. 1990: Herd behavior and investment. *American Economic Review*, June, 465–79.

Scheinkman, J.A. and LeBaron, B. 1989: Nonlinear dynamics and stock returns. *Journal of Business*, 62 (3), 311–38.

Schmerken, I. 1991: LOR to launch new risk product, complexity notwithstanding. *Wall Street Computer Review*, January.

Scholes, M. 1996: Global financial markets, derivative securities, and systemic risks. *Journal of Risk and Uncertainty*, 12, 271–86.

Schwert, G.W. 1990a: Stock market volatility. *Financial Analysts Journal*, 46 (3), 23–34.

Schwert, G.W. 1990b: Stock volatility and the crash of '87. *Review of Financial Studies*, 3 (1), 77–102.

Securities and Exchange Commission (SEC). 1987: *The Role of Index-Related Trading in the Market Decline on September 11 and 12, 1986*. Washington, D.C.: Division of Market Regulation, SEC.

Securities and Exchange Commission (SEC). 1988: *The October 1987 Market Break*. Washington, D.C.: Division of Market Regulation, SEC.

Securities and Exchange Commission (SEC). 1990a: *Market Analysis of October 13 and 16, 1989*. Washington, D.C.: Division of Market Regulation, SEC.

Securities and Exchange Commission (SEC). 1990b: *Trading Analysis of October 13 and 16, 1989*. Washington, D.C.: Division of Market Regulation, SEC.

Securities and Exchange Commission (SEC) 1991: Market decline on November 15, 1991 (memorandum from William H. Hayman, director, Division of Market Regulation, to SEC Chairman Breeden). Washington, D.C.: Division of Market Regulation, SEC, December 24.

Seff, E. 1988: Evidence proved hedging worked. *Pensions & Investment Age*, February 8.

Seyhun, H.N. 1990: Overreaction or fundamentals: some lessons from insiders' response to the market crash of 1987. *Journal of Finance*, 45 (5), 1363–88.

Sharpe, W.F. 1975: Likely gains from market timing. *Financial Analysts Journal*, 3 (2), 60–9.

Sharpe, W.F. 1978: *Investments*. Englewood Cliffs, NJ: Prentice-Hall.

Shiller, R.J. 1981: Do stock prices move too much to be justified by subsequent changes in dividends? *American Economic Review*, 71 (3), 421–36.

Shiller, R.J. 1984: Stock prices and social dynamics. *Brookings Papers on Economic Activity*, 2, 457–510.

Shiller, R.J. 1987: Comments. In R. Hogarth and M. Reder (eds), *Rational Choice: the contrast between economics and psychology*, 317–21. Chicago: University of Chicago Press.

Shiller, R.J. 1988: Portfolio insurance and other investor fashions as factors in the 1987 stock market crash. In *NBER Macroeconomics Annual*, 287–95. Cambridge, MA: MIT Press.

Shiller, R.J. 1989: Investor behavior in the October 1987 stock market crash: survey evidence. In R.J. Shiller, *Market Volatility*, 379–402. Cambridge, MA: MIT Press.

Shiller, R.J. 1993. *Macro Markets: creating institutions for managing society's largest economic risks*. Oxford: Clarendon Press.

Shirreff, D. 1998: Another fine mess at UBS. *Euromoney*, November, 41–3.

Shleifer, A. and Summers, L.H. 1990: The noise trader approach to finance. *Journal of Economic Perspectives*, 4 (2), 19–33.

Shleifer, A. and Vishny, R.W. 1997: The limits of arbitrage. *Journal of Finance*, 52 (1), 35–55.

Siegel, J.J. 1992a: Equity risk premia, corporate profit forecasts, and investor sentiment around the stock crash of October 1987. *Journal of Business*, 65 (4), 557–70.

Siegel, J.J. 1992b: The equity premium: stock and bond returns since 1802. *Financial Analysts Journal*, 48 (1), 28–38.

Siegel, J.J. 1998a. Comment. In R.E. Litan and A.M. Santomero (eds), *Brookings–Wharton Papers on Financial Services*, 103–10. Washington, D.C.: Brookings Institution Press.

Siegel, J.J. 1998b. *Stocks for the Long Run: the definitive guide to financial market returns and long-term investment strategies*, 2nd edn. New York: McGraw-Hill.

Siegel, J.J. and Thaler, R.H. 1997: Anomalies: the equity premium puzzle. *Journal of Economic Perspectives*, 11 (1), 191–200.

Siegel, L.B. 1997: Are stocks risky? Two lessons. *Journal of Portfolio Management*, Spring, 29–34.

Singleton, C. and Grieves, R. 1984: Synthetic puts and portfolio insurance strategies. *Journal of Portfolio Management*, 10 (3), 63–9.

Sloan, A. and Stern, R. 1988: How Black–Scholes led to Black Monday. *Forbes*, January 25.

Smith, D.J. 1997: Aggressive corporate finance: a close look at the Procter & Gamble-Bankers Trust leveraged swap. *Journal of Derivatives*, Summer, 67–82.

Smith, V.L., Suchanek, G.L. and Williams, A.W. 1988: Bubbles, crashes, and endogenous expectations in experimental spot asset markets. *Econometrica*, 56 (5), 1119–52.

Somes, S. and Zurack, M.A. 1987: Pension plans, portfolio insurance and FASB Statement No. 87: an old risk in a new light. *Financial Analysts Journal*, 43 (1), 10–3.

Star, M.G. 1992: LOR raising cash for debut of SuperTrusts. *Pensions & Investment Age*, June 8.

Stoll, H.R. and Whaley, R.E. 1987: Program trading and expiration-day effects. *Financial Analysts Journal*, 43 (2), 16–28.

Stoll, H.R. and Whaley, R.E. 1990: The dynamics of stock index and stock index futures prices. *Journal of Financial and Quantitative Analysis*, 25 (4), 441–68.

Stulz, R.M. 1982: Options on the minimum or the maximum of two risky assets. *Journal of Financial Economics*, 10 (2), 161–85.

Summers, L.H. 1986: Does the stock market rationally reflect fundamental values? *Journal of Finance*, 41 (3), 591–601.

Tate, R. 1988: The insurance company guarantee. In D. Luskin (ed.), *Portfolio Insurance: a guide to dynamic hedging*, 182–5. New York: John Wiley.

Telser, L. 1989: October 1987 and the structure of financial markets: an exorcism of demons. In R.J. Barro et al. (eds), *Black Monday and the Future of Financial Markets*, 101–12. Homewood, IL: Mid-America Institute for Public Policy Research and Dow Jones–Irwin.

Thaler, R.H. 1985: Mental accounting and consumer choice. *Marketing Science*, 4, 199–214.

Thaler, R.H. 1993. *Advances in Behavioral Finance*. New York: Russell Sage Foundation.

Thaler, R.H., Tversky, A., Kahneman, D. and Schwartz, A. 1997: The effect of myopia and loss aversion on risk taking: an experimental test. *Quarterly Journal of Economics*, May.

Thorley, S.R. 1995: The time-diversification controversy. *Financial Analysts Journal*, 51 (3), 68–76.

Tilley, J.A. and Latainer, G.D. 1985: A synthetic option framework for asset allocation. *Financial Analysts Journal*, 41 (3), 32–43.

Tinic, S.M. 1995: Derivatives and stock market volatility: is additional government regulation necessary? *Journal of Financial Services Research*, 9 (3), 351–62.

Toft, K.B. and Prucyk, B. 1997: Options on leveraged equity: theory and empirical tests. *Journal of Finance*, 52 (3), 1151–80.

Trennepohl, G.L., Booth, J.R. and Tehranian, H. 1988: An empirical analysis of insured portfolio strategies using listed options. *Journal of Financial Research*, 11 (1), 1–12.

Treynor, J.L. 1988: Portfolio insurance and market volatility. *Financial Analysts Journal*, 44 (6), 71–3.

Treynor, J.L. 1998: Bulls, bears, and market bubbles. *Financial Analysts Journal*, 54 (2), 69–74.

Trippi, R.R. and Harriff, R.B. 1991: Dynamic asset allocation rules: survey and synthesis. *Journal of Portfolio Management*, Summer, 19–27.

Vaga, T. 1990: The coherent market hypothesis. *Financial Analysts Journal*, 46 (6), 36–49.

Van Eaton, R.D. and Conover, J.A. 1997: Put prices and PEN participation rates at longer horizons: is equity risk in the eye of the beholder? *Financial Analysts Journal*, 53 (6), 67–73.

Van Eaton, R.D. and Conover, J.A. 1998: Misconceptions about optimal equity allocation and investment horizon. *Financial Analysts Journal*, 54 (2), 52–9.

Von Furstenberg, G.M. and Nam Jeon, B. 1989: International stock price movements: links and messages. *Brookings Papers on Economic Activity*, 1, 125–67.

Wadhwani, S. 1989: Commentary: price volatility, international market links, and their implications for regulatory policies. *Journal of Financial Services Research*, 3 (2/3), 255–9.

Wang, G.H.K., Moriarty, E.J., Michalski, R.J. and Jordan, J.V. 1990: Empirical analysis of the liquidity of the S&P 500 index futures market during the October 1987 market break. *Advances in Futures and Options Research*, 4 (1), 191–218.

Welch, I. 1992: Sequential sales, learning and cascades. *Journal of Finance*, 47 (2), 695–732.

West, K.D. 1988: Bubbles, fads and stock price volatility tests: a partial evaluation. *Journal of Finance*, 43 (3), 639–56.

Whalley, A.E. and Wilmott, P. 1997: Key results in discrete hedging and transaction costs. In A. Konishi and R.E. Dattatreya (eds), *Frontiers in Derivatives: state-of-the-art models, valuation, strategies & products*, 183–95. Chicago: Irwin Professional Publishing.

White, E.N. 1990: When the ticker ran late: the stock market boom and the crash of 1929. In E.N. White (ed.), *Crashes and Panics: the lessons from history*, 143–87. Homewood, IL: Dow Jones–Irwin.

Wigmore, B.A. 1998: Revisiting the October 1987 crash. *Financial Analysts Journal*, 54 (1), 36–48.

Wood, R.A. 1989: The volatility of the S&P 500: an intraday examination. College Station, PA: Pennsylvania State University.

Wunsch, R.S. 1984: Stock index futures: weekly commentary. New York: Kidder Peabody Financial Futures Department, December 11.

Wunsch, R.S. 1985a: Stock index futures: weekly commentary. New York: Kidder Peabody Financial Futures Department, January 15.

Wunsch, R.S. 1985b: Stock index futures: weekly commentary. New York: Kidder Peabody Financial Futures Department, April 23.

Wunsch, R.S. 1985c: Stock index futures: weekly commentary. New York: Kidder Peabody Financial Futures Department, June 11.

Wunsch, R.S. 1986: Stock index futures: weekly commentary. New York: Kidder Peabody Financial Futures Department, June 17.

Wunsch, R.S. 1987: Stock index futures: weekly commentary. New York: Kidder Peabody Financial Futures Department, October 20.

Wunsch, R.S. 1988: Stock index futures: weekly commentary. New York: Kidder Peabody Financial Futures Department, February 9.

Wunsch, S. 1997: The illusion of liquidity. *Auction Countdown* (Arizona Stock Exchange), November 30.

Zhu, Y. and Kavee, R.C. 1988: Performances of portfolio insurance strategies. *Journal of Portfolio Management*, 14 (3), 48–54.

Zurack, M.A. and Hill, J.M. 1997: US index implied volatility and market breaks: a historical perspective. New York: Goldman Sachs Equity Derivatives Research, November 20.

Name Index

Subject Index